LEARNING AND MOTIVATION
IN THE CLASSROOM

LEARNING AND MOTIVATION IN THE CLASSROOM

Edited by

SCOTT G. PARIS
GARY M. OLSON
HAROLD W. STEVENSON
The University of Michigan

LAWRENCE ERLBAUM ASSOCIATES, PUBLISHERS
1983   Hillsdale, New Jersey   London

Lawrence Erlbaum Associates, Inc., Publishers
365 Broadway
Hillsdale, New Jersey 07642

Library of Congress Cataloging in Publication Data
Main entry under title:

Learning and motivation in the classroom.

Based on papers presented at the Institute on Learning and Motivation in the Classroom, June
1981, at the University of Michigan.
    Bibliography: p.
    Includes indexes.
    1. Learning—Addresses, essays, lectures.   2. Motivation in education—Addresses, essays,
lectures.
3. Classroom management—Addresses, essays, lectures.
I. Paris, Scott G., 1946–   . II. Olson, Gary M.
III. Stevenson, Harold William, 1924–   . IV. Institute on Learning and Motivation in the
Classroom (1981:
University of Michigan) [DNLM: 1. Learning—Congresses.
2. Motivation—Congresses. 3. Psychology, Educational
—Congresses. LB 1065 L438 1981]
LB1060.L423   1983   370.15′23   83-8962
ISBN 0-89859-273-9

Printed in the United States of America
10 9 8 7 6 5 4 3 2 1

Contents

PART II: MOTIVATION AND ACHIEVEMENT

Preface

Throughout this century there have been substantial links between scientific psychology and education. Binet, Dewey, Thorndike, and other early pioneers were strongly interested in both realms. Significantly, two deep strands in the early twentieth century American consciousness shaped the relationship between education and psychology: the commitment to public education as a vital and important force within a democratic society, and an abiding faith in the scientific method. Thus, it is scarcely an accident that such educationally relevant topics as learning, motivation, and intelligence were dominant in the early development of psychology.

However, the fact that many significant figures had deep interests in education and psychology was no guarantee of rapid progress toward scientifically based educational reform. Indeed, there were factors which guaranteed difficulties. On the one hand, scientific psychology, as any new and developing field, experienced considerable conceptual and methodological uncertainty. Theoretical frameworks, experimental paradigms, and specific domains of study went through cycles of popularity. This meant there was little accumulating knowledge about learning, motivation, and intelligence. On the other hand, in the face of technological development, increasing international competition, and profound changes in family goals and organization, researchers received more pressure from society to "produce results." Educators eager to improve schools often adopted psychological theories or findings prematurely, and were later disillusioned when anticipated benefits were not observed. Throughout the century cycles of enthusiasm and wariness have characterized the relationship between education and psychology.

We are currently in a period of enthusiasm. It is too soon to tell whether this represents a new level of understanding and sophistication or only another cycle between the disciplines. We suspect it is the former. Why? First, most of the mainstream psychological research on learning and motivation is being conducted currently in substantive areas with direct relevance to school learning. Much of this research is either based in the classroom or focuses on domains that are at the center of the curriculum. Second, after a long period in which cognitive phenomena were largely studied in isolation from emotional and motivational variables, researchers now see the need to examine these two realms together. Finally, the role of social science research in establishing social policy has been recognized and it requires examination. We need to understand the complex processes whereby research influences social policy if we hope to link educational practices with psychological research and theory to provide better schooling experiences for children.

In thinking about these matters, we felt the time was ripe for an amalgamation of recent advances in theory and research in education and psychology, with a particular focus on cognition, motivation, and social policy. Thus, we convened an Institute on Learning and Motivation in the Classroom that was held during June of 1981 at the University of Michigan. The goal of the Institute was to provide a forum for psychologists and educators to exchange ideas and findings, and to discuss the implications of recent work on learning and motivation for educational policy. To this end, a series of guest speakers were invited, and an intensive three weeks of public lectures, seminars, and informal discussions were held. This volume presents chapters based on the presentations of the speakers at the Institute. They are organized into three sections to conform to the topical organization of the three weeks of the Institute. A brief introduction preceding each section highlights the issues contained in the chapters of that section.

No enterprise of this scope can proceed without the help and support of a variety of organizations and people. The Combined Program in Education and Psychology, the Bush Program in Child Development and Social Policy, and the Program in Cognitive Science at the University of Michigan were the source of intellectual and administrative expertise for the Institute. Financial support came from the School of Education and the Horace H. Rackham School of Graduate Studies at the University, and through grants from the Bush Foundation to the Bush Program in Child Development and Social Policy and the Alfred P. Sloan Foundation to the Program in Cognitive Science.

A group of competent and enthusiastic colleagues and students assisted us in the planning and coordination of the daily sessions: Craig Barclay, Susan Duffy, Richard Newman, Paul Pintrich, Jim Stigler, and Shirley Willard worked hard and effectively. Without their efforts the Institute could not have been carried out.

A number of people have helped us both in the running of the Institute and in the subsequent preparation of this volume. These include Linda Shultes from the Combined Program in Education and Psychology, Eileen Blumenthal and Margot Michael from the Bush Program, and Mary Jo Blahna and Ed Sammons from the Program in Cognitive Science.

Finally, we are grateful to the scholars who attended the Institute, and whose participation in the formal and informal activities throughout the three-week period provided the energy and ideas that gave the Institute both coherence and substance: Mary Ahlum, Piraye Bayman, Susan Burns, John Burton, David Cross, Jeanne Day, Ann Marie DeBritto, Shari Ellis, Judith Golub, Randy Isaacson, Janis Jacobs, Carolyn Jagacinski, Joe Lapides, Kris Mika, Evelyn Oka, Suzanne Randolph, Mike Reiner, David Saarnio, Kevin Spratt, Mary Trepanier, Todd VandenAkker, Nancy Vye, Keri Weed, and Arthur Woodward.

Our goal in convening the Institute and in publishing these chapters is to stimulate discussion which can lead to the improvement of classroom instruction in America. Education is at the foundation of a democratic and technological society. Only through research and through continuing discussion of the implications of research for practice can we hope to have the best educational system that our resources and our determination will allow.

S. G. Paris
G. M. Olson
H. W. Stevenson

LEARNING AND MOTIVATION IN THE CLASSROOM

INSTRUCTIONAL ISSUES

The classroom is, fundamentally, a place to learn. Educators have always believed that the psychology of learning is directly relevant to classroom activities. But direct *relevance* and direct *application* are quite different things. Despite the intensity with which learning has been studied, the efforts to apply what has been learned to the classroom have been filled with confusion and frustration. During the period when the study of learning focused on rats and pigeons, there were many attempts to generate applications to human learning. As Resnick points out in her chapter, theorists like Thorndike and Skinner had strong interests in educational applications of their principles. But extrapolations from experimental observations in the learning laboratory to the classroom were based on a fragile chain of assumptions. Even when the psychology of learning shifted to studies of verbal learning and memory of adults, there was still a big gap between the world of the psychological experiment and the world of the classroom.

We are now in a different era. The study of learning and cognition is centered in domains that are at the heart of educational curricula: reading, mathematics, and science. Such topics as comprehension, induction, abstraction, inference, understanding and categorization—all of which appear to be related to what students ought to be doing in the classroom—now represent the central focus of much cogni-

1

tive science research. Of course, just because research is being done on the learning of geometry or physics, on arithmetic or reading, does not mean that the step from basic work to applications is immediate. Resnick points out that cognitive science so far has done a much better job of decomposing tasks and states of understanding than in describing how transitions between states of understanding occur. Thus, even in the domains of reading, mathematics, and science, the task of deriving basic principles is just beginning. Nonetheless, without an understanding of relevant basic principles, the issue of applications is moot. The chapters in this section survey a broad sample of recent research aimed at developing such an understanding. The authors represent diverse substantive interests, research philosophies, and theoretical goals. Nevertheless, there is a central focus throughout these five chapters: the attempt to derive instructional implications from research and theory on cognition.

Lauren Resnick seeks to link research on basic cognitive processes with instructional practices. She points out that cognitive science research in the domains of reading comprehension, science, and math has provided us with thorough analyses of cognitive objectives for instruction although it has not yet provided detailed analysis of learning processes on which to construct a theory of instruction. But the effort to do so has begun, and Resnick describes characteristics that she believes are important for a cognitive theory of learning and ultimately a cognitive theory of instruction. In particular, she suggests that instructional theories will be fairly domain-specific and that a goal of deriving broad principles for all instructional practices may be too simplistic.

Is it possible to construct a model of reading instruction based on present knowledge of theory and practice? David Pearson and Rob Tierney pursue this goal in their chapter. They examine five different areas in search of general principles: models of reading, existing classroom practices, correlations of classroom observations with achievement, program evaluation research, and experiments on instructional practices. They conclude that their examination of the five areas pinpoints three factors that affect the success of a reading program, and thus constitute factors that a model of reading instruction will need to address. These factors are: the orientation toward reading, or the relative emphasis given to meaning versus decoding; the explicitness of instruction, specifically the extent of teacher intervention in the learning of component skills; and finally, the role of practice. The chapter serves as a useful guide to issues in instructional research on reading.

Marlene Scardemalia and Carl Bereiter elaborate a novel theme, viewing the child as co-investigator in the research enterprise. They asked children to think aloud while engaged in a complex cognitive task, in this instance, writing. A frequent "side effect" of their efforts to get children to reveal more about their mental processes was found: the children became interested themselves in discovering what they could about their mental processes. Because research has already shown that awareness of how one's own mental processes work (i.e., metacognition) may be an important part of cognitive development, they elaborate on the hypothesis that encouraging the child to serve as co-investigator with the experimenter or instructor may facilitate the development of such awareness.

The goal of James Greeno's chapter is to characterize students' understanding in high school geometry. This in turn should provide a description of cognitive objectives of instruction in the domain. Many agree that understanding, not rote memorization, should be the objective of school learning. However, objective descriptions of what is meant by understanding are rare. Greeno uses think-aloud protocols, observations of students' behavior, and computer simulations of their performance to construct descriptions of what it means to understand within these domains. This kind of research represents the first steps toward a cognitive theory of instruction in the sense described by Resnick.

What are the relationships between cognitive development and school learning? Anton Lawson discusses a series of studies on the interrelations of basic principles of cognitive development—primarily derived from Piaget—and science learning in the classroom. Starting from the claim that adolescents are deficient in formal operational thought, he evaluates evidence on the contribution of science curricula to developmental changes in logical thinking. He argues that science learning does help students develop better reasoning skills and he identifies a number of issues that must be considered in assessing the relationship between developmental changes and school learning.

Collectively these chapters offer several provocative hypotheses for cognitive theories of classroom instruction. Although no single theory has emerged within any of these academic domains, these five chapters represent bold attempts to identify cognitive objectives, learning processes, and classroom practices that are relevant to direct educational applications.

1 Toward a Cognitive Theory of Instruction

Lauren B. Resnick
Learning Research and Development Center
University of Pittsburgh

We are now well accustomed to noting the cognitive "revolution" that has characterized the last decade or two of psychology. The human mind has been rediscovered, or at least reaffirmed; reasoning and thought are central objects of scientific study; and the nature of human cognitive abilities is being examined in fresh ways. It seems evident that the new conceptions of human competence that are emerging ought to affect the practice of education—that a cognitive theory of instruction ought to be emerging alongside our increasingly elaborated theories of cognitive performance and development. What would such a theory look like, how close are we to having one, and what directions must be followed to further its development? These are the questions explored in this chapter. The goal of this inquiry is to build an agenda for research that will result in a cognitive theory of instruction capable of informing educational practice and at the same time extending the limits of our knowledge about how people learn and develop.

Let us begin with some definitions that will serve to set the boundaries of the inquiry. First, I define as instruction *anything that is done in order to help someone else acquire a new capability*. This is an intentionally broad definition. It means that instruction is not limited to traditional "teacher's tasks," such as lecturing or conducting recitations or setting homework assignments—although these are certainly activities that may qualify as instruction. Rather, any act that intentionally arranges the world so that somebody will learn something more easily qualifies as instruction. I think it will become clear as the chapter proceeds why this broad definition of instruction is essential—indeed is dictated by—the view of human learning that is being elaborated by current cognitive psychology.

With this view of instruction as a point of departure, we can now consider the elements of a theory of instruction. Such a theory must be both descriptive,

5

explaining why instruction works and why it does not, and prescriptive, suggesting what to do the next time for better results. For these purposes three requirements must be met. First, a theory of instruction must specify the new capabilities that we are trying to help somebody acquire—that is, the goal of the instructional effort. Second, it must provide a theoretical account of how people acquire these desired capabilities. Finally, an instructional theory must specify how something done by an instructor interacts with the individual's processes of acquisition so that something new is acquired. There are, then, three components to a theory of instruction: (1) specification of capabilities to be acquired; (2) description of acquisition processes; and (3) principles of intervention.

A BRIEF HISTORY OF PSYCHOLOGICAL THEORIES OF INSTRUCTION

The effort to build a theory of instruction is rooted in today's cognitive psychology and poses a new challenge, but this is by no means the first time that psychologists have addressed this task. A brief review of some past efforts at drawing instructional implications from psychological theory will help us to appreciate both the goals and the potential pitfalls of our new venture.

E. L. Thorndike and the Theory of Bonds

Our account begins with Edward L. Thorndike, the prominent American associationist. Thorndike had a well-developed instructional theory that grew directly out of his general associationist theory of how the human mind works. For Thorndike, new capabilities to be acquired could be described as collections of "bonds"—that is, associations between stimuli or between stimuli and responses. Thorndike took so seriously the notion of defining instructional goals in these terms that he actually undertook an analysis of school subject matter. In 1922 he published a book entitled *The Psychology of Arithmetic,* which contains many lists of the bonds he thought made up the subject matter of arithmetic. The book thus essentially offered what we might now call a *task analysis* of arithmetic, in terms consonant with associationist learning theory. In keeping with associationist principles, there was minimal organization imposed on the lists of bonds. Thorndike implicitly recognized some deeper structure than that reflected in a simple collection of bonds; he proposed that bonds that "go together" should be taught together. Thus, he clustered addition bonds in one list and subtraction bonds in another, and so forth, largely following common sense views of arithmetic content. But his book offered little guidance as to what made things go together.

Despite this limitation, Thorndike's task analysis proved very powerful. This was in large part because it was accompanied by a strongly articulated theory of acquisition. This theory specified that one acquires new bonds through a trial-and-error process in which associations that are rewarded become stronger, whereas those that are punished or ignored gradually die out. This is the "law of effect." The law of effect pointed in turn to a very clear theory of instructional intervention: An instructor should organize practice in a way that would strengthen correct bonds, by reward, and weaken incorrect ones. This theory led to several decades of research in mathematics education in which investigators tried to determine empirically which bonds were easiest to form and which were hardest, so that practice could be organized from easiest to hardest. Such practice would give maximum opportunities for rewarding correct answers and thus strengthening correct bonds.

This approach to mathematics teaching still continues. For example, much computer-assisted drill-and-practice instruction can be viewed as a sophisticated manifestation of Thorndike's theory. The Stanford CAI (computer-assisted instruction) programs for math (Suppes & Morningstar, 1972), for example, fit that theory very well even though there is no mention in any of the program descriptions of association theory. Thus the Thorndikian theory of instruction has had a real influence on educational practice.

Skinner and Operant Conditioning

Another psychologist who has had a profound impact on the theory and practice of instruction is B. F. Skinner (Glaser, 1978; Skinner, 1958). His effect was to lead instruction even further away from a central concern with the structure of knowledge and its interrelatedness. Skinner and other radical behaviorists denied that a science of mental life was possible because mental events were not open to public observation. With respect to instruction, the radical behaviorist position dictated a definition of the capabilities to be taught entirely in terms of observable performances. This has led to an entire technology of behavioral objectives (cf. Mager, 1961), still one of the more powerful influences on curriculum design and teaching practice.

Although the Skinnerian formulation was explicit about the terms in which capabilities to be induced through instruction should be stated, Skinner himself never did the kind of detailed work on the analysis of instructional subject matter that Thorndike did. Thus, there were no guidelines in Skinner's own writing explaining how to arrive at the content of objectives or how to order them. Robert Gagné's theory of cumulative learning (Gagné, 1962, 1968) and the methods of task analysis and learning hierarchy specification based on it (cf. Resnick, 1973) filled this gap, providing a method of task analysis that is still very influential.

As was the case with associationism, there was a strong acquisition theory associated with the Skinnerian view of learning. Much was shared with Thorndike, since learning was seen to be the result of patterns of reinforcement, or reward. But Skinner went beyond Thorndike. He proposed that wrong responses produce such negative side effects in learning that it would be best to avoid them completely. He and his associates (e.g., Terrace, 1963) showed that "errorless learning" was possible through shaping of behavior by small successive approximations. This led naturally to an interest in a technology of teaching by organizing practice into carefully arranged sequences through which an individual gradually acquires the elements of a new and complex performance without making wrong responses en route. This was translated for school use into "programmed instruction"—a form of instruction characterized by very small steps, heavy prompting, and careful sequencing so that children would be led step by step toward ability to perform the specified behavioral objectives. Meanwhile, the same general principles were applied to methods of organizing and maintaining desired social behavior in the classroom and keeping children's attention on the assigned work. This line of application became known as "behavior modification" (Kazdin, 1981).

Both associationism and behaviorism, then, provided a coherent theory of instruction that included methods of specifying the capabilities to be taught, a general theory of acquisition, and principles for intervention. Neither, however, offered a thorough analysis of thinking or knowledge, and so both were often judged inadequate by educators and psychologists interested in promoting reasoning and understanding. These groups found the theories of Piaget and other psychologists, such as those of the Gestalt school, more compatible with their concerns. We turn next to these early cognitive psychologists.

Gestalt Psychology and the Structures of Thinking

Although they do not come to mind immediately as instructional theorists, Gestalt psychologists—especially Max Wertheimer (1945/1959)—were in fact very interested in education. Wertheimer spent time in schools and tried to develop a theory of education that would promote "productive thinking" and "meaningful" learning. Compared with the formulations offered by associationists and behaviorists, the instructional theory that can be induced from Wertheimer's writing is very sketchy. Nevertheless, it represents an early cognitive theory of instruction and thus is of considerable interest to our present inquiry.

For Wertheimer, the important capabilities to be promoted through instruction were principles and structured knowledge rather than unordered collections of bonds or behaviors specified without reference to the thoughts behind them. The essential character of Gestalt thought on education is well illustrated by reference to Wertheimer's famous parallelogram problem. Wertheimer reports going into a classroom of children who had been taught to find the area of a parallelogram by dropping a perpendicular line and then multiplying the perpendicular by the base of the parallelogram. Performance on this task was excellent as long as the parallelogram was presented in the standard way, as shown in the top of Fig. 1.1. But when Wertheimer asked the class to find the area of a parallelogram in a

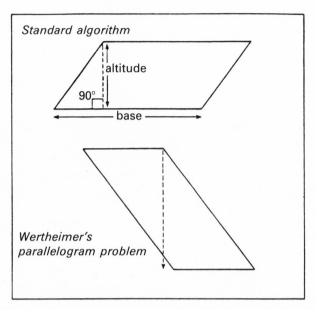

FIG. 1.1.   Finding the area of a parallelogram using the standard algorithm. Children were confused when applying it to Wertheimer's problem figure. (From Resnick and Ford, 1981. Reprinted with permission.)

different position (as in the bottom of the figure) the typical response was "That's not fair" or "We haven't had that yet"—from teacher as well as children! The difficulty was that the standard formula did not seem to apply with the "up-ended" figure when a perpendicular was dropped from a top angle.

Wertheimer used this negative example to point to what one ought *not* to seek as an educational outcome—rote learning of procedures and answers—and to an alternative goal. He was interested in instruction that would lead children to recognize the principles that lay behind procedures so that they could solve problems that were not identical to those they had already encountered. For the parallelogram, this would mean recognizing: (1) that "area" refers to the number of unit squares that can be superimposed on a figure, but that this requires a figure that has right angles; (2) that nonrectangular figures can be converted into rectangular ones by cutting and repiecing figures; and (3) that the added perpendicular in the standard formula for the parallelogram is simply a convenient way of simulating the effects of this cutting and repiecing. Recognition of these three principles is what Wertheimer would have viewed as essential to a "structural" solution to the parallelogram problem. It was that kind of structural knowledge that he proposed as the appropriate objective of instruction.

Wertheimer thus proposed the terms in which capabilities for instruction should be analyzed. Unfortunately, however, the other portions of a theory of instruction—a theory of acquisition and a theory of intervention—are largely missing in the Gestaltist formulation. For the Gestaltists, structural knowledge was essentially either present or absent. Little attention was paid to how it developed.

With respect to intervention, the Gestalt emphasis on underlying structures of knowledge led to an interest in "discovery" methods of teaching. The notion was that if one discovered something rather than being told or shown it, then the underlying principles rather than just a performance pattern would be acquired. This theme was directly pursued in work by Katona (1940/1967), who tried in a number of experiments to show that learning by memorizing actually interfered with the recognition of principles and organized structures. The theme of discovery learning was also picked up by a number of educational psychologists (see Shulman & Keislar, 1966). However, a close analysis of a number of the discovery learning experiments suggests that it was not the discovery *methods* of teaching so much as the different *content* made available to students that accounts for different learning outcomes (see Resnick & Ford, 1981, pp. 144–146).

A more robust principle of intervention that can be drawn from Gestalt theory is the importance of providing instructional *representations* that highlight the relations and structural features that we want students to acquire. This principle—well illustrated by the variety of "structural materials" for teaching mathematics that were developed during the 1950s and 1960s—is also in accord with developmental theories of instruction offered by Bruner (1960, 1966) and by Piaget.

Piaget

One can hardly consider the possibilities for a cognitive instructional theory without attending to Piaget. Piaget himself had little to say about instruction; yet despite this, there have been numerous efforts to draw educational implications from his work, and a variety of different educational programs have been labeled "Piagetian" (Collis, 1975; Furth & Wachs, 1975; Kamii & DeVries, 1977). Is there a coherent instructional theory to be found beneath the label? The answer requires a look at the work of a number of psychologists and educators who consider themselves to be applying Piagetian theory.

Consider first the question of the capabilities to be fostered through instruction. A central core of Piaget's work has been concerned with characterizing the emergence in children of the general logical deductive capacities that are the structural bases of thinking. This led some educators, especially in the first flush of excitement over Piaget, to propose the teaching of operational thinking—assessed by the various "Piagetian tasks" such as conservation—as the goal of instruction (e.g., Kamii, 1972; Lavatelli, 1970; Weikart, Rogers, Adcock, & McClelland, 1971). Improvement of performance on various Piagetian scales, which are themselves based on the tasks used in Piaget's studies, has sometimes been proposed as a criterion of effective education even when the actual instruction focuses on traditional school subject matter (Almy, 1970). Others have proposed Piagetian reinterpretations of school subject matter, especially in mathematics (e.g., Lovell, 1971) and science (Lawson, this volume); or early education programs aimed at general forms of operational thinking (e.g., Furth & Wachs, 1975; Kamii & DeVries, 1977). Often, however, it is not very clear in what sense the goals are specifically Piagetian, since the concepts to be taught have not been studied by Piaget. In any case, this kind of interpretive analysis of subject matter is quite different from the very detailed instructional task analyses of Thorndike or Gagné.

The difficulty in making clear connections between Piagetian theory and the tasks of school instruction persists when we consider the question of acquisition. Piaget does, of course, offer a broad theory of development and hence of the acquisition of capabilities. (See Gallagher & Reid, 1981, for an introduction to Piaget's theory of learning; see Inhelder, Sinclair, & Bovet, 1974, for some Genevan instructional studies.) The key elements in this theory are *interaction* and *equilibration*. Broadly, the interactionist position specifies that biological endowment interacts with the environment so that a child growing up in its appropriate socio-ecological niche will develop in certain directions. Equilibration refers to the complementary processes of assimilation and accommodation by which the child constructs successively more complex and powerful schemes that are used to interpret the stimuli encountered in the environment. The process of equilibration is sparked by cognitive conflict, or the noting of contradictions. Clearly, there is a good deal more of an acquisition theory here than in the Gestalt work. Nevertheless, the Piagetian acquisition theory remains quite general. The actual *processes* involved in assimilation and accommodation are not specified, so the *nature* of the organism–environment interaction is not made clear.

As a result, Piagetian theory provides a very weak guide for instructional efforts. This becomes apparent as one attempts to derive an intervention theory from Piaget's writing. Only some very general principles are forthcoming: Set up an environment in which the child can interact and be actively engaged with things, with other children, and with adults. Promote the natural activities of children in interaction with their environments. Do not do too much drill and practice as this leaves little room for the construction of ideas and relationships by the child. Leave room for invention and discovery. Point out contradictions and let the child work on resolving them.

It is, for the moment, very hard to derive anything more than these general principles from the Piagetian view. Although the principles have been inspiring to many educators, they have proved difficult to translate into specific practices for the classroom. Again, we see a contrast with the explicit prescriptions of behavioral and associationist theories of instruction.

These, then, are some of the predecessors we have to build upon as we approach the task of developing a cognitive theory of instruction. As we have seen, the theories that are strong on prescribing interventions are theories that do not have much to say about thought processes. Even worse, they are theories that almost entirely ignore structure, organization, and meaning as central aspects of learning. On the other hand, the more cognitive theories—those that treat mental life as real and important and that are concerned with the structure of knowledge—have been very weakly developed as instructional theories. Despite some elegant examples of the *kinds* of instructional goals that might be promoted, neither Gestaltist nor Piagetian analyses have proceeded very far in specifying these outcomes. Further, we can draw only very general theories of acquisition or intervention from Piaget, and virtually none from Wertheimer and the Gestaltists.

Is this choice between cognition and a vigorous instructional theory necessary? Or can we envisage a strong theory of acquisition and intervention based on cognitive analyses of instructionally relevant tasks? That is the question addressed in the remainder of this chapter. I will consider the characteristics of current cognitive science research as they bear on these instructionally relevant tasks in order to suggest directions for a cognitive science of instruction. My account begins by characterizing the current state of cognitive task analysis and then turns to the implications of information-processing theories for cognitive theories of acquisition and intervention.

COGNITIVE TASK ANALYSIS: NEW DEFINITIONS OF CAPABILITIES TO BE DEVELOPED THROUGH INSTRUCTION

A central concern of cognitive science today is the analysis of complex task performances. As basic principles of cognitive processing have become established, largely through work on simple, laboratory-like tasks, cognitive scientists (including psychologists, linguists, and computer scientists) have increasingly turned their attention to the more complex tasks that occur in the real world. Among the kinds of tasks now under study are comprehension of extended written and spoken messages, solving physics problems, solving mathematics problems ranging from simple arithmetic to geometry and algebra, programming computers, repairing electrical equipment, reading X-ray films, and performing medical diagnoses. All these tasks are the kinds that form part of school, university, or technical curricula. Because cognitive analyses of performance on instructionally relevant tasks automatically afford descriptions of capabilities to be fostered by instruction, it is possible to characterize a large part of current mainstream cognitive psychology as directly contributing to a theory of instruction.

The flavor of the research on cognitive task analysis, and the kinds of capabilities that are being identified, can best be conveyed by considering examples of this research. I focus here on three domains from the school curriculum—reading comprehension, science, and mathematics.

Reading Comprehension

There is no instructionally relevant domain of investigation that has experienced as spectacular a growth in the past several years as reading comprehension. Furthermore, work on the understanding and comprehension of natural language points to some of the major themes in cognitive theory. Thus, this is a good place in which to begin a consideration of cognitive task analysis. Current work on text comprehension represents a blending of questions and methods from at least three disciplines: psychology, linguistics, and artificial intelligence. My examples come largely from psychology, but it is a psychology that is by now heavily influenced by and influential in the other two fields; the sources of influence and points of collaboration are mentioned as I proceed.

Three major themes can be detected in the current line of research on understanding and learning from text. These are: (1) the importance of prior knowledge in understanding a text passage, (2) the central role of inference in reading, and (3) the flexibility of the reading process—its adaptation to local conditions and demands. Each of these is considered in turn.

Prior Knowledge.   In 1972, Bransford and Johnson offered a dramatic example of the extent to which texts become comprehensible by virtue of being assimilated into existing cognitive structures. To make the demonstration, they showed that certain especially ambiguous passages could not be understood at all until some hint of what they were "about" was provided. For example, the passage in Fig. 1.2 is incomprehensible until a picture related to the story is seen (Fig. 1.3).

Following Bransford and Johnson, there came a number of other demonstrations that ambiguous (but perhaps not so totally obscure) passages took on meaning either according to hints provided in advance by the experimenter or according to the subjects' predilections. Anderson, Reynolds, Schallert, and Goetz (1977), for example, showed that music students interpreted a passage as describing an evening of playing music, whereas physical education students interpreted the same passage as an evening of playing cards. Others showed that the context in which information in a passage was conveyed could influence what was remembered from the passage and how the memory was organized. For example, in research by Anderson, Spiro, and Anderson (1978) a "restaurant" story produced a different pattern of recall for an identical set of food items than did a "supermarket" story.

These various demonstrations of the role of organizing schemata on understanding and recall echoed an earlier line of work, by Ausubel (1968), on "advance organizers." Ausubel had published a series of studies that showed

If the balloons popped the sound wouldn't be able to carry since everything would be too far away from the correct floor. A closed window would also prevent the sound from carrying, since most buildings tend to be well insulated. Since the whole operation depends upon a steady flow of electricity, a break in the middle of the wire would also cause problems. Of course, the fellow could shout, but the human voice is not loud enough to carry that far. An additional problem is that a string could break on the instrument. Then there could be no accompaniment to the message. It is clear that the best situation would involve less distance. Then there would be fewer potential problems. With face to face contact, the least number of things could go wrong.

FIG. 1.2. Ambiguous textual passage. (From Bransford & Johnson, 1972. Reprinted with permission.)

that learning of information from text could be improved if, in advance of reading the text, students were provided with an organization or structure within which to interpret it. Recent reviews and experiments (e.g., Mayer, 1979) have made it clear that advance organizers are an advantage when certain conditions hold: (1) the learner does not already know enough about the topic to provide the organizer for himself or herself; (2) the organizer is at least somewhat more "abstract" than the text itself, so that it provides a general structure, rather than just a preview of what is to come; (3) the material to be learned does not itself contain the necessary organizing and anchoring ideas; (4) the test comes long enough after the exposure to organizer and text that the learner cannot recall the material directly but must create an interpreted version.

Work on "story grammars" is a particularly well-developed example of how prior knowledge works in the process of understanding. Dealing with a particular kind of text, the narrative story, a number of investigators (Mandler, 1978; Stein & Glenn, 1979; Thorndyke, 1977) have shown that stories have a prototypical structure in which several categories of information must occur in order: a setting, an initiating event, an internal response, an attempt (to obtain a goal), an outcome or consequence, and a reaction. Some of the categories in this structure are more central than others. This is shown by substantial regularities in which portions of stories people omit in their retellings or in the stories they make up (Goldman, 1979). Story grammars represent an attempt to develop a domain-specific theory of text understanding. That is, it is proposed that in order to understand stories people must already have an idea of what a story is supposed to be like. This idealized story—a "schema" of a story—organizes and directs their interaction with the particular story they are now reading or hearing.

The idea that a prototypic version of a situation is used to interpret specific instances is shared by much of the recent artificial intelligence (AI) work on natural language understanding (Schank & Abelson, 1977). A number of computer programs have been constructed that are capable of "understanding" and answering questions about texts on a number of topics. Much of the ability of these AI programs to understand derives from their domain specificity, which allows them to use previously stored knowledge to interpret the new text. But the specificity is also a shortcoming, for it makes it difficult to develop a general program for text comprehension.

Inference.   The most comprehensive attempt to build a generalized model of text understanding is that of Kintsch and van Dijk (1978). Their efforts are, in a sense, the necessary complements to models of processing that depend on representing an individual's knowledge of a particular domain. Their theory focuses on the extent to which a text is internally "coherent" (i.e., explicitly interconnected) and on the processes required for a reader to infer connections that are not explicit in the text. A text is coherent in the Kintsch and van Dijk analysis to the extent that each new proposition (i.e., actor–action–object sequence) makes explicit reference to prior propositions. In Fig. 1.4, for example, propositions 1–4 and 5–11 are fully coherent because the actor (subject) in each proposition has already been named in a close prior proposition. Line 5 is not explicitly coherent with its predecessors, however. To understand the text—that is, to construct a fully coherent representation of it—the reader must infer a linking proposition: for example, "The Swazi tribe had warriors." The number of missing propositions and the distance in the text that must be traversed to find explicit links affect not only the processing time for a text but also the short-term memory demands it makes. Too much local incoherence can render a text incomprehensible, but a completely explicit text would be uninteresting—like a primer. Optimal texts thus require "just the right amount" of inferential work by the reader—as if there were an implicit contract between the writer and the reader.

The Kintsch and van Dijk theory highlights the central role of *inference* in understanding a text. This is a feature of comprehension that emerges in virtually every cognitive analysis. Texts and oral messages are rarely, if ever, complete in specifying everything that has to be known to make sense of the situation described or the argument being made. It is the task of the reader to fill in the gaps. To do this, when one reads a text one builds up in the mind a knowledge structure that fits the situation in the text. This knowledge structure is not a direct match to the text; it leaves out some things that the text mentions and adds some things

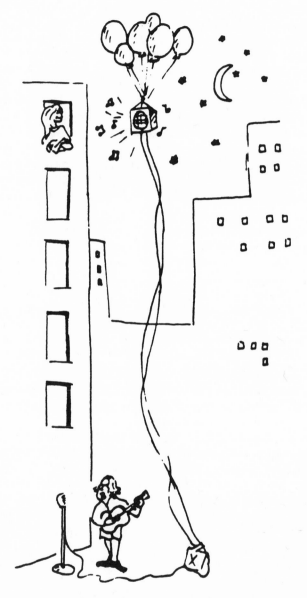

FIG. 1.3.   Appropriate context for ambiguous passage. (From Bransford & Johnson, 1972. Copyright 1972 by Academic Press. Reprinted with permission.)

Text:
The Swazi tribe was at war with a neighboring tribe because of a dispute over some cattle. Among the warriors were two unmarried men named Kakra and his younger brother Gum. Kakra was killed in a battle...

Propositional analysis of text:

1. The Swazi tribe was at war.
2. The war was with a neighboring tribe.
3. The war had a cause.
4. The cause was a dispute over some cattle.

5. There were warriors.
6. The warriors were two men.
7. The men were unmarried.
8. The men were named Kakra and Gum.
9. Gum was the younger brother of Kakra.
10. Kakra was killed.
11. The killing was in a battle.

FIG. 1.4.   A text and its propositions. (Adapted from Kintsch, 1979.)

that the text does not mention. What it leaves out is what the reader construes as not being important or central to the main argument of the text. What it adds are things that the text has failed to specify but which "have to" be true if the situation being represented is to make sense.

The ability to detect and use centrality to a theme is an important part of the inference process. For a given story line or line of argument, readers tend to agree fairly well on what statements are important or central and which ones are subordinate, perhaps functioning only as elaborations. Meyer (1975) has used this regularity to develop a method for coding the statements in a passage for their relative centrality; other less systematic ways of judging centrality have also been developed. Using measures of this kind, it has been possible to show that the material most likely to be forgotten or left out of a summary is the material lowest in the hierarchy of importance. Conversely, if material high in the hierarchy is not specified in the text, people will have trouble interpreting the text at all, will tend to insert missing high-level propositions in their summaries, and will spend a long time "studying" the portion of the passage where the high-level organizing material is expected to be (Kieras, 1977). Also, when asked whether a given statement was or was not present in the text, people are likely to assert with great confidence that highly central material that is consonant with the gist of the text was there—even when it was not. In a series of studies that further link the Kintsch general coherence-plus-inference model with schema theories, Voss and his colleagues (Chiesi, Spilich, & Voss, 1979; Spilich, Vesonder, Chiesi, & Voss, 1979) have shown that readers' ability to make inferences depends on what they already know about the topic of the text.

Flexibility. Various studies have shown that skilled readers adapt their reading to local features of the text as well as to their own purpose for reading. For example, reading rates are slower and there is more checking back at points in a text where ambiguous, inconsistent, or incoherent information is encountered (Kieras, 1977). Eye-movement data demonstrate additional processing activity at points where information from important clauses must be integrated and inferences made (Just & Carpenter, 1981), and on parts of the text that are relevant to a particular kind of information the reader is trying to get from a passage (Rothkopf & Billington, 1979). Skilled readers also adjust their reading rates to the general readability of the text (Bassin & Martin, 1976; Coke, 1976) and to the kinds of information they seek to acquire (McConkie, Rayner, & Wilson, 1973; Samuels & Dahl, 1975). Finally, the number and types of inferences made depend on the purpose for which a text is read.

Although this flexibility on the part of skilled readers has been frequently documented, the processes underlying it have only recently begun to be studied. This recent research has made it clear that the likelihood of using varied processes under normal reading conditions must depend on individuals' abilities to monitor their own comprehension (Brown, 1980). These "metacomprehension" abilities, which are at least partly a function of age, seem to depend critically on sensitivity to important relationships among the propositions in a text. Thus, flexibility, like inference, depends on prior knowledge of the topic of the text.

Science and Mathematics

A growing body of work in the learning and performance of science and mathematics tasks is pointing to some general characteristics of performance in these domains that accords well with the emphasis on prior knowledge, inferences, and flexible strategies in reading comprehension. In particular, research on science and problem solving suggests that the knowledge structures of individuals who are highly skilled in a domain are different in kind from the knowledge structures of novices. As a result, experts solve problems in different ways from novices, and—we may conjecture—they go about learning new information in their domain of expertise differently. At the same time, it is becoming clear that even very young children invent theories that allow them to construct procedural and predictive rules in simple mathematics and science domains.

Novice–Expert Differences in Physics. Chi, Feltovich, and Glaser (1981) have shown that the initial representation of a problem in mechanics is different for expert physicists (advanced graduate students) than for novices (undergraduate students). When asked to sort and classify problems, the novices did so on the basis of the kind of apparatus involved (lever, inclined plane, balance beam, etc.), the actual terms used in the problem statement, or the surface characteristics of the diagram presented. Experts, however, classified problems according to the underlying physics principle needed to solve them (e.g., Energy Laws, Newton's Second Law). Some typical novice classifications are shown in Fig. 1.5; the contrasting expert classifications are shown in Fig. 1.6.

Larkin, McDermott, Simon, and Simon (1980), in a complementary set of studies, have shown that the process of solution is also different for novices and experts. The novices seem to directly translate the given information into for-

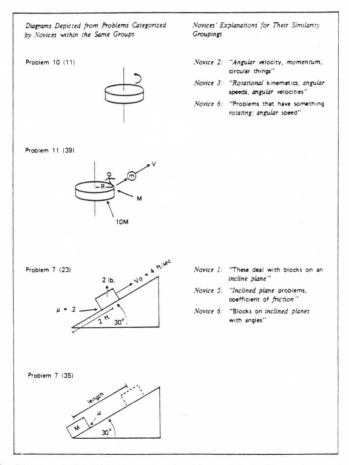

FIG. 1.5. Diagrams depicted from two pairs of problems categorized by novices as similar and samples of three novices' explanations for their similarity. Problem numbers given represent chapter, followed by problem number from Halliday and Resnick, 1974. (From Chi et al., 1981. Copyright 1981 by Ablex Publishing Corp. Reprinted with permission.)

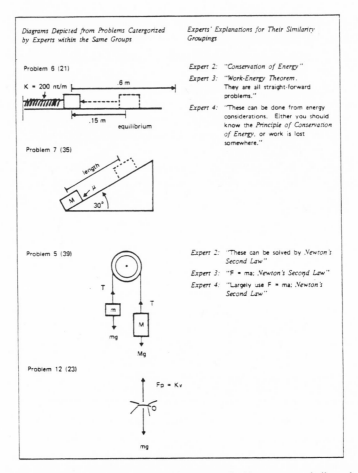

FIG. 1.6.   Diagrams depicted from pairs of problems categorized by experts as similar and samples of three experts' explanations for their similarity. Problem numbers given represent chapter, followed by problem number from Halliday and Resnick, 1974. (From Chi et al., 1981. Copyright 1981 by Ablex Publishing Corp. Reprinted with permission.)

mulas and then work more or less algebraically on the formulas, looking for substitutions and transformations that will yield the required answer to the problem. Experts, by contrast, do a fair amount of interpretation that allows them to represent the problems as instances of certain general laws of physics and to restructure the relationships between elements of the problem. As a result, they usually have only one or two equations to write and the problem is virtually solved by the time they figure out what it is about. A general characterization of Larkin's finding is that the novices behave as if they are doing puzzles in which the terms to be manipulated have little external reference—their protocols look very much like those of people solving cryptarithmetic and other puzzlelike problems (Newell & Simon, 1972). They are characterized by what has come to be called "means–end analysis," in which they work backward from a goal. Experts, by contrast, seem to be working forward from the information given in the problem.

Invented Routines and Rule-Driven Behavior.   Examination of school text-books does not reveal in any direct way what children actually do when they perform arithmetic tasks. This is revealed in a striking way by consideration of simple, single-digit addition and subtraction. Textbooks typically teach addition as a process of counting out the two named subsets and then recounting the combined set, and everyone expects children rather quickly to give up any kind of counting in favor of memorizing the addition "facts." However, experiments have now revealed that there is an intermediate period during which children continue to solve addition problems by counting—but not by the method initially taught in school. Instead, they use a procedure that seems to imply an under-standing of commutativity and that is elegantly simpler than the procedure taught. This procedure, typical of 6-year-olds and up, is known as the *min* model, because the smaller (minimum) of the two addends is added to the other in a counting-on procedure. For example, to add 3 + 5, the child starts at 5 (even though it is named second) and counts on: "5 . . . 6, 7, 8." This procedure has been documented in reaction-time and interview studies of a number of children in different countries and of different measured mental abilities (Groen & Park-man, 1972; Svenson, 1975; Svenson & Broquist, 1975). A study by Groen and Resnick (1977) shows that the *min* procedure can be invented by 4- and 5-year-old children.

A similar story can be told for subtraction. The textbooks demonstrate either a counting-out procedure in which the minuend set is established, a specified number of objects is removed, and the remainder counted; or a matching pro-cedure in which sets to represent the minuend and the subtrahend are established, objects from these sets are paired one-for-one, and the remaining unmatched objects are counted. However, after practice, children do something rather dif-ferent from either of these: they *either* count down from the minuend *or* count up from the subtrahend, *whichever will take the fewest counts.* Thus for 9 − 2 they say, "9 . . . 8, 7," but for 9 − 7, they say, "7 . . . 8, 9" (Svenson & Heden-borg, 1979; Woods, Resnick, & Groen, 1975). Children who invent these pro-cedures behave as if they understand the commutativity principle of addition and the complementarity of addition and subtraction. However, it is not yet clear how explicit such understanding actually is (cf. Resnick, in press).

These inventions by children are no doubt heartening for those who would apply a constructivist theory of learning and development to education by leaving children free to explore and discover within only loosely defined boundaries. But the presence of inventions tells only part of the story, for not all inventions are mathematically successful. Several investigators (Brown & Burton, 1978;

Ginsburg, 1977; Lankford, 1972) have shown that children's errors on slightly more complex arithmetic tasks (e.g., multidigit written subtraction) are actually systematic applications of the wrong algorithmic procedure, rather than random failures to recall the appropriate "facts." These wrong procedures are variants of the correct ones; they are analogous to computer algorithms with "bugs" in them and have thus been christened "buggy algorithms." A finite number of bugs, which in various combinations make up several dozen buggy algorithms, have been identified for subtraction—which is the most often studied arithmetic domain so far. The children who display these buggy algorithms are systematically applying rules that no one could have taught them (for no one would deliberately teach a wrong rule). Buggy algorithms are thus clear examples of inventions that are unsuccessful.

Despite their failure as rules of calculation, buggy algorithms demonstrate an important characteristic of human learning and performance. Close analysis of the various incorrect algorithms that have been observed among children makes it clear that most of them are rather sensible and often quite small departures from the correct algorithm. As the examples in Fig. 1.7 reveal, they tend to "look right" and to obey a large number of the important rules for written calculation: The digit structure is respected, there is only a single digit per column, all the columns are filled, and so forth. In the sense of being an orderly and reasonable response to a new situation, the buggy algorithm looks quite sensible.

To illustrate this point, consider the third bug shown in Fig. 1.7. The written response looks more or less correct and follows most of the rules for written subtraction, such as operating on each column only once, having only a single digit in each column, and showing a borrow digit with a crossed-out and decremented digit. The syntax of the procedure is more or less correct. Yet the algorithm violates some fundamental mathematical constraints. In particular, it behaves as if its inventor does not understand that the borrow digit adds units via an exchange with another column, and that the exchange must maintain equivalence of the overall quantity. This knowledge, if applied, would not permit what this particular buggy algorithm does: It "borrows" 100 but "returns" only 10. Other bugs, too, have the character of respecting much of the syntax of written arithmetic but violating the "semantics"—or underlying meaning (Resnick, 1982).

A similar emphasis on the sensible, rule-driven character of "wrong" responses appears in Siegler's (1978) work on the balance beam and other similar tasks. In the balance task various numbers of weights can be hung at various distances from the fulcrum; the child must predict which, if either, side will go down. Children do not completely solve this problem successfully until adolescence. Siegler showed, however, that at each of several preceding stages children actually follow algorithmic rules for deciding which side of the balance will go down. The rules that are followed become successively richer, not only in the amount of information that children call on but in the extent to which they are

1. **Smaller-From-Larger.** The student subtracts the smaller digit in a column from the larger digit regardless of which one is on top.

```
    3 2 6            5 4 2
  - 1 1 7          - 3 8 9
  ───────          ───────
    2 1 1            2 4 7
```

2. **Borrow-From-Zero.** When borrowing from a column whose top digit is 0, the student writes 9 but does not continue borrowing from the column to the left of the 0.

```
    6'0,2            8'0,2
  - 4 3 7          - 3 9 6
  ───────          ───────
    2 6 5            5 0 6
```

3. **Borrow-Across-Zero.** When the student needs to borrow from a column whose top digit is 0, he skips that column and borrows from the next one. (Note: This bug must be combined with either bug 5 or bug 6.)

```
    '8 0,2           7,
  - 3 2 7            8'0,4
  ───────          - 4 5 6
    2 2 5          ───────
                     3 0 8
```

4. **Stops-Borrow-At-Zero.** The student fails to decrement 0, although he adds 10 correctly to the top digit of the active column. (Note: This bug must be combined with either bug 5 or bug 6.)

```
    7 0,3            6 0,4
  - 6 7 8          - 3 8 7
  ───────          ───────
    1 7 5            3 0 7
```

5. **0 − N = N.** Whenever there is 0 on top, the digit on the bottom is written as the answer.

```
    7 0 9            6 0 0 8
  - 3 5 2          -   3 2 7
  ───────          ─────────
    4 5 7            6 3 2 1
```

6. **0 − N = 0.** Whenever there is 0 on top, 0 is written as the answer.

```
    8 0 4            3 0 5 0
  - 4 6 2          -   6 2 1
  ───────          ─────────
    4 0 2            3 0 3 0
```

7. **N − 0 = 0.** Whenever there is 0 on the bottom, 0 is written as the answer.

```
    9 7 6            8 5,6
  - 3 0 2          - 4 0 9
  ───────          ───────
    6 0 4            4 0 7
```

8. **Don't-Decrement-Zero.** When borrowing from a column in which the top digit is 0, the student rewrites the 0 as 10, but does not change the 10 to 9 when incrementing the active column.

```
    6
    7 0,2            1
  - 3 6 8            2,0,5
  ───────          -     9
    3 4 4          ───────
                     1 1 0 6
```

9. **Zero-Instead-Of-Borrow.** The student writes 0 as the answer in any column in which the bottom digit is larger than the top.

```
    3 2 6            5 4 2
  - 1 1 7          - 3 8 9
  ───────          ───────
    2 1 0            2 0 0
```

10. **Borrow-From-Bottom-Instead-Of-Zero.** If the top digit in the column being borrowed from is 0, the student borrows from the bottom digit instead. (Note: This bug must be combined with either bug 5 or bug 6.)

```
    7 0,2            5 0,8
  - 3 6 8          - 4 8 9
  ───────          ───────
    4 5 4            1 0 9
```

FIG. 1.7. Samples of Brown and Burton's (1978) buggy subtraction algorithms invented by children. (Adapted from Resnick, 1982. Copyright 1982 by Lawrence Erlbaum Associates. Reprinted by permission.)

able to coordinate that information. The early rules consider either weight or distance alone; the child seems to be unable to consider both at once. Subsequently, weight and distance are combined; but, at first, not in an accurate computation of torque on the balance beam. Nevertheless, the rules are systematic and produce predictable patterns of responses. Here, too, is evidence for the principled character even of errors.

The preceding sketch of the status of cognitive task analysis provides convincing evidence that one part of the agenda of building a cognitive theory of instruction is well under way. Analyses of the kind that have been described are capable of providing rigorous and formal statements of instructional objectives concerned with meaning and understanding and their relation to performance skills. We no longer have to accept the choice between the rigor of behavioral objectives and our desire for explicit recognition of cognitive structures and thought. We are moving closer to being able to make useful specifications of *cognitive* objectives for instruction (cf. Greeno, 1976).

COGNITIVE THEORIES OF ACQUISITION

When we move to a consideration of the other parts of the instructional theory agenda, however, we are on less well-developed ground. The reemergence of cognition in American psychology was accompanied by a loss of interest in learning and acquisition processes. Until very recently, cognitive psychologists have been focusing almost exclusively on the issue of cognitive performance while ignoring the issue of how these performances are acquired. In contrast, the older learning theories—those represented by Thorndike and Skinner, for example—were deeply interested in transitions. Their theories were largely intended to account for changes in performance as a result of certain kinds of experiences in the environment.

Although work toward cognitive theories of acquisition is relatively recent, such work is now recognized by many cognitive scientists as a major agenda for the field (see, e.g., Anderson, 1981). Further, the research on cognitive task analysis—some of which I have reviewed here—points both to the standards of rigor to be expected in eventual cognitive learning theories and to some of the broad characteristics that these theories are likely to have. I consider some of these characteristics in the following section.

Constructivism

Even a cursory consideration of the emerging findings from cognitive task analyses makes it clear that our new theories of acquisition will have to take account of the important role of mental constructions and interpretations by the learner. The central role of inference in text understanding, the evidence for inventions of mathematical procedures, and the characterization of expert problem solvers as individuals who reformulate problems before beginning to work on them all point toward the active role that the learner himself plays in acquiring new knowledge. For those who have been committed to cognitive interpretations of development, this emphasis on active construction of knowledge by the learner is not new. It has been a central theme in Piaget's work and theory for decades and has been much emphasized in many of the most sensitive and influential explorations of the implications of Piaget's work for education (Duckworth, 1979;

Furth, 1970; Ginsburg & Opper, 1969; Kamii & DeVries, 1977). Yet, curiously, this central theme has been little elaborated even within cognitive developmental theory. As noted earlier, Piaget's theory of construction of new schemes via assimilation and accommodation provides only a skeleton of a theory of acquisition. It has not been fleshed out, nor has it been developed for any particular domain of knowledge to a degree sufficient to provide a useful example of how the processes might actually work in the course of cognitive construction.

Sensible Constructions on Limited Data.   A central feature of the constructions that characterize acquisition is that they operate without complete information. Rather than waiting until all the evidence is in, people seem to work to make sense of the world on the basis of the information they have. The research on buggy algorithms, on rule-based developmental sequences, and on inference in text comprehension all point to the fact that people seek sensible solutions and explanations within the limits of their knowledge.

A close consideration of buggy arithmetic algorithms and their origin highlights this point. Brown and VanLehn (1982) have developed a formal theory, in the form of a computer simulation, of the origin of bugs in arithmetic. According to their "repair" theory, buggy algorithms arise when an arithmetic problem is encountered for which the child's current algorithms are incomplete or inappropriate. The child, trying to respond, eventually reaches an impasse, a situation for which no action is available. At this point, the child calls on a list of "repairs"—actions to try when the standard action cannot be used. The repair list includes strategies such as performing the action in a different column, skipping the action, swapping top and bottom numbers in a column, and substituting an operation (such as incrementing for decrementing). The outcome generated through this repair process is then checked by a set of "critics" that inspect the resulting solution for conformity to some basic criteria, such as no empty columns, only one digit per column in the answer, only one decrement per column, and the like.

Together, the repair and critic lists constitute the key elements in a "generate and test" problem-solving routine. This is the same kind of "intelligent" problem solving that characterizes many successful performances in other domains (cf. Simon, 1976, pp. 65–98). With buggy algorithms, the trouble seems to lie not in the reasoning processes but in the inadequate data base applied. Inspection of the repair and critic lists makes it clear that the generation and the test rules in this particular system can all be viewed as "syntactic." That is, they all concern the surface structure of the procedure and do not necessarily reflect what we can call the "semantics" of subtraction (Resnick, 1982).

Repair theory is, in fact, a detailed theory of acquisition for a small domain of arithmetic. Its broader implications for cognitive theories of acquisition is that these theories must recognize people's tendency to organize and structure whatever information they have—even though the information may be grossly incomplete or downright inaccurate. They do not simply acquire information passively until there is enough of it for "correct" rules and explanations to emerge. This tendency to construct ordered explanations and routines even in the absence of adequate information can account at least partly for another phenomenon, observed thus far mainly in science learning: robust beliefs that are resistant to change even when instruction (and thus better information) *does* come along. We will consider this phenomenon again, in the context of coherence and integration in learning.

Coherence in Learning: The Integration of Old and New Knowledge

As we have seen, research on reading comprehension makes it clear that the job of the reader is to connect new information in a text to the old, and it shows how comprehension falters when these "given-new" (cf. Clark & Haviland, 1977) links are difficult to establish. An extension of these notions of coherence-building suggests that we view the acquisition of new capabilities as a process of building appropriate links between knowledge already held and new knowledge. Stated this way, the role of coherence in learning sounds deceptively simple. The established behaviorist notion of building new performances out of the components of old ones, stated most elegantly in Gagné's (1962) theory of prerequisites and cumulative learning, appears to describe its role almost completely. It might seem that all that is needed to extend the coherence principle to a cognitive theory of acquisition are the detailed task analyses that would allow us to specify the mental structures that are to be extended at the next stage of learning. Even this would be no small task, but there is evidence that the problem of coherence will prove even more complicated than cumulative learning theory would suggest.

A growing body of evidence, mostly collected in studies of science learning, is now showing how prior knowledge can actually interfere with new learning. A recurrent finding in studies of physics instruction is that people bring with them to the study of physics a quite powerful set of beliefs about how the physical world works. These beliefs are robust and resistant to the new data and theoretical principles that are taught in physics courses (Champagne, Gunstone, & Klopfer, in press; Selman, Krupa, Stone, & Jaquette, in press; Viennot, 1979). Their "naive" beliefs allow people to construct explanations of various phenomena that accord quite well with their perceived experiences. The difficulty is that these beliefs do not match well with the Newtonian principles taught in physics courses, yet they are not always abandoned as the result of instruction in Newtonian physics. Some students can perform adequately on the textbook problems in a high school or college physics course, yet when given practical problems that are not easily recognized as applications of the textbook formulas—problems that force them to construct their own representation of the situation—they will revert to the conceptions they had before the course began. These students show evidence of having well-integrated knowledge structures that will have to be given up or altered radically before they can acquire Newtonian conceptions at a level beyond mechanical equation solving.

These findings force us to broaden our thinking about the relations between established and new knowledge in the course of acquisition. We must think not only about the cumulation and linking of knowledge structures, but also about what kind of *confrontation* between old conceptions and new ones may be needed for the new to take hold. If schema theories of discourse comprehension and the performances of expert physicists point toward the positive role that prior knowledge can play in performance and learning, these studies of difficulties in physics teaching reveal its negative role. This is a far more subtle role for "entering capabilities" than was allowed in the Gagné analyses of prerequisites. Now that the phenomenon has been demonstrated, the task ahead is to analyze it. How, precisely, do already held schemata drive attention *away* from competing interpretations? Is the process simply preemptive, or is there a more complex relationship between the two schema systems to be uncovered? And what happens to old schemata as new ones take over? Are they simply "left behind" or are they incorporated into a new framework? As answers to questions like these begin to take shape, we will have a theory of acquisition capable of more directly guiding instruction in these complex subject matters.

The Nature of Theory Change: Insight Versus Incremental Change

The preceding discussion suggests that it may be useful to view cognitive acquisition as a process of knowledge restructuring, a definition that immediately brings to mind both Gestalt and Piagetian theory. These structuralist theories both stressed the role of invention and insight in the process of such restructuring. The notion that insight, presumably resulting in an immediate restructuring of knowledge, is characteristic of learning contrasts sharply with traditional theories of learning in which acquisition is described as a gradual and incremental process—a function of extended practice. Debates among learning theorists concerning incremental versus "all-or-none" learning of simple discriminations can, in fact, be viewed as one of the important predecessors of the cognitive revolution in experimental psychology. Given this history, it is not surprising that there has been a general tendency to equate cognitive theories of human behavior with insight-oriented theories of acquisition. In fact, a cognitive view of education has up to now almost always carried the implication that learning does not proceed in smooth steps, but instead is marked by occasional moments of insight resulting in immediate qualitative differences in the nature of thinking.

It is no longer so likely, however, that cognitive theories of acquisition will emphasize momentary insightful restructurings rather than the gradual acquisition of new understanding. A number of cognitive scientists are now turning their attention to the question of acquisition. A recent edited volume (Anderson, 1981) provides an excellent overview of the direction that one major class of these theories—the ones committed to formalization through computer simulation—is taking. Work of this kind by Neches (1981) is directly relevant to the examples of task analysis presented earlier in this chapter and illustrates well the power of incremental theories. Neches has constructed a computer program that invents the *min* model of mental addition. That is, it begins with a procedure for addition in which both addends are counted in the order presented; but after a period of practice on addition problems, it performs by "naming" the larger addend and then counting up by the amount of the smaller. The conversion is accomplished by a set of mechanisms that seek performance efficiency by eliminating redundant steps and by strengthening responses that are made while weakening potentially competing responses. The program is self-modifying; all transformations of knowledge are its own. It makes a major transformation in its procedure, yet there is no single moment of insight. Indeed, it is not clear that the system needs to "understand" commutativity in order to behave in accord with it.

The Neches program, like other self-modifying systems, provides a plausible account of how acquisition might proceed. But the account is only that: *plausible*, but by no means proven. One difficulty with this line of work is that up to now it has proceeded with only a limited amount of data on the actual human processes that are being modeled. Typically, as with Neches, there exists strong evidence for a particular initial performance and a final one. However, there is usually no observation of the acquisition process itself. As a result, the theorist is free to build a self-modifying system without the requirement that any particular features of the acquisition sequence itself be matched. Intriguing as the current self-modifying programs are, then, we must withhold acceptance of them as actual descriptions of cognitive activity until they can be more fully constrained by observations of human learning.

We must not, however, assume that as a more substantiated theory of acquisition is developed it will necessarily support insight as opposed to incremental accounts of acquisition. Over the past 3 years my colleagues and I have spent several hundred hours studying protocols taken on a small number of children as they were taught subtraction using a method intended to induce understanding of the meaning of the various scratch marks and manipulations involved in subtraction with borrowing. This instruction emphasizes the analogy between two different representations of subtraction—one, the symbols used in standard written notation and the other, a concrete representation using blocks designed to highlight the quantitative meaning of place value. The child is required to make alternating moves in the two representations, in order to build a mental mapping between operations in each. This procedure helps the child to apply his or her understanding of the blocks action to the writing. The procedure is summarized in Fig. 1.8.

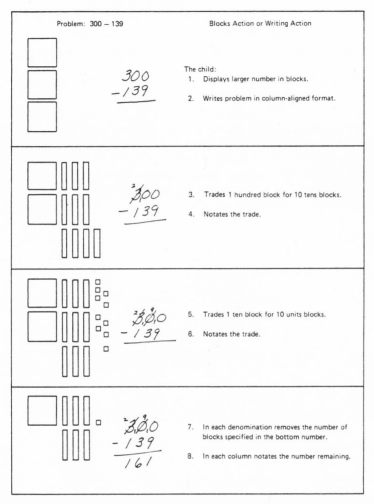

FIG. 1.8.   Instructional procedure for mapping blocks action to writing in teaching subtraction with borrowing. (From Resnick, 1982. Copyright 1982 by Lawrence Erlbaum Associates. Reprinted by permission.)

We have paid special attention to the case of one child, Molly, who quite clearly experienced a moment of insight in the course of this instruction. She told us so by her exclamation, "Oh, neat! Now I get it," at Step 2 (Fig. 1.8), and an accompanying change in the pace and rhythm of her working through the remaining steps. Recently, impelled by the need to begin serious work on a theory of acquisition for this domain of mathematics understanding, we have begun to reexamine this child's protocol. There is no doubt that Molly *felt* that she had understood something new at the moment of her exclamation. But on closer examination it is not at all clear what it was that she really "got." She certainly did not suddenly know the correct algorithm to use, nor did she automatically and quickly generate correct descriptions of the operations she was doing. In fact, it took a delay of several weeks and another hour or so of probing for Molly to generate an explanation of written subtraction that convinced us that she understood *why* the written subtraction algorithm "worked." There was, in other words, no immediate restructuring of knowledge at Molly's moment of felt insight.

Yet something clearly happened at that moment. What? Our best current interpretation is that at the moment of insight, Molly learned *where* to look for explanations. That is, she learned that the blocks and the writing are analogous and thus, perhaps, the schemata she had for blocks might also apply to writing. This insight allowed her to inspect the two routines and to apply her understanding of one to the other—a process, however, that was to take considerable time beyond the actual moment of insight.

The story of Molly's insight is, for the moment, more a conjecture than a theory. I offer it now, despite its very tentative status, to make two points. First, the feeling of having an insight does not necessarily mean that a complete restructuring of knowledge has taken place; it may only mark a moment in which some clue as to how to go about the process of restructuring becomes apparent. Second, our study of Molly highlights the kind of detailed observations—freed of assumptions about insight and immediate mental restructuring as the foundation of acquisition—that we are going to need as we build a cognitive theory of acquisition.

A COGNITIVE THEORY OF INTERVENTION

We come finally to the question of intervention. If the route has been long, I think it has not been unnecessarily circuitous. For to propose principles of intervention in the absence of a strong theory of acquisition is to operate in the kind of theoretical vacuum that can only produce an endless series of empirical experiments on different instructional methods, with no basis for interpretation.

It should not be surprising that with a cognitive theory of acquisition only beginning to emerge, we can hardly point to a vigorous cognitive theory of intervention at this time. Nevertheless, the developments outlined in the course of this chapter surely suggest the kind of instructional theory that we can expect to build. Specifically, the accumulated body of cognitive task analysis and the emerging work on cognitive theories of acquisition clearly signal the need for a *constructivist theory of instruction*. It now seems absolutely certain that our task is to develop a theory of intervention that places the learner's active mental construction at the very heart of the instructional exchange. Instruction cannot simply put knowledge and skill into people's heads. Instead, effective instruction must aim to place learners in situations where the constructions that they naturally and inevitably make as they try to make sense of their worlds are *correct* as well as sensible ones.

A constructivist theory of instruction need not avoid prescriptions for intervention; nor need it specify only a very general environmental arrangement, as in some of the Piagetian proposals for designing schools and classrooms. Instead, a constructivist intervention theory must address all the traditional concerns of instructional design: how to present new information to students, what kinds of responses to demand from students, how to sequence and schedule learning episodes, and what kinds of feedback to provide at what points in the learning sequence. These traditional instructional concerns take on new substance and direction when approached from a constructivist perspective. Although the enterprise of building a constructivist instructional theory has barely begun, it is possible to sketch some of the questions that will need to be addressed as work proceeds. I do this in the concluding pages of this chapter.

Instructional Representations

One of the central questions for any theory of instructional intervention concerns the form in which information is best conveyed to the learner. In traditional instructional design it was tacitly assumed that a task analysis that specified the performance or knowledge of skilled people in a domain would automatically yield not only "objectives" for instruction in that domain but an outline of the form in which information should be presented to learners. Implicit in this assumption was the notion that instruction should communicate as directly as possible the "mature" or "expert's" form of a concept or skill. Research of the kind discussed in this chapter, however, makes it clear that this assumption does not adequately recognize the work of the learner in *constructing* the mature form of knowledge. Novice–expert contrastive studies have shown that the mental representations of beginners differ qualitatively from those of people more experienced in a domain of knowledge. Furthermore, there are hints that novices may not be able to assimilate or use the categories and representations of experts when these are directly presented; yet we know that extensive practice allows people who begin as novices to discover the representations and skillful performances of experts. If this is so, then the task of the instructor is not to search for ways of presenting information that directly match the thought or performance patterns of experts. Rather, it is to find instructional representations that allow learners to gradually construct those expert representations for themselves.

Until quite recently, the question of representations for instruction has been the almost exclusive concern of curriculum developers and pedagogical subject-matter specialists. Mathematics educators, for example, have developed an extensive repertoire of concrete and pictorial representations of mathematical concepts (Resnick & Ford, 1981, chap. 5). Only recently have psychologists begun to analyze these materials and their function in the learning process. In an earlier paper (Resnick, 1976), I suggested that instructional representations must: (1) represent the concept or idea to be acquired in a veridical, if simplified way; (2) be "transparent" to the learner (i.e., represent relationships in an easily apprehended form or decompose procedures into manageable units); (3) map well onto expert modes of understanding and skill. As an example, Dienes blocks (of the kind displayed in Fig. 1.8) seem to meet these requirements nicely for the principles of place value. They represent the relations among numbers that are embedded in place value notation, and they are in a form that is easy for children to recognize and manipulate. The ten-for-one relationship between adjacent denominations is visible and physically verifiable by superimposition or alignment of the blocks, and exchanges between denominations can be made in a way that parallels the steps in calculation algorithms. In another domain of learning, Gentner (1980) has been analyzing the role of analogies in learning and teaching scientific concepts. Research on instructional representations in a variety of subject matters should eventually lead to a generalizable theory of representations for teaching that is capable of guiding instructional design efforts. Such a theory will need to take explicit account of how learners interpret representations and how they build mental representations and procedures from the instructional materials that are presented.

Interventions That Take Account of Previous Knowledge

As I have noted earlier, the theme of building on past learning is an old one in instructional psychology. In behavioral theories, it has generally been assumed that previous knowledge, when present, facilitated subsequent learning. That is, new capabilities were to be built of the components of older ones, and knowledge and skill would thus cumulate hierarchically. As we have seen, however, prior knowledge can also interfere with acquiring new concepts. This means that instructional methods are needed that explicitly take this interference into account. A theory of intervention quite different from the one derived from cumulative learning theory will be needed to guide instruction of this kind. As a point of departure, the Piagetian notion that cognitive growth occurs as the result of conflict between competing schemes might be elaborated in the context of instructional subject matters and perhaps linked more explicitly to schema-driven theories of comprehension and acquisition. This could provide one basis for intervention studies that explore different approaches to relating new learning to old. What is best: ignoring prior incompatible conceptions and helping students construct strong new ones, or directly confronting the conflicts between the old and the new conceptions? These kinds of questions have rarely been raised in the context of instruction, except by people exploring the educational implications of Piaget (e.g., Duckworth, 1979). They will surely have to be addressed in the constructivist instructional theory of the future.

A New Theory of Practice in Learning

The time is also ripe for a new look at an old instructional question: the role of practice in learning. It is interesting to contrast our current views of practice with those of Thorndike. For Thorndike, the role of practice was straightforward and self-evident. It "stamped in" correct associations through reward. The assumption, maintained in subsequent associationist and behaviorist instructional theories, was that competencies did not change in any fundamental qualitative way as a result of practice; they merely became stronger, faster and more reliable. The evidence from recent cognitive research is that practice also provides the occasion for productive cognitive inventions and that skill and understanding may undergo qualitative changes in the course of practice. This, I believe, forces a reconsideration of the role of practice in learning. Why does practice sometimes lead to productive inventions, and sometimes to the kind of rigid, "distorted" thought deplored by Wertheimer? A recent paper by Anderson, Greeno, Kline, and Neves (1981) suggests that the same mechanisms that account for the acquisition of skill in constructing high school geometry proofs may also explain phenomena such as set and functional fixedness. We do not know how general such a "trade-off" between the benefits of smooth and skillful performance and the disadvantages of rigid performance sequences may be. Anderson's theory accounts nicely for data on the developing abilities of a group of high school students in a traditional geometry course in which daily practice in proving theorems of a fairly standard type is provided. However, this does not mean that forms of instruction and practice might not be devised that would foster skill acquisition without promoting set or functional fixedness.

If practice is to provide the occasion—and perhaps the motivation—for the invention and testing of new procedures, then the traditional distinction between skill acquisition and understanding may need to be substantially modified. Practice, leading to skillful performance, may turn out to be necessary to the development of deep understanding, at least in certain domains of learning. Piaget's insistence on reflexive abstraction and his demonstration that successful performance often precedes understanding of certain phenomena (Piaget, 1974/1978) suggest such a possibility, as do our own demonstrations of procedural inventions by children (Groen & Resnick, 1977). Surely the *kinds* of practice afforded by instruction and the ways in which procedural practice is interspersed with invitations to reflect and construct explanations will influence the development of understanding. Here, then, is another set of questions about practice that a constructivist theory of intervention will have to address.

Assessing Understanding: The Links Between Knowledge and Performance

Assessment of students' entering capabilities and of the results of their learning efforts is an integral part of an instructional intervention. A cognitive theory of intervention must therefore include principles for assessment that are capable of revealing a learner's state of knowledge. Although the need for diagnostic assessment has long been recognized by instructional and test theorists (Glaser, 1981; Greeno, this volume) existing tests fall far short of permitting strong inferences about the cognitive state of learners. Traditional achievement tests are designed more to facilitate comparisons between people than to permit strong descriptions of individual competence. Meanwhile, content-referenced tests (Glaser, 1963), which *are* intended to reveal directly the learner's capabilities, lack any principled basis for linking observations of performance to inferences about cognitive competence. This is hardly surprising when one considers the behavioral roots of the content-referenced testing movement. According to strict behavioral theories, a person's competence is nothing more than the sum of that person's performances. There was thus no reason to try to develop a method for inferring underlying knowledge from the observed performances.

A cognitive theory of instruction, by contrast, requires exactly such a method. By focusing on the knowledge to be inferred, rather than on the performances per se, the objectives of instruction are likely to change—in directions that promote transfer and further learning (cf. Greeno, 1976, this volume). Principled bases for inferring that knowledge from performance must therefore be developed. Cognitive psychologists regularly make such inferences in their laboratories. But the effort is usually intensely individual and ad hoc: Those inferences survive that, after inspection of a large amount of data and research findings of other scientists, remain plausible. For instructional assessment, tasks and allowable inferences about underlying competence will need to be specified more systematically. The translation of methods of cognitive analysis into forms usable for instructional assessment constitutes another major agenda for a cognitive theory of intervention.

CONCLUSION

I have tried in this chapter to sketch an emerging revolution in the psychology of instruction. The cognitive perspective that now permeates psychology and its related disciplines has profound implications for the ways in which we ought, in the future, to think about instruction. As I have suggested here, the new view of the learner as an active constructor of knowledge forces a deep reconsideration of many of the assumptions of the instructional theories we have been living with. Some of the directions in which the new constructivist assumptions may lead instructional theory have been suggested in the final section of the chapter. But the particular questions addressed there are only early examples of the ways in which the traditional concerns of instructional theory can be expected to take on new substance as work toward a cognitive theory of instruction gathers momentum.

One of the more important influences on the direction of research in cognition is the cumulating evidence for the central and complicated role of prior knowledge in performance and learning. As this phenomenon has been recognized it has had the effect of directing the efforts of cognitive scientists toward intensive study of human performance in particular domains of skill or knowledge. Instead of searching for general laws of learning or development many cognitive scientists are now devoting attention to the analysis of specific task domains—including many that are of direct interest to the educator. Although this has the effect of making large segments of basic cognitive science immediately relevant to the task of developing an instructional theory, it also renders the task more complex than it might have seemed in the past. If we are to find general laws of cognitive learning that can be applied to instruction, it will be only through the detailed study of particular domains of knowledge. It is only in this way that we will be able to understand how knowledge accumulates and influences new cognitive constructions.

REFERENCES

Almy, M. *Logical thinking in second grade*. New York: Teachers College Press, 1970.

Anderson, J. R. *Cognitive skills and their acquisition*. Hillsdale, N.J.: Lawrence Erlbaum Associates, 1981.

Anderson, R. C., Reynolds, R. E., Schallert, D. L., & Goetz, T. E. Frameworks for comprehending discourse. *American Educational Research Journal, 1977, 14*, 367–381.

Anderson, R. C., Spiro, R. J., & Anderson, M. C. Schemata as scaffolding for the representation of information in connected discourse. *American Educational Research Journal 1978, 15*(3), 433–440.

Ausubel, D. *Educational psychology: A cognitive view*. New York: Holt, Rinehart, & Winston, 1968.

Bassin, C. B., & Martin, C. J. Effects of three types of redundancy reduction on comprehension, reading rate, and reading time of English prose. *Journal of Educational Psychology, 1976, 68*(5), 649–652.

Bransford, J. D., & Johnson, M. K. Contextual prerequisites for understanding: Some investigations of comprehension and recall. *Journal of Verbal Learning and Verbal Behavior, 1972, 11*, 717–26.

Brown, A. L. Metacognitive development and reading. In R. J. Spiro, B. C. Bruce, & W. F. Brewer (Eds.), *Theoretical issues in reading comprehension*. Hillsdale, N.J.: Lawrence Erlbaum Associates, 1980.

Brown, J. S., & Burton, R. R. Diagnostic models for procedural bugs in basic mathematical skills. *Cognitive Science, 1978, 2*, 155–192.

Brown, J. S., & VanLehn, K. Toward a generative theory of bugs in procedural skills. In T. Carpenter, J. Moser, & T. Romberg (Eds.), *Addition and subtraction: A cognitive perspective*. Hillsdale, N.J.: Lawrence Erlbaum Associates, 1982.

Bruner, J. S. *The process of education*. Cambridge, Mass.: Harvard University Press, 1960.

Bruner, J. S. *Toward a theory of instruction*. Cambridge, Mass.: Harvard University Press, 1966.

Champagne, A. B., Gunstone, R. F., & Klopfer, L. E. Cognitive research and the design of science instruction. *Educational Psychologist, 1982, 17*(1), 31–53.

Chi, M. T. H., Feltovich, P., & Glaser, R. Categorization and representation of physics problems by experts and novices. *Cognitive Science*, 1981, *5*, 121–152.

Chiesi, H. L., Spilich, G. J., & Voss, J. F. Acquisition of domain-related information in relation to high and low domain knowledge. *Journal of Verbal Learning and Verbal Behavior*, 1979, *18*, 257–274.

Clark, H. H., & Haviland, S. E. Comprehension and the given-new contract. In R. O. Freedle (Ed.), *Discourse production and comprehension* (Vol. 1). Norwood, N.J.: Ablex, 1977.

Coke, E. V. Reading rate, readability in variations in task-induced processing. *Journal of Educational Psychology*, 1976, *68*, 167–173.

Collis, K. F. *The development of formal reasoning* (Project No. HR2434/1 Report). Social Research Council of Great Britain, May 1975.

Duckworth, E. Either we're too early and they can't learn it or we're too late and they know it already: The dilemma of "applying Piaget." *Harvard Educational Review*, 1979, *49*(3), 297–312.

Furth, H. G. *Piaget for teachers*. Englewood Cliffs, N.J.: Prentice-Hall, 1970.

Furth, H. G., & Wachs, H. *Thinking goes to school: Piaget's theory in practice*. New York: Oxford University Press, 1975.

Gagné, R. M. The acquisition of knowledge. *Psychological Review*, 1962, *69*(4), 355–365.

Gagné, R. M. Learning hierarchies, *Educational Psychologist*, 1968, *6*(1), 1–9.

Gallagher, J., & Reid, D. K. *The learning of Piaget and Inhelder*. Belmont, Calif.: Brooks-Cole, 1981.

Gentner, D. *The structure of analogical models in science*. (BBN Report No. 4451) Cambridge, Mass.: Bolt Beranek & Newman, Inc., 1980.

Ginsburg, H. *Children's arithmetic: The learning process*. New York: Van Nostrand, 1977.

Ginsburg, H., & Opper, S. *Piaget's theory of intellectual development*. Englewood Cliffs, N.J.: Prentice-Hall, 1969.

Glaser, R. Instructional technology and the measurement of learning outcomes: Some questions. *American Psychologist*, 1963, *18*, 519–521.

Glaser, R. The future of testing: A research agenda for cognitive psychology and psychometrics. *American Psychologist*, 1981, *36*, 923–936.

Glaser, R. The contributions of B. F. Skinner to education and some counterinfluences. In P. Suppes (Ed.), *Impact of research on education*. Washington, D.C.: National Academy of Education, 1978.

Goldman, S. R. *Knowledge children use in producing stories about problem solving*. Paper presented at the annual meeting of the American Psychological Association, New York, 1979.

Greeno, J. G. Cognitive objectives of instruction: Theory of knowledge for solving problems and answering questions. In D. Klahr (Ed.), *Cognition and instruction*. Hillsdale, N.J.: Lawrence Erlbaum Associates, 1976.

Groen, G. J., & Parkman, J. M. A chronometric analysis of simple addition. *Psychology Review*, 1972, *79*(4), 329–43.

Groen, G. J., & Resnick, L. B. Can preschool children invent addition algorithms? *Journal of Educational Psychology*, 1977, *69*, 645–652.

Halliday, D., & Resnick, R. *Fundamentals of physics*. New York: Wiley, 1974.

Inhelder, B., Sinclair, H., & Bovet, M. *Learning and the development of cognition*. Cambridge, Mass.: Harvard University Press, 1974. (Originally published, 1974.)

Just, M. A., & Carpenter, P. A. Inference processes during reading: Reflections from eye fixation. In J. W. Senders, D. F. Fisher, & R. A. Monty, (Eds.), *Eye movements and higher psychological functions*. Hillsdale, N.J.: Lawrence Erlbaum Associates, 1981.

Kamii, C. An application of Piaget's theory to the conceptualization of a preschool curriculum. In R. K. Parker (Ed.), *The preschool in action: Exploring early childhood programs*. Boston, Mass.: Allyn & Bacon, 1972.

Kamii, C., & DeVries, R. Piaget for early education. In M. C. Day & R. K. Parker (Eds.), *The preschool in action*. Boston, Mass.: Allyn & Bacon, 1977.

Katona, G. *Organizing and memorizing: Studies in the psychology of learning and teaching*. New York: Hafner, 1967. (Originally published, 1940.)

Kazdin, A. E. Behavior modification in education: Contributions and limitations. *Developmental Review*, 1981, *1*, 34–57.

Kieras, D. Problems of reference in text comprehension. In M. A. Just & P. A. Carpenter (Eds.), *Cognitive processes in comprehension*. Hillsdale, N.J.: Lawrence Erlbaum Associates, 1977.

Kintsch, W. On modeling comprehension. *Educational Psychologist*, 1979, *14*, 3–14.

Kintsch, W., & van Dijk, T. A. Toward a model of text comprehension and production. *Psychological Review*, 1978, *85*, 363–394.

Lankford, F. G. *Some computational strategies of seventh grade pupils* (Final report, Project No. 2–C–013). HEW/OE National Center for Educational Research and Development and the Center for Advanced Studies, University of Virginia, October 1972.

Larkin, J. H., McDermott, J., Simon, D. P., & Simon, H. A. Expert and novice performance in solving physics problems. *Science*, 1980, *80*(4450), 1335–1342.

Lavatelli, C. S. *Piaget's theory applied to an early education curriculum: A Piaget program*. New York: Learning Research Associates, 1970.

Lovell, K. *The growth of understanding in mathematics: Kindergarten through grade three*. New York: Holt, Rinehart, & Winston, 1971.

Mager, R. F. *Preparing objectives for programmed instruction*. San Francisco: Fearon, 1961.

Mandler, J. M. A code in the node: The use of a story schema in retrieval. *Discourse Processes*, 1978, *1*, 14–35.

Mayer, R. E. Can advance organizers influence meaningful learning? *Review of Educational Research*, 1979, *49*, 371–383.

McConkie, G. W., Rayner, K., & Wilson, S. J. Experimental manipulation of reading strategies. *Journal of Educational Psychology*, 1973, *65*(1), 1–8.

Meyer, B. J. F. *The organization of prose and its effect on recall*. Amsterdam: Elsevier, 1975.

Neches, R. *Models of heuristic procedure modification*. Unpublished doctoral dissertation, Carnegie-Mellon University, 1981.

Newell, A., & Simon, H. A. *Human problem solving*. Englewood Cliffs, N.J.: Prentice-Hall, 1972.

Piaget, J. *Success and understanding*. Cambridge, Mass.: Harvard University Press, 1978. (Originally published, 1974.)

Resnick, L. B. (Ed.). Hierarchies in children's learning: A symposium. *Instructional Science*, 1973, *2*, 311–362.

Resnick, L. B. Task analysis in instruction design: Some cases from mathematics. In D. Klahr (Ed.), *Cognition and instruction*. Hillsdale, N.J.: Lawrence Erlbaum Associates, 1976.

Resnick, L. B. Syntax and semantics in learning to subtract. In T. Carpenter, J. Moser, & T. Romberg (Eds.), *Addition and subtraction: A cognitive perspective*. Hillsdale, N.J.: Lawrence Erlbaum Associates, 1982.

Resnick, L. B. A developmental theory of number understanding. In H. Ginsburg (Ed.), *The development of mathematical thinking*. New York: Academic Press, 1983.

Resnick, L. B., & Ford, W. W. *The psychology of mathematics for instruction*. Hillsdale, N.J.: Lawrence Erlbaum Associates, 1981.

Rothkopf, E. Z., & Billington, M. J. Goal-guided learning from text: Inferring a descriptive processing model from inspection times and eye movements. *Journal of Educational Psychology*, 1979, *71*(3), 310–327.

Samuels, S. J., & Dahl, P. R. Establishing appropriate purpose for reading and its effect on flexibility of reading rate. *Journal of Educational Psychology*, 1975, *67*(1), 38–43.

Schank, R., & Abelson, R. *Scripts, plans, goals, and understanding: An inquiry into human knowledge structures*. Hillsdale, N.J.: Lawrence Erlbaum Associates, 1977.

Selman, R. L., Krupa, M. P., Stone, C. R., & Jaquette, D. S. Concrete operational thought and the emergence of the concept of unseen force in children's theories of electromagnetism and gravity. *Science Education*, 1982, *66*, 181–184.

Shulman, L. S., & Keislar, E. R. (Eds.). Learning by discovery: A critical appraisal. Chicago: Rand McNally, 1966.

Siegler, R. The origins of scientific reasoning. In R. Siegler (Ed.), *Children's thinking: What develops*. Hillsdale, N.J.: Lawrence Erlbaum Associates, 1978.

Simon, H. A. Identifying basic abilities underlying intelligent performance of complex tasks. In L. B. Resnick (Ed.), *The nature of intelligence*. Hillsdale, N.J.: Lawrence Erlbaum Associates, 1976.

Skinner, B. F. Teaching machines. *Science*, 1958, *128*, 969–977.

Spilich, G. J., Vesonder, G. T., Chiesi, H. L., & Voss, J. F. Text processing of domain-related information for individuals with high and low domain knowledge. *Journal of Verbal Learning and Verbal Behavior*, 1979, *18*, 275–290.

Stein, N. L., & Glenn, C. G. An analysis of story comprehension in elementary school children. In R. O. Freedle (Ed.), *New directions in discourse processing* (Vol. 2). Norwood, N.J.: Ablex, 1979.

Suppes, P., & Morningstar, M. *Computer-assisted instruction at Stanford, 1966–1968: Data, models and evaluation of the arithmetic programs*. New York: Academic Press, 1972.

Svenson, O. Analysis of time required by children for simple additions. *Acta Psychologica*, 1975, *39*, 289–302.

Svenson, O., & Broquist, S. Strategies for solving simple addition problems: A comparison of normal and subnormal children. *Scandinavian Journal of Psychology*, 1975, *16*, 143–151.

Svenson, O., & Hedenborg, M. L. Strategies used by children when solving simple subtractions. *Acta Psychologica*, 1979, *43*, 1–13.

Terrace, H. S. Discrimination learning with and without errors. *Journal of Experimental Analysis of Behavior*, 1963, *6*, 1–27.

Thorndike, E. L. *The Psychology of Arithmetic*. New York: Macmillan, 1922.

Thorndyke, P. W. Cognitive structures in comprehension and memory of narrative discourse. *Cognitive Psychology*, 1977, *9*(1), 77–110.

Viennot, L. Spontaneous reasoning in elementary dynamics. *European Journal of Science Education*, 1979, *1*(2), 205–221.

Weikart, D., Rogers, L., Adcock, C., & McClelland, D. *The cognitively oriented curriculum: A framework for preschool teachers*. Urbana: University of Illinois, 1971.

Wertheimer, M. *Productive thinking*. New York: Harper & Row, 1959. (Originally published, 1945.)

Woods, S. S., Resnick, L. B., & Groen, G. J. An experimental test of five process models for subtraction. *Journal of Educational Psychology*, 1975, *67*(1), 17–21.

2 In Search of a Model of Instructional Research in Reading

P. David Pearson
Rob Tierney
University of Illinois, Urbana–Champaign

The relationship between science and technology has been debated by philosophers, scientists, and practitioners for centuries. For many technological disciplines (e.g., engineering, agriculture, pharmacology, medicine), the bridge from basic scientific research has been well paved and easy to travel over the last century within the Western world. In these fields advances in technology often can be traced directly to discoveries made in pursuit of theory in a basic science. The history of the relationship between changes in education, particularly reading, and advances in psychological theory has not provided as many examples of bridging. Although there was much concern about such bridges early in the history of reading research (Huey, 1908/1968; Woodworth, 1938), the decades of the 40s, 50s, and 60s witnessed little such concern. The 70s, on the other hand, brought together a renewed interest in reading from psychologists and a new interest in cognition from reading educators; hence, bridging concerns have been rekindled with a fervor never before witnessed.

In such a milieu, people like ourselves (who call themselves reading educators) seek to strengthen the relationship between psychology and the practice of teaching reading in order:

1. To apply ideas and methods from research on basic processes in reading.
2. To understand and improve curriculum and instruction in reading comprehension.
3. To inform, through school-based research, theories of basic processes.

Our guiding principle is that above all, reading researchers be held accountable for improving instruction, regardless of whether ideas emanate from basic process research or school-based research.

The fundamental paradigm from which many reading educators generate instructional research hypotheses is straightforward: (1) basic process research helps us to build a model of the competent reader. We are able to identify the types of knowledge and kinds of strategies good readers employ in trying to understand varieties of texts; (2) acquisition research, by focusing on age and ability variables, allows us to pinpoint differences between novice and competent, or poor and good readers at various levels of development. Hence potential breakdowns are identified; (3) instructional practice research allows us to determine whether or not interventions at key points can help students either "fix up" knowledge or process breakdowns or prevent breakdowns from occurring in the first place.

We believe that the best instructional research is based on what we have learned and will learn from basic research on skilled reading and developmental research on reading acquisition. However, it is important to recognize that basic research knowledge about skilled reading and acquisition is not enough to build successful instructional programs. Indeed the path from basic to applied research is often difficult to follow because having an analysis of an idealized competent reader does not directly indicate the means for helping a child become a competant reader. Equally important is our commitment to the notion that it is not only logically possible, but reasonable to expect that research about instruction should inform basic process research.

A PLAN FOR DISCOVERING A MODEL OF READING INSTRUCTION

Although the past decade has witnessed unprecedented growth in ideas about expert reading and some growth in ideas about acquisition, the work of building a good model of reading instruction has only started. To be sure, there are longstanding "armchair metaphors" about how reading should be taught; however, they suffer on two counts. First, they are generally limited to the development of early reading skill, getting the student from a novice stage to a stage in which he or she can read simple, familiar material. Rarely do they say anything about comprehension instruction save that it is important, ought to be practiced, or is a complex process. Second, they have not undergone the kind of careful decomposition, hypothesis testing, and recomposition that recent research has imposed upon models of skilled reading.

The purpose of this chapter is to report an omnibus search for the principles upon which to base a model of reading instruction. Beginning with William James' pragmatic advice to "Never question the origin of good," we review and try to gather insight from the following sources:

1. We examine models of skilled reading to determine the implications they might carry for instructional models.

2. We look at the research that has characterized and analyzed current practices of teaching reading. We ask whether the test of time that graces the conventional wisdom has given us useful methods and materials.

3. We evaluate the growing body of literature labeled "process/product" research, a paradigm in which researchers look for correlations between instructional variables and student achievement or growth in achievement.

4. We review a body of literature in which researchers have conducted long-term evaluations of instructional programs.

5. We review pedagogical experiments designed to test the importance of variables that school personnel can actually control (as opposed to individual difference and social class variables that are not under school control).

EXTRAPOLATIONS FROM GENERAL THEORIES OF READING

Goodman and His Colleagues

Goodman and his colleagues, although they do not propose a model of instruction per se, do have a set of guidelines that they use to evaluate instruction. They begin with what they call a "whole-language" orientation toward the reading. This orientation stipulates that one can never examine the reading process in isolation from language processes in general (Goodman & Goodman, 1979), the context in which language is acquired (Goodman & Goodman, 1979; Harste, Burke, & Woodward, 1982), and the functions that language and reading serve in a social context (Carey, Harste, & Smith, 1981). They believe that reading should never be decomposed in order to study component processes (Goodman & Goodman, 1979).

According to the Goodmans and their colleagues (Cambourne, 1976–1977), learning to read "ought not to be very much more difficult or mystical than the process by which one learns the oral mode of language. That is, provided that the same principles of relevance, meaningfulness, and motivation for communication which characterized the learning of oral language have been adhered to [p. 610]." The ramification of this notion for instruction is that helping students learn to read involves providing context within which students can learn about learning and learn about reading for themselves. To this end, teachers should aim to involve students in meaningful reading situations that do not distract them from reading with understanding. It is assumed that within such contexts readers' use of language clues will be supported and strengthened. Goodman is eloquent on the point that teachers must make the fullest possible use of the language competence and total experiential background that children bring to school with them by providing material that is meaningful and that deals with familiar situations and ideas and is written in a language that is like their own oral language. Then and only then can the child apply his or her language strength to the task

(Goodman, 1969). In other words, it is Goodman's argument that any instruction that does not build on the process of natural language learning is at cross-purposes with the child's natural language learning strengths and may even become counterproductive (Goodman & Goodman, 1979).

The role of the teacher in the instructional model implied by this point of view is that of a humanistic, supportive colearner rather than a purveyor of knowledge. It is the teacher's task to create relevant learning situations and in these situations provide readers reliable feedback whereby they can read to learn for themselves.

In the past 10 years, many suggestions for teachers have been forthcoming from Goodman and his colleagues (Goodman, 1975; Goodman & Burke, 1972, 1980). Their explicit suggestions are based largely on the notion that increasing students' awareness of the language and thought clues available during reading may help readers focus on aspects of written language not being processed effectively as well as help support and strengthen readers' use of clues already being used. Accordingly, they suggest a general lesson framework, guidelines, and a number of example lessons that illustrate how teachers might help readers effectively use the cuing systems (graphophonic, systatic, and semantic) available to them.

They expect that lessons can be implemented to benefit all learners, including proficient readers, readers who exhibit evidence of effective, but inconsistent use of strategies, and readers for whom the development of strategies has been disrupted. They believe that some readers (those whose development is disrupted) need first to realize that they are effective language users and that these abilities can help in reading. For example, within the context of a lesson, cloze procedures might be used to enable students to become more aware of their ability to use grammatical and semantic cues.

For those readers who make effective but inconsistent use of reading strategies, they have suggested encouraging them to make judgments while reading and developing their awareness of the transfer value of effective reading strategies from easy to difficult material. With respect to having readers make judgments, they suggest that readers should be encouraged to ask self-monitoring questions such as "Does what I am reading make sense? If it doesn't what should I do about it?" If the material is not making sense, readers should read on to see if later context will begin to clear things up *or* to decide on their own to move to an alternative selection. To develop a reader's awareness of the transfer value of strategies, they suggest, for example, in the context of a successful reading experience, focusing a reader's attention on the strategies he or she used to deal with unfamiliar words and to discriminate important from unimportant words. Hopefully the reader can then transfer these strategies to reading situations where they incur difficulty.

For the readers who are proficient, such lessons provide an opportunity to develop confidence in the use of strategies. For example, proficient readers might be encouraged to examine the influence of background knowledge upon interpretation. Also, according to Goodman and Burke (1980), teachers might help readers become consciously aware their own responsibility to become active participants in the negotiation that must occur between reader and author.

Thus, the lesson procedures proposed by Goodman and his colleagues represent planned situations in which the use and availability of selected reading strategies or cuing systems are highlighted and reinforced. In terms of general guidelines for implementing lessons, they suggest that: (1) lessons can and should be planned; and (2) they have to represent naturally occurring language learning situations in which readers discover an awareness of their own language processing procedures. With this in mind, they suggest a number of guidelines for material selection and lesson implementation. They suggest two guidelines for material selection: (1) the language of the material used should be similar to the oral language of the reader, unambiguous, replete with natural redundancy; and (2) the content of the material used should be both interesting and significant to readers. Their guidelines for lesson implementation specify four phases—initiating, interacting, applying, and expanding. In initiating, they emphasize the importance of catching the readers' interests and the need, wherever possible, to involve the students in evaluating and planning their own reading experiences. In the interacting phase, they emphasize the importance of challenging students to interact with each other in exploring issues. In the applying and extending phases, students should be given opportunities to develop and extend strategies across a variety of learning situations and texts. In general, however, although Goodman offers several suggestions for planning and teaching lessons, he emphasizes the overriding need to place students at the center of their own problem-solving experiences in naturally occurring settings—ones that are likely to facilitate their discovery of the rules and wonder of reading.

From the Goodmans' point of view the notion that there could exist a model of reading instruction distinct from a model of reading (or a model of reading distinct from a model of language use and development) makes no sense at all. They are all different facets of the same phenomenon. There are probably few philosophies of reading instruction so intimately related to underlying process models.

LaBerge and Samuels

In contrast to language-centered views of reading stand models such as that developed by LaBerge and Samuels (1974). Their competent reader behaves almost identically to Goodman's good reader; that is, he or she samples from a variety of information sources (graphic, semantic, or syntactic) to build a model of the meaning of a text. However, LaBerge and Samuels believe that before a reader can achieve that level of sophisticated interactive processing, he or she must proceed through stages in which lower-level processes, like decoding from print to speech, are learned consciously and then automated. This necessity stems from LaBerge and Samuels' limited capacity constraint on the information processor: When the reader allocates a great deal of attention to decoding, he or she has little attention left over for monitoring meaning. When decoding becomes automatic (i.e., requires little conscious attention), a reader can allocate more attention to building a model of the meaning of the text. Samuels has gone on to suggest that the explicit teaching of decoding skills coupled with practice in reading fluency (lots of practice to develop rapid and errorless oral reading) helps children reach an appropriate state of automaticity vis-à-vis decoding. Samuels further argues that such subskill instruction is particularly important for the poor reader, who seems to need the order, system, and sequencing inherent in such an approach. Good readers, he concedes, often discover efficient strategies on their own.

One point deserves emphasis here. Both basic and applied researchers have to be aware of the possibility that there will be a discontinuity between models of a process and instructional models that intend to make readers competent at that process. To take an extreme case, it may be that the best way to produce the kind of reader Goodman wants is to teach him or her to read on the basis of implications from Samuels and LaBerge's model. We suspect this is not true; nonetheless, we raise the possibility as a check on overenthusiastic extrapolation from models of processes to models of instruction.

Schema-Theoretic Notions

A third model of the reading process that has served as the basis for instructional practices has emanated from schema-theoretic notions of reading comprehension advanced by cognitive psychologists in recent years (Perfetti & Lesgold, 1977; Rumelhart, 1977). At the core of schema-theoretic notions is that the reader is an active information processor whose goal it is to construct a model of meaning for the text. The reader varies his or her processing strategies and reliance on various information sources (e.g., stores of schemata versus data in the text) as a function of what he or she knows about the topic and what he or she perceives the task to be (e.g., to update knowledge or to prepare for a quiz). There are at least two compelling implications for the classroom that have been schema-theoretic notions. One is the central role of background knowledge in building models of text meaning. The other is the necessity of a range of dynamic processing strategies.

If background knowledge is so important, then educators are obligated either to select materials and reading activities that allow students to engage it or to help students develop it prior to or during reading. For example, we have ample evidence that comprehension varies as a function of the sophistication of children's schemata for "stories," yet we persist in providing young readers with narratives that lack the structure of true stories (Brewer & Lichtenstein, in press; Mandler & Johnson, 1977; Stein & Glenn, 1979). In effect, we block their use of background knowledge in constructing meaning. An earlier emphasis on real stories seems advisable. Similar arguments can be made for content or topical schemata as well as for structural schemata (Johnston & Pearson, 1982; Steffensen, Joag dev, & Anderson, 1979). But sometimes students have to read content that is novel to them, particularly in the content areas such as social studies and science. When this occurs, educators must accommodate in one of two ways: Either they can intervene and supply appropriate links between what is known and what is new (in the form of prereading concept development activities) or they can use texts that provide such linkages for the reader. In this regard, the recent work of Hayes and Tierney (1982) is important because it suggests that providing such links in text is useful.

As important as background knowledge is the development, in every reader, of processing, control, and monitoring strategies. What we have in mind here are the mechanisms outlined by researchers such as Spiro (1980)—schema selection, schema maintenance, schema combination, etc.—and Baker and Brown (in press)—comprehension monitoring, planning, checking, and summarization strategies. Of relevance to instructional practices, schema-theoretic notions have extended our understanding of how good readers comprehend and what it is they do as compared to poor comprehenders or when they themselves break down. These notions provide the basis, at least, for determining what might be taught or highlighted within alternative instructional contexts. As with other models of the reading process schema theory offers extrapolations to practice but nothing approaching a truly explicit model for instruction. Toward the identification of instructional variables, schema-theoretic notions leave unspecified procedures by which learning might be facilitated.

EXTRAPOLATIONS FROM EXISTING PRACTICE

Another potential source for developing a model of reading instruction is existing instructional practice. The research paradigm is straightforward: Examine what exists in classrooms, programs, and materials and look for regularities (Beck, McKeown, McCaslin, & Burkes, 1979; Duffy & Roehler, 1980; Durkin, 1978–79, 1981).

What type of picture of instruction do we get when we examine teacher behavior in classrooms (Duffy, 1981; Duffy & McIntyre, 1980; Durkin, 1978–79)? We find a teacher who apparently perceives his or her role as a technician whose job it is to arrange practice and drill conditions so that learning will occur. There is very little in the way of what Duffy (1981) calls "proactive" teaching; that is, making clear to students what the task is, modeling how to perform it, and guided practice in doing it. Instead there is a great deal of "mentioning" or assignment giving (Durkin, 1978–79), during which time teachers make certain that students understand the directions to the workbook or worksheet assignments. The most substantive of teacher–student interactions occur during question/answer sessions following silent reading. Those are best characterized as assessment rather than discussion: low-level questions in search of single correct answers (Durkin, 1978–79). What feedback occurs can hardly meet Duffy's (1981) definition of "reactive" teaching because the feedback given is not substantive. It provides little help to the students who make errors; instead it is little more than an acknowledgment that an error occurred (Duffy & Roehler, 1980). Students spend a great deal of time engaged in the completion of workbook, worksheet, or chalkboard copying activities (Mason & Osborn, in press). Teachers spend a lot of time giving assignments, clarifying assignments, or asking questions.

Turning from classrooms to basal reading curricula (Beck et al., 1979; Durkin, 1981), the picture changes very little. Durkin (1981) was struck by the similarity between what teachers do during reading lessons, especially related to comprehension activity, and what is recommended in the teachers' manuals of basal reader programs. There was little in the way of suggestions for what Duffy (1981) has labeled proactive or reactive teaching; instead, lots of assessment, lots of monitoring. Beck et al.'s analysis goes a step further in pointing out how certain suggestions for building background, setting purposes, and assessing comprehension via questions may actually hinder rather than help the comprehension of basal stories and articles.

What kind of model of instruction could conceivably underlie such practices? We think such a model would be based on the assumption that the primary role of the teacher in the classroom is to "arrange conditions" and set up independent activities that will either occupy students' time or permit students to discover the regularities of print, text, and reading skill activities on their own. As Duffy (1981) has pointed out: "Rather than being driven by goal-oriented and theoretically consistent instructional models, teachers appear to be preoccupied with activities which maintain activity flow. Consequently, teachers look like technicians and managers rather than like reflective professionals [p. 35]." Ironically, reading educators may promote such a model of instruction in at least two ways (Brophy, 1980): (1) by providing teachers with such primitive knowledge about the reading process that professional reflection is not possible; and (2) by providing pre- and in-service education focusing on the niceties of materials such as games, kits, and worksheets rather than on teaching and interaction strategies.

A model of reading instruction consistent with these findings from analyses of instruction and basal program suggestions would include principles such as these:

1. Select a reading program with lots of practice materials for various reading skills.

2. Spend as little time as possible explaining comprehension tasks; however, take time to explain the task directions.

3. If students do poorly on a task, give them more practice material.

4. When students do not understand an assignment, answer only specific questions from specific individuals.

5. After students have read a story (and, for primary children, while students are reading a story), ask lots of literal comprehension questions focusing on story details in order to make certain that the students have paid attention to the story.

6. If conflicts about an answer arise, give students the right answer.

7. If a student fails to answer a question, ask another student.

We grant that these extrapolations from current practice are somewhat harsh and fail to take into account the hundreds of examples of good instruction that we and others have observed in classrooms. But we let the harshness stand, if for no other reason than to emphasize the point that the materials and management emphasis of the 70s has created a milieu in which active teaching is no longer at the core of the teacher's role. Materials are. And a major goal seems to be to march the students through the materials. To add credibility to this harshness, let us point out that Shannon (1981) found that many teachers and most administrators regard materials as the primary concern in developing a reading program.

PROCESS–PRODUCT RESEARCH

"Process–product" research correlates measures gleaned from classroom observation (the process) with standardized measures of academic growth (the product). A typical process–product study proceeds as follows: A range of classrooms, teachers, and students are sampled. Data are collected on a variety of teaching and learning process measures such as content covered, time allocated, engaged time, teacher questions, student success rate, numbers and types of disciplinary actions, and feedback. Process variables that have high correlations with product measures are assumed to represent characteristics of successful programs. For purposes of establishing causal connections, some investigators (e.g., Anderson, Evertson, & Brophy, 1979; Good & Grouws, 1979; Stallings, 1978) have conducted experimental studies in which variables previously found to be correlated with achievement have been systematically manipulated over some period of time. Usually the cycle ends with someone like Medley (1977, 1979), Rosenshine (1971, 1979, 1980), Good and Grouws (1979), or Brophy (1979) summarizing the consistent findings across studies.

The variables that emerge in study after study (see Duffy, 1981; Rosenshine & Stevens, in press, for recent summaries) as the strongest correlates of achievement or achievement gain are engaged time on task (more time on task yields greater gains), content covered/mastered (the more covered, the better), error rate (low error rates for low achievers—80% correct; moderate error rates for high achievers—70% correct), and grouping pattern (tutoring > small group > large group > individualized). Duffy (1981) has summarized these and other findings into a generalization he feels emerges consistently from the data: The most effective teachers of basic skills generate the most opportunity to learn.

In generating "opportunity to learn," Duffy argues, teachers rely on various tools. They elicit higher student engagement rates, monitor student behavior more closely, provide more substantive feedback, prevent misbehavior, and elicit cooperation. Furthermore, they believe in themselves as teachers and believe their students can learn.

A model of effective instruction consistent with these process–product findings would include principles such as teaching students in small groups, developing a system for monitoring behavior, assigning tasks with a high probability of success, establishing high expectations for all students, and pacing instruction briskly. In creating this list of principles, we have relied on the interpretations of those who have conducted and reviewed this body of research. We regard the list as a source of hypotheses to be tested in future experiments rather than canons for classroom instruction that can now be accepted without question.

PROGRAM EVALUATIONS

Another potential source of instructional models comes from research in which certain instruction has been systematically evaluated in order to examine effects on student learning. Some of the studies, such as the Follow-Through Study (Becker, 1977), have evaluated total programs over several years. Others (Tharp, 1982) have examined fairly specific strategies over long periods of time.

DISTAR

The broad scale research that has been done in the Follow-Through program is both interesting and controversial. The controversy centers on the various interpretations that have been offered to explain the achievement differences among the various models (Becker, 1977; Bereiter & Kurland, in press; House, Glass, McLean, & Walker, 1978a, 1978b; Wisler, Burns, & Iwamoto, 1978). In particular, the Direct Instruction programs (Abt associates) have alternatively been interpreted to be *more effective* than the other more individualized and more student-centered models used by other models in the study (Becker, 1977) *no more effective* (House, Glass, McLean, & Walker, 1978a, 1978b), and *again more effective* (Bereiter & Kurland, in press).

What is most relevant to the purpose of generating a general model of reading instruction are some of the principles of learning and teaching that underlie the programs that have been created for use in the apparently successful Direct Instruction Model classrooms. In formulating these principles, the Direct Instruction researchers have incorporated some of the psychological literature on concept acquisition and learning. Four key principles that are to be used when creating instructional programs are listed by Becker (1977; Becker, Engelman, & Carnine, 1979).

The first principle is: Teach the general case. When, after having been taught some members of a set, a student can identify all the members of that set, the general case has been used to teach the set. They believe that the use of the general case in designing instruction will make both teaching and learning more efficient. They describe three major types of general cases: concepts, operations, and problem-solving rules. In order to construct tasks that teach the general case they advocate: (1) sequenced discrimination of positive and negative instances that will lead to a clear picture of the distinctive features of the concept, operation, or rule; (2) planned variation of irrelevant features; and (3) gradual enlargement of the set of nonexamples.

Although trial and error is acknowledged as a viable way of learning new information, the second principle is: Errors should be kept to a minimum so that less time will be required to learn new information. The principle of minimizing errors requires that teachers preteach concepts in simple tasks and then move to complex tasks. Errors will be minimized if component building blocks are taught before the general case; for example, letter–sound correspondences would be taught before the children read the words in which those letters occur. They also say that the task analysis that precedes any program writing should locate and buttress against error-inducing possibilities; for example, the more similar two concepts are, the greater the probability of error and the greater the need to emphasize distinctive features. In the sequencing of examples, they recommend that only one feature at a time be changed. Finally, they favor separating highly similar concepts in sequencing instruction. Thus the sequence b–r–t–w–d is superior to the sequence b–d–p–q–g for sound-symbol instruction.

The third principle is: Teach the essentials. By including only the essentials in a program, they believe it is possible to minimize the number of examples to learn a concept. Efficiency of example presentation can be accomplished because students can interpolate (for example, if shown four widely varying shades of red, each of which is labeled *red,* students will induce that the in-between shades are also red) and extrapolate (if a wolf is not a dog, then surely a cat—which is even more dissimilar from a dog—is not a dog). The overriding concern is that instructional time is limited and that it should be devoted to teaching the essentials of any subject.

The fourth principle is: Provide for adequate practice. The amount of practice necessary will vary as a function of the size of the learning set and of the intraset similarity, as well as the amount of time it takes a student to learn what is being taught.

Inherent in all the instructional programs that have been developed for the Direct Instruction Model classrooms is the notion of the central importance of task analysis and the sequencing of instruction based on task analysis. This analysis and sequencing provide the framework for the development of instructional tasks that permit the teacher to clearly demonstrate a concept, operation, or rule to the students. In constructing the tasks, the program developers incorporate the general principles of learning and teaching described previously (teach the general case, keep errors to a minimum, teach the essentials, provide for adequate practice). As they sequence tasks, they attend to providing students with massed practice of new information and to using cumulative programming that permits information taught in earlier lessons to be incorporated into the more complex tasks found in later lessons.

How teachers present tasks receives a lot of the attention of the program developers, both in the scripted lessons and in the training that is provided for teachers using the programs. A variation of the presentation sequence mode model → lead → test is used in many of the instructional tasks: A teacher demonstrates a concept, operation, or rule (model), then guides the students in practicing what has been taught (lead), and finally assesses student mastery of the task by checking out the performance of the students immediately as well as later on by evaluating their independently completed written activities (test). Not all tasks utilize all three parts of this presentation mode. Some are only ''model and test'' tasks. Others (for example, most of the synthesis and application tasks) are ''test only'' tasks; the intent of these tasks is to determine if students can assemble what they have learned into a complex task or apply it to new situations.

Teachers are trained to use several variations of the model, lead, and test procedures to correct a variety of student errors. They are also trained to use information the students have mastered to correct errors in synthesis and application tasks.

During Direct Instruction lessons about 80% of student responses are in choral form, that is, all the students in a group respond together. This procedure is intended to maximize student engaged time during each lesson and to give a teacher feedback about what each student has mastered. For more precise individual feedback, teachers intersperse individual turns with choral responses. Tests are used to estimate the additional teaching and practice time necessary for each student.

According to Becker and Carnine (1978), the Direct Instruction Model is governed by two rules: (1) beat the clock, or teach more in less time; and (2) control the details of what happens during instruction.

The beat-the-clock rule is intended to increase classroom efficiency. Becker and Carnine suggest these strategies: (1) in the early grades, use classroom aides as well as teachers to teach lessons to children in order to maximize engaged instructional time for each student; (2) carefully organize the schedule to avoid "wasted time" (for example, a teacher and an aide each teach small groups of children in different corners of the room while a third group works independently on carefully correlated activities); (3) train, supervise, and monitor teachers to help them become more efficient in their use of time in the classroom; and (4) teach the general case whenever possible.

The second rule, control the details, applies to instruction. They suggest that it is important to: (1) have the teachers use scripted lessons that contain carefully worked out instructional sequences; (2) train teachers to use these materials; (3) observe teacher and student progress in the lessons and provide help for teachers and students who are having trouble.

Although we find the program content and teaching procedures of the programs that have been developed for use in Direct Instruction Model classrooms different from the focus of our own research, we believe there is much to learn about principles of instructional effectiveness from the model. There is also something to be learned from how the Direct Instructional Model has implemented its programs in classrooms.

KEEP

The Direct Instruction Model, with its emphasis on task analysis and the sequencing of tasks, is an interesting contrast to the Kamehameha Early Education Project (KEEP), which has been discussed extensively in two recent articles (Au & Mason, 1981; Tharp, 1982). KEEP claims to operate a direct instruction model that focuses primarily on comprehension, but with instruction that is both child focused *and* task focused.

Two characteristics of the KEEP program make it a particularly interesting model source: (1) its students are high-risk, low-income, native Hawaiian children; and (2) it is remarkably effective in increasing student performance as measured by standardized tests (Tharp, 1982). The program has evolved over several years, with each succeeding cohort of students gaining over (or maintaining equity with) its immediate predecessor. It is labeled a direct instruction model, though it lacks several of the characteristics of direct instruction as defined by others (cf. Rosenshine, 1979). What it does have are these characteristics:

1. At least 20 minutes per day (and about 2/3 of the total time teachers spend interacting with groups of students) is devoted to comprehension activity with each reading group (K–3).

2. Instruction occurs in small ($5 < N < 10$) groups.

3. Much of the instruction occurs during story discussion; that is, what distinguishes KEEP from other programs is the systematic use of thought-provoking questions. The questions form a "line of questions," thus avoiding the problems pointed out by Durkin (1978–1979) and Beck et al. (1979).

4. The program has been designed to maximize consistency with native Hawaiian culture. Notably, whereas most teachers use participation structures in which one person (teacher or student) at a time has the floor, teachers in this program allow responses and comments and questions from two or more students at a time and from the *joint* effort of two or more students (Au & Mason, 1981).

5. Student progress (via criterion-referenced tests) and teacher adherence to suggested methods (via observation) are monitored regularly and extensively.

The program emphasizes high engagement rates, extensive monitoring, and group instruction. However, unlike DISTAR there are no explicit rules (general cases) taught for completing comprehension tasks and the model–lead–test framework is not adhered to in any serious way. The KEEP program really uses an inundation–discovery approach to improving comprehension. The rationale seems to be, if students are constantly barraged with well-conceived interrogations of text, eventually they will learn what to attend to when they read texts on their own. On the other hand, the data suggest that a frontal assault on comprehension-oriented activity encourages growth in comprehension, with no apparent decrement on decoding skills, which are mainly taught in individual exercises.

Looking at both DISTAR and KEEP, some general principles do emerge, even though the content of the two programs is vastly different. Both programs stress the necessity to keep students on the task, teach in groups instead of individually (at least initially), provide many opportunities to apply skills to be learned, and monitor progress and offer feedback where breakdowns occur.

INSTRUCTIONAL EXPERIMENTS

Experimental research has focused on issues of comprehension and instruction at a much more micro level. The studies reviewed here share a set of features in common. First, all are derived rather directly from basic research on the reading process; that is, they represent attempts to bridge the gap from basic research to real instruction. Second, all have evaluated the efficacy of instructional treatments using transfer tasks; they have asked the question, What happens to student performance when instructional crutches are removed? Third, all have obtained positive results; they have shown that an intervention produces gains in some aspect of comprehension. Fourth, all have emphasized techniques that allow students to monitor for themselves whether or not they understand task demands or know when they are performing the task appropriately.

Several studies have aimed at improving children's ability and predisposition to draw inferences. Hansen and Pearson (1980) began with the observation that children were best at answering the kinds of questions teachers ask most often, namely literal recall of story details. They wondered whether this observation represented a robust developmental trend, an accident of children's instructional history (they have more practice at literal questions), or the fact that literal questions are inherently easier than inferential questions.

Hansen and Pearson devised three instructional treatments. In the first, a business as usual approach, average second-grade students were given a traditional diet of questions of about 80% literal and 20% inferential questions. In the second, a practice-only treatment, literal questions were removed from these children's basal reader activities altogether; they received only inferential questions. In the third, called a strategy training group, students received the traditional question diet but, prior to each story, they were asked to perform two tasks: (1) relate what they knew (from their prior knowledge) about what to do in circumstances like those the upcoming story characters would experience; and (2) predict what the story protagonist would do when confronted with these critical situations from the to-be-read story. They then read the story to compare their predictions with what actually occurred (as in the KEEP Directed Reading–Thinking Activity). As a part of this prereading discussion, the experimenters emphasized the principle that comprehension requires relating the new (what's in a story) with the known (what students already knew before reading the story). This activity represented an attempt to help change students' conceptions about "the process of reading"—to help them become explicitly aware of the "known-to-new" principle.

On four different measures including, notably, a standardized reading comprehension test, Hansen and Pearson found that the two experimental groups outperformed the control group. The conclusion from these data is that inference performance, even for young students, is amenable to alteration, either through direct strategy training or through changing the kinds of questions they practice answering.

In a follow-up, Hansen and Pearson (1982) combined their earlier strategy training and question practice approaches into a single treatment. They trained four teachers to administer the treatments instead of teaching the classes themselves, as they had done earlier. Also they used good and poor fourth-grade readers instead of average second-grade students. The combined approach proved somewhat advantageous for good readers in comparison to the control group. However, it proved extremely effective for the poor readers. Poor readers in the experimental group exceeded their control counterparts on inference measures taken from the materials in which the instruction was embedded as well as on measures from three new passages on which no instruction had been offered. From these data, and the data from the earlier study, Hansen and Pearson concluded that younger and older poor readers benefit from explicit attempts to alter comprehension strategies; older good readers, on the other hand, did not seem to benefit nearly so much, perhaps because they have developed adequate strategies on their own.

Gordon (1980) extended the inference training to fourth-graders. Over a period of 8 weeks, she contrasted the effects of a group explicitly trained to draw inferences with a control group that received language experience and immersion activities, and a second experimental group whose instruction focused on activating and fine-tuning content schemata (the topics addressed in the stories) and structural schemata (helping students develop an abstract framework for what is entailed in a story) before and after reading.

Gordon's results were consistent with those obtained by Hansen and Pearson (1980, 1982). There were statistically reliable differences favoring the inference training group on new inference items derived from the instructional stories. Also, high-achieving but not low-achieving students in that group did better than other groups on the inference items on the delayed post test. The most remarkable differences favored the schemata activation group on the free-recall protocols; their scores were often two or three standard deviations above the inference group and the control group, particularly on recall measures that were sensitive to the development and use of a story schema. In this study, there were no significant differences between groups on a standardized test.

Raphael and Pearson (1982) applied a more general approach to both literal and inference questions. During four 45-minute sessions, fourth-, sixth-, and eighth-grade students were taught to distinguish between questions that required, in different measure, information in the text versus knowledge the child already had. The children learned to generate answers to questions that invited textually explicit answers (derive an answer from the same text sentence from which the question was generated), textually implicit answers (derive an answer from a text sentence different from the one from which the question was derived), or scriptally implicit answers (derive an answer from one's store of prior knowledge). The three types of questions were labeled RIGHT THERE, THINK AND SEARCH, and ON MY OWN, respectively.

Using a Model → Guided Practice → Independent Practices → Direct Feedback instructional design, they taught the students to apply the strategy to increasingly longer texts, ranging from one paragraph to 600 words, with an increasingly larger number of questions per lesson, and increasingly fewer feedback prompts from the instructor. On all the comprehension measures there were reliable differences favoring the training group over the control group. Trained students became better at discriminating questions of the different types, evaluating their own question-answering behavior, and giving quality responses. Raphael and Pearson concluded that students had developed improved comprehension and comprehension-monitoring strategies that gave them more control over the kind of routine question-answering activity they experience daily in basal reader and content area material.

A study conducted by Day (1980) provides an interesting application of many of these same issues about instructional effectiveness with a very different population and a very different instructional objective. Working with low ability community college students, Day (1980) contrasted approaches to training students to write summaries for prose passages. The treatments differed systematically from one another in terms of how rules for writing summaries were integrated with self-management strategies designed to help students monitor their own progress in summary writing. Treatment 1 consisted of self-management alone (a fairly traditional self-checking procedure to determine whether the summary conveyed the information the student intended to convey). Treatment 2 was rules alone; that is, subjects were trained to use van Dijk and Kintsch's (1978) five rules for summarizing narratives: Delete redundancy, delete irrelevancies, subordinate subtopics, select topic sentences, create topic sentences. Treatment 3 simply put Treatments 1 and 2 together in sequence. First do one, then the other. Treatment 4 *integrated* the rules and self-management strategies into a single coherent routine. One might say that the four treatments varied along a continuum of integration of explicit training and explicit monitoring devices. A model–feedback–practice instructional design was used. The data from the experiment showed that overall the integrated treatment produced the greatest gains from pretest to posttest. Day (1980) concluded that, particularly with slower students: "explicit training in strategies for accomplishing a task coupled with routines to oversee the successful application of those strategies is clearly the best approach [p. 15]."

Palincsar (1982) evaluated the effects of explicit instruction (modeling and corrective feedback) of four comprehension-monitoring activities with learning disabled junior high students who were efficient at decoding but deficient in comprehension. The four activities included summarizing, question generating, predicting what might be discussed next in the text, and clarifying unclear text. The activities were taught through a procedure referred to as reciprocal teaching; the teacher and students took turns assuming the role of teacher in a dialogue about segments of expository text.

The research involved two studies. Both studies employed a multiple base line across groups. All students experienced four conditions: base line, intervention, maintenance, and follow-up. In Study 1 the investigator worked with six students, in pairs, in a setting analogous to a resource room. In Study 2, four remedial reading teachers worked with a total of 21 students in small groups in their classrooms.

Palincsar found that students' ability to answer comprehension questions, as assessed on passages independent of the training materials, improved significantly; they typically achieved 70% accuracy the 15th day of training. The effects were also apparent on an 8-week delayed measure. Students' verbal behavior during training indicated that they became more adept with summarizing and question generating as the intervention progressed. Also, modest but reliable transfer was suggested on three or four tasks similar to but distinct from the training tasks. Finally, gains observed in the experimental setting generalized to the classroom setting (regular social studies and science assignments) for five of the six students in Study 1.

The results of this investigation provide further support to a small body of instructional research in reading comprehension that suggests that students can indeed, through explicit instruction, be taught to acquire and independently apply reading strategies that will enhance reading comprehension.

These six studies appear to warrant the conclusion that we can teach comprehension skills if we are able to define them carefully, model for students methods they can use to complete skill activities, offer plenty of guided practice (with the teacher offering feedback as the tasks are completed), and then allow students to practice the skills on their own. The interesting thing to note about these conclusions is their similarity with those derived from the previous section on program evaluations. Although the tasks in the two sets of studies are quite different, the principles leading to effective performance are remarkably similar.

One could probably infer that such research would have yielded positive results by examining the gaps in instruction found by Durkin (1978–79) and the positive correlations between existing instructional practices and achievement noted by people like Rosenshine and Stevens (in press). That the few instructional studies on reading comprehension also support such a line of research is encouraging.

HAVE WE FOUND A MODEL OF READING INSTRUCTION?

Any search for a model of reading instruction is limited by the resources enlisted. Our present analysis is by no means an exception. There are numerous studies, examples, and commentaries from which instructional principles might be extrapolated that we did not review. Furthermore, there are countless variables and variations on these variables that might have been gleaned from the studies reviewed that we might be accused of failing to highlight. Despite these limitations, we would like to identify a few variables that we consider sufficiently potentially important to warrant further investigation.

The first can be called orientation toward reading. A classroom program can have a meaning emphasis or a decoding emphasis—providing instruction that gives students a set to construct meaningful representations for texts they encounter or a set for fast and accurate identification of words. The orientation toward reading subsumes many specific aspects of instruction. For example, in providing feedback about oral reading miscues, should a teacher give students a clue about meaning (it's a kind of animal), a clue about the code (it starts like "dad"), or a direction that might lead to a self-generated, meaning-induced strategy (read on and see if you can figure it out later)? In asking comprehension questions, should a teacher emphasize "the facts" in the form stated by the text by asking low-level literal questions or "interpretations" by asking inference questions that require integration across text segments or between text and existing schemata? In introducing stories, how much time should a teacher spend building background, a step that is likely to encourage students to integrate existing knowledge and new text information rather than compartmentalizing the new information for veridical recall?

The second theme is explicitness of instruction. How much (and when) should teachers intervene in students' discovery of specific comprehension strategies and comprehension-monitoring strategies? Should teachers adopt a heavy-handed approach and model these strategies for students at the outset of the instructional sequence in the hope that the modeling will reduce initial failure and lead to better strategy application and control? Is it enough to let students start doing these tasks on their own, offering feedback only where breakdowns surface? Or should the learning be left primarily in the hands of the students, who, after all, are ultimately responsible for acquiring and applying the strategies? These questions reveal at least three points along a continuum of degree of teacher intervention in student learning. Although we have cited much research favoring explicitness, we feel its impact must yet be demonstrated in a wide range of instructional tasks and contexts. Also we suspect that the value of explicit instruction may depend on variables such as student ability and task characteristics. That is, some students may be able to discover appropriate strategies on their own, whereas others may need much guidance, depending on the task. Previous research also points to the importance of providing students with explicit routines for monitoring how they are comprehending or how they are proceeding to complete the assigned task. Some students may discover task-monitoring procedures on their own, but we are especially interested in whether it is helpful to explicitly teach unsuccessful readers to monitor their comprehension.

A third theme has to do with who controls the learning environment. We believe, and we suspect few would disagree, that the overall goal of instruction is to nurture students who assume ownership of their own learning. Few of the studies we have reviewed have addressed student ownership of comprehension strategies or have chosen to be satisfied with measures indicative of a relatively low level of skill or strategy transfer or generalization. Granted, the Gordon (1980), Raphael and Pearson (1982), Day (1980), and Palinscar (1982) efforts worried about taking students from a state of dependence to a state of independence in strategy application, but even in those studies the process of turning the reins over to students was itself under teacher control. And, also, the Goodman perspective on learning assumes that control is a negotiable process between teacher and student. Yet, we still know little about what it means for a student to own a strategy let alone how students achieve that ownership. We have some clues in the work we have reviewed, but the definition and means of achieving responsibility for one's own learning await further work.

A fourth theme is the dominant role seemingly played by practice. All the process–product research and program evaluation research points to the importance of "time on task" as a potent variable. Yet, the review of classroom practices suggests that there is something missing in a "practice only" approach to strategy learning. Furthermore, the practice issue probably interacts with the orientation to reading issue (*What* do the students practice and in *what contexts?*) the explicitness issue (*When* do they practice on their own?), and the ownership issue (What kinds of practice either index or nurture independence?).

We are sure that these are not the only themes or variables that will emerge in the next decade as we begin to fine-tune our models of instructional research in reading. But we are also sure that good instructional research will have to account for these factors; they are too important to overlook.

ACKNOWLEDGMENT

The research reported herein was supported by the National Institute of Education under Contract No. US-NIE-C-400-76-0116. We gratefully acknowledge the assistance of Richard C. Anderson, Jean Osborn, and Meg Gallagher for their reactions to earlier versions of this manuscript.

REFERENCES

Anderson, L., Evertson, C., & Brophy, J. An experimental study of effective teaching in first-grade reading groups. *Elementary School Journal,* 1979, *79,* 193–223.

Au, K. H., & Mason, J. M. Social organizational factors in learning to read: The balance of rights hypothesis. *Reading Research Quarterly,* 1981, *17*(1), 115–152.

Baker, L., & Brown, A. L. Metacognitive skills of reading. In P. D. Pearson (Ed.), *Handbook of reading research.* New York: Longmans, in press.

Beck, I. L., McKeown, M. G., McCaslin, E. S., & Burkes, A. M. *Instructional dimensions that may affect reading comprehension: Examples from two commercial reading programs.* Pittsburgh: University of Pittsburgh, Learning Research and Development Center, 1979. (ERIC Document Reproduction Service No. ED 197 322).

Becker, W. C. Teaching reading and language to the disadvantaged: What we have learned from field research. *Harvard Educational Review,* 1977, *47,* 518–543.

Becker, W. C., & Carnine, D. *Direct instruction—A behaviorally based model for comprehensive educational intervention with the disadvantaged.* Unpublished manuscript, University of Oregon, 1978.

Becker, W. C., Engelman, J., & Carnine, D. The direct instruction model. In *Encouraging change in America's schools: A decade of experimentation.* New York: Academic Press, 1979.

Bereiter, C., & Kurland, D. M. A constructive look at follow-through results. *Interchange,* in press.

Brewer, W. F., & Lichtenstein, E. H. Event schemas, story schemas, and story grammars. In A. D. Baddeley & J. D. Long (Eds.), *Attention and performance IX.* Hillsdale, N.J.: Lawrence Erlbaum Associates, in press.

Brophy, J. Teacher behavior and its effects. *Journal of Educational Psychology,* 1979, *71,* 733–750.

Brophy, J. *Recent research in teaching.* Paper presented as an invited address at the annual meeting of the Northeastern Educational Research Association, October 1980.

Cambourne, B. Getting to Goodman: An analysis of the Goodman model of reading with some suggestions for evaluation. *Reading Research Quarterly,* 1976–77, *12,* 605–636.

Carey, R. F., Harste, J. C., & Smith, S. L. Contextual constraints and discourse processes: A replication study. *Reading Research Quarterly,* 1981, *16*(2), 201–212.

Day, J. D. *Teaching summarization skills: A comparison of training methods.* Unpublished doctoral dissertation, University of Illinois, August 1980.

Duffy, G. Teacher effectiveness research: Implications for the reading profession. *Directions in reading: Research and instruction,* 30th Yearbook of the National Reading Conference, Washington, D.C.: The National Reading Conference, 1981.

Duffy, G., & McIntyre, L. *A qualitative analysis of how various primary grade teachers employ the structured learning component of the direct instruction model when teaching reading.* Research Series No. 80, Institute for Research on Teaching, Michigan State University, June 1980.

Duffy, G., & Roehler, L. *Classroom teaching is more than opportunity to learn.* Unpublished paper, Michigan State University, 1980.

Durkin, D. What classroom observations reveal about reading comprehension instruction. *Reading Research Quarterly,* 1978–79, *14,* 481–533.

Durkin, D. Reading comprehension instruction in five basal reading series. *Reading Research Quarterly,* 1981, *16,* 515–544.

Good, T. L., & Grouws, D. A. The Missouri mathematics effectiveness project: An experimental study in fourth-grade classrooms. *Journal of Educational Psychology,* 1979, *71,* 355–362.

Goodman, K. S. Analyses of oral reading miscues: Applied psycholinguistics. *Reading Research Quarterly,* 1969, *5,* 9–30.

Goodman, K. S. The reading process. In S. Smiles & J. Towner (Eds.), *Proceedings of the Sixth Western Symposium on Learning.* Bellingham, Wash., 1975.

Goodman, K. S., & Goodman, Y. M. Learning to read is natural. In L. B. Resnick & P. A. Weaver (Eds.), *Theory and practice of early reading* (Vol. 1). Hillsdale, N.J.: Lawrence Erlbaum Associates, 1979.

Goodman, Y. M., & Burke, C. L. *Reading miscue inventory: Procedure for diagnosis and evaluation.* New York: Macmillan, 1972.

Goodman, Y. M., & Burke, C. L. *Reading strategies: Focus on comprehension.* New York: Holt, Rinehart, & Winston, 1980.

Gordon, C. J. *The effects of instruction in metacomprehension and inferencing on children's comprehension abilities.* Unpublished doctoral dissertation, University of Minnesota, 1980.

Hansen, J., & Pearson, P. D. *The effects of inference training and practice on young children's comprehension* (Tech. Rep. No. 166). Urbana: University of Illinois, Center for the Study of Reading, April 1980. (ERIC Document Reproduction Service No. ED 186 839)

Hansen, J., & Pearson, P. D. *An instructional study: Improving the inferential comprehension of good and poor fourth-grade readers* (Tech. Rep. No. 235). Urbana: University of Illinois, Center for the Study of Reading, 1982.

Harste, J., Burke, C., & Woodward, V. Children's language and world: Initial encounters with print. In J. Langer & M. Smith-Burke (Eds.), *Bridging the gap: Reader meets author.* Newark, Del.: International Reading Association, 1982.

Hayes, D. A., & Tierney, R. J. Developing readers' knowledge through analogy. *Reading Research Quarterly,* 1982, *17,* 256–280.

House, E. R., Glass, G. V., McLean, L. F., & Walker, D. F. Critiquing a follow through evaluation. *Phi Delta Kappan,* 1978, *59,* 473–474. (a)

House, E. R., Glass, G. V., McLean, L. D., & Walker, D. F. No simple answer: Critique of the follow-through evaluation. *Harvard Educational Review,* 1978, *48,* 128–160. (b)

Huey, E. B. *The psychology and pedagogy of reading.* Cambridge, Mass.: MIT Press, 1968. (Original publication New York: McMillan Co., 1908).

Johnston, P., & Pearson, P. D. *Prior knowledge, connectivity, and the assessment of reading comprehension* (Tech. Rep. No. 245). Urbana: University of Illinois, Center for the Study of Reading, June 1982.

LaBerge, D., & Samuels, S. J. Towards a theory of automatic information processing in reading. *Cognitive Psychology,* 1974, *6,* 293–323.

Mandler, J. M., & Johnson, N. S. Remembrance of things parsed: Story structure and recall. *Cognitive Psychology,* 1977, *9,* 111–151.

Mason, J. M., & Osborn, J. *When do children begin "reading to learn"? A survey of classroom reading instruction practices in grades two through five* (Tech. Rep.). Urbana: University of Illinois, Center for the Study of Reading, in press.

Medley, D. *Teacher competence and teacher effectiveness: A review of process–product research.* Washington, D.C.: American Association of Colleges for Teacher Education, 1977.

Medley, D. Research on teacher effectiveness. In P. Peterson & H. Walberg (Eds.), *Research on teaching: Concepts, findings, and implications.* Berkeley, Calif.: McCutchan, 1979.

Palincsar, A. M. *The reciprocal teaching of comprehension monitoring activities.* Unpublished doctoral dissertation, University of Illinois, Urbana–Champaign, 1982.

Perfetti, C. A., & Lesgold, A. M. Discourse comprehension and sources of individual differences. In M. Just & P. Carpenter (Eds.), *Cognitive processes in comprehension.* Hillsdale, N.J.: Lawrence Erlbaum Associates, 1977.

Raphael, T. E., & Pearson, P. D. *The effects of metacognitive strategy awareness training on students' question-answering behavior* (Tech. Rep. No. 238). Urbana: University of Illinois, Center for the Study of Reading, March 1982.

Rosenshine, B. *Teaching behaviors and student achievement.* Windsor, England: National Foundation for Educational Research in England and Wales, 1971.

Rosenshine, B. V. Content, time, and direct instruction. In P. Peterson & H. Walberg (Eds.), *Research on teaching: Concepts, findings, and implications.* Berkeley, Calif.: McCutchan Publishing Co., 1979.

Rosenshine, B. V. How time is spent in elementary classrooms. In C. Denham & A. Lieberman (Eds.), *Time to learn.* Washington, D.C.: National Institute of Education, May 1980.

Rosenshine, B. V., & Stevens, R. Advances in teacher education research. *Journal of Special Education,* in press.

Rumelhart, D. E. Toward an interactive model of reading. In S. Dornic (Ed.), *Attention and performance VI.* London: Academic Press, 1977.

Shannon, P. *Teachers self-perceptions and reification of instruction within reading instruction.* Unpublished doctoral dissertation, University of Minnesota, 1981.

Spiro, R. J. Constructive processes in prose comprehension and recall. In R. J. Spiro, B. C. Bruce, & W. F. Brewer (Eds.), *Theoretical issues in reading comprehension.* Hillsdale, N.J.: Lawrence Erlbaum Associates, 1980.

Stallings, J. *Teaching basic reading skills in the secondary schools.* Paper presented at the annual meeting of the American Educational Research Association, 1978. (ERIC Document Reproduction Service No. ED 166 634)

Stein, N., & Glenn, C. G. An analysis of story comprehension in elementary school children. In R. Freedle (Ed.), *New directions in discourse processing.* Norwood, N.J.: Ablex, 1979.

Steffensen, M. S., Joag-dev, C., & Anderson, R. C. A cross-cultural perspective on reading comprehension. *Reading Research Quarterly,* 1979, *15,* 10–29.

Tharp, R. *The direct instruction of comprehension: Results and description of the Kamehameha Early Education Program.* Paper presented at the American Educational Research Association, Boston, April 1980.

Tharp, R. G. The effective instruction of comprehension: Results and description of the Kamehameha Early Education Program. *Reading Research Quarterly,* 1982, *17,* 503–527.

van Dijk, T. A., & Kintsch, W. Cognitive psychology and discourse: Recalling and summarizing stories. In W. U. Dressler (Ed.), *Current theories in text linguistics.* New York: de Gruyter, 1978.

Wisler, C. E., Burns, G. P., & Iwamoto, D. Follow-through readers: A response to the critique by House, Glass, McLean and Walker. *Harvard Educational Review,* 1978, *48,* 171–185.

Woodworth, R. S. *Experimental psychology.* New York: Holt, 1938.

3

Child as Coinvestigator: Helping Children Gain Insight into their own Mental Processes

Marlene Scardamalia
York University

Carl Bereiter
Ontario Institute for Studies in Education

This chapter is based on a simple premise—that children's metacognitive development may be aided by giving them greater access to data arising from their own cognitive processes. It seems to be generally agreed that children are less aware of their cognitive processes than adults are (Brown, 1978; Flavell, Speer, Green, & August, 1981; Flavell & Wellman, 1977; Paris & Lindauer, 1982). Certainly one important factor retarding the growth of metacognitive knowledge is the limited availability of data from which such knowledge may be constructed. Not only are the data elusive because of the rapid and fleeting nature of mental events, but also because when people are engaged in mental activity their attention is normally taken up with the task at hand or with the content of cognition rather than being directed toward the process itself.

We are assuming, as others have (Brown, 1977; Flavell, 1979; Paris, Newman, & McVey, 1982), that metacognitive knowledge must be constructed like any other kind of knowledge. Insight into one's own mental processes does not occur because of a window opening on the mind but because in the course of long experience one manages to piece together some kind of coherent knowledge on the basis of fragmentary data.

A corollary to this premise is that not all experiences are equal in their ability to provide data for the construction of metacognitive knowledge. Activities may differ not only in the kinds of cognitive processes they elicit but also in the extent to which the cognitive processes that are brought into play yield instructive data. Let us consider an obvious example. The person solving a problem silently and the person solving a problem while thinking aloud are carrying out some of the same cognitive processes (no need to argue that they are altogether the same).

The person thinking aloud, however, generates data that cognitive researchers will often find to be more informative than the data yielded by the silent problem solver (Ericsson & Simon, 1980). Is it not reasonable to suppose that thinking aloud might also yield data helpful to the thinker in understanding his or her own cognitive processes, bringing events to light that might otherwise pass unnoticed? Thinking aloud is one among a variety of ways that cognitive researchers try to get cognitive behavior to yield more informative data. In setting out to devise ways of giving children greater access to data on which they could base metacognitive knowledge, therefore, a good starting place might be the kinds of activities that have proved illuminating in cognitive research.

For the past 5 years we have been doing cognitive–developmental research on children's writing. The nature and findings of this research are not germane to this chapter and therefore are not discussed here. (See instead Bereiter & Scardamalia, 1982; Scardamalia, Bereiter, & Goelman, 1982.) What is germane is that in the course of some 70 experiments we have employed numerous methods for probing mental processes in young people, and a frequent side effect has been that the children themselves became actively interested in what the experimental procedures were allowing them to discover about their mental processes. For the most part we have employed experimental designs that permitted us to inform subjects about the purpose of the inquiry and to discuss matters freely with them as we proceeded. This allowed children, in effect, to participate as coinvestigators—to function not only as sources of data but as seekers and interpreters of data as well.

Involvement and enthusiasm have generally been high. Students who have not liked writing have nonetheless seemed to like analyzing the task and the process. We have consequently been led to think about possible educational uses of this sort of collaborative inquiry. The educational use we explore in this chapter is coinvestigation as a way of fostering metacognitive knowledge, considered as a type of self-knowledge. Coinvestigation might also have promise as a way of developing theoretical or scientific knowledge—we have exploited it for that purpose ourselves—but that is a different matter. In this chapter we are not concerned with promoting the kind of formalized knowledge possessed by the psychologist but rather with promoting the more informal self-knowledge that appears to constitute a natural part of intellectual maturity.

This is mainly a how-to chapter. It describes a variety of techniques that we have found helpful for getting children profitably involved in inquiry into their cognitive processes. In presenting these techniques, we do not presume at all to advocate a ''method'' or to promote an already developed educational program. On the contrary, we offer these techniques in the hope that they may be helpful to researchers and instructional designers who are exploring ways of assisting metacognitive development. We do not foresee courses in metacognition being taught in schools. Rather, we foresee that instruction in many areas of intellectual skill might be enriched by designing activities so that they bring more of the cognitive processes out into the open where teachers and students can examine and try to understand them. The illustrations offered in this chapter come almost entirely from work on writing. It would remain for educators or researchers to devise comparable procedures in other areas. Finally, the techniques discussed in this chapter are only techniques for making data from cognitive processes more accessible. What is done with the data—what kinds of discussions, comparisons, analyses, and planning of further explorations might ensue between teacher and child—also remains an open question. Simply getting cognitive data out into the open where it can be dealt with is no small accomplishment, however, especially when the data in question come from children who have had little experience in contemplating or consciously regulating their mental processes. We hope that the development of techniques for bringing cognitive behavior out into the open will create educational possibilities of exciting and unforeseen kinds.

WHERE COGNITIVE INQUIRY MAY HELP

It is possible to agree with the points made in the preceding section and nevertheless question the advisability of encouraging children to focus attention on their own cognitive processes. We trust that some of these concerns will be allayed as we offer concrete examples, and so we reserve to the final section discussion of the overall merits of cognitive inquiry by children.

The ensuing discussion may be clarified, however, if at this point we consider how cognitive inquiry relates to more typical approaches to the teaching of intellectual skills. Most intellectual skills, after all, are taught reasonably successfully without any need for the learners to investigate what is going on in their own minds. Most of us probably have very little idea of how we read, for instance, and we probably had even less idea at the time we were learning; yet we do not feel that our capacity for intelligent reading has been hampered. Apparently, through practice and self-monitoring, we gain sufficient insight to hold us in good stead.

Not everyone acquires effective cognitive strategies for reading, writing, problem solving, and the like, however (Bereiter & Scardamalia, in press a; Flavell et al., 1981; Paris & Myers, 1981). The normal processes for aquiring procedural knowledge may be reliable for attaining the rudimentary skills of literacy and other major types of cognitive behavior, but they do not appear reliable for acquiring the strategies that characterize expert performance. The normal processes of acquiring procedural knowledge or "know-how" include observation, practice, and rule learning. The conditions under which we believe inquiry into cognitive processes is likely to prove valuable are the conditions in which these typical methods are not sufficient. Let us consider briefly what those conditions might be.

Observational Learning

Strategy learning through observation has been frequently demonstrated (Rosenthal & Zimmerman, 1978). Strategies themselves, being mental phenomena, cannot be observed, of course. Behavior is observed and the strategy must in some sense be inferred. The problem with many cognitive strategies is that observable behavior gives only a limited and sometimes misleading basis for reconstructing the underlying mental operations.

An anecdote provided by a colleague illustrates the problem. Her young son one day announced that he had learned to revise. He proudly showed her an essay with sentences crossed out and with arrows directing the reader to insert chunks of text and to reorder different parts. The trouble was that the revised draft did not make sense, so she asked her son what he was trying to accomplish. What he was trying to do was make his papers look like a manuscript she was working on. He mimicked the observables of the revision process but not the accompanying mental operations that gave purpose to the observables.

We should not underestimate the value of such observational learning. It provides a concrete framework to which the more elusive mental operations may be attached. Thus, we would expect this colleague's son to be at a considerable advantage compared to many young students with whom we work, whose only concrete model for revision is the producing of a clean copy. Observational learning may also be helpful in creating a motivational context for cognitive strategy learning. Although not yet grasping what revision was for, our colleague's son must have sensed that it was a valued activity and one worth emulating. Similarly, children who observe their parents reading may not thereby learn much about the process of reading, but they are likely to learn something about its place in life.

As we see it, the observable manifestations of cognitive behavior provide an excellent starting point for coinvestigation of the process, for adult and child to discover, for instance, what is different in the ways they decide what to cross out and where to draw the arrows in revising a manuscript. But if children are left too much on their own to fill in the mental activities lying behind observables, there is a danger that they will remain dominated by what they observe. Thus, in writing, we find children's composing processes to be dominated by the observable part of the process—the manuscript. When asked to plan texts aloud, they yield protocols that are little different from what we receive if we ask them to dictate essays (Burtis, Bereiter, Scardamalia, & Tetroe, in press). Expert writers, on the other hand, display a large and varied amount of thinking during composition that is relevant to but never appears as part of the manuscript (Hayes & Flower, 1980). In order for children to grasp these other kinds of thinking, they need sources of information beyond ordinary observation.

One of the ways that instructional researchers have tried to overcome the limitations of ordinary observation has been by rendering more of the cognitive process observable, often through the use of thinking aloud while modeling

(Bird, 1980; Brown, 1978; Burtis et al., in press). Studies so far reported all seem to indicate that cognitive modeling, unless it is supported by more active instructional procedures, is not effective in changing children's strategies. As we shall see, however, thinking aloud by both child and adult can provide a valuable source of data for use in coinvestigation of cognitive strategies.

Practice

Groen and Resnick (1977) have shown that through practice alone young children develop increasingly sophisticated strategies for simple addition, moving from laborious finger counting to methods using increasingly efficient mental operations. A necessary condition for practice to be sufficient is a large amount of redundancy in operations and content. It is the repeated counting of the same small set of numbers, Neches (1979) suggests, that creates the possibility of discovering shortcuts.

Every skill has its redundant elements. The danger in relying on practice alone is that the redundant parts will be worked into a streamlined procedure that is insensitive to novel or nonredundant aspects of the activity. Singing, for instance, is highly redundant. One sings the same limited set of notes with the same limited set of durations over and over again in various combinations. With practice one can become proficient at this. But singers who are serious musicians must struggle continually to rise above the effects of mere practice and to perfect ways of singing that are attuned to the distinctive qualities of each composition. This requires both effort and insight (Pavarotti & Wright, 1981). Effort and insight mark the ways in which *studying* singing is different from simply practicing it.

We have reason to believe that what is true of singing is also true of such intellectual skills as reading and writing. Here, too, there is much redundancy, so that with practice students can develop efficient strategies that allow them to meet the routine demands of school reading and writing tasks with a minimum of effort. The result, however, is comprehension strategies that are insensitive to the distinctiveness and complexity of text information (Scardamalia & Bereiter, in press c), and writing strategies that are insensitive to the distinctive requirements of different writing goals (Bereiter & Scardamalia, in press a). Rising above these routine "cognitive coping strategies," as we call them, requires sustained effort directed toward one's own mental processes. Prime candidates for coinvestigations with children, then, are skill areas in which "practice makes perfect" is an untrustworthy slogan.

Rule Learning

Strategy learning can be greatly simplified whenever students can be taught rules that they are able to follow. Not all rules that describe expert performance are followable by novices, however. Consider the following rule of writing style, for instance:

Omit needless words (Strunk & White, 1959).
It seems likely that anyone sophisticated enough to be able to apply this rule would not need to be taught it.

One may, of course, strive for simpler or more explicit rules, but there will surely remain many cases in which children lack the knowledge necessary to apply a procedural rule and cannot be readily taught it. An alternative in such cases is to teach children a self-regulatory procedure that permits them to make optimum use of the knowledge they do possess. For editing out "needless" language, for instance, children may be taught to experiment with deletions, testing to see whether meaning is disrupted by the deletion (Bereiter, Scardamalia, & Cattani, 1981). Coinvestigation is relevant in these situations because the procedure does not depend on the children's conceptual understanding of rules but rather on their ability to direct and monitor their cognitive processes.

Overarching all the problems we have been considering is the problem of motivation or purpose. In the case of highly specific skills such as high jumping or playing chess, learners can have from an early stage a fairly clear idea of what they are trying to achieve. If they are motivated to achieve it, then they will likely make the most of the opportunities offered by observation, practice, and rule learning, and show progress to more sophisticated strategies even when the learning conditions are far from ideal.

In the case of more general intellectual skills such as comprehension, composition, and explanation, however, students who have not yet achieved a sophisticated strategy are not in a good position to appreciate what the strategy could do for them. With these kinds of activities, the goals tend to emerge from strategy execution rather than to precede it (Scardamalia & Bereiter, in press d). Consequently there is a serious motivational problem, not in the sense of students' unwillingness to exert effort but in the sense of their not having a clear notion of what their efforts are supposed to yield. In the absence of such a notion, it is natural for students to stick with the cognitive strategies they have and to assimilate new learning to them. We have repeatedly found that our efforts to guide students to more complex composing strategies are thwarted unless we can convey to the students some sense of a cognitive outcome to strive for. Coinvestigation of cognitive strategies has so far appeared to have its most significant function in this motivational context. It gives children an opportunity to grasp the potentialities of cognitive strategies that they have not yet mastered, and this allows them to engage in strategy learning activities with a greater sense of purpose.

OPEN INQUIRY

The techniques discussed in this section are general-purpose techniques for bringing cognitive events out into the open in working with children. Although children may be as mentally active as adults, and often even more willing to expose their mental activity to scrutiny, it is usually more difficult with children than with adults to bring forth information on their cognitive processes. This is partly because children are less accustomed to paying attention to their mental processes and consequently lack some of the metacognitive skills needed to extract metacognitive knowledge. Also, they lack the large repertoire of mentalistic terms that the sophisticated adult possesses, and this limits their ability both to understand questions and to formulate statements related to cognitive events. This does not make cognitive inquiry with children any the less rewarding, either for the adult or for the child; it only means that the adult must come equipped with appropriate techniques for helping children surmount the obstacles to inquiry and communication.

The simplest way to engage children in collaborative interchange is to have them introspect—simply talk to you about how they typically do something or try to monitor their mental activities as they engage in some activity. In our experience with such techniques, major difficulties in employing them come not so much from limitations in what children can contribute, as from the adult's misunderstanding of what the child can be expected to contribute.

It is true that the child cannot keep up as active an interchange as an adult coinvestigator can. Adult coinvestigators have a good deal of sophistication in making points clearly, coming back to points not made clear on first go-around, noting when there is a mismatch between what has been conveyed and what is intended, and so on. A rule of thumb we seldom find ourselves regretting having followed is to assume that when a child is telling us something that seems either insignificant or very confused, we are probably missing something important. Also, the child is probably struggling to explain something at the edge of current awareness. This is precisely the point at which we must try harder to make sense of what is happening.

What follows is a list of techniques for supporting discussion under such circumstances. Before proceeding with this list, however, a list that might make it appear that the adult is not assuming the role of coinvestigator so much as the role of coach, we would like to clarify the sense in which the effort is a collaborative one, with mutual benefits for investigator and child.

It is important to remember that the adult is involved in the first place because the kinds of complex activities being dealt with are not well understood. If the adult knew the procedures underlying the phenomena in enough detail to model them clearly or reduce them to specific rules, then the problem would not be so difficult. The truth of the matter is, however, that adults are novicelike in this respect and are trying themselves to understand procedures being used. In interchange with children we typically start by explaining that our purpose for being there is that we would like to learn more about how people write. It is precisely because this process is not well understood that we seek their help. We believe they have important knowledge to contribute about how children their age do things. The message is a sincere one, because it is true, and it establishes their legitimacy as coinvestigators. We remind the reader that our concern here is with bringing cognitive phenomena out into the open so that they are available for discussion by adult and child. We do not deal with the inferential processes that may go on in such discussions nor with the scientific uses to which the resulting information might be put (see, however, Bereiter & Scardamalia, in press b).

a. *Teach Children to Think Aloud.*   The purpose behind teaching the child to think aloud is that the thinking-aloud experience itself provides data for comment. That is, it appears to make normally covert processes more accessible to the person doing the thinking aloud, as well as to the person listening.

However, we have found that young children find thinking aloud a more difficult task than adults do. Adults, asked to say aloud all the things that naturally occur to them as they engage in some task, can proceed with little additional instruction. In contrast, younger children tend to need someone beside them to provide encouragement and to ask questions when they fall silent (see sections d and e). Practice also seems to help, as does learning to think aloud while doing some nonverbal activity such as drawing a picture.[1]

The rewards of engaging students in think-aloud experiences are substantial. The following discussion took place in a class of Grade 10 students who had just completed one session of thinking aloud while reading. First one student put up his hand: "I think that when you have to read out loud you slow down the whole process of reading. I read much faster when I read to myself. Don't you think that if information goes into your head faster that better things might come out?" This child seems to have some insight into the concept of coding efficiency as currently represented in the literature (Perfetti & Lesgold, 1977). Another student put up her hand in response and said: "Well, I think it's not the speed that's the big thing. I think it's the fact that when you make me say everything out loud I'm using up a lot of what's in my head to do the job of thinking aloud so I don't have so much [mental working space] left to do the thinking about what I'm reading." (This student appears to have some insight into limited capacity information-processing models). Another student, in a tone suggesting embarrassment, confessed: "I have a problem. When I read, I like to read the last paragraph first. That way when I start again from the beginning, I have some idea of what's going to happen." She seemed delighted to discover that we thought her strategy was a sophisticated one, and other children seemed interested in the possible advantages and disadvantages of this strategy.

The point of these examples is not that students have sophisticated ideas about

---

[1]The use of nonverbal tasks in series with verbal tasks was investigated by Tetroe (1981).

cognitive processes, although they sometimes do. The point is that they are very interested in analyzing their cognitive processes, and that they are interested in them in much the same way as cognitive psychologists are. On the toughest of teaching days we find children will give us their full attention if either another student or the teacher engages in some thinking-aloud activity.

b. *Give Students Something Concrete to Talk About.*   Vague questions such as "How do you decide what to write when you're given a writing assignment?" are likely to result in vague or stereotyped answers. We find, in fact, that questions of this broadly "metacognitive" kind make for a tense interview. The student wants to be cooperative but is never quite sure what you are trying to get at. It is much better to give the students something to do—moving things, underlining, searching, etc.—and then discuss what they are doing as they do it. In studying text comprehension, for instance, we have found that a task of arranging sentences provides the basis for a richer discussion of comprehension strategies than does ordinary reading, because the task involves discrete decisions that can be questioned and justified (Scardamalia & Bereiter, in press c).

Hayes-Roth & Hayes-Roth (1979) have a task they use to study planning that illustrates the advantages of tasks that are not strictly dependent on verbal report. Subjects are provided with a shopping list and a city map and are asked to plan a day of shopping where they try to accomplish a great number of things in a limited time. The nice feature of the task for purposes of uncovering planning procedures used by young children is that their planning strategy shows up concretely in the way they track things on the map and refer to the shopping list. What an experimenter can see from observing such activity is that adults get themselves oriented to the map as a whole, determining sections of the city where with little travel they can get much accomplished (Hayes-Roth & Hayes-Roth, 1979); by comparison, young children get themselves located at one point on the map, see if the building next to it is one where they can accomplish any one of the specified tasks; if not, they move to the next building and repeat the same procedure. Planning, with this task, becomes something like a board game, making it possible to discuss and compare strategies as one might, for instance, with a game like checkers.

Tasks that manage to uncover strategies for adult investigators tend also to provide children with data they need to understand their own activity. Children frequently can describe their activity *after* such an exercise, although they would not do so before. Further, seeing an adult do the task after they have themselves had the opportunity to "see" how they perform, appears to create interest in and appreciation of the adult strategy.

In one study (Bereiter, Scardamalia, & Turkish, 1980), we wanted to investigate children's conceptual knowledge of written genres. Questions like "What kinds of things would you include in a story?" obtained results from high school students, but elementary school children did not know what to make of the question. In this case giving them an actual story to talk about would only serve to focus attention on specific story content rather than on general properties of the genre. What finally worked was to show them an actual composition but not let them read it, saying, for instance, "This is an essay I wrote trying to convince somebody of something. What kind of thing do you think I probably said at the beginning, in order to make this a good essay?" Although getting children to discuss abstract characteristics of text was still not easy, this minimal amount of concretizing at least made it possible.

   c. *Have Students Prescribe Rather Than Describe.*   Students who are inarticulate in trying to describe how they go about doing some mental task often come forth with clear statements of procedure when asked to give advice to another student, particularly a younger one, for carrying out the task. Even formulating instructions for themselves can be helpful, as Meichenbaum (1973) has shown. The benefits that peer tutoring has been found to yield for the child doing the tutoring (Cloward, 1967) may be partly due to this effect. Children seem to have a better vocabulary for prescribing than for describing. It is also possible that the task of prescribing gives better direction to their search of long-term memory than does a task of describing.

   d. *Attend to Nonverbal Cues and Use Them as Points for Discussion.*   Here are some examples of observable behavior and related questions:

Observable Behavior	*Possible Question*
Eye shift	You just noticed something, didn't you?
Change in rate	You're going faster now. Is this part easier?
Discouraged look	You look discouraged. Is something particularly hard here?
Satisfied look	Did you just figure something out?
Long pause	What's going on in your mind now?

   e. *Enlist the Student's Help in Getting You to Understand.*   When a child makes an unclear statement, novice interviewers tend to err in either of two ways. They either take the statement at face value, which means the child gets classified as the one who doesn't understand, or they resort to courtroom procedures of insistent questioning, which often confuses or intimidates the child. In coinvestigation, however, adult and child should be trying equally to help each other understand what is going on.

We have found conversational moves like the following to be useful in getting students to take an active role in helping us to understand, rather than responding passively to the questions they are asked:

Ask student to fill in gaps: "You've lost me here. How did you get from thinking about *X* to thinking about *Y?* Did I miss something?"

Ask student to restate more slowly: "Wait, you're going too fast for me. Could you say that a little slower so I can write it all down?" (This often leads to restatement in different terms, yielding more clues for understanding.)

Confess incomprehension: "I just don't get it. If this is so hard that you can't do it, then how did you know to write down what you've written so far?"

Check distortions: "I think I got something wrong here. I wrote down _____ but I don't think that's quite what you said." (By getting a chance to correct misstatements children not only clarify what they said originally, but they begin to feel free about correcting the adult and consequently may begin to do so when the adult isn't aware of a need to be corrected.)

With all the foregoing statements, the essential thing to convey is that it is you, the adult, who has a problem with the verbal interchange—not the child. That is, you are failing to get some piece of information that you believe is quite important. When children clearly get this message we find them taking on more assertive roles, correcting the adult's misconceptions, asking the adult to rewrite something because it is not quite right, and we've even had children suggesting to us questions we might ask them if we really wanted to know what they were thinking.

f. *Use a Series of Tasks of Increasing Complexity.*   Because change is usually more salient than constancy, children can often gain awareness of cognitive strategy features by noticing what things get harder to do as a task increases in difficulty. The task sequence must be carefully designed, of course, so that changes are clear-cut and psychologically interesting. One would not, for instance, derive much from presenting students with a sequence of miscellaneous reading passages selected so as to be graded in readability level. They would differ in too many ways at once, and some of the major factors in difficulty, such as vocabulary, are probably not very fruitful ones for coinvestigation.

A simple task sequence that we found productive for studying composing processes was a sequence that involved planning a paragraph that would incorporate two given sentences (Paris, Scardamalia, & Bereiter, 1982). At the easiest level the two sentences contained common topical words. At an intermediate level they contained related but not identical topical words. At the most difficult level the two sentences did not directly suggest a common topic at all, so that the student had to invent a unifying theme. Task sequences suitable for coinvestigation of cognitive strategies can be found scattered throughout the experimental cognitive–developmental literature; see for instance the balance scale tasks in Siegler (1981), and the equivalent fraction tasks cited by Case (in press).

For use in coinvestigation it is important that the tasks start at an easy enough level that the students can build confidence in their basic ability to handle the type of task, and they should if possible increase in difficulty by steps sufficiently fine that students can experience points that give them real difficulty, short of total failure.

Again, it is vital for children to understand that the point of the activity is not successful or unsuccessful task performance but rather understanding the mental processes involved in the task. Once children catch on to the idea that each step in task difficulty means an interesting new phenomenon to investigate, they seem to lose their anxiety about success and failure and can even begin to regard failure, when it comes, as itself an interesting phenomenon to be explained. A further possibie benefit from this kind of activity is metacognitive awareness by students of their own capabilities, with an accompanying ability to predict what will and will not cause them difficulty.

g. *Turn the Task the Child Must Work on Into a Discrimination or Comparison Task.* Rather than requiring students to describe the strategies they use to solve a task, have them evaluate some strategy that you propose or demonstrate.

We have found three different presentation formats useful. Each assumes that the child has worked previously on the task and therefore has something to compare the adult's procedure with.

The first is the most straightforward. Simply think aloud while you do the precise task the child was just asked to do. Then ask the child if what you did was anything like what he or she did.

One child we had been working with struggled for a long time trying to figure out which of several stories fitted a particular proverb. His strategy, as far as could be determined from what he did, was to find a topic that the proverb and story shared, and match proverb to story on this topical basis (i.e., they are both about monkeys), rather than on the basis of underlying meaning. We then modeled how we went about the task, matching elements in the story with elements in the proverb and checking to see whether the story elements could fit into the proverb and still make sense. Upon seeing this (the strategy was not described to the child, the child just looked on while the adult talked aloud) the child proceeded to accurately describe the adult's strategy, compare it to his own, and consider how he might go about the task differently in the future. Prior to this the child had seemed neither to be able to describe his own strategy nor to appreciate what the adult was saying about how he might do things differently.

Another format is to lead students through the execution of a different strategy themselves and then have them compare it to what they normally do. This only works, of course, with procedures that are straightforward enough that one can coach students in carrying them out. But a variety of important cognitive strategies are of this kind, such as those involving rehearsal, review, apportionment of study time, and elaboration in memorizing (Brown, 1978; Paris et al., 1982; Rohwer, 1973).

The third format, easiest for the child, requires the most work on the part of the adult. The adult identifies cognitive procedures that the child appears to be using and puts these in a list along with other procedures that the child does not appear to use. Some of these other procedures reflect less mature strategies, some of them more mature strategies than the child appears to employ. This method has been employed by Paris and Myers (1981) to identify reading strategies. We have found it useful, from the child's point of view, for gaining insight into strategic choices related to more and less successful task performance. One child, for instance, had been working on revising stories to accommodate new information. When presented with a list of procedural rules, he could identify procedures he once followed but no longer did (keep the story the same and add the new information at the end), as well as identify useful procedures that he had not previously thought of (e.g., think of different ways the ideas already in your story and the new idea can fit together, then choose the one that makes most sense).[2]

The methods of open inquiry described in this section are all ones that can be used without any great deal of formal psychological knowledge. This fact naturally raises a question of validity. If one were proposing student inquiry in physical science, one would want to be sure it didn't result in the learning of a lot of wrong principles. What is to prevent coinvestigation of cognitive processes from resulting in a lot of false psychological knowledge?

False knowledge is not likely to be a problem so long as the responsible adult tries to keep attention focused on strategy description and evaluation, avoiding the temptation to formulate general laws about how the mind works. The cognitive inquiry we have been talking about is largely a matter of observing events and trying to relate them coherently to one another. Naturally the observing and the relating will both be limited, but that would be true for any other kinds of events. In discussing a field trip, for instance, students will have failed to see much of what was there to be seen, will have misperceived some things, and will interpret events in ways that reflect their lack of background knowledge and concepts. The teacher, furthermore, will often not be an expert in the area pertinent to the field trip. But those are not reasons to avoid field trips and much less are they reasons to avoid describing and discussing what was observed. On

---

[2]This procedure was devised by Sonja Dennis in course work at the Ontario Institute for Studies in Education, and the example is from her report.

the contrary, it is through just such experiences that one hopes to build the experiential basis that will give meaning to later, more disciplined study.

MODEL-BASED INQUIRY

Techniques of open inquiry, such as those described thus far in the chapter, serve mainly as a way of putting children in touch with the cognitive strategies they presently use. A whole other dimension of metacognitive knowledge, however, is awareness of strategy change—being aware not only of one's current cognitive behavior but of developments that lie ahead. Again, some of this knowledge can be imparted by conventional means—by demonstrating or explaining more advanced strategies, for instance. Although these didactic approaches, if based on sound knowledge, can be extremely valuable, we believe the ideal circumstance for learning would be one in which students can actually experience strategy change. In other words, although it may be very useful to understand "This is how I do it and this is how an expert does it," a sizable increment in self-knowledge occurs if the terms can be shifted to "This is how I usually do it and this is how it feels to do it like an expert." Needless to say, such a foretaste of expert competence can also be expected to have a strong motivating effect.

But how does one get a child to experience expertlike performance, short of turning the child into an expert? The answer may lie in a technology that has only recently begun to take shape among instructionally oriented developmental psychologists—a technology that we have called *simulation by intervention* (Bereiter & Scardamalia, in press b; Brown & Campione, 1981; Butterfield, Siladi, & Belmont, 1980). In scientific applications, simulation by intervention involves testing theoretical notions about cognitive development by experimentally introducing either facilitations that the theory predicts will cause younger subjects to act like older ones, or impediments that the theory suggests will cause older subjects to act like younger ones (see, for instance, Case, Kurland, & Goldberg, 1982). Simulation by intervention thus requires a fairly strong model of the cognitive process under investigation, in order to have a basis for making and testing predictions.

Educational applications of simulation by intervention also require a fairly strong model of the process in question, which is why we have labeled this section "model-based inquiry." The idea is to intervene in children's typical cognitive processes in such a way as to induce cognitive behavior that formally resembles or contains significant elements of more mature cognitive behavior. Because students find themselves involved in mental activities that are new to them, the situation is a natural one for coinvestigation of cognitive processes.

In this section we discuss and illustrate three approaches to model-based inquiry. Whereas in the section on open inquiry we could discuss a variety of detailed techniques that are applicable in a wide range of activities, model-based inquiry tends to require different techniques, depending on the model employed. Consequently the material in this section is intended mainly to suggest general ways of going about model-based inquiry.

a. *Induce a Simplified Version of the More Advanced Strategy.* This approach, known as procedural facilitation, is described at length in Scardamalia and Bereiter (in press d). The advanced strategy may be simplified by reducing open-ended decisions to choices among a few alternatives and by establishing routines that bypass certain difficulties. The child is helped to execute the strategy by the use of externalized procedures and cues. However—and this is a key point as far as coinvestigation of cognitive processes is concerned—the child still has to do all the productive thinking. Procedural facilitation simply helps to structure the process. Hence, children find themselves engaging in mental activities that are new to them, and this frequently fascinates them, providing a natural focal point for coinvestigation. By providing an explicit contrast to routine procedures such methods tend to highlight two kinds of data: (1) how one typically goes about the task—information that naturally arises out of the child's efforts to cope with changes forced by the new routine; and (2) the nature of more sophisticated performance—information that follows from what the routine enables the child to do that is in advance of normal procedures.

One of the most elaborate procedural facilitations we have tried was concerned with getting students to evaluate, diagnose, and revise their texts (Scardamalia & Bereiter, in press b). Normally, children's revision procedures consist essentially of proofreading. In the induced procedure, students used a simplified routine that involved making evaluations of their writing at the end of each sentence. They chose, from a diverse but small set of evaluative statements, ones that were applicable to their text, explained their choice of evaluations, chose from a small set of remedial activities an appropriate one, and then carried out the chosen action. The overall effect was that elementary students did make more adultlike revisions. Moreover, they unanimously reported that the procedure had taught them to do things they didn't normally do—consider the coherence of consecutively presented ideas, consider how an idea might confuse a reader— and to stop doing things they normally did. The procedure stood directly in the way of their carrying out typical revision activities of producing clean copy, and most children claimed it was the first time they had any idea *how* one might go about doing things in ways other than those they were accustomed to, even though they knew all along that they should.

The same principles of coinvestigation apply here as with the more informal procedures discussed in the preceding section. Purposes need to be open and shared. Students need to feel that the emphasis is on mutual understanding of the mental phenomena, not on successful performance. And the same methods for achieving fruitful discussions are applicable. The difference is that procedural facilitation opens up rich possibilities for turning the spotlight of coinvestigation on mental growth itself.

b. *Use Tasks That Transfer Existing Strategies to New Domains.*   In writing, as in a variety of intellectual tasks, children fail to evidence capabilities they evidence in more practical contexts. For example, although in their daily lives children clearly demonstrate planning toward goals, they rarely show evidence of explicit goal-directed planning in composition (Burtis et al., in press). There are some profound reasons, that we cannot go into here, why composition goals should be harder for children to get a fix on than many other kinds of goals (Scardamalia & Bereiter, in press d). But by altering the composition task somewhat, it may be possible to get students to apply their already existing abilities in goal-directed planning to writing.

A series of studies by Jacqueline Tetroe (1981; Tetroe, Bereiter, & Scardamalia, 1981) explored the possibilities of doing this by giving students ending sentences that it was their job to write compositions leading up to. Introducing this concrete kind of goal was, in fact, found to induce a higher level of planning (Tetroe et al., 1981).

In order for interventions of this kind to have a lasting effect, it seems essential that students gain as much insight as possible into what they are doing. Planning to reach an ending sentence is not the same as the planning mature writers do to achieve a rhetorical goal, but it has similarities that students may be able to recognize through discussion and reflection—through considering, for instance, why the ending sentence task is harder than the typical writing task and what it is that they do differently in coping with it. In this particular case the task enabled children to distinguish between their "what next" approach to text production—thinking of an idea and then considering what they should say next—and the strategy of considering multiple task constraints simultaneously—the strategy that writing to an ending sentence encourages.

An extensive collection of writing tasks that use concrete goals to mobilize strategies that students do not spontaneously apply to writing is presented in Scardamalia, Bereiter, and Fillion (1981). We are not aware at this time of other domains in which strategy-mobilizing or strategy-transferring tasks have been devised.

c. *Have Students Provide Procedural Support for Others.*   In the "Open Inquiry" section we mentioned the benefits for cognitive inquiry of having students prescribe procedures for others. A more refined version of this approach is one in which children administer procedural facilitations to an adult or to other children. This approach has the significant advantage that it permits the child to participate in or actually to induce in someone else a cognitive strategy that the child himself or herself has not yet mastered.

We have tried this with children providing procedural support to someone else who is planning a composition. The child is provided with a list of sentence openers like "An even better idea is . . . ," "I could make my main point clearer if . . . ," and "But many readers won't agree that . . ." The child's task was to use these planning cues, as we call them, to help an adult plan a composition. The adult planned out loud and the child was to listen closely and hand the adult a planning cue whenever the adult was stuck or when it seemed appropriate to help the adult think harder or more completely about the composition. When handed a planning cue, the adult was supposed to start the next planning sentence (not text sentence) with it, if possible.

What we find consistently, even with children of age 8 who use this procedure, is such close monitoring of what the adult is saying that the cards selected at "stuck points" are those the adult might well have selected were she conducting the procedure herself. The data the child is made privy to under such conditions should serve both to illuminate the nature of mature processes and to provide the child with a means of entering into the mature process.

Children can be shown to produce thought judged more reflective than that produced by children not using the cards under conditions where roles are reversed—where the adult is handing cards to the child (Scardamalia & Bereiter, in press a). This suggests once again that, given insight into more mature processes, children will make use of that insight (see also Paris et al., 1982).

One distinct advantage of having a child provide procedural support for someone else is a division of mental labor. When students tried to use planning cues by themselves they usually found this more difficult. As one 11-year-old put it, "You've asked me to both think of ideas and to look at them at the same time! I can't do that. And if I think of the idea, then stop to think about it, I forget what I'm supposed to be thinking of." By dividing cognitive tasks and switching roles, students have the opportunity to see a process from different viewpoints and to avoid cognitive overload while doing so. They also get a picture of why the task they are being asked to do is so difficult.

Model-based inquiry clearly has advantages in directing inquiry toward the growing edge of the child's competence rather than toward the child's habitual practices. It is clear, however, that one needs to make strong assumptions about the nature of this growing edge and where it is growing to in order to design procedural facilitations and other model-based interventions.

Two concerns might occur to the reader. One is, what if the model is wrong? That is, what if the supposedly more mature strategy that we are trying to give children a feeling for isn't really the way mature people function but is instead some psychologist's mistaken idea of how they function? In our experience this problem has seemed to be self-correcting. If we try to persuade children to use a poorly conceived procedure, they either can't do it, find it silly or unnatural, or—which is most frequent—transform the procedure in such a way as to make it work within their existing strategies. Fortunately, a model-based procedure can be satisfactory even though the model it is based on is only a very rough approximation. So long as the procedure leads children somewhere into the neighborhood of a more mature process, they can start to have experiences that open their eyes to possibilities for further growth and learning.

Another concern educators might have about model-based inquiry is that it seems to impose on children standard ways of doing things, whereas open inquiry gives scope to individual differences in cognitive strategies and styles. This might be a problem if we were talking about extended programs of instruction in which model-based procedures were engrained as habits. As it is, however, we are talking about their more episodic use as vehicles for exploration, insight, and novel experience. In this regard, we think it is vital to keep the inquiry aspect at the forefront of students' attention. They should never be told that the procedures they are experimenting with represent the *right* way to do things.

The procedures should not be treated as mere games or gimmicks, either, however. Students need to realize that they are experimenting with ways to extend their mental capabilities. They are not experimenting with neat tricks to make work easier, but rather with procedures that involve thinking more deeply about more things. In our experience students respond marvelously well to this kind of opportunity, provided they are supplied with procedures that enable them to act. It is being asked to think harder when they have no available means for thinking harder that makes students retreat from intellectual challenges.

CONCLUSION

In the preceding sections we have presented a number of specific techniques whereby adult and child can collaborate in the investigation of cognitive activities. Our emphasis has been on techniques the adult may use to facilitate communication and to bring into the open the kinds of phenomena that will make coinvestigation fruitful. In concluding, however, we want to reemphasize the mutual nature of the investigative enterprise and take a broader view of its purpose.

One of the reasons that inquiry learning in the schools may not live up to the glowing words in which it has been advocated is that, for the most part, children are finding out things that the teacher already knows. The result is that the teacher can, at best, share vicariously in the children's curiosity and joy of discovery. At worst, inquiry turns into puzzle solving, where the teacher knows the answer and the children's job is to find out what it is.

Inquiry into people's own cognitive processes is a different story. Here, teachers and students can work as genuine partners in inquiry. Partly this may be because everyone is rather ignorant about how the mind works. But there is more to it than that. We have perhaps done more cognitive research on children's writing than anyone else has or will ever care to, yet we have experienced no decline in the amount of new insight we can gain by sitting down with a child and engaging in one of the kinds of shared inquiry described in this chapter. Quite the contrary. The more we understand the composing process, it seems, the more we can learn and the more we can help a child to learn.

The crucial thing seems to be that we are learning about ourselves (and we, the experimenters, always are learning about ourselves in coinvestigation, as well as learning about the children—and the children, also, are learning about us as well as learning about themselves). Understanding of self and others appears to be nonterminating, and this is probably because it aims to be holistic. Consequently every new detail is a potential challenge to our understanding of the whole.

The principal value that we see in acquiring personal (as contrasted with theoretical) knowledge of cognitive processes is that it enables students to take a more self-directive role in their mental development. Cognitive development in young children is largely unintentional. As Montessori (1967) pointed out, the young child does things that result in learning, but does not do them in order to learn. Cognitive development is a natural consequence of activity carried out for other purposes. The child's actions may be driven by curiosity, but the curiosity is "aroused" by external events. Later we begin to see the emergence of what we have elsewhere analyzed in detail as *intentional cognition* (Bereiter & Scardamalia, in press c).

In its largest sense, intentional cognition means having a *mental life* that is carried on consciously and purposefully, just as one's outer life is, but that is not simply a projection of that outer life. Rather, mental life has purposes and activities of its own, which are primarily concerned with the active construction of knowledge.

Perhaps the most far-reaching consequence of developing a self-directed mental life is that meaningfulness ceases to be a property that is "found" or not "found" in external activities and contexts. It becomes a property that people invest activities with, by virtue of assigning them a role in their mental lives.

Such coinvestigation appears to hold promise at two levels. One is at the level of cognitive strategy acquisition. As we indicated in an earlier section, coinvestigation is most applicable for cognitive strategies that cannot reliably be acquired through observation, practice, and the learning of explicit rules. Strategies involved in the construction of personal knowledge are preeminently of this kind—remote from observation, inaccessible to assigned practice, and difficult to formalize under rules.

The other level is the level of direction and purpose. Students cannot be expected to take a self-directive role in their cognitive development unless they themselves, and not just the teacher, have a sense of where development is heading—where the growing edge of their competence is and what possibilities lie ahead. Studying theories of developmental psychology is not likely to give students such knowledge in a usable form. Active investigation of their own cognitive strategies could do so, however—especially if it is done in collaboration with an adult who can help them recognize and reflect upon what is happening and help them experiment with possible next stages in development.

ACKNOWLEDGMENTS

This chapter is based primarily on work made possible by a grant from the Social Sciences and Humanities Research Council of Canada. Additional support came from the Alfred P. Sloan Foundation and from the Ontario Institute for Studies in Education. We wish to thank Robbie Case for helpful suggestions, and the editors of this book for their careful review of a draft of this chapter.

REFERENCES

Bereiter, C., & Scardamalia, M. From conversation to composition: The role of instruction in a developmental process. In R. Glaser (Ed.), *Advances in instructional psychology* (Vol. 2). Hillsdale, N.J.: Lawrence Erlbaum Associates, 1982.

Bereiter, C., & Scardamalia, M. Cognitive coping strategies and the problem of "inert knowledge." In S. S. Chipman, J. W. Segal, & R. Glaser (Eds.), *Thinking and learning skills: Current research and open questions* (Vol. 2). Hillsdale, N.J.: Lawrence Erlbaum Associates, in press. (a)

Bereiter, C., & Scardamalia, M. Levels of inquiry in writing research. In P. Mosenthal, S. Walmsley, & L. Tamor (Eds.), *Research in writing: Principles and methods*. New York: Longman International, in press. (b)

Bereiter, C., & Scardamalia, M. Schooling and the growth of intentional cognition: Helping children take charge of their own minds. In Z. Lamm (Ed.), *New trends in education*. Tel-Aviv: Yachdev United Publishing Co., in press. (c)

Bereiter, C., Scardamalia, M., & Cattani, C. *Recognition of constraints in children's reading and writing*. Paper presented at the annual meeting of the American Educational Research Association, Los Angeles, April 1981.

Bereiter, C., Scardamalia, M., & Turkish, L. *The child as discourse grammarian*. Paper presented at the annual meeting of the American Educational Research Association, Boston, 1980.

Bird, M. *Reading comprehension strategies: A direct teaching approach*. Unpublished doctoral dissertation, The Ontario Institute for Studies in Education, 1980.

Brown, A. L. Development, schooling, and the acquisition of knowledge about knowledge: Comments on Chapter 7 by Nelson. In R. C. Anderson, R. J. Spiro, & W. E. Montague (Eds.), *Schooling and the acquisition of knowledge*. Hillsdale, N.J.: Lawrence Erlbaum Associates, 1977.

Brown, A. L. Knowing when, where, and how to remember: A problem of metacognition. In R. Glaser (Ed.), *Advances in instructional psychology* (Vol. 1). Hillsdale, N.J.: Lawrence Erlbaum Associates, 1978.

Brown, A. L., & Campione, J. C. Inducing flexible thinking: A problem of access. In M. Friedman, J. P. Das, & N. O'Connor (Eds.), *Intelligence and learning*. New York: Plenum, 1981.

Burtis, P. J., Bereiter, C., Scardamalia, M., & Tetroe, J. The development of planning in writing. In C. G. Wells & B. Kroll (Eds.), *Exploration of children's development in writing*. Chichester, Eng.: John Wiley & Sons, in press.

Butterfield, E. C., Siladi, D., & Belmont, J. M. Validating theories of intelligence. In H. W. Reese & L. P. Lipsitt (Eds.), *Advances in child development and behavior* (Vol. 15). New York: Academic Press, 1980.

Case, R. A developmentally based approach to the problem of instructional design. In S. S. Chipman, J. W. Segal, & R. Glaser (Eds.), *Thinking and learning skills: Current research and open questions* (Vol. 2). Hillsdale, N.J.: Lawrence Erlbaum Associates, in press.

Case, R., Kurland, D. M., & Goldberg, J. Operational efficiency and the growth of short-term memory span. *Journal of Experimental Child Psychology,* 1982, *33,* 386–404.

Cloward, R. D. Studies in tutoring. *Journal of Experimental Education,* 1967, *36,* 14–25.

Ericsson, K. A., & Simon, H. A. Verbal reports as data. *Psychological Review,* 1980, *87,* 215–251.

Flavell, J. H. Metacognition and cognitive monitoring: A new area of cognitive–developmental inquiry. *American Psychologist,* 1979, *34,* 906–911.

Flavell, J. H., Speer, J. R., Green, F. L., & August, D. L. The development of comprehension monitoring and knowledge about communication. *Monographs of the Society for Research in Child Development,* 1981, *46*(5, Serial No. 192).

Flavell, J. H., & Wellman, H. M. Metamemory. In R. V. Kail & J. W. Hagen (Eds.), *Perspectives on the development of memory and cognition.* Hillsdale, N.J.: Lawrence Erlbaum Associates, 1977.

Groen, G. J., & Resnick, L. B. Can preschool children invent addition algorithms? *Journal of Educational Psychology,* 1977, *69,* 645–652.

Hayes, J. R., & Flower, L. Identifying the organization of writing processes. In L. W. Gregg & E. R. Steinberg (Eds.), *Cognitive processes in writing.* Hillsdale, N.J.: Lawrence Erlbaum Associates, 1980.

Hayes-Roth, B., & Hayes-Roth, F. A cognitive model of planning. *Cognitive Science,* 1979, *3,* 275–310.

Meichenbaum, D. Cognitive factors in behavior modification: Modifying what clients say to themselves. In C. M. Franks & G. T. Wilson (Eds.), *Annual review of behavior therapy: Theory and practice.* New York: Brunner-Mazel, 1973.

Montessori, M. *The absorbent mind.* New York: Holt, Rinehart, & Winston, 1967.

Neches, R. *Promoting self-discovery of improved strategies.* Paper presented at the annual meeting of the American Educational Research Association, San Francisco, April 1979.

Paris, P., Scardamalia, M., & Bereiter, C. *Synthesis through analysis: Facilitating theme development in children's writing.* Paper presented at American Educational Research Association, New York, March 1982.

Paris, S. G., & Lindauer, B. K. The development of cognitive skills during childhood. In B. Wolman (Ed.), *Handbook of Developmental Psychology.* Englewood Cliffs, N.J.: Prentice–Hall, 1982.

Paris, S. G., & Myers, M. Comprehension monitoring in good and poor readers. *Journal of Reading Behavior,* 1981, *13,* 5–22.

Paris, S. G., Newman, R. S., & McVey, K. A. Learning the functional significance of mnemonic actions: A microgenetic study of strategy acquisition. *Journal of Experimental Child Psychology,* 1982, *34,* 490–509.

Pavarotti, L., & Wright, W. *My own story.* New York: Doubleday & Company, Inc., 1981.

Perfetti, C., & Lesgold, A. Discourse comprehension and sources of individual differences. In M. Just & P. Carpenter (Eds.), *Cognitive processes in comprehension.* Hillsdale, N.J.: Lawrence Erlbaum Associates, 1977.

Rohwer, W. D., Jr. Elaboration and learning in childhood and adolescence. In H. W. Reese (Ed.), *Advances in child development and behavior* (Vol. 8). New York: Academic Press, 1973.

Rosenthal, T. L., & Zimmerman, B. J. *Social learning and cognition.* New York: Academic Press, 1978.

Scardamalia, M., & Bereiter, C. *Development of dialectical processes in composition.* In D. Olson,

N. Torrance, & A. Hildyard (Eds.), *Literacy, language and learning: The nature and conse-quences of reading and writing.* Cambridge University Press, in press. (a)

Scardamalia, M., & Bereiter, C. The development of evaluative, diagnostic, and remedial ca-pabilities in children's composing. In M. Martlew (Ed.), *The psychology of written language: A developmental approach.* London: John Wiley and Sons, in press. (b)

Scardamalia, M., & Bereiter, C. Development of strategies in text processing. In H. Mandl, N. Stein, & T. Trabasso (Eds.), *Learning and comprehension of texts.* Hillsdale, N.J.: Lawrence Erlbaum Associates, in press. (c)

Scardamalia, M., & Bereiter, C. Fostering the development of self-regulation in children's knowl-edge processing. In S. S. Chipman, J. W. Segal, & R. Glaser (Eds.), *Thinking and learning skills: Current research and open questions* (Vol. 2). Hillsdale, N.J.: Lawrence Erlbaum Associ-ates, in press. (d)

Scardamalia, M., Bereiter, C., & Fillion, B. *Writing for results: A sourcebook of consequential composing activities.* Toronto: OISE Press, 1981. (Also, La Salle, Ill.: Open Court Publishing Company, 1981.)

Scardamalia, M., Bereiter, C., & Goelman, H. The role of production factors in writing ability. In M. Nystrand (Ed.), *What writers know: The language, process, and structure of written dis-course.* New York: Academic Press, 1982.

Siegler, R. S. Developmental sequences within and between concepts. *Monographs of the Society for Research in Child Development,* 1981, *46*(2, Serial No. 189).

Strunk, W., Jr., & White, E. B. *The elements of style.* New York: Macmillan, 1959.

Tetroe, J. *The effects of children's planning behavior on writing problems.* Paper presented at the annual meeting of the American Educational Research Association, Los Angeles, 1981.

Tetroe, J., Bereiter, C., & Scardamalia, M. *How to make a dent in the writing process.* Paper presented at the annual meeting of the American Educational Research Association, Los Angeles, 1981.

4 Forms of Understanding in Mathematical Problem Solving

James G. Greeno
University of Pittsburgh

One important contribution of psychological science to education has been to provide concepts and principles for formulating behavioral objectives in much of the school curriculum. As we achieve greater understanding of cognitive processes, the concepts and principles that we develop can be used in formulating objectives of instruction in more cognitive terms. These objectives are in the form of cognitive analyses of instructional tasks; Resnick (this volume) summarizes several examples of such analyses. This chapter presents two examples of cognitive task analysis in some detail.

The theoretical issue studied in this research is the nature of understanding. The goal that students should acquire understanding of concepts and principles of mathematics, rather than merely acquire rote procedures, is widely accepted. However, in comparison to goals involving concrete skills such as computational algorithms, objectives of understanding have not been formulated in definite, specific ways. Instructional objectives of the form, ''the students should understand [a concept]'' have not been considered sufficiently specific to be assessed behaviorally and therefore have played a decreasing role in instructional design.

In the research described in this chapter, the goal was to develop definite theoretical characterizations of understanding in a specific domain of problems. The general strategy used was to choose some performance that provides persuasive evidence of understanding and to develop hypotheses about cognitive structures and processes that cause the performance to occur. Assuming that the performance does require understanding, then the cognitive structures and processes that bring it about constitute understanding, and hypotheses about those structures and processes are hypotheses about the nature of understanding. If the hypotheses are approximately correct, they describe knowledge that constitutes understanding, and thus can be adopted as meaningful and definite cognitive objectives for instruction.

The research described here involved analyses of performance on two tasks in the domain of high school geometry. These two analyses illustrate several general points. First, the analyses provide definite hypotheses about understanding, illustrating the feasibility of developing such hypotheses for school tasks and showing the kinds of cognitive objectives for instruction for understanding that can be obtained from such analyses.

A second point is one emphasized by Resnick (this volume). She notes that cognitive scientists have begun to give more attention to processes of acquisition and instructional intervention, following a period of almost exclusive focus on analyses of performance of relatively complex tasks. The examples I discuss here are consistent with that trend, in that some aspects of acquisition and instructional intervention are included in the theoretical analyses, along with questions about characteristics of cognitive structures and processes that constitute understanding.

A third point is that analyses of knowledge structures involved in performing school tasks can address questions of theoretical interest as well as potential instructional utility. The examples I discuss are concerned with two significant theoretical issues in the psychology of understanding.

One example considers knowledge for solving problems with structural understanding. Important discussions by Judd (1908), by Katona (1940), and especially by Wertheimer (1945/1959)[1] distinguished problem solving with understanding from problem solving of a rote, mechanical nature. Previous discussions have consisted mainly of examples that illustrate the phenomenon of structural understanding in compelling ways. A goal of the analysis presented here is to clarify the concept of structural understanding by providing a definite and specific hypothesis about cognitive structures and processes that constitute this kind of understanding in the context of a specific problem domain.

The second example considers understanding of a general formal principle related to solutions of specific problems. This issue has been especially salient in relation to questions of cognitive development, where Piaget's (e.g., 1941/1965) research was interpreted as indicating that young children lack understanding of important general logical and mathematical concepts, but more recent studies (e.g., Gelman & Gallistel, 1978) indicate that significant understanding of those concepts should be attributed to young children. A theoretical problem arises from the obvious fact that this understanding cannot be construed as explicit

---

[1]Wertheimer's analysis is the most widely known; indeed it would be appropriate to use the label "Wertheimer's problem" to refer to the question of learning to solve problems with understanding. It is a pleasure to note that the XXII International Congress of Psychology, for which the initial version of this chapter was prepared, was held very near in time to the 100th anniversary of Wertheimer's birth, and near his birthplace as well. Wertheimer was born 15 April 1880, in Prague.

knowledge—for example, preschoolers obviously do not know the concept of cardinality in an explicit way. The theoretical problem is how to characterize understanding of a principle that is not explicit. The analysis presented in the second example provides a characterization of knowledge that constitutes one form of implicit understanding of a formal principle.

A fourth general point illustrated in these examples is that understanding is not a uniform cognitive state. There are different knowledge structures that constitute understanding in different forms. This is important for theory, because it implies that there will not be a single correct cognitive model of the understanding of a concept or a procedure. It also is important for educational practice, because it implies that goals of teaching for understanding must be formulated in more precise and differentiated terms than is customary in order to play an effective role in instruction. The examples presented, involving structural understanding and implicit understanding of a general principle, involve related but distinct forms of understanding. Both are desirable outcomes of instruction, but adoption of them as instructional objectives would lead to the design of quite different sets of materials and tasks.

The first example includes theoretical analyses of alternative knowledge structures that can be acquired in learning to solve some proof exercises that are included in geometry courses. One alternative has knowledge that constitutes understanding of a structure of relations in the problem; the other lacks that understanding. The alternative that simulates knowledge for understanding provides a definite hypothesis in which problem-solving procedures are integrated with a general schema for part–whole relationships. The analysis also provides a definite hypothesis about cognitive structures that can enable such transfer to occur. In observations reported here, substantial variation was found among students in their performance on a transfer problem that has the same structure as a set of problems that the students had previously learned to solve. In the model that was developed to represent understanding of structure, the schematic knowledge that provides the basis of understanding also provides a basis for transferring problem-solving procedures to novel problems. Thus, the analysis is consistent with the view that ability to transfer knowledge to novel problems provides evidence that students understand the structure that the problems share.

The second example, involving understanding of a formal principle, analyzes implicit understanding of the principle of deductive consequence. This is a metaprinciple in relation to solutions of proof problems; it constitutes a general criterion of validity for proofs. Understanding of the principle involves knowledge about what proofs are, which may be distinct from knowing how to construct correct proofs in specific situations. One form of understanding of deductive consequence is knowledge of the logical requirements for a deductively valid inference. Evidence that a student knows these requirements can be obtained in a task of checking proofs. In this task, the student must distinguish valid proofs from invalid arguments; thus successful performance requires knowledge of the defining features of valid deduction. In the study reported here, we first found that students taking a high school geometry course did not acquire this understanding to a significant degree. Then an analysis was formulated of a cognitive process that would provide a basis for successful performance on the task of proof checking. This analysis was used in designing instruction that had a beneficial effect on students' performance on proof checking, and thus, I propose, on their understanding of the principle of deductive proof.

STRUCTURAL UNDERSTANDING

The analysis of structural understanding that I conducted was focused on processes of learning and transfer. Discussions of structural understanding such as those by Judd (1908), Katona (1940), and Wertheimer (1945/1959) have distinguished meaningful learning from rote learning of problem-solving procedures. Meaningful learning occurs when the material that is learned is related to some general structure or principle, whereas in rote learning the new procedure or information is simply associated with the specific problem situation in which it is experienced. Evidence for understanding resulting from meaningful learning often is obtained by showing that after meaningful learning, individuals are better able to transfer their knowledge to new kinds of problems.

One of the classical examples of meaningful learning given by Wertheimer is learning the proof in geometry that opposite vertical angles are congruent. Figure 4.1 shows the problem, along with representations of two ways to think about the solution. Wertheimer pointed out that children often learn this proof in a mechanical way, represented by the equations in Fig. 4.1, memorizing the algebraic steps. Wertheimer contrasted this mechanical kind of thinking with a more meaningful version, in which the proof is understood in relation to spatial relationships among the angles. He used a diagram like the one at the bottom of Fig. 4.1 to explain these relationships. The spatial pattern can be seen as a pair of overlapping structures, each involving a pair of angles that form a straight line and containing a shared part.

Empirical Observations

I present some data that illustrate the range of understanding that can occur regarding problems like Fig. 4.1. The data consist of thinking-aloud protocols that were obtained from six students during the year they studied geometry in high school. During the year, each student was interviewed approximately once a week. In each interview, the student solved a few geometry problems and thought aloud as he or she worked on the problems. The major use of this set of data has been in developing a computational model that simulates the problem-

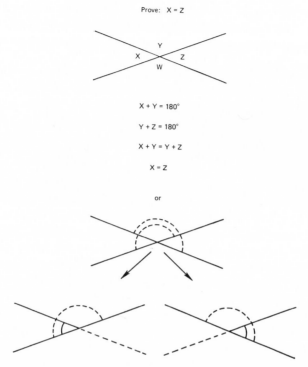

FIG. 4.1.   The problem of vertical angles, with two solutions.

solving performance of the students. The model has been described in other reports (Greeno, 1976, 1978; Greeno, Magone, & Chaiklin, 1979).

The third interview, which occurred during the fifth week of the course, included three problems involving the structure of two whole units each composed of two parts, with one of the parts shared by the two wholes. The first problem, given to all six of the students, is shown in Fig. 4.2. A second problem, given to four of the six students after they worked on Fig. 4.2, is about segments, rather than angles. It is shown, along with its solution, in Fig. 4.3. Finally, the problem of vertical angles, shown in Fig. 4.1, was given to four of the six students.

At the time this interview occurred, the students had completed a section of the geometry course in which they learned to solve proof problems involving segments. Thus, problems like Fig. 4.3 were review problems for them; in fact Fig. 4.3 was an example problem in the section that had been completed. They had begun to learn about angles; concepts such as right angles, adjacent angles, and supplementary and complementary angles had been introduced. However, proof problems involving angles had not yet been studied in class. One of the students was working independently and had done some proofs involving angles. For the other five students, problems such as Figs. 4.1 and 4.2 were novel, and presented tests of transfer of knowledge about solving related but distinct problems, such as Fig. 4.3.

To anticipate results that I describe later, the theoretical analysis is a simulation of learning that can occur from example problems involving segments. Two versions of learning were simulated: I refer to these as stimulus–response learning and meaningful learning. The difference between the versions is a hypothesis about the knowledge that enables transfer to occur between problems like Fig. 4.3 and problems like Figs. 4.1 and 4.2.

In both simulations of learning, study of example problems leads to acquisition of knowledge used in solving problems, consisting of procedures for writing lines of proof. The simulations differ in the representations of problems that provide the cues for use of the procedures. In the simulation of stimulus– response learning, problems like Fig. 4.3 are represented quite specifically; the cues for writing lines of proof include segments that are perceived in the diagram of a problem, with features involving the ends of the segments that are needed for the additivity of their lengths.

In the simulation of meaningful learning, a more abstract representation is involved. The learner represents the problem using a schema that identifies part–whole relations among the objects in the problem. The problem-solving procedures that are acquired have arguments that are specified in terms of the slots of the part–whole schema. This enables the procedures to be used for problems that have different kinds of objects, providing that the objects in the new problem can be represented using the schema of part–whole relationships.

For example, in stimulus–response learning, a procedure is acquired in which the length of a segment is subtracted from both sides of an equation. This corresponds to Step 6 of the proof in Fig. 4.3. In meaningful learning, the

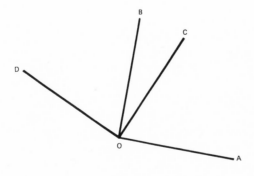

Given: ∠AOB and ∠COD are right angles
Prove: ∠AOC ≅ ∠BOD

FIG. 4.2. A problem used to test transfer.

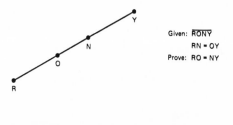

Given: $\overline{RONY}$

$RN = OY$

Prove: $RO = NY$

FIG. 4.3.   A problem from previous learning for students, and the third example problem for simulation of learning.

Statement	Reason
1. $\overline{RONY}$	1. Given
2. $RN = OY$	2. Given
3. $RN = RO + ON$	3. Segment addition (Step 1)
4. $OY = ON + NY$	4. Segment addition (Step 1)
5. $RO + ON = ON + NY$	5. Substitution (Steps 2, 3, 4)
6. $RO = NY$	6. Subtraction property (Step 5)

procedure learned from Step 6 involves subtracting a part that is shared in two whole units from each of them. The conditions for applying the procedure acquired in stimulus–response learning include the existence of segments, whereas the conditions for applying the procedure acquired in meaningful learning include objects designated as parts and wholes. Thus, the procedure acquired in meaningful learning is potentially applicable in a new problem involving angles, whereas the procedure acquired in stimulus–response learning cannot be applied unless there are segments in the problem.

The protocols that were obtained provided an impressive range of performance. Some of the students gave quite clear evidence that their representations of the problems included the part–whole relationships that provide the basis for transfer from segment problems like Fig. 4.3 to angle problems like Figs. 4.1 and 4.2. Other students gave quite clear evidence that these general relationships were not included in their representations. A summary of the six students' performances on Fig. 4.2 is in Table 4.1. Two students, S3 and S5, gave proofs that seemed to result directly from use of the overlap–part–whole schema described previously. These proofs were not correct technically; they involved subtraction of the shared angle $\angle BOC$ before statements about addition of angles were included. This property of the errors is consistent with the hypothesis that the schema was used, because the subtraction procedure is a salient component of the schematic knowledge. For a correct proof, some lower-level operations have to be performed first, and it is plausible to expect that the schema would lead students to think of the top-level operations earlier, and this would lead to the kinds of errors that S3 and S5 committed. Both S3 and S5 gave correct solutions to the segment problem (Fig. 4.3) and remarked about the similarity of that problem and Fig. 4.2.

Two students, S2 and S6, gave correct proofs but did not provide evidence of using the schema. S2 was the student who was working independently and had worked on proofs about angles. There was no evidence in S2's protocol that the schema was used. S6 worked out a proof that involved an analogy to proofs for segment problems, but it apparently was based on the substitution procedure rather than the structure of part–whole relations. S6 seemed to realize that if expressions involving addition could be found, they could serve as arguments in a procedure that involves substitution, and solved the problem by finding those expressions.

A fifth student, S4, may have used the overlap–part–whole schema for representing the problem, or at least was aware of the general similarity of the structure of Fig. 4.2 and problems with segments. S4 mentioned subtraction as a component of the solution and asked whether the "definition of betweenness" should be used. "Definition of betweenness" was the name given in the course text for addition of lengths of segments, and S4's use of this rather awkward term provided evidence of appreciating the similarity between Fig. 4.2 and corresponding problems that involved segments. S2 did not succeed in solving Fig. 4.2. S2 was asked to solve the problem with segments shown in Fig. 4.3 and had considerable difficulty with it. A reasonable interpretation is that S2's representation of Fig. 4.2 may have included the important part–whole relationships, but that S2's knowledge of the problem-solving operations was too weak to enable a solution to be found for the problem.

Performance on the vertical angles problem, Fig. 4.1, is summarized in Table 4.2. This problem was not given to students S4 and S1.

When the vertical angles problem was presented, S3 gave strong evidence of understanding its relation to Fig. 4.2 and Fig. 4.3, saying "You know something, I'm getting sort of tired of that problem." S3 gave a proof of the vertical angles theorem that was similar to the one that S3 gave for Fig. 4.2, with subtraction incorrectly used before addition of angles was asserted.

S5 did not succeed in finding a proof for the vertical angles theorem. However, there was further evidence that S5 had used the overlap–part–whole relationships in solving Fig. 4.2. When that problem was shown again and S5 was asked

TABLE 4.1
Performance on Fig. 4.2

Students	Performance
S3, S5	Conceptually correct proofs with technical errors. Protocol evidence for overlap-part–whole schema—e.g., "I have to subtract." "These are the same."
S2	Correct proof. No protocol evidence for schema.
S6	Correct proof using substitution procedure. Protocol evidence against schema: "I'm trying to find a way that I can substitute."
S4	Failed to find a proof. Protocol evidence for schema: "I would have to subtract . . . would I have to use the definition of betweenness?"
S1	No progress toward proof.

TABLE 4.2
Performance on Fig. 4.1

Student	Performance
S3	Proof with technical errors like Fig. 2. Protocol: "It's the same problem again; I'm getting sort of tired of that problem."
S5	Did not find a proof. Saw the way to proceed using subtraction when Fig. 4.2 was shown again.
S2	Correct proof using supplementary angles. Found an analogous proof involving complementary angles for Fig. 4.2
S6	Did not find a proof. Was trapped by perceptual distraction.

whether a similar method could be used for Fig. 4.1, S5 apparently saw that the structure provided a way to proceed, saying, "I could say if I had this, I could subtract the supplementary angle from that one."

S2 gave a correct proof for the vertical angles theorem, using a theorem that two angles that are supplementary to the same third angle are congruent to each other. When S2 was asked whether there was a connection between the vertical angles theorem and Fig. 4.2, S2's response did not provide evidence for use of the overlap–part–whole schema. S2 assimilated Fig. 4.2 to the solution scheme used for the vertical angles theorem, saying that Fig. 4.2 could be solved using complementary angles.

S6 was unable to prove the vertical angles theorem, and gave performance that Wertheimer (1945/1959) noted as evidence for a lack of structural understanding. S6 proceeded with the problem by noting that $X + Y = 180°$ and that $W + Z = 180°$. There probably are perceptual factors that produce the tendency to think of the problem in this way. S6 was trapped in this view of the problem and never escaped from it. A representation with two distinct pairs of angles is inconsistent with the overlap–part–whole schema, so S6's performance provides further strong evidence that those relationships were not in S6's representation.

In summary, three students gave quite strong evidence that the structure of relationships in the overlap–part–whole schema was in their representation of Fig. 4.2. None of these students gave proofs that were entirely correct; however, S3 and S5 gave proofs that showed a good grasp of the problem. S3 showed good transfer to the vertical angles problem, and S5 recognized the structure of that problem when Fig. 4.2 was shown again. The third of these students, S4, failed to find a proof for Fig. 4.2, apparently because of weak knowledge of problem-solving procedures. A fourth student, S2, solved both Fig. 4.2 and the vertical angles problem successfully, but did not provide any protocol evidence of using the overlap–part–whole schema. It is possible, of course, that the relationships in that structure were recognized and used by S2 in an implicit way. A fifth student, S4, solved Fig. 4.2 successfully and gave relatively clear evidence of not being cognizant of the overlap–part–whole relationships, especially in the vertical angles problem that S4 was unable to solve. The sixth student, S1, made no progress on any of the problems, apparently lacking a great deal of the knowledge required for successful performance.

Theoretical Analysis

The goal of the theoretical analysis was to identify a set of learning processes and knowledge structures that could simulate acquisition of learning with structural understanding. In developing this model I collaborated with John Anderson; some of the results were presented in Anderson, Greeno, Kline, & Neves (1981) as part of a general discussion of the acquisition of problem-solving skill.

To clarify the specific structures responsible for understanding, two versions of the learning simulation were formulated. One of these is called stimulus–response learning, and the new problem-solving procedures acquired by this system are associated with relatively specific situational cues. In the other system, called meaningful learning, the new problem-solving procedures are acquired as integral parts of schemata that represent problem-solving situations in terms of general part–whole relations.

The models that were formulated simulate learning of procedures from worked-out examples, as do many recent computational models of learning procedures (Neves, 1981; Vere, 1978). The learning that was simulated is based on two tasks that are given early in the geometry course and one task that produces learning that should occur some years earlier.

The first two example problems used for simulation of learning are shown in Fig. 4.4, and the third example is shown in Fig. 4.3. The examples were used to investigate three different aspects of learning in which new material is related to a schema. In the first problem, meaningful learning involves an existing schema and the model simulates learning to apply that schema in a situation where it was not applicable previously. Meaningful learning in the second problem involves elaborating an existing schema by forming new problem-solving procedures that become part of the schema. In the third problem situation, meaningful learning involves building a new schema, which has previously existing schemata as subschemata. In all three cases, rote learning was simulated by a process that acquires problem-solving procedures and associates them with relatively specific representations of the problem situation.

The simulation models were programmed in ACTP (Greeno, 1978), a variant of Anderson's (1976) ACT production system. In this system, there is declarative knowledge represented by a semantic network and procedural knowledge in the form of production rules. In learning from examples, the input for learning is the solution of a problem, and the system learns by adding productions to its procedural knowledge or by adding semantic-network structures to the declarative knowledge that it has available for solving problems. The procedures for learning used in this simulation were not the same as those developed and

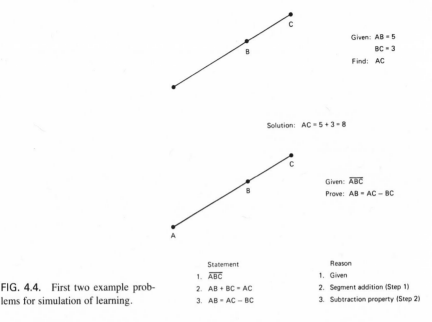

FIG. 4.4. First two example problems for simulation of learning.

Given: AB = 5
       BC = 3
Find: AC

Solution: AC = 5 + 3 = 8

Given: ABC
Prove: AB = AC − BC

Statement	Reason
1. ABC	1. Given
2. AB + BC = AC	2. Segment addition (Step 1)
3. AB = AC − BC	3. Subtraction property (Step 2)

investigated by Anderson in his use of ACT as a model of learning (Anderson, 1981).

For learning new productions, a process was developed for keeping a representation of the problem situation in working memory. This representation determines the information that is included in the conditions of new productions when they are added to the system. The representation includes semantic information that is taken from the problem situation (either the diagram or the system's semantic knowledge) that increases the coherence of the problem representation. The process for selecting the added semantic information is similar to that used by Kintsch and VanDijk (1978) for forming coherent representations in their model of text comprehension, although the one developed for ACTP adds more information than Kintsch and VanDijk's does.

Processes also were implemented for schema-based learning. The process for learning to apply an existing schema in a new situation uses the problem representation in working memory to form the condition of the schematizing production, and uses the action performed in the example to determine how to assign components of the situation to slots in the schema. Acquisition of new procedures and synthesis of a new schema required knowledge of general structural features of schemata in the system. This knowledge constitutes a kind of meta-schema—a schema that enables the system to acquire new schematic knowledge. For example, procedures attached to schemata include information about consequences that are matched against goals to determine whether use of the procedure is desirable, and information about prerequisites that are tested in the problem

TABLE 4.3
General Components   Schemata

Schema
Slots
Schematizing Productions
Contextual Associations
Procedural Attachments
—Prerequisites
—Performances
—Consequences

situation to determine whether the procedure can be applied. The process for acquiring new procedures identifies conditions in the problem situation that are included as prerequisites, and a generalized form of the action in the example is included as a consequence of the procedure. The process for synthesizing a new schema also includes knowledge about the general structure of schemata, in the form of actions that store new semantic knowledge in the form required by the procedures that retrieve and utilize schemata for problem solving.

The schemata that are critical for the system's meaningful learning are included in its declarative knowledge.[2] The structure of schematic knowledge in this model is not unusual; it is a somewhat simplified version of the concept that Bobrow and Winograd (1977) used in the Knowledge Representation Language, (KRL). The main components are listed in Table 4.3. Like all schemata, those used here provide a set of relationships among some objects. The objects fit into the structure in positions called slots. There are procedures for applying the schema in specific situations; these are referred to as schematizing productions. There is some information that identifies features of the situation that are relevant for performing procedures; these are called contextual associations. An important feature of these schemata is that they have procedures associated with them, in the manner of KRL. The organization of these procedure descriptions is patterned after Sacerdoti's (1977) model of planning in problem solving, called Network of Action Hierarchies (NOAH). Information stored about each procedure includes prerequisite conditions, consequences, and specific actions that are carried out in performing the procedure.

Learning New Applicability Conditions.   The first example problem that the model learns from is the first problem in Fig. 4.4. I assume that students learn to

---

[2]I consider the use of declarative structure for representing schemata as a detail of implementation, rather than a substantive psychological hypothesis. In fact, I am inclined to believe that the relationships incorporated in these schemata probably are represented in humans as cognitive procedures, rather than as declarative structures. I believe that a model could be formulated in which schemata would be represented procedurally, and that it would be functionally equivalent to the model that I describe here.

solve problems like this some years before they study geometry. The problem was included in the analysis to clarify the requirement of having knowledge about applying schemata to represent problems.

In the simulation of stimulus–response learning from the first example problem, the action of adding lengths is associated with a representation of the problem situation that specifies some relevant properties such as the collinearity of the segments. The knowledge acquired by rote learning enables the system to solve new problems that are closely similar to the one in which learning occurred, but generalization is very limited. For example, the rote learner does not generalize to a problem in which the total length and one subsegment are given, and the other subsegment is to be calculated.

Meaningful learning occurs in the first example problem when there is an active schema that is assumed as prior knowledge: the relationship between parts that are combined to form a whole. The components of this schema are shown in Table 4.4. We have evidence from studies of children's performance on arithmetic story problems (Riley, Greeno, & Heller, 1983) that this schema has been acquired by most 8-year-old children. The schema is used in understanding problems such as the following: "There are five girls and eight children; how many boys are there?" The schematizing production identifies the set of boys and the set of girls as the parts and the set of children as the whole. Then, using the information stored in procedural attachments, the procedure of separation is chosen and the numbers are subtracted to find the answer.

When the system learns meaningfully from the first example problem it learns to apply this schema to problems involving segments. It acquires a new schematizing production, which is sketched in Fig. 4.5. As a result, in future problems like this one the model can interpret the segments as a part–whole structure.

TABLE 4.4
Components of Whole/Parts Schema

Whole/Parts

Slots: Whole, Part 1, Part 2
Context: Set → Number
Schematization:

Set 1 — Kind of
  → Set 3
Set 2 — Kind of

Procedures:
  Combine/Calculate
  Separate/Calculate
  Adjust Parts

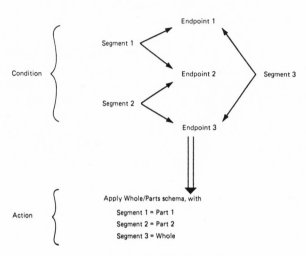

FIG. 4.5.   Schematizing production learned from the first example with meaningful learning.

One consequence is that the whole collection of procedures associated with the schema is then available for solving a variety of problems, which is not the case when simple stimulus–response learning occurs. For example, the knowledge acquired in meaningful learning generalizes to problems in which the total length and one subsegment are given and the other subsegment is to be calculated, because when the whole/parts schema is applied, the procedure of separating the whole into parts is made available.

Learning New Procedural Attachments.   The second example is the second problem in Fig. 4.4. From this problem the model learns procedures required for writing steps of proof. (Previously, the model's only procedures involved calculations with numbers.) The stimulus–response learning system simply learns actions of writing lines of proof like Steps 2 and 3 in the example when the stimulus conditions are equivalent to those of the example problem, including collinear points and a goal to prove that the length of one segment is the difference between lengths of two other segments.

Meaningful learning from the second example involves an addition of structure to the part–whole schema that is already known by the system. The new structures are procedures that are associated with the schema. They are sketched in Table 4.5. Note that the prerequisites of these procedures include problems that have been schematized as part–whole structures. The actions of the procedures are defined in terms of the slots of the whole/parts schema. This means

TABLE 4.5
Procedures Learned from the Second Example

A. Write–segment–addition:
    Prerequisite: Whole/Parts schema.
                              Statement: Collinear Points
    Perform: Write statement:
                              "Part 1 + Part 2 = Whole"
                              Write reason: "Segment Addition"
B. Write–subtraction
    Prerequisite: Whole/Parts schema,
                              Statement: Part 1 + Part 2 = Whole
    Perform: Write statement:
                              "Part 1 = Whole − Part 2"
                              Write reason: "Subtraction Property"

that the actions involve writing steps of proof that refer to objects that occupy the slots of an instantiation of the schema. The main consequence of this learning, in contrast to the stimulus–response learning from this example, is that the procedures that are learned are applicable in any problem situation that is represented using the whole/parts schema. The procedures acquired in stimulus–response learning can only be applied in situations involving segments with collinear endpoints.

Learning a New Schema.   The final learning task that was simulated used the problem in Fig. 4.3. Stimulus–response learning from this example acquires the procedures for writing proof steps involving substitution and the subtraction property, based on Steps 5 and 6, and associating them with relatively specific problem conditions, as in the earlier examples.

The meaningful version of learning from this example results in a new schema, sketched in Table 4.6, in which two part–whole schemata are included as

TABLE 4.6
Schema Acquired from Fig. 4.3

Overlap/Whole/Parts

Slots:
    Part 1, Part 2, Part 3, Whole 1, Whole 2
Subschemata:
    Whole/Parts 1, (Part 1, Part 2, Whole 1)
    Whole/Parts 2 (Part 2, Part 3, Whole 2)
Procedures:
    Write–Substitution
    Write–Subtraction (2 sides)

subschemata. The problem solver represents the segments *RO, ON,* and *RN* as a part–whole structure, and also represents the segments *ON, NY,* and *OY* as a second part–whole structure. This enables it to apply the procedures for writing steps based on segment addition, corresponding to Steps 3 and 4 of the example. Steps 5 and 6 of the example involve new procedures for the model. They also involve both of the part–whole structures represented in the problem. This leads to the formation of a new schema, with two part–whole structures that share one of their parts. Problem-solving procedures corresponding to Steps 5 and 6 of the example are acquired and associated with the new schema.

Conclusions

The simulation of meaningful learning provides a definite hypothesis about a process that can acquire problem-solving procedures with structural understanding. Although transfer to problems about angles was not implemented, it is clear that the knowledge acquired in meaningful learning from examples about segments is applicable in problems like Figs. 4.1 and 4.2. For a student to make that application, schematizing productions would have to be learned to enable the appropriate schemata to be used to represent relationships among angles, or the student could use more general interpretive processes to comprehend the problems as instances of the overlap–part–whole structure.

It is significant that a plausible simulation of meaningful learning could be formulated using only knowledge structures of relatively standard kinds. Schemata with characteristics that are standard in knowledge representation systems and learning processes that are commonly proposed for learning from examples were combined in a straightforward way to form a simulation of learning with significant structural understanding. This seems quite encouraging for the prospect of developing definite hypotheses about understanding over a substantial range of instructional tasks.

UNDERSTANDING A GENERAL FORMAL PRINCIPLE

The second analysis I present was concerned with a somewhat different aspect of understanding, involving a formal principle. This study, in which I collaborated with Maria Magone, was concerned with geometry students' understanding of the general concept of proof. This constitutes a metaprinciple in relation to the tasks that students are taught to perform in their study of geometry. The skills that students are required to learn involve constructing proofs. The question addressed in this study is whether students understand what proofs are—that is, whether they know the general features that are required for something to be a proof.

The concept we focused on can be called the principle of deductive consequence. In a formal proof, each assertion that is made is deductively required by the premises of the problem or by other assertions that have been made explicitly. This imposes a strong criterion for statements to be acceptable for inclusion in a proof. For each statement that is put into a proof, there must be a sufficient basis in earlier statements that the added statement *must* be true if the earlier statements are accepted. This criterion contrasts with ordinary exposition, in which statements are expected to be reasonable in the light of previous information—for example, new statements should not directly contradict statements made earlier—but there is not a general constraint that each new statement is required by the assertions made previously.

The task that we used to investigate understanding of deductive consequence involved checking proofs. We presented proof problems with solutions worked out, and asked students to check whether each proof was correct. If the student said that there was an error, we asked what was wrong.

Our study had three parts. First, we gave proof-checking problems to some students who were taking a course in geometry. (These were different students than those who gave the protocols described in the first section.) Six problems were given in interviews held in November, and four of the same problems were given in May. Fifteen students participated each time, with ten students participating in both interviews and five additional students who were different in the two interviews. The performance of students on proof-checking tasks was not very good, especially on a problem in which the error to be detected was that an assertion needed to justify a step had been omitted.

The second part of our study was a theoretical investigation. We developed a computational model of correct performance on the proof-checking task, including problems with errors of omitted information. Because the students whom we observed had not performed these tasks successfully, the model we developed was not a simulation of performance that had been observed. However, we attempted to develop a model that was psychologically plausible, in the sense that it used procedural and propositional knowledge that we felt could be acquired by human learners, and would simulate performance of human problem solvers who had acquired that knowledge.

The third part of the study was an instructional experiment to test whether the proof-checking knowledge incorporated in the model could be acquired by human learners. We developed instructional materials for training the procedure of checking proofs. A group of 15 college-student subjects who had studied geometry in high school received this instruction, along with sufficient review of basic geometry to make the instruction possible. A control group was given only the review materials. The experimental group succeeded better on proof checking and other geometry problems than the control group, both in the domain of problems that was used in the instruction and in another domain of problems that was used in a test of transfer.

Performance on Proof Checking

One of the proof-checking problems that we used is shown in Fig. 4.6. The proof shown is not valid. For Step 1 to be justified, lines *AC* and *BD* should have been asserted as parallel. Because this was neither given nor proved in prior steps, Step 1 is not justified.

Performance of the geometry students on proof-checking problems is shown in Table 4.7. The problem in Fig. 4.6 was the one that is called "Missing given" in Table 4.7. Note that performance on that problem was poor both in November and in May. Performance on other problems was somewhat better. The valid proof had a diagram in which the statement to be proved appeared false; apparently some students came to disregard the appearance of the diagram between November and May. Other sources of errors included reasons given in the problem that are not theorems of geometry, and reasons whose antecedents did not apply to the objects that the statements referred to. In two problems, the diagrams were consistent with the statements to be proved; in the other two problems, the statements to be proved were incorrect in the diagrams. About half the students found the errors in the problems with consistent diagrams, both in November and in May. Performance in November was somewhat better on the problems where the discrepancy could be seen visually; these problems were not included in the May interviews.

Theoretical Analysis

The goal of the theoretical analysis was to develop a definite hypothesis about knowledge that would enable students to solve proof-checking problems successfully. To do this we formulated a computational model of correct proof-checking performance.

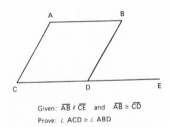

Given: $\overline{AB} \parallel \overline{CE}$ and $\overline{AB} \cong \overline{CD}$
Prove: $\angle ACD \cong \angle ABD$

Statement	Reason
1. $\angle ACD \cong \angle BDE$	corresponding $\angle$s
2. $\angle BDE \cong \angle ABD$	alternate interior $\angle$s
3. $\angle ACD \cong \angle ABD$	transitive property

FIG. 4.6. A difficult proof-checking problem.

TABLE 4.7
Performance on Proof Checking

Problems	Number	November	May
Valid proof	1	.50	.93
Missing given	1	.06	.19
Other invalid:			
Diagram consistent	2	.46	.46
Other invalid:			
Diagram inconsistent	2	.72	—

The procedure that we implemented is sketched in Table 4.8. This procedure is applied to each step in the proof. If all the steps are accepted, and the final step corresponds to the problem goal, then the proof is accepted.

First, the reason that is given in the proof step is checked against a list of theorems that are available for use. (The list includes definitions and postulates as well as theorems; the model does not recognize this technical distinction.) Each theorem is associated with its "deep structure," in which the antecedent and consequent of the conditional proposition are represented with variables that can be matched with objects in the statement and in previous statements and the given information.

The second step of the procedure involves retrieving the antecedent and consequent of the theorem that is given as the reason. Then there is a matching process, in which the consequent of the theorem is matched with the statement and the variables in the consequent are replaced by the objects that are mentioned in the statement. If the consequent cannot be matched to the statement, the step is rejected. This happens if the property or relation asserted in the statement does not match the property or relation of the consequent.

In the fourth step of the procedure, the objects that were found in the statement are substituted for the variables in the antecedent, forming one or more propositions that should have been asserted in previous steps or in the given information. Finally, there is a search for those propositions in the set of previous

TABLE 4.8
Procedure for Verifying a Step

(a) Test whether reason is a theorem.
(b) Retrieve deep structure of reason.
(c) Instantiate consequent in statement.
(d) Form corresponding instantiation in antecedent.
(e) Determine whether antecedent has been asserted.
(f) Determine whether statement matches problem goal.

statements and given information of the problem. If they are found, the proof step is accepted; otherwise, it is rejected.

To clarify the procedure, consider its application to the first step of the problem in Fig. 4.6. First, the reason "Corresponding angles" is checked with the list of available theorems. This is successful; there is a theorem (actually, a postulate) called "Corresponding angles" on the list.

Next, the deep structure of this theorem is retrieved. The antecedent is "If angles X and Y are corresponding angles with lines L and M as sides, and lines L and M are parallel, and line N contains their other sides," and the consequent is, "Then X and Y are congruent."

In the third step, the consequent of the reason is matched with the statement of the proof step. The step says that $\angle ACD$ and $\angle BDE$ are congruent. Therefore, X and Y in the consequent are replaced by these angles.

In the fourth step, the propositions that have to be asserted are formed. This includes a pattern in which $\angle ACD$ and $\angle BDE$ are corresponding angles, with two of their respective sides collinear. There also must be an assertion, either in given information or a previous statement, that the other sides are parallel.

Finally, in a search for these propositions, the system fails to find the assertion about parallel lines that is needed. The system rejects the first step of the proof.

The knowledge required for checking proofs can be compared with knowledge for constructing proofs, especially as a model for solving proof construction problems was formulated earlier (Greeno, 1978). The knowledge needed for proof checking is much simpler in one way than the knowledge that is needed for constructing proofs, but is somewhat more complex in two other ways.

The factor that makes knowledge for checking proofs simpler is that steps of the proof are already shown. This eliminates the need to search for a sequence of problem-solving inferences to achieve the goal of the problem. As a result, the strategic knowledge used for choosing plans and goals that guide the search for inferential operators is not needed for proof checking.

On the other hand, two components of knowledge are required for proof checking that are not needed for constructing proofs. First, the procedures for verifying steps of proof and checking whether the main goal has been satisfied must be added. The other complexity involves the way in which postulates and theorems are represented in the models of proof construction and checking. In the model of proof construction, postulates and theorems are represented implicitly as problem-solving operations in the form of production rules, with the antecedents as conditions that are tested and the consequents as actions that assert properties or relations that are inferred. However, in the model of proof checking there is an explicit representation of postulates and theorems, which are stored in a list so that reasons can be checked to determine whether they are theorems and their antecedents and consequents can be retrieved in the process of determining whether the needed assertions have been made.

Instructional Experiment

We performed a test of our ideas about proof checking by designing some instructional materials based on the computational model of proof checking that we had implemented. This instruction was given to some human learners. The subjects were able to use the procedure that was taught in the instruction, and it resulted in some improvement in their performance in proof checking. We take this as evidence that the model of proof checking has some psychological validity, in the sense that it simulates a cognitive procedure that human problem solvers can learn to perform.

Materials. Instructional materials were designed for presentation to small groups of student subjects. A description was given of a five-step procedure, referred to as the "if–then" procedure because of its emphasis on the antecedent–consequent structure of reasons for proof steps. The steps are: (1) Check if the reason is a valid theorem, postulate, or definition; (2) Divide the reason into its "if" and "then" components; (3) Check the antecedent: has it previously been shown in the given information, the diagram, or in previous steps of the proof? (4) Check the consequent: does it match the relationship of the statement? (5) If the statement is the last one in the proof, does it match the goal of the problem? Note that the steps of the procedure correspond to the steps shown in Table 4.8, except that instantiation of the reason is left implicit. In the instruction, instantiation was shown implicitly in examples, in which the antecedents and consequents of reasons were converted to appropriate propositions about the objects in the problems.

After the procedure was explained, two example problems were worked by the group of student subjects working together, with supervision by the instructor–experimenter. Then booklets were provided that contained proof-checking problems. On each problem, the students first worked individually on the problem, then one student was asked to check the proof aloud, going thorugh the "if–then" procedure for each line of the proof. Any errors or omissions were corrected by the instructor, and questions asked by the students were discussed. Two booklets of proof-checking exercises were prepared for use in two training sessions.

In addition to the materials for instruction in proof checking, there also were materials that reviewed basic concepts of geometry and construction of proofs. Initially, the instructor reviewed basic definitions, postulates, and theorems needed to solve proof problems involving congruence of triangles. Booklets were provided that contained problems of constructing proofs, and students worked individually, then reviewed each problem, as described previously. Two booklets of problems in proof construction were prepared for use in two review sessions. All problems used in the review of proof construction and in training of proof checking were in the domain of congruent triangles.

Materials also were prepared for assessing the results of instruction. A set of problems involving congruence of triangles was prepared as a test, designed to be given individually to the students. The test problems included 10 proof-checking problems and three problems of constructing proofs.

Finally, materials were prepared for testing transfer. These included a brief review of definitions, postulates, and theorems involving angles formed by parallel lines intersected by a transversal. These concepts and propositions had not been included in the previous instruction or testing, and there was no discussion of proof checking during the review of concepts about parallel lines. A transfer test was presented, consisting of 11 proof-checking problems and three problems of constructing proofs, all concerned with angles formed by parallel lines intersected by a transversal.

Subjects and Procedure.   Subjects were 30 students at the University of Pittsburgh who had studied geometry in high school but were not majoring either in mathematics or computer science. Subjects were paid for their participation in the experiment.

The study was conducted in 1-hour sessions on consecutive days. Subjects in an experimental condition received the review of triangle congruence and proof construction in two group sessions; then training in checking proofs about congruent triangles was given in two further group sessions; and finally the test problems and the transfer to parallel lines were given in two individual sessions. Subjects in a control condition received the two review sessions and the test and transfer sessions, without the intervening instruction in proof checking. Fifteen subjects (nine women and six men) participated in each of the conditions.

The subjects in the experimental condition participated on 6 consecutive days; subjects in the control condition participated on 4 consecutive days. For each day on which they participated, subjects chose a convenient time from among a number of available sessions. Group sessions usually had three or four students. In the test and transfer sessions, involving individual subjects, students were asked to think aloud as they worked on problems, and their protocols were recorded on audio tape.

Results.   Performance of the students in the control and experimental conditions is summarized in Table 4.9. The instruction apparently had a positive effect, enabling students in the experimental condition to detect a higher proportion of errors than the control students. The difference in performance on invalid proofs was significant ($t(28)$ 2.35, $p < .05$), and there clearly was not an interaction between training conditions and sessions. The data in Table 4.9 are based on strict scoring of error detection, in which errors had to be identified and the reasons for the errors given correctly. Data also were tabulated using a more lenient criterion, where errors had to be identified correctly but the subject's

TABLE 4.9
Proportion Correct

Problem Type	Session	Number of Problems	Control	Experimental
Invalid	Test	7	.42	.62
	Transfer	8	.50	.70
Valid	Test	3	.87	.89
	Transfer	3	.87	.89
Proof construction	Test	3	.20	.53
	Transfer	3	.33	.49

explanation of the error was incorrect in some way. With the lenient criterion, there was a significant main effect of training ($t(28)$ 2.89, $p < .01$) and a nonsignificant interaction with sessions ($t(28) = 0.59$, $p > .50$), as with the strict criterion.

An examination of the individual problems failed to reveal any systematic differences in the kinds of problem for which the instruction in proof checking was especially effective. For example, some errors in proof involve incorrect reasons; others involve antecedents that have not been established. There was a somewhat larger effect of instruction on problems with incorrect reasons in the test session, but the effect on problems with antecedents not established was greater in the transfer session. One specific problem for which instruction had an especially large effect is the problem shown in Fig. 4.6, which was included in the transfer session. One of the 15 control subjects detected the error in this problem correctly, whereas eight of the experimental subjects did.

The thinking-aloud protocols were examined to determine whether the subjects used the proof-checking procedure in an explicit way. Three of the subjects in the experimental condition used the procedure on nearly all the steps in every problem. Most of the students in the experimental condition applied the procedure when they appeared to be uncertain about a step. Only two of the subjects in the control condition used a form of the proof-checking procedure that included explicit checking of the antecedents and consequents of reasons.

The experimenters formed two general impressions of differences between subjects in the two conditions. First, experimental subjects appeared to read the statements of the proof more carefully than did the control subjects, even when the experimental subjects were not using the proof-checking procedure explicitly. Second, the control participants typically checked steps by comparing the statements with the problem diagrams. Only one student in the experimental condition appeared to use the strategy of comparing statements with diagrams. The rest attended primarily to the reason and related it to information from previous steps in the proof.

There was a substantial difference between the two conditions in performance on proof construction problems in both the test and transfer sessions. The difference was significant ($t(28)$ 2.94, $p < .01$) and the interaction with sessions was not significant ($t(28) = 1.02, p > .50$). A substantial part of the difference was due to one problem in the test session that used a pattern of overlapping triangles on which experimental subjects had some specific practice that was not given to control subjects. Even without that problem, however, there was an advantage for the experimental subjects: .43 to .30 on proof construction problems. It seems likely that the training in proof checking gave subjects some skills that facilitated their performance in proof construction problems as well.

Discussion.   The subjects who were given training in proof checking did not become experts on that task, but they clearly acquired some skill that subjects without that training lacked. The result provides general support for the computational model of proof checking, showing that it is learnable at least to an extent. The fact that students still failed to detect some errors may be attributable simply to the relatively small amount of training, combined with the absence of any constraints on the subjects to use the procedure they had learned in the test and transfer problems. As a methodological point, the experiment has the interesting feature that human problem solvers were trained to perform in agreement with a model that existed earlier; thus, we succeeded in getting human performance to simulate a computer program, rather than the other way.

An important conceptual question is whether the skill represented in the computational model and acquired to some extent by the student subjects constitutes significant understanding of the concept of proof. It seems to us that it does. Knowledge of the procedure enables an individual to analyze relations between each step of a proof and the information in previous statements and the premises of the problem. The relation that is examined is deductive consequence, the defining characteristic of formal proof. It seems reasonable to characterize a procedure for testing the features of deductive consequence as a form of significant implicit understanding of the concept of formal proof.

The view that ability to check proofs reflects understanding of the principle of deductive consequence is strengthened by contrasting correct performance on proof checking with performance by students who have not received instruction in the task. Typical untutored performance strongly resembles comprehension of narrative or expository text, where each new statement is accepted if it is consistent with previous information and can be added to it in a coherent structure. In a proof, a stronger criterion of acceptance should be applied to each new statement: It must not only be consistent with prior information, it must follow from it deductively. The procedure for checking applies this stronger criterion, and knowledge of the procedure therefore provides a form of knowledge that relates directly to characteristics that distinguish formal proof from ordinary texts.

CONCLUSIONS

In the introduction to this chapter I mentioned four general points that are illustrated by aspects of the analyses that I have discussed. I now return to those points as a framework for presenting some conclusions.

First, the analyses illustrate the applicability of methods of analysis developed in cognitive science to school tasks, and show how those methods can lead to formulation of cognitive objectives of instruction. The analyses summarized by Resnick (this volume) involving reading, physics, and elementary mathematics, and the investigations reported by Scardamalia and Bereiter (this volume) involving writing, should leave little doubt as to the feasibility of research into the cognitive requirements of significant instructional tasks using currently available concepts and methods of cognitive science. Of course, this should not be interpreted as suggesting that more powerful and valid concepts and methods will not be developed in the future, but only that significant and useful insights can be obtained with the tools that we have at present.

These analyses also provide characterizations of knowledge that can be adopted as definite objectives of instruction. The analysis of structural understanding given here identifies a specific cognitive structure of general relationships as the knowledge that constitutes understanding of the structure of a class of geometry problems. The analysis of understanding of the principle of deductive consequence identifies a cognitive procedure that incorporates defining features of valid deductive inference. Both these characterizations could provide objectives for instruction that are specific enough to be incorporated into instructional materials, if it is thought that their acquisition would be valuable.

The second general point involves analysis of acquisition and instructional intervention. In the example of structural understanding, a theoretical analysis of acquisition was developed. This analysis was ad hoc in many ways, and much work remains for the development of a general model of schema-based learning. Even so, some suggestions for instruction can be taken from the analysis. A major condition for meaningful learning to occur in the model is the activation of an appropriate schema in the learner's knowledge structure. This suggests that at a minimum, instruction with the goal of structural understanding should include an effort to activate general schematic knowledge that can provide an appropriate structure for the material being learned. A straightforward method would involve simple discussion of the structure involved; in the case of the part–whole schema, pointing out to students that segments or angles in the problems have other segments or angles as their parts, and discussing the way in which these part–whole structures are involved in the inferences that are made in solving the problems. Another instructional method involves structural mapping, where an analogy is used involving the problem that is the target of instruction and a problem from another domain that has the same structure in a salient form. The efficacy of analogical mapping for geometry problems has not been studied systematically;[3] however, its general usefulness is widely recognized, and it has been studied systematically in other domains such as electricity and electronics (Gentner, 1980; Riley, Bee, & Mokwa, 1981) and in elementary mathematics (Resnick, in press, this volume).

In the example of understanding the principle of deductive consequence, instructional materials were developed for teaching the procedure of proof checking that incorporates defining features of valid deductive inference. Instruction using the materials was modestly successful, and because we gave only 2 hours of instruction, it seems quite likely that sustained use of the method in a geometry course would have substantial benefit for students. This example, involving an instructional objective in procedural form, is particularly adaptable for instructional purposes, as a procedure can both be taught and assessed in a straightforward way.

The third general point involves theoretical significance of the analyses. Development of definite models as hypotheses about cognitive structures that constitute understanding should provide some clarification of understanding in relation to general concepts of psychological theory. The major psychological concept involved in the example of structural understanding is that of a schema. This concept has been central in the theory of language understanding that has been developed recently (e.g., Norman & Rumelhart, 1975), and it would be reasonable to expect that it would also be useful in the analysis of understanding in nonlinguistic domains. A satisfying conceptual continuity is provided by the finding that a schema organized in essentially the same way as those hypothesized in analyses of language understanding and knowledge representation (Bobrow & Winograd, 1977) can provide a plausible account of structural understanding of a class of mathematical problems.

The theoretical contribution of the analysis of understanding the principle of deductive consequence involves a characterization of implicit understanding. We attribute implicit understanding of a principle to an individual when the principle plays a significant functional role in the individual's performance. One way in which a principle can be functional is in a procedure for evaluating examples to determine whether they satisfy the principle. The procedure for proof checking that was formulated and that students acquired in instruction evaluates solutions

---

[3]I can report an anecdote in which the method of analogical mapping provided a successful instructional experience for the vertical angles problem. An eighth-grade student was shown the proof of the theorem, but was unable to recall it about two weeks later. Two analogous situations were then discussed. One of these involved distances on a map, with two equal total distances and a shared component, and the conclusion of equal partial distances with the shared component removed. The other situation involved a person standing on a scale holding one of two filled suitcases; the combined weights of the person with either of the suitcases was equal, and the conclusion was that the suitcases had to be equal. With these items of background, the student generated the proof of equal vertical angles and remembered it on two later occasions, one 2 days later and the other 7 months later.

of proof problems according to the principle of deductive consequence, and thus illustrates this form of implicit understanding.

Using performance in an evaluation task such as proof checking as a criterion for knowledge of a general concept has two important precedents. First, in experimental studies of concept identification, subjects' ability to distinguish correctly between positive and negative examples is taken as the criterion of their acquisition of the concept. In a more complex domain, knowledge of the grammar of a language is tested by the ability of a human subject or computational system to discriminate correctly between strings that are sentences of the language and strings that are not sentences according to the grammar.

The final general point mentioned in the introduction was that "understanding" refers to numerous distinct forms of knowledge. The examples discussed in this chapter illustrate two major categories of understanding: intrinsic and theoretical understanding. Intrinsic understanding of a problem involves cognizance of relationships among elements of the problem or steps in its solution. Theoretical understanding involves cognizance of relationships between the problem and general principles that constrain or justify aspects of the solution. (A more extended discussion of these forms of understanding has been given by Greeno & Riley, 1981.) Structural understanding, in the characterization given here, is a form of intrinsic understanding, involving cognizance of a set of relationships among problem components. Understanding the principle of deductive consequence is an example of theoretical understanding, involving cognizance of a significant constraint on valid solutions of proof problems.

The difference between these two forms of understanding emphasizes the importance of identifying the cognitive structures and processes that are intended when we ask whether someone understands a problem or a procedure. The cognitive structures identified in each of the analyses constitute significant understanding of proof problems. We would say that a student with cognizance of the part–whole relations in the vertical angles problem has more understanding of that problem than a student without that cognizance. Similarly, a student with cognizance of the defining features of valid deductive inference has more understanding of any proof problem than a student without that cognizance. Furthermore, there are other significant forms of understanding in the domain of proof problems that could be taken into account in a theoretical analysis or in design of instruction.

Although an undifferentiated concept of understanding is inadequate for both theoretical and instructional purposes, a more differentiated and specific characterization of understanding is both important and feasible. Concepts and methods of cognitive psychology have now been developed that make it possible to formulate objectives for instruction that are specific enough to be used as the basis of instructional design and assessment, and that also correspond to significant forms of understanding.

ACKNOWLEDGMENTS

This research was supported by the Personnel and Training Research Programs, Office of Naval Research, under Contract Number N00014–79–C–0215. Contract Authority Identification Number NR 667–430. The study of proof checking was a collaborative study by Maria Magone and me. James Rowland assisted in collecting and analyzing the data of the instructional experiment, and James Mokwa assisted in implementing models.

This chapter is an expanded version of a paper presented at the XXII International Congress of Psychology in Leipzig, in July 1980. The original version has been published in R. Glaser & J. Lompscher (Eds.), *Cognitive and motivational aspects of instruction,* a volume of proceedings of the Congress, and in Japanese, in *Psychology,* 1982, 60–64.

REFERENCES

Anderson, J. R. *Language, memory, and thought.* Hillsdale, N.J.: Lawrence Erlbaum Associates, 1976.

Anderson, J. R. *Acquisition of cognitive skill.* (Technical Report 81–1). Pittsburgh: Carnegie–Mellon University Department of Psychology. 1981.

Anderson, J. R., Greeno, J. G., Kline, P. J., & Neves, D. M. Acquisition of problem-solving skill. In J. R. Anderson (Ed.), *Cognitive skills and their acquisition.* Hillsdale, N.J.: Lawrence Erlbaum Associates, 1981.

Bobrow, D. G., & Winograd, T. An overview of KRL, a knowledge representation language. *Cognitive Science,* 1977, *1,* 3–46.

Gelman, R., & Gallistel, C. R. *The child's understanding of number.* Cambridge, Mass.: Harvard University Press, 1978.

Gentner, D. *The structure of analogocal models in science.* (Report No. 4451). Cambridge, Mass.: Bolt, Beranek, & Newman, 1980.

Greeno, J. G. Indefinite goals in well-structured problems. *Psychological Review,* 1976, *83,* 479–91.

Greeno, J. G. A study of problem solving. In R. Glaser (Ed.), *Advances in instructional psychology* (Vol. 1). Hillsdale, N.J.: Lawrence Erlbaum Associates, 1978.

Greeno, J. G., Magone, M. E., & Chaiklin, S. Theory of constructions and set in problem solving. *Memory & Cognition,* 1979, *7,* 445–461.

Greeno, J. G., & Riley, M. S. *Processes and development of understanding.* (Report 1981/8). Pittsburgh: University of Pittsburgh Learning Research and Development Center, 1981.

Judd, C. M. The relation of special training to general intelligence. *Educational Review,* 1908, *36,* 2842.

Katona, G. *Organizing and memorizing.* New York: Columbia University Press, 1940.

Kintsch, W., & VanDijk, T. A. Toward a model of text comprehension and production. *Psychological Review,* 1978, *85,* 363–394.

Neves, D. M. *Learning procedures from examples.* Unpublished doctoral dissertation, Carnegie–Mellon University, 1981.

Norman, D. A., & Rumelhart, D. E. *Explorations in cognition.* San Francisco: W. H. Freeman, 1975.

Piaget, J. *The child's conception of number.* New York: W. W. Norton, 1965. (Originally published 1941).

Resnick, L. B. A developmental theory of number understanding. In H. P. Ginsburg (Ed.), *Development of mathematical thinking.* New York: Academic Press, in press.

Riley, M. S., Bee, N. V., & Mokwa, J. J. *Representations in early learning: The acquisition of problem-solving strategies in basic electricity/electronics.* Pittsburgh: University of Pittsburgh Learning Research and Development Center, 1981.

Riley, M. S., Greeno, J. G., & Heller, J. I. *Development of word problem-solving ability.* In H. P. Ginsburg (Ed.), *Development of mathematical thinking.* New York: Academic Press, 1983.

Sacerdoti, E. D. *A structure for plans and behavior.* New York: Elsevier–North Holland, 1977.

Vere, S. A. Inductive learning of relational productions. In D. A. Waterman & F. Hayes-Roth (Eds.), *Pattern-directed inference systems.* New York: Academic Press, 1978.

Wertheimer, M. *Productive thinking* (Enlarged ed.). New York: Harper & Row, 1959. (Originally published 1945.)

5 Investigating and Applying Developmental Psychology in the Science Classroom

Anton E. Lawson
Department of Physics, Arizona State University

My introduction to developmental psychology took place about 12 years ago while teaching science in California. I recall being astounded at reading that some children think that changing the shape of a piece of clay changes its weight and that some children even believe a change in shape changes the amount of clay. Since that time I have had the opportunity to investigate what these sorts of student misconceptions mean to the science teacher. In this chapter I would like to raise a number of questions and discuss a series of investigations undertaken to answer these questions to understand better the nature of intellectual development and what it means to the science teacher. At the conclusion I would hope that you will have a reasonably clear notion of how developmental psychology can be applied to improve instruction in the science classroom as well as an awareness of some important unresolved issues.

INITIAL STUDIES OF THE DEVELOPMENT OF ADVANCED REASONING

Although research has shown that nearly everyone attains the reasoning abilities commonly associated with Piaget's stage of concrete operational thought, data collected by many investigators in the 1960s and 1970s suggested that the advanced reasoning abilities of Piaget's formal operational thinker were attained by only some 50% of adolescents and adults (Chiappetta, 1976; Cohen, Hillman, & Agne, 1978; Kolodiy, 1975; Lawson, Karplus, & Adi, 1978; McKinnon & Renner, 1971; Piaget, 1972; Towler & Wheatley, 1971).

Data such as these raise a number of important questions for the science teacher. For example, are large percentages of adolescents and adults really concrete operational in Piaget's sense or is their failure to perform satisfactorily on the tasks due simply to the lack of some specific science or mathematics knowledge? If high school students are indeed concrete operational, then what factors are responsible for the failure of advanced reasoning to develop? How does this apparent lack of advanced reasoning ability affect performance outside of science and mathematics? In other words, how general is this apparent intellectual deficit? Does taking science courses help students to develop advanced reasoning abilities? If not, can science be taught in such a way that it does? If advanced reasoning can be taught does it generalize to problems beyond the science classroom? These questions have been the targets of our research efforts.

How Does the Apparent Lack of Advanced Reasoning Ability Affect Performance in the Science Classroom?

Because many high school students appear to have poorly developed advanced reasoning abilities, Lawson and Renner (1975) conducted a study to determine how this apparent lack of formal reasoning affects scientific understanding. First, they selected a high school and with the help of its science teachers identified the major concepts taught in biology, chemistry, and physics classes. Those concepts were then classified into one of two groups: concrete concepts and hypothetical concepts. Consider, for example, the biological concepts of "gene," "species," "DNA replication," "environment," and "natural selection." In my opinion, "species" and "environment" can readily be understood in terms of familiar actions, observations, and examples. In other words, these concepts can be derived from direct experience by using concrete reasoning. Such concepts are called *concrete concepts.*

The concepts of "gene," "DNA replication," and "natural selection" must be understood in terms of other concepts (trait, heredity, cell, molecular structure, competition, environmental factors), functional relationships, inferences, and/or idealized models. These understandings are not the result of direct experiences and require application of advanced reasoning. Such concepts are called *hypothetical concepts.*

Some concepts, of course have more than one meaning and may, therefore, be "concrete" or "hypothetical," depending on their treatment. For example, the concept of habitat, if defined as a place where an organism lives, is a "concrete" concept. Indeed this meaning of habitat has been successfully taught to first-graders. However, if habitat is defined as Hutchinson defines niche, as "an *n*-dimensional hypervolume every point of which corresponds to an environmental state permitting the species in question to maintain a steady state," the concept is

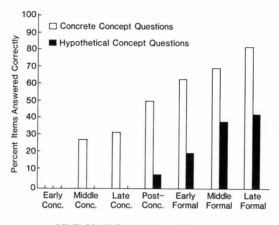

FIG. 5.1.   A comparison of success on concrete and hypothetical science concepts with chance eliminated—combined disciplines.

clearly a "hypothetical" one. This concept is difficult to understand for some graduate students.

Lawson and Renner hypothesized that students classified as concrete operational based on responses to advanced reasoning tasks would be able to acquire understanding of the concrete concepts but would not be able to acquire understanding of hypothetical concepts. The limitation would be due presumably to their failure to acquire the general operational structures of the advanced hypothetico–deductive thinker that would allow the concepts' assimilation. Using a battery of individually administered tasks, students were classified into developmental stages and substages. They were then administered a multiple-choice pencil-and-paper test of their understanding of the concrete and hypothetical concepts taught during the semester. The results of the study for the combined disciplines are shown in Fig. 5.1.

Note the positive relationship between developmental level and science concept understanding in the figure. As hypothesized, the concrete operational students demonstrated no understanding of hypothetical science concepts. Because biology courses include some hypothetical concepts, whereas chemistry and physics courses deal almost exclusively with hypothetical concepts, the justifiable conclusion would seem to be that intellectual capabilities are poorly matched to the intellectual demands of the courses for a substantial percentage of high school students. (See also Lawson, 1980; Lawson & Nordland, 1977; Lawson & Wollman, 1980.) This seems a reasonable explanation of why many forewarned high school students choose not to enroll in science courses when given a choice. It also raises the question of how effective high school science courses are in promoting the intellectual development of students.

DO HIGH SCHOOL SCIENCE COURSES HELP STUDENTS DEVELOP INTELLECTUALLY?

Although few studies have dealt specifically with this question, the data that have been gathered would seem to indicate that the answer for most classes is no (e.g., McKinnon & Renner, 1971; Pallrand, Bady, Braun, & Moretti, 1978). Consider, for example, the effect of 10th-grade biology on the intellectual development of students. One of the major investigative techniques of the biologist is the establishment of correlations between isolated variables (referred to by Piaget and others as correlational reasoning—a formal reasoning skill). Consequently, one might hope that a 10th-grade biology course would help students develop their ability to analyze and interpret data for the degree to which two isolated variables are correlated.

A problem that requires just such abilities, called the Fish Puzzle (Fig. 5.2), was administered to students before and after enrolling in 10th-grade biology (grades 6 and 8 before high school biology and grades 10, 12, and college after 10th-grade biology (Lawson, Adi, & Karplus, 1979)). Although the data in Fig. 5.3 clearly show that correlational reasoning develops across adolescence, they fail to show that the 10th-grade biology course (taken between observations O_2 and O_3) had anything to do with its development. If the course had an effect, the line would have reflected relatively greater improvement after the course.

Perhaps the fact that this biology course, and presumably others as well, did not help students develop correlational reasoning is not surprising. After all, most biology teachers do not set out expressly to teach students to analyze data for possible correlations. My point, however, is that this ability is an important one not only for learning science but also for answering many everyday questions of importance (e.g., is there a correlation between smoking and lung cancer, between coffee drinking and cancer of the pancreas, between cholesterol and heart disease?). Many adolescents and adults do not know what the word *cor-*

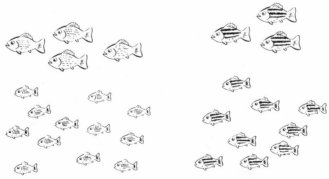

FIG. 5.2.   The fish puzzle. Students are asked to examine pictures and decide if there is a relationship between size of fish and width of stripes.

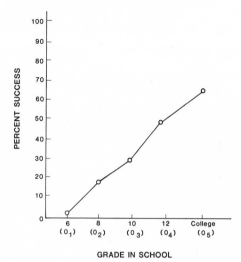

FIG. 5.3. Percentage of subjects at each grade successfully using correlational reasoning to solve the fish puzzle. The biology course was taken between observations O_2 and O_3.

relation means, much less how to identify and analyze data that would establish whether or not one exists. In my opinion, courses should teach those abilities. What better place to teach them than in science classes?

CAN ADVANCED REASONING BE TAUGHT?

If it is the case that many students do not acquire advanced reasoning abilities spontaneously or as a consequence of specific high school experiences, and if these abilities are in fact necessary for comprehension of much of what is taught in high school and college science courses, then either curricula must be changed or students must be taught the necessary reasoning. Can specific instruction be designed and carried out to help students develop advanced reasoning abilities? If so, are the acquired abilities of a generally useful nature (i.e., transferable) or does their use remain restricted to the context in which they were learned?

Before we become too optimistic about the possibility of teaching transferable advanced reasoning abilities it might be appropriate to recall the sobering words of Piaget and David Ausubel. Piaget, when asked about the possibility of teaching students the method of designing controlled experiments replied: "It would be completely useless. The child must discover the method for himself [Piaget, in Hall, 1970]." Ausubel (1979) in discussing the possibility of teaching transferable problem solving skills stated: "Knowledge of scientific method, in other words, tends to be discipline-specific and cannot be learned apart from the context of the discipline, and once learned it cannot be transferred to discovery learning or problem solving in other disciplines [p. 174]."

In spite of these pessimistic statements, the question of learning and transfer of advanced reasoning has been and remains an important issue. Piaget's statement notwithstanding, research suggests that the answer to the question, "Can students acquire advanced reasoning abilities as a consequence of specific instruction?'' is a definite *yes*. The answer to the question, ''Are the learned abilities transferable?'' appears to be a qualified *maybe*. In deference to Piaget, it should be noted that in a sense he was correct. The child must ''discover the method himself,'' yet the teacher can conduct classes in such a way that almost insures that the child *will* discover the method. I shall now turn to research studies that substantiate these assertions.

Our initial attempt to teach students advanced reasoning took place in a high school biology class in Delphi, Indiana, in 1974 (Lawson, Blake, & Nordland, 1975). Students from four 10th-grade biology classes were randomly divided into two groups—an experimental group that received training in the ability to control variables, and a control group that received no training. The training involved materials identical to those used by Inhelder and Piaget (1958) in their pendulum task, which involves the isolation and control of variables. Training also involved materials obtained from the Science Curriculum Improvement Study's *Energy Sources* unit (SCIS, 1971). These materials, called ''rotoplanes,'' provided subjects with additional experiences requiring the control of variables.

Following the training phase, both experimental and control groups were posttested using three advanced reasoning tasks: the pendulum, the bending rods, and the balance beam (Inhelder & Piaget, 1958). Use of the pendulum task allowed determination of the effectiveness of the training to facilitate the ability to control variables with materials identical to the training materials. The bending rods task was used to determine whether or not the training was generalizable to a problem also involving the control of variables but using novel materials (specific transfer). The balance beam task requiring proportional reasoning was used to determine the extent to which the training was generalizable to other areas of advanced reasoning (nonspecific transfer). Piaget claims that proportional reasoning ability develops concomitantly with the ability to control variables—at least under natural conditions.

The experimental group participated in four instructional sessions of 50 minutes each. Two instructors participated in each of the sessions. Subjects worked in teams of two, at tables upon which the experimental materials had been distributed. Each session involved concrete experiments requiring identification and control of variables for successful completion. The basic procedure employed in the sessions followed the SCIS exploration–invention–discovery learning cycle. The learning cycle was designed to be compatible with Piaget's equilibration model of intellectual development (Renner & Lawson, 1973; SCIS, 1974).

In general, *exploration* involves the students in concrete experience with materials. As a consequence of these initial explorations, which sometimes may be highly structured by the teacher or on other occasions relatively free, the learner encounters new information that does not fit his or her existing structures. This produces disequilibrium. At the appropriate time, the teacher suggests a way of ordering the experiences. In essence, the teacher invents a new structure, which often involves a new concept. This phase, termed *invention,* is analogous to Piaget's structure building and promotes a new state of understanding or equilibrium. The question now is, ''Can the new situation be applied in other situations?'' During phase three, *discovery,* further application of the inventions are discovered by students. Discovery experiences serve to reinforce, refine, and enlarge the content of the invention.

During the first training session in this specific instance, subjects were given an opportunity for *exploration* into the pendulum materials and problem. The concepts of *period of the pendulum* and *variable* were introduced (invented) during the second training session. The word ''variable'' was introduced by having students list all the factors that they thought might affect the period on the chalkboard. The students were then told that each of the factors was called a variable. Following introduction of these terms, subjects were provided opportunities to test which variables did or did not affect the period. During the third training session, the concept of a *controlled experiment* was introduced (invented) in relation to the identified variables in the pendulum problem. This was done by first pointing out that the only way to arrive at an unambiguous test of the effect of a single variable was to change that variable while keeping the others the same. This process was discussed at length with respect to each of the variables. Subjects were then allowed further opportunities to measure the period of the pendulum, assuming that all variables except the one being tested were kept the same. The fourth session involved experiments in which the concepts of variables and controlled variables were applied to problems with novel materials (i.e., the rotoplanes). This activity would be considered to be part of the *discovery* phase of the SCIS learning cycle.

Following the treatment all subjects were interviewed individually on the three reasoning tasks. Scores were awarded on the basis of the quality of subjects' verbal responses and their ability to exhibit appropriate behaviors (i.e., to control variables on the pendulum and bending rods tasks and to hang weights in correct locations on the balance beam task).

Table 5.1 shows the mean posttest scores for the experimental and control groups on the three reasoning tasks. The experimental group's mean score on the pendulum task (the trained task) was significantly greater than on the control group's ($t = 2.74; p < .01$). The experimental and control groups did not differ significantly on the bending rods or the balance beam task.

The results suggest that the exploration–invention–discovery learning cycle was effective in enabling subjects to perform at a higher level on the trained task. Thus training can increase subjects' performance on a task using materials similar to those used in the training sessions. However, the fact that the experimental group did not perform better than the control group on the two tasks designed to measure transfer of training suggests that the superior performance on the trained task was probably not due to increased understanding or development of reasoning ability but rather was simply a matter of rote learning. This tends to support

TABLE 5.1
Comparison of Experimental and Control Group
Mean Posttest Scores

| Task | Experimental | | Control | | T |
	Mean	S.D.	Mean	S.D.	
Pendulum	3.12	.93	2.53	.80	2.74*
Bending rod	2.57	.61	2.56	.62	.09
Balance beam	2.57	.61	2.69	.64	−.72

*$p < .01$

Piaget's position that a direct attempt to teach students to control variables is of little value.

Why was the instruction not more successful? Piaget states that four factors are necessary for intellectual development: (1) maturation; (2) concrete experience; (3) social transmission; and (4) self-regulation (equilibration). Because all subjects in this study were over 14 years of age, it seems highly unlikely that a lack of physical maturation was the reason for the relative ineffectiveness of the training. The instructional procedures certainly contained concrete materials and all the subjects were actively engaged in physically manipulating those materials. Also social transmission was a component incorporated into instruction. The concepts of variables, controlled variables, and controlled experiment were all introduced, discussed, and rediscussed at length. This was done not only with groups of students but with every individual student as well. Students also worked in teams, which encouraged students' interaction. It would seem that according to Piaget's statements, the factor most likely missing from the training sessions was the self-regulation or equilibration factor.

A possible reason for the apparent lack of self-regulation by the students was a lack of a sufficient number and variety of experiences that would enable the students to arrive at the desired understanding at their own rates. Further, the training sessions may have failed due to students' lack of familiarity with the materials and terms used during the sessions or perhaps due to the excessive complexity of the training materials. A follow-up study was undertaken to see if this were indeed the case.

A FURTHER ATTEMPT TO TEACH AN ADVANCED REASONING ABILITY

Results of the follow-up study were reported by Lawson and Wollman (1976). Fifth-grade students and seventh-grade students served as subjects in which students in each grade were given training in how to isolate and control variables in a series of four individual training sessions. The training sessions involved the presentation of problems involving the determination of cause-and-effect relationships. The first session involved bouncing tennis balls, which presumably was more familiar to the students than pendulums and far less complex as well. In other words, fewer and more familiar variables were involved. The second session involved bending rods (materials used during the posttest), the third session involved an apparatus called a "Whirlybird" (SCIS, 1970), and the fourth session involved two biology experiments presented in a pencil-and-paper format.

The overall intent of the training was to start with a simple and familiar context to capitalize on subjects' intuitive understanding and later to provide familiar symbolic notions (the phrases "fair" and "unfair tests"). These were to remain invariant across changes in context and to help students identify what must stay the same across those contexts. This was seen as essential for abstraction of the necessary reasoning.

It should be pointed out that our approach assumed that the necessary reasoning abilities already existed in young students, albeit only as intuitions useful in familiar contexts. Therefore the training was designed not to give students new ways of reasoning but to help them extract intuitive notions from familiar contexts (i.e., make the intuitions explicit verbal rules that could serve as anticipatory schemata useful in problem solving in novel contexts).

Posttesting followed the training sessions in two phases. The first phase consisted of individual interviews in which three tasks (bending rods, the pendulum, and the balance beam) were administered. The bending rods task was used to determine whether or not the training was effective in facilitating the ability to control variables with materials identical to those used during the training. The pendulum task was used to determine whether or not the training was generalizable to a problem also involving controlled variables but using novel materials (specific transfer). The balance beam task was also used to determine the extent to which the training encouraged a general development in advanced reasoning (nonspecific transfer). Students also responded orally to a written question involving value judgment, adapted from Peel (1971), that presumably requires hypothetical reasoning. Responses were tape-recorded and later classified into developmental categories.

During the second phase of posttesting, pencil-and-paper problems were group administered. Students responded to a spheres task involving the control of variables, a logic question involving the logical fallacy known as affirming the consequent, and one combinatorial question. These problems, like the balance beam task and the Peel question, were administered to determine the extent to which the training encouraged a general advance in reasoning rather than a specific advance limited to the control of variables. The spheres task, like the pendulum task, tested for specific transfer of the trained concept. It was, however, an additional step removed from the training in that it did not involve the manipulation of materials. Instead of the combinatorial question, the seventh-grade students were administered a shortened version of the Longeot examina-

TABLE 5.2
Mean Pretest and Posttest Levels of Intellectual Development as
Measured by the Bending Rods Task

Group	Pretest	Posttest
Fifth grade		
Experimental	3.93	7.06*
Control	4.00	4.42
Mean	3.96	5.75
Seventh grade		
Experimental	4.50	7.37*
Control	4.75	5.43
Mean	4.62	6.41

*$p < .001$

tion (Longeot, 1962, 1965) that incorporated problems of class logic, propositional logic, proportional reasoning, and combinatorial reasoning as the measure of nonspecific transfer of training.

Table 5.2 shows the mean pretest and posttest levels of intellectual development for both the fifth- and seventh-grade students as measured by the bending rods task. The fifth-grade experimental group showed a gain in level from 3.93 (slightly less than fully concrete-operational-IIB) to 7.06 (between early formal-IIIA and full formal-operational-IIIB), which was highly significant (Wilcoxon T

TABLE 5.3
Means, Standard Deviations, and Mann–Whitney μ Values for
Experimental and Control Group Posttest
Measures—Fifth-Grade Sample

Posttest Measure	Experimental		Control		μ
	M	S.D.	M	S.D.	
Trained task					
Bending rods	7.06	.99	4.43	1.02	10.5**
Specific transfer tasks					
Pendulum	5.38	2.13	4.14	.95	83.5*
Spheres	4.75	2.77	3.00	1.18	78*
Nonspecific transfer tasks					
Balance beam	4.63	1.15	4.14	.54	89
Peel	2.00	.37	2.00	.39	105.5
Combinatorial	5.74	.45	5.29	1.07	88

*$p < .01$
**$p < .001$

= .0, p < .001). The fifth-grade control group's slight gain from 4.00 to 4.42 was not significant. The seventh-grade experimental group also showed a significant gain in level from 4.50 to 7.37 (T = .0, p < .001), whereas the control group's gain from 4.75 to 5.43 was not significant.

Means and standard deviations for the trained task, the specific transfer tasks, and the nonspecific transfer tasks for the fifth-grade students are shown in Table 5.3. The Mann–Whitney values show that the experimental group performed significantly better than the control group on the bending rods, pendulum, and spheres tasks. However, on the remaining measures, group differences did not reach significance.

Means and standard deviations for the six posttest measures for the seventh-grade subjects are shown in Table 5.4. Inspection of the table shows that the experimental group performed significantly better than the control group on the bending rods, pendulum, and spheres tasks and on one measure of nonspecific transfer—the Longeot examination—as well. However, on the balance beam task and on the Peel question, group differences failed to reach significance.

The results clearly indicate that advances in reasoning can be made as a consequence of direct intervention. It is my belief that the primary cause of success in this study as opposed to the general lack of success in the previous study was that instruction began with materials and problems that were simple and familiar to the students. Instruction proceeded gradually through a variety of increasingly complex and novel (yet concrete) situations insuring that the students had to reason through each situation before going on to the next. Students

TABLE 5.4
Means, Standard Deviations, and Mann–Whitney μ Values for
Experimental and Control Group Posttest
Measures–Seventh-Grade Sample

	Experimental		Control		
Posttest Measure	M	S.D.	M	S.D.	μ
Trained task					
Bending rods	7.37	.81	5.43	1.50	24***
Specific transfer tasks					
Pendulum	7.56	.73	5.13	1.54	20***
Spheres	6.88	2.78	3.94	2.02	53**
Nonspecific transfer tasks					
Balance beam	4.63	1.15	4.63	.96	121
Peel	2.31	.60	2.38	.72	181
Longeot	4.13	1.45	3.44	1.36	69*

*p < .05
**p < .01
***p < .001

were forced to reflect on their actions, an aspect of intellectual functioning seen as crucial for intellectual development. For example, in the second training session involving the bending rods, when a student set out to demonstrate that a thick rod bends more than a thin one, but did so in an incorrect fashion, rather than telling him he was wrong we attempted to guide him to this discovery and to a means of correcting his approach. *E:* "Are you sure that this rod bends less because it's thicker? Could there be another reason it is bending less?" *S:* "Well, the thick rod is made of steel and the thin one is brass. Maybe that would make a difference." *E:* "How could you do the test to be sure it's bending less because it's thicker and not because it's steel?" *S:* "Use two steel rods?"

The fact that the training sessions took place on an individual basis made this sort of exchange possible. In the classroom this would happen much less frequently. Therefore, a reasonable prediction would be that the same sort of approach carried out in the classroom would take longer to achieve comparable results. This led us to the next logical step in our series of investigations. Can this instructional approach be carried out successfully in the classroom setting? Can it improve other aspects of advanced reasoning such as correlational reasoning and proportional reasoning?

TEACHING ADVANCED REASONING IN THE SCIENCE CLASSROOM

Lawson and Snitgen (1982) tested the hypothesis that substantial gains in advanced reasoning can be attained in the classroom setting provided that a variety of experiences occurred, the instruction capitalized on the student's intuitive understanding, and instruction allowed students to reflect upon their initially incorrect or incomplete reasoning. A one-semester experimental biology course was taught with students' entry and exit levels of reasoning ability assessed. The experimental course, entitled "Biological Science for the Elementary Teacher," was designed for prospective elementary school teachers and used the exploration–invention–discovery learning cycle to introduce key biological concepts and advanced reasoning abilities. The course consisted of a series of laboratory investigations that initially were relatively structured, yet later allowed students considerable freedom in their design and completion. Aspects of advanced reasoning were introduced during discussions at specific points in the course only when needed by the investigations. After the introduction of a reasoning pattern, subjects were given additional information about its use, and problems requiring its application in "Reasoning Modules" that were part of the course study guide. The reasoning patterns were then reinforced by their subsequent use in later investigations and by the inclusion of problems on examinations that required their use.

The general teaching strategy was to let students generate and discuss experimental designs in teams. They could reflect upon similarities and differences in the results as a means of identifying mistakes or inadequacies in the original designs and therefore in the reasoning that led to those designs. The correct reasoning was then introduced and named by the instructor (i.e., control of variables, proportional reasoning, correlational reasoning). Subsequent lessons then allowed students opportunities to apply the reasoning in designing, conducting, or interpreting data from new experiments. Such a strategy includes provisions for social interaction and concrete experience—both identified as necessary for intellectual development. The strategy also includes provision for reflection upon past reasoning and past errors, which is also seen as necessary.

As an example of this technique, consider the introduction of the reasoning required in the design of controlled experiments. As part of the study of the ecosystem, students began by attempting to identify the energy source(s) for developing plants. Investigations required that seed parts be identified and germinated in various combinations to determine the role played by each. Although controlled experimentation was required by the nature of the problem, this was not mentioned. Rather, working in teams, students were challenged to design their own experiments as best they could. Later the teams' experimental results were graphed and compared. Differences in data led students to question one another to determine the source of the differences. It was discovered that not all groups had experimented in the same way (e.g., some had not watered the seed parts the same, the amount of light varied, different seed combinations had been tried).

At this point the idea of a controlled experiment was introduced in the context of the experiment just conducted. The terms "fair and unfair test" were initially used, as earlier research (Lawson & Wollman, 1976) had indicated that those terms were more easily understood than the terms "controlled" and "uncontrolled experiments." This discussion was meant to help initiate the self-regulation process—to help students begin to develop the reasoning necessary to design controlled experiments.

Students were then instructed to work through a "Reasoning Module" entitled "Is That Really Fair?" The module included an introduction to "fair tests" in which two boys at a lake were arguing over who could do more push-ups. To prove that he could do more push-ups the first boy got down on the beach and proceeded to do 25 push-ups. At that the second boy jumped into shallow water and using the water to partially buoy up his body did 26 push-ups. At this point the students were asked to judge whether or not a fair test had been conducted and to justify their response. Such an introduction takes advantage of the fact that in familiar contexts even concrete operational students can comprehend when tests have been conducted fairly (i.e., in a controlled fashion).

The introduction was followed by an essay in which the terms "fair" and "unfair tests" and "controlled" and "uncontrolled experiments" were used in the context of comparing bouncing tennis balls to determine which ball was inherently bouncier. The students were then instructed to conduct a series of controlled experiments to determine the effect of a number of variables on the number of times the arm of a whirlybird (SCIS, 1970) will spin before stopping. The students then answered a series of seven pencil-and-paper questions about the essays, experiments, and other situations that tested their understanding of controlled experiments. The intent of the reasoning module was to begin with familiar contexts that take advantage of student's intuitive understanding (Ausubel, 1964) and progress to unfamiliar contexts to enable the students to gradually abstract or disembed the necessary reasoning from the contexts in which it is embedded (Bruner & Kenney, 1970).

Additional laboratory investigations followed, involving such things as the role of light, water, fertilizer, and crowding on plant growth, the role of soil particle size on water holding ability and the role of crowding on the growth of fruit fly populations. These allowed students to apply the concept of controlled experimentation to a variety of novel situations. It was hoped that such redundancy in reasoning and novelty in context would lead to satisfactory self-regulation. Hence, transfer of training would be evidenced on posttest measures.

The pretest and posttest data presented in Fig. 5.4 show that substantial gains in reasoning were made by the students with respect to conservation reasoning, the ability to isolate and control variables, and use of proportional, correlational, probabilistic, and combinatorial reasoning. Scores of 0–5 represent concrete reasoning, whereas scores of 6–11 represent transitional reasoning, and scores of 12–15 represent formal reasoning (see Lawson, 1978). The pretest was given at the beginning of the semester and the posttest was given at the end. Note that on

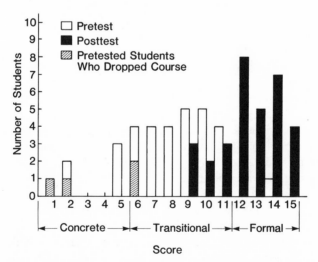

FIG. 5.4.   Frequencies of pretest and posttest scores of subjects on the Classroom Test of Formal Reasoning. Note that four pretest subjects dropped the course prior to the posttest. Scores of 0–5 represent concrete reasoning. Scores of 6–11 represent transitional reasoning. Scores of 12–15 represent formal reasoning.

the pretest only 4 students (11%) were in the formal range, with 26 (72%) in the transitional range and 6 (17%) in the concrete range. On the posttest 24 students (75%) were in the formal range, 8 (25%) were in the transitional range, and 0 (0%) were in the concrete range. It should be noted, however, that two of the concrete students and two of the low transitional students found the reasoning demands of the course too much and dropped before taking the posttest. Nonetheless, the overall gains in reasoning by the class were considerable, thus supporting the hypothesis that advanced reasoning can be taught successfully in the classroom. Note that a control group was not used in this study. A potential weakness is our inability to assess the relative contribution of maturation and/or history to the pretest to posttest gains. However, in the present case this was not viewed as a major problem in that previous data suggested little if any measurable development of advanced reasoning during a one-semester interval for students of the type used (Lawson & Snitgen, 1982). Indeed, in the present sample, no significant pre- to posttest gains were made on two uninstructed aspects of advanced reasoning and, on one of them, the posttest scores were actually lower than pretest scores. Also in the present sample, the calculated correlation coefficient between pretest developmental level and year in school (freshman–senior) was $r = -.04$. This alone does not indicate lack of development of advanced reasoning with time spent in school. Longitudinal data would be needed for convincing evidence. Yet it does suggest that the completion of college courses alone is not sufficient for development.

WHO WILL PROFIT FROM INSTRUCTION IN REASONING AND WHO WILL NOT?

Although it seems clear that most students can gain in their ability to reason, some students seem surprisingly resistant to instruction. What psychological factors can account for this? Age seems to be a factor. Consider the data presented earlier for the fifth- and seventh-grade students. Although both groups showed significant and generalizable improvement in their ability to control variables, the seventh-grade students were easier to train and performed better than the fifth-graders on the posttests. Danner and Day (1977) report similar results.

Studies by Kuhn, Ho, and Adams (1979) and by Lawson (1982) compared concrete operational, early adolescents' (age 11–13) ability to learn advanced reasoning to that of concrete operational college students (age 20–25). In both studies it was found that the college students were more responsive to instruction. Just what happens as a child becomes older to cause this improvement is not clear. Of course, experience increases with age. Perhaps older students, such as the college students, simply have more familiarity with issues like the possible links between smoking and lung cancer, food preservatives and stomach cancer, the possibilities of winning raffles, horse races, or magazine publishers sweepstakes, which provide a needed supply of connecting or generalizing experiences that make the instruction more meaningful, hence better understood and recalled. Brain growth continues up until about age 15–16 (Epstein, 1978) and perhaps mental capacity (Pascual-Leone, 1976) does as well.

One factor that is known to increase with age and is known to be related to the development of advanced reasoning is field independence (Case, 1975; Lawson, 1976; Niemark, 1977). The Lawson (1976) study found sixth-graders' ability to reason successfully on the bending rods and balance beam tasks to correlate .81 and .77 respectively with field independence. It seems that developing advanced reasoning ability either as a consequence of general experience or specific instruction requires the child to disembed relevant information from the background of irrelevant noise, something that field dependent individuals find extremely difficult.

Perhaps for older students, such as the college students in my biology course, an important source of failure to acquire the reasoning abilities was a smaller than normal mental capacity. Support for this hypothesis comes from the finding that the Raven Progressive Matrices test, which is in large part a measure of mental capacity (Bereiter & Scardamalia, 1979), was found to correlate .66 with reasoning posttest performances (Lawson & Snitgen, 1982).

At this point little else about individual differences can be said. The issue of individual differences in the acquisition of advanced reasoning is one that needs considerably more research. Nonetheless, the following general picture has emerged: Developing advanced reasoning abilities involves the disembedding of problem-solving strategies (sequences of mental operations) from the general social and physical milieu in which they are embedded. For people who are field independent (high mental capacity processors and insensitive to misleading gestaltlike cues) the strategies are disembedded spontaneously during adolescence. The disembedding seems to require a sufficient mental capacity that, if one were to adopt Pascual-Leone's position, increases with age (Pascual-Leone, 1976). For field dependent people the disembedding is more difficult due to their tendency to be oversensitive to misleading gestaltlike cues. Yet if field dependent people have sufficient mental capacity and are given specific instruction with the reasoning patterns introduced in such a way as to highlight them and suppress misleading cues, the patterns can be assimilated and applied correctly in novel contexts. On the other hand, in field dependent people who are low information processors due to habitual failure (or perhaps inability) to use large amounts of mental capacity, learning is more difficult and perhaps, for all practical purposes, not possible. Results reported by Stage (1981) are consistent with this view. She found mental capacity to be the best predictor of a person's use of advanced reasoning in at least one occasion (competence), whereas she found field independence to be the best predictor of a person's use of advanced reasoning on a variety of problems (performance). Scardamalia (1977) also reports data that suggest reasoning performance is a function not only of logical competence but of mental capacity and task variable saliency.

DO ADVANCES IN REASONING GENERALIZE BEYOND THE SCIENCE CLASSROOM?

In addition to my biology course, a number of other science curriculum development projects (e.g., Project SOAR, J. W. Carmichael, Project Director, Xavier University, New Orleans; Project ADAPT, R. Fuller, Project Director, University of Nebraska, Lincoln; Project DOORS, Thomas Campbell, Project Director, Illinois Central College, East Peoria; Project DORIS, Frank Collea, Project Director, California State University, Fullerton) have been initiated with the explicit objective of increasing students' ability to employ advanced reasoning patterns. The assumption underlying these projects is that an increased ability to reason will not only enhance problem solving and achievement in science but will improve performance in other academic pursuits as well. Indeed, the reasoning improvements should facilitate performance beyond the confines of academia into problems of everyday life. Are such projects working toward a realistic goal? Or is improvement in advanced reasoning, if possible at all, limited to the field in which it was developed? Recall Ausubel's previous statement that problem-solving skills, once learned, cannot be transferred to problem solving in other disciplines.

To date, as far as I am aware, no convincing evidence has been gathered to argue that the goal of general achievement advance is realistic. It would seem that only longitudinal data of specific students' achievement, who have acquired advanced reasoning abilities as a consequence of specific instruction, would provide that evidence. Nevertheless descriptive data that I have gathered do at least argue for the plausibility of the general hypothesis and suggest the importance of testing the hypothesis through longitudinal studies.

STATISTICAL RELATIONSHIP WITH ACADEMIC ACHIEVEMENT

The descriptive data of interest were gathered in conjunction with data reported by Lawson (1978) and Lawson (1980) some of which is shown in Table 5.5. The table shows intercorrelations among three measures of advanced reasoning and measures of achievement in four academic areas for a sample of 72 ninth-grade students (mean age 15.1 years) selected from English classes of a high school in an upper middle-class community in the San Francisco Bay area. The reasoning measures were the group-administered Lawson Classroom Test of Formal Reasoning and two individually administered tasks, the bending rods and the balance beam. Achievement in reading, language arts, mathematics, social studies, and science was measured by the *Iowa Tests of Educational Development, Grades 9–12, Form X5* (Science Research Associates, Inc., 1970).

Note that the coefficients among the reasoning measures and achievement in the various areas are all substantial ($r = .42$ to $.72$) and generally similar for all

TABLE 5.5
Pearson Product Moment Correlation Coefficients Among Measures of Formal Reasoning and Achievement

Variables	Formal Reasoning			Achievement				
	Classroom Test	Bending Rods	Balance Beam	Reading	Language Arts	Mathematics	Social Studies	Science
Formal reasoning								
Classroom test	1							
Bending rods	.75	1						
Balance beam	.65	.78	1					
Achievement								
Reading	.69	.66	.61	1				
Language arts	.60	.51	.42	.79	1			
Mathematics	.70	.55	.53	.74	.69	1		
Social studies	.72	.69	.58	.88	.70	.73	1	
Science	.69	.68	.58	.85	.67	.73	.79	1

All p's $< .01$

areas of achievement. That is, they are not substantially higher for science and mathematics than for, say, social studies. If the measures of reasoning were essentially measures of specific science and mathematics knowledge then the measures should correlate more highly with science and mathematics achievement than with achievement in the nonscience areas. The fact that the classroom test correlated as well with social studies achievement ($r = .72$) as with science or mathematics achievement ($r = .69$ and $.70$ respectively) demonstrates clearly that this is not the case. This is an important result because it demonstrates that the type of reasoning we are dealing with is related to *general* achievement and not achievement in science and mathematics alone.

THE CONFOUNDING WITH INTELLIGENCE

The previous analysis at least suggests the plausibility of the hypothesis that increasing students' abilities to employ advanced reasoning patterns may improve their achievement in a wide variety of areas. However, the data could be interpreted in quite another way that would argue that general advances in academic achievement are not feasible. This interpretation would argue that the observed correlations between measured advanced reasoning ability and the various measures of achievement are not due to achievement's dependence on advanced reasoning but are due to the codependence of performance on tasks of advanced reasoning and academic achievement on some general intelligence factor. This could be fixed either genetically or fixed very early in life, perhaps what Spearman (1951) has called his innate educative ability or "g" factor, or what Cattel (1971) calls fluid intelligence. This position would argue that those students high in fluid intelligence will perform well on reasoning tasks and likewise on achievement tests because of their codependence on some basic and fixed intelligence factor or factors. Some support for this position comes from studies by Cloutier and Goldschmid (1976), Keating (1975), and DeVries (1974) that have shown formal reasoning and various measures of intelligence to be correlated. On the other hand studies by Diamond, Keller, and Mobley (1977) and Clayton and Overton (1976) have found formal reasoning and fluid intelligence to be largely uncorrelated.

Data are needed that assess advanced reasoning ability, achievement, and fluid intelligence for a single sample of subjects. The correlation between advanced reasoning ability and achievement must be computed with the influence of fluid intelligence held constant. If the correlation between achievement and reasoning drops to near zero when fluid intelligence is partialled out, then the second position will have been supported. That is, the observed correlation between advanced reasoning ability and general achievement is due to their codependence on fluid intelligence. However, if the correlation remains substantial, then support for the hypothesis that the advanced reasoning ability does significantly influence achievement will have been found. Hence improving one's ability to reason will improve general achievement.

PARTIALLING OUT FLUID INTELLIGENCE

Such data were recently gathered for a sample of biology students (Lawson, 1980). The subjects were 72 college students (mean age 23.6 years, S.D. = 5.81) enrolled in my biology course for preservice teachers at Arizona State University. Advanced reasoning ability was measured using a slightly modified version of my Classroom Test of Formal Reasoning. Fluid intelligence was measured by the verbal (abstractions) section of the Shipley–Hartford Intelligence Scale (Shipley, 1940). The section consists of 20 word-series completion items administered within a 10-minute time limit. Items range in degree of difficulty (e.g., (a) white–black, short–long, down–_____; (b) tar–pitch– throw, saloon–bar–rod, fee–tip–end, plank–_____–meals). A subject's score on the section is simply the number of items correctly completed. Numerous studies have demonstrated the validity of the Shipley–Hartford Scale as a measure of fluid intelligence (Paulson & Lin, 1970; Wahler & Watson, 1962; Wiens & Banaka, 1960). Achievement in biology was measured by a test consisting of 70 multiple-choice items assessing understanding of biological concepts such as biological classification, organism, population, species, photosynthesis, community, environment, predator, food web, decomposition, and evolution. The items were assembled from the Biological Science Curriculum Study resource books of items (BSCS, 1971a, 1971b).

Advanced reasoning ability and biology achievement were found to correlate at $r = .56$, a figure somewhat lower, but similar to the .69 correlation found between the Classroom Test of Formal Reasoning and science achievement for the high school students reported earlier. The somewhat lower correlation could be due partly to the lower reliability of the measures used with the college students. Advanced reasoning ability was found to correlate with fluid intelligence at $r = .48$, whereas achievement and fluid intelligence correlated at $r = .27$. The partial correlation coefficient between reasoning and achievement with fluid intelligence held constant was .51. Further, the partial correlation coefficient between achievement and fluid intelligence with reasoning held constant was essentially zero ($r = .03$).

The fact that the partial correlation coefficient between reasoning and achievement after partialling out fluid intelligence is still substantial represents support for the hypothesis that the observed high correlations between advanced reasoning ability and general achievement are not primarily due to the codependence on fluid intelligence. This conclusion is underscored by the finding that the partial correlation coefficient between achievement and fluid intelligence, with reasoning held constant, was essentially zero. In other words, support has been gathered for the hypothesis that advanced reasoning ability (apart from fluid intelligence) is an important contributor to general academic achievement. This finding is important, for it makes plausible the hypothesis that teaching advanced reasoning patterns may produce general gains in achievement. It would seem that the curriculum development projects cited earlier are working toward a realistic goal. Ausubel's view seems, at this point at least, to be prematurely pessimistic. These descriptive data should encourage those concerned with teaching reasoning abilities to conduct longitudinal studies of subsequent achievement by graduates of their courses to provide needed experimental evidence.

CORRELATION OR CAUSALITY?

The careful reader will no doubt have noticed that a number of my statements, including the basic assumption underlying the cited curriculum development projects, is that improvements in reasoning will *cause* improvements in general achievement. It should be noted that, although the descriptive data reported suggest a correlational relationship between advanced reasoning and general achievement, they do not imply a causal relationship. This, of course, is why experimental studies are needed.

Nonetheless, from a theoretical point of view I find it far more satisfying to believe that advanced reasoning ability causes achievement rather than vice versa. Certainly one can view advanced reasoning as achievement, but I believe it should be viewed as achievement of the basic underlying mental operations that unify intellectual endeavors in all walks of life. The failure of Piaget's attempts to explain the unity of formal reasoning should not dissuade educators from the attempt to identify those basic mental operations and their basic psychological unity. In short, what we seek is the identification of a basic unified set of mental operations that can be taught and that will improve achievement in a general sense.

REFERENCES

Ausubel, D. P. The transition from concrete to abstract cognitive functioning: Theoretical issues and implications for education. *Journal of Research in Science Teaching*, 1964, 2, 261–266.

Ausubel, D. P. Education for rational thinking: A critique. In A. E. Lawson (Ed.), *The psychology of teaching for thinking and creativity*, AETS 1980 Yearbook. Columbus: ERIC/SMEAC, 1979.

Bereiter, C., & Scardamalia, M. Pascual-Leone's *M* construct as a link between cognitive developmental and psychometric concepts of intelligence. *Intelligence*, 1979, 3, 41–63.

Biological Sciences Curriculum Study. *Resource book of test items for biological science: An inquiry into life* (2nd ed.). Boulder, Colo.: 1971. (a)

Biological Sciences Curriculum Study. *Resource book of test items for biological science: Molecules to man* (Rev. ed.). Boulder, Colorado: 1971. (b)

Bruner, J. S., & Kenney, H. J. Representation and mathematics learning. In W. Kessen & C.

Kuhlman (Eds.), *Cognitive development in children*. Chicago: University of Chicago Press, 1970.

Case, R. *The relationship between field dependence and performance on Piaget's tests of formal operations*. Unpublished research report, University of California, Berkeley, 1975.

Cattell, R. B. *Abilities: Their structure, growth and action*. New York: Houghton Mifflin, 1971.

Chiappetta, E. L. A review of Piagetian studies relevant to science instruction at the secondary and college level. *Science Education*, 1976, *60*(2), 253–262.

Clayton, V., & Overton, W. F. Concrete and formal operational thought processes in young adulthood and old age. *International Journal of Aging and Human Development*, 1976, *7*(3), 237–245.

Cloutier, R., & Goldschmid, M. L. Individual differences in the development of formal reasoning. *Child Development*, 1976, *47*(4), 1097–1102.

Cohen, H., Hillman, D., & Agne, R. Cognitive level and college physics achievement. *American Journal of Physics*, 1978, *46*, 1026.

Danner, F. W., & Day, M. C. Eliciting formal operations. *Child Development*, 1977, *48*, 1600–1606.

Devries, R. Relationships among Piagetian, IQ, and achievement assessments. *Child Development*, 1974, *45*, 746–756.

Diamond, S. R., Keller, H. R., & Mobley, L. A. Adults performance on formal operations: General ability or scientific interest. *Perceptual and Motor Skills*, 1977, *44*, 249–250.

Epstein, H. T. Growth spurts during brain development: Implications for educational policy and practice. In J. S. Chall & A. F. Mirsky (Eds.), *Education and the brain*. The 77th Yearbook of the National Society for the Study of Education, University of Chicago Press, 1978.

Hall, E. A conversation with Jean Piaget and Barbel Inhelder. *Psychology Today*, 1970, *3*, 25.

Inhelder, B., & Piaget, J. *The growth of logical thinking from childhood to adolescence*. New York: Basic Books, 1958.

Keating, D. P. Precocious cognitive development at the level of formal operations. *Child Development*, 1975, *46*, 276–280.

Kolodiy, G. The cognitive development of high school and college science students. *Journal of College Science Teaching*, 1975, *5*(1), 20–22.

Kuhn, D., Ho, V., & Adams, C. Formal reasoning among pre- and late adolescents. *Child Development*, 1979, *50*(4), 1128–1135.

Lawson, A. E. Formal operations and field independence in a heterogeneous sample. *Perceptual and Motor Skills*, 1976, *42*, 981–982.

Lawson, A. E. The development and validation of a classroom test of formal reasoning. *Journal of Research In Science Teaching*, 1978, *15*(1), 11–24.

Lawson, A. E. Relationships among level of intellectual development, cognitive style, and grades in a college biology course. *Science Education*, 1980, *64*(1), 95–102.

Lawson, A. E. The relative responsiveness of concrete operational seventh grade and college students to science instruction. *Journal of Research in Science Teaching*, 1982, *19*(1), 63–77.

Lawson, A. E., Adi, H., & Karplus, R. Development of correlational reasoning in secondary schools: Do biology courses make a difference? *The American Biology Teacher*, 1979, *41*(7), 420–425; 430.

Lawson, A. E., Blake, A. J. D., & Nordland, F. H. Training effects and generalization of the ability to control variables in high school biology students. *Science Education*, 1975, *59*(3), 387–396.

Lawson, A. E., Karplus, R., & Adi, H. The acquisition of propositional logic and formal operational schemata during the secondary school years. *Journal of Research in Science Teaching*, 1978, *15*(6), 465–478.

Lawson, A. E., & Nordland, F. H. Conservation reasoning ability and performance on BSCS blue version examinations. *Journal of Research in Science Teaching*, 1977, *14*(1), 69–76.

Lawson, A. E., & Renner, J. W. Relationships of science subject matter and developmental levels of learners. *Journal of Research in Science Teaching*, 1975, *12*(4), 347–358.

Lawson, A. E., & Snitgen, D. A. Teaching formal reasoning in a college biology course for pre-service teachers. *Journal of Research in Science Teaching,* 1982, *19*(3), 233–248.

Lawson, A. E., & Wollman, W. T. Encouraging the transition from concrete to formal cognitive functioning: An experiment. *Journal of Research in Science Teaching,* 1976, *13*(5), 413–430.

Lawson, A. E., & Wollman, W. T. Developmental level and learning to solve problems of proportionality in the classroom. *School Science and Mathematics,* 1980, *80*(1), 69–75.

Longeot, F. Un essai d'application de la psychologie genetique a la psychologie differentielle. *Bulletin de l'Institut National D'Etude,* 1962, *18*(3), 153–162.

Longeot, F. Analyze statistique de trois tests genetiques collectifs. *Bulletin de l'Institut National D'Etude,* 1965, *20*(4), 219–237.

McKinnon, J. W., & Renner, J. W. Are colleges concerned with intellectual development? *American Journal of Physics,* 1971, *39,* 1047–1052.

Niemark, E. C. *Toward the disembedding of formal operations from confounding with cognitive style.* Symposium paper read at the Seventh Annual Meeting of the Jean Piaget Society, May 1977.

Pallrand, G., Bady, R., Braun, R., & Moretti, V. *Cognitive development and science teaching.* Paper presented at the National Association for Research in Science Teaching Annual Convention, Toronto, April 1978.

Pascual-Leone, J. Metasubjective problems of constructive cognition: Forms of knowing and their psychological mechanism. *Canadian Psychological Review,* 1976, *17*(2), 110–125.

Paulson, M. J., & Lin, T. Predicting WAIS IQ from Shipley–Hartford scores. *Journal of Clinical Psychology,* 1970, *26,* 453–461.

Peel, E. A. *The nature of adolescent judgment.* New York: Wiley-Interscience, 1971.

Piaget, J. Intellectual evolution from adolescence to adulthood. *Human Development,* 1972, *15,* 1–12.

Renner, J. W., & Lawson, A. E. Promoting intellectual development through science teaching. *The Physics Teacher,* 1973, *11*(5), 273–276.

Scardamalia, M. *The interaction of perceptual and quantitative load factors in the control of variables.* York University Department of Psychology Reports, 1977.

Science Curriculum Improvement Study. *Subsystems and variables teacher's guide.* Chicago: Rand McNally, 1970.

Science Curriculum Improvement Study. *Energy sources teacher's guide.* Chicago: Rand McNally, 1971.

Science Curriculum Improvement Study. *SCIS teacher's handbook.* University of California, Berkeley, 1974.

Science Research Associates, Inc. *Iowa Tests of Educational Development,* Grades 9–12, Form X5. Chicago, 1970.

Shipley, W. C. A self-administering scale for measuring intellectual impairment and deterioration. *Journal of Psychology,* 1940, *9,* 371–377.

Spearman, C., & Wynn-Jones, L. *Human ability.* London: MacMillan, 1951.

Stage, E. K. *Formal operational reasoning: Format, content and intervention.* Symposium paper presented at the National Association for Research in Science Teaching Annual Convention, Grossinger's in the Catskills, April 1981.

Towler, J. O., & Wheatley, G. Conservation concepts in college students: A replication and critique. *The Journal of Genetic Psychology,* 1971, *118,* 265–270.

Wahler, H., & Watson, L. A comparison of the Shipley–Hartford as a power test with the WAIS verbal scale. *Journal of Consulting Psychology,* 1962, *26,* 105.

Wiens, A., & Banaka, W. Estimating WAIS IQ from Shipley–Hartford scores: A cross validation. *Journal of Clinical Psychology,* 1960, *16,* 452.

MOTIVATION AND ACHIEVEMENT

As we have seen, classroom learning is facilitated by mastery of sequential steps in complex tasks, informed practice, acquisition of problem-solving strategies, and the fit between the developmental level of individual students and the materials used. These principles of cognitive and educational psychology, though, merely set the stage. An effective agenda for classroom learning must also include consideration of patterns of successes and failures experienced by students. Effective teachers must be sensitive to students' motivation to approach tasks, to persevere in spite of setbacks, and to feel pride in their accomplishments because students' attitudes, values, and learning are related. In the following chapters, five distinguished psychologists discuss the interaction between motivation and learning and how they are interwoven in classroom interactions.

Martin Covington integrates cognitive and motivational concepts to help explain achievement behavior. In his view, neither personality variables, such as need for achievement, nor attributions for success and failure are sufficient to account for student achievement. Covington uses the term *motivated cognitions* to capture the purposeful and self-serving nature of students' attitudes and behaviors. Thus, improvements in students' abilities to understand their own abilities, to allocate effort appropriately, and to manage their resources for learning are considered to be important goals of education.

Bernard Weiner extends his well-known research on attributions for success and failure to the emotional consequences of those thoughts. He discusses situations and research that illustrate how different causal attributions (e.g., ability, effort, luck) give rise to emotions such as competence, shame, and surprise. In particular, he focuses on pity, anger, and guilt as common emotions experienced by children in the classroom. Weiner illustrates how each of these reactions can have debilitating effects on achievement and learning.

Why do boys excell in scientific achievement more frequently than girls? This important academic and social question is analyzed by Martin Maehr. He rejects explanations based on educational curricula and offers instead an intriguing hypothesis about sex-related differences in achievement motivation. He focuses on the subjective definitions of achievement and the importance of personally constructed goals to distinguish how boys and girls approach courses in science. Four types of goals—ego, task, social solidarity, and extrinsic rewards—are delineated, and descriptions are provided of how each goal elicits different types of behavior. Maehr discusses the implications for gender differences in achievement and offers suggestions for improving the education of both boys and girls.

The authors of the remaining two chapters consider students developing motivational orientations to schooling. John Nicholls distinguishes between task and ego goals and concludes that ego goals often foster competition, social comparison, and failure for many children. He argues persuasively that schools should promote intrinsic standards and sustained task involvement—learning for its own sake—in order to maximize student's achievement and satisfaction. Carol Dweck and Janine Bempechat examine children's conceptions of their own abilities. They note that young children often equate ability with striving and regard their achievements as continually growing. Older children, however, separate effort and ability and regard intelligence as a fixed entity that is limited and relatively unaffected by motivation. Dweck and Bempechat discuss classroom activities that foster these developmental conceptualizations and suggest ways of influencing children's orientations to learning.

In each of these chapters readers will recognize familiar mainstays of motivational theory such as need for achievement, causal attributions, achievement goals, intrinsic motivation, and learned helplessness. What is exciting and novel is the creative way in which each author has synthesized traditional ideas with new data on developmental, cognitive, and emotional processes within educational settings. Researchers and teachers alike should find the synthesis provocative and the implications compelling for motivated classroom learning.

6 Motivated Cognitions

Martin V. Covington
University of California, Berkeley

> *Your soul is oftentimes a battlefield upon which your reason and judgment wage war against your passion and your appetite. Your reason and your passion are the rudder and the sails of your seafaring soul.*
>
> —Kahlil Gibran

The contemporary Syrian poet and philosopher, Kahlil Gibran, speaks convincingly of human behavior as a seamless process in which reason and passion act simultaneously; on occasion as antagonists, and at other times as cocreators. As human beings we are constantly caught up in the struggle for a blending and reconciliation of these factors, or at least a truce. Yet our theories of behavior rarely attend to this balancing. Indeed, motivational theorists and researchers of an information-processing persuasion seem to maintain a studious disregard for one another's accomplishments and insights. Yet to understand emotions fully in the absence of a concern for rationality is impossible, and to study both separately is insufficient. Reason and passion must be considered together. In contemporary terms this implies such questions as "How does affect drive cognitions?" and in turn, "How do rational, information-processing factors influence, channel, and mediate affect?" Certainly the call for such a rapprochement is not new. Many of the classic, general theories of an earlier day addressed the issue of motivated intellectuality. The most ambitious effort was that of Sigmund Freud, whose voluminous outpourings he himself summarized succinctly as follows: "For thought is not the slave of impulse to do its bidding. . . . What intelligence has to do in the service of impulse is to act not as its obedient servant, but as its clarifier and liberator. . . . Intelligence converts desire into plans.''

Because so much has already been written on this topic, the question of why we should say more can fairly be asked. There are two reasons. First, within the last decade new developments have occurred that deserve critical review. Specifically, some researchers within the information-processing tradition have attempted to integrate motivational concerns within a cognitive framework, with the result that motivation is relegated to the status of an epiphenomenon rather than an explanatory concept in its own right. At the same time, in a parallel but separate development, theories of human coping and defending have evolved sufficiently to allow for a more balanced, integrated treatment of motivation and cognition. Such a potential rapprochement promises more explanatory power than would otherwise be obtained by the treatment of either motivation or cognition alone or by considering motivation as simply a by-product of cognitive processes. I employ the phrase *motivated cognitions* to refer to this complex interplay in which cognition is at once the servant of motives, as Freud put it, and also the planner and clarifier. The second reason for this chapter is that the notion of motivated cognitions holds implications for instructional theory that have not yet been widely recognized, especially as it relates to classroom achievement, fear-of-failure dynamics and learned helplessness phenomena.

However, before turning to these points, it may prove useful to present a brief overview of the theoretical context in which cognition and motivation have been treated. A constructionistic view of humankind serves this purpose well (Covington, in press; Haan, 1977). This view holds that individuals create their own subjective realities and act upon them. When individuals are free to pursue legitimate developmental needs such as establishing a sense of belonging, cognitive processes act in an integrated way both as a clarifier and a servant of needs. Here constructions of reality are essentially veridical and lead to flexible, adaptive coping responses. In contrast, whenever the satisfaction of these motives is frustrated or threatened, cognitions serve a defensive, self-protective purpose. A defensive mode involves the dogmatic, rigid application of cognitive strategies and the expectation that problems can be resolved and stressful feelings banished by private, magical means without ever really confronting the issues. Although such resulting personal realities may be internally consistent, even logical and entirely self-justified, they nonetheless lead to behavior that is ultimately counterproductive.

In this dynamic context, cognitions refer to the person's *perceptions of causality*. This is the domain of attribution theory that derives from a naive theory of action first purposed by Heider (1958), and more recently formalized and extended by Kelley (1967, 1973), Weiner (1972, 1974, 1979) and others (Covington & Beery, 1976). Attribution theorists investigate attempts by individuals to make sense of their own behavior and that of others. One main research focus is on the explanations that people invoke to account for their successes and failures in achievement settings. Four kinds of explanations are primary, those relating to the individual's self-perceived ability level, effort (study) expenditure, task difficulty, and luck. Thus, for example, one student might ascribe success largely to good fortune, whereas another attributes it to personal skill and ability. These are two entirely different constructions of reality, either of which may or may not be realistic.

Rational processes take center stage in the search to create a sensible, causally consistent picture of one's world. Basic to this process is the conviction that all of us create our own purposes and determine our own fate at least in part. We may leave aside, as ultimately unprofitable, the deterministic/freewill debate by assuming with Lefcourt (1973) that it does not really matter where the truth lies, but rather what counts is the *belief* that one is in control or is being controlled. When the belief in personal efficacy is destroyed so is a major share of our humanness; when it flourishes so does creativity, flexibility, and compassion.

In this constructive schema, the concept of motivation lends a sense of purposefulness and direction to human activity. Thus cognitions are motivated in that they serve a larger goal, that of creating personal meaning for one's experiences, or as variously expressed by researchers, the need to establish and maintain a sense of personal worth (Beery, 1975; Covington & Beery, 1976); to stabilize a sense of identity (Erikson, 1950), or to achieve mastery over one's environment (deCharms, 1968; White, 1959).

One of the best laboratory-based illustrations of the exercise of logic and reason in the service of such basic human goals as achieving a sense of competency is the phenomenon of levels of aspiration (Diggory, 1966). Here individuals strive to master complex psychomotor activities such as those involved in the tossing of rings on pegs at various distances from the target. Self-evaluations of skill improvement as well as judgments about temporary successes and failures are defined in terms of the relationship between one's goals and one's actual performance. When individuals select and modify performance goals in a naturally occurring fashion, their aspirations are typically placed slightly above their present achievement levels (Gould, 1939). This dynamic imbalance draws a person toward more competent performances. Yet these expectations remain quite flexible in the short run so that by raising one's aspirations after successful performances and lowering them after disappointments, learners maintain a balance between success and failure experiences. Such flexible goal setting is known to enhance cognitive explanations for success and failure that favor continual motivational involvement. Specifically, success is attributed to skillful effort and failure to insufficient or improper effort (Ames & Felker, 1979; Weiner, 1972, 1974, 1979; Weiner & Kukla, 1970). This dynamic interplay between realistic goal setting, self-monitoring, cognitive feedback, and a growing sense of competency has been astutely described by Diggory (1966):

[The individual] . . . seldom needs anyone to tell him when he succeeds or fails because he sets his own standards of performance. At first these standards are likely to be modest, relatively easy to achieve, but he moves always towards standards more difficult to achieve. The standards he uses are quite varied and may change from one attempt to the next. Now he tries to produce a result as good as the last one, but quicker. Next, he may disregard time altogether and try to improve the product [pp. 125–126].

In this description we see the constructive side of human nature at its best with motives and reason operating in joint harness. Needless to say, however, this constructive model holds no guarantee for the eventual attainment of this or any other goal; the approach is not a recipe for success but rather a lens through which we may observe and describe the processes by which individuals approach a task in either effective or maladaptive ways. The divisive side of this process is also illustrated in the same ringtoss example by the phenomenon of the *atypical shift* (Diggory, 1966). Here people tend to raise rather than to lower self-expectations after failure. This occurs when competitive pressure is added to the achievement context. When people are placed in competition, satisfaction comes to depend not so much on bettering one's own previous performances, as in Diggory's example, but instead on doing better than others. Rewards become more scarce because a person can succeed only at the expense of others and, as a consequence, the maintenance of a sense of competency shifts away from approaching success and toward the avoidance of failure. In this context, atypical shifts are thought to be a reasonable, one might even say logical response to circumstances in which the individual cannot be expected to succeed. Here the mere statement of a worthy goal, and not its actual attainment, becomes a source of gratification. In effect, the person enters an imaginary realm where fantasies substitute for actual accomplishments.

To summarize, rationality per se is not the primary goal of behavior (except perhaps among some logicians!). Rather it is through the exercise of logic, accurate observation, and proper deductions that individuals create personal, causal realities in which they work toward the goals of competency, affiliation, and self-acceptance. Sometimes rationality prevails in this process, whereas at other times—principally where motivational goals are frustrated—strategies are adopted that allow for the superficial appearance of achievement or growth when in fact none has been made. This latter mode describes the domain of self-deception and defensiveness.

There remains one final point of definition. The difference between rationally derived perceptions of causality and defensively driven cognitions remains elusive and difficult to demonstrate empirically. For example, all too often the available evidence on defensiveness lends itself equally well to cognitive, non-motivational interpretations (for a critical review, see Miller & Ross, 1975). Although definitional and methodological issues are far from settled, we are on reasonably firm ground in assuming that defensiveness occurs whenever an individual constructs personal realities that cast the self in a better or poorer light than available external evidence warrants. However, note that this working definition does not necessarily implicate a behavior as being defensive solely because it is maladaptive. Individuals may reach false, counterproductive conclusions simply because they are not in possession of all the facts. For instance, the child who declares that trying harder will not improve his or her grades is not necessarily acting defensively, and may even be correct as far as this reasoning goes if, in fact, there has been a chronic history of personal effort/outcome noncontingency. Very likely the child is being victimized by an incomplete understanding of the difference between sheer amount of effort and the quality of one's study.

The distinction between rationality and defensiveness is further drawn by the case of developmentally immature individuals. The young child can possess the requisite, correct information, but its meaning and relevance to rational decision making may be distorted through the imperfect filter of childhood perceptions. For example, we shall soon see that primary-grade children interpret precisely the same achievement information in an opposite fashion from that of high school students. For the younger group, an achievement failure may lead to positive or at least neutral conclusions about one's competency, whereas for older individuals the same facts cause shame and denial. Here the young child is acting rationally simply because he or she doesn't know better! These examples make clear that we need to maintain a conceptual distinction between developmentally immature cognitions, logically derived yet maladaptive explanations, and defensively driven cognitions.

These general remarks set the stage for a more detailed examination of the notion of motivated cognitions. I turn first to the question of whether or not explanatory power is lost when motives are viewed only as a special case of cognitions.

Motives as Attributions

The most widely known theory of achievement motivation (Atkinson, 1957, 1964; Atkinson & Raynor, 1977) holds that achievement behavior is the result of an emotional conflict between fear of failure and hope of success. Although various facets of this model are not incompatible with a rational, information-processing interpretation—especially the concern for realistic goal setting—the main emphasis nonetheless remains on noncognitive factors including motive level, task incentive value, and dynamic conflict resolution. In what was to become a crucial test of the conceptual viability of cognitive attribution theory, Bernard Weiner and his colleagues proposed a radical reinterpretation of this traditional achievement theory (Weiner, 1972, 1974, 1977, 1979; Weiner, Frieze, Kukla, Reed, Rest, & Rosenbaum, 1971). The major elements of this revised model and the main causal pathways of presumed cognitive influence are shown in Fig. 6.1. For sake of simplicity, specific predictions for these direct and indirect paths are not presented here. Also, only those dynamics presumed to follow a failure are discussed.

In essence, this model asserted that need for achievement (nAch) is mediated by perceptions of causality that in turn influence affective reactions to failure (shame), expectancy of future success, and subsequent test performance. Thus achievement motivation, originally conceived in terms of differential emotional anticipations, became heavily imbued with cognitive elements. In this new schema, nAch was assigned a subordinate status as one of many antecedents to achievement, with cognitive attributions becoming the major causal determinants of achievement behavior. It was well known that people differing in nAch gave different explanations for the causes of their successes and failures. Individuals motivated to approach success tended to attribute failure to a lack of effort, and success to their ability, whereas failure-prone people ascribed failure to lack of ability, and success to external factors such as luck (Weiner et al., 1971; Weiner & Kukla, 1970). It was precisely these attributional differences that were taken by Weiner and his associates to be the essence of individual differences in achievement motivation. Once nAch acted to trigger differential attributions in response to success and failure, it was assumed to play no further role as a major determinant of subsequent events. At stake, then, was the basic assumption that attributions are in themselves a sufficient explanation for achievement behavior, and that we are justified in deleting the concept of need achievement from theories of achievement behavior.

Only recently have all the causal assumptions of this cognitive reinterpretation been tested simultaneously and in real-life settings. In the first of several studies,

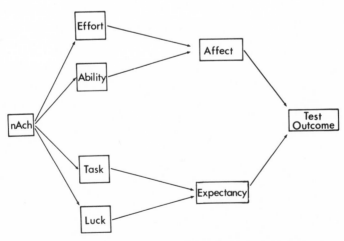

FIG. 6.1.   Cognitive attribution theory of achievement behavior.

my colleague, Carol Omelich, and I gathered data on all the crucial elements indicated in Fig. 6.1 in the context of test taking in the college classroom (1979a). After receiving feedback on a first test performance, students made attributions for initial failures, indicated degree of felt shame, and estimated the likelihood of success on a second, upcoming test. The primary method for analyzing this system of nonmanipulated variables was path analysis, a procedure that allowed for all determining factors as specified by a causal model to be incorporated into an overall predictive analysis. Our results offered little support for the cognitive model of achievement behavior. First, the kinds of causal explanations made by individuals for their failure (e.g., "not enough effort") accounted for little of the subsequent variation either in shame reactions, in expectancies for future success, or in later retest performance. Second, nAch status emerged as an important causal influence on all these variables in its own right, independent of cognitions. Of special significance here was the fact that the deletion of all attributional sources from the path analysis did not reduce appreciably the amount of explained variance in retest performances beyond that already accounted for by the classic elements of Atkinson's original motivation-based model. The assumption of the centrality of retrospective attributions has fared little better in other evaluation studies (Bernstein, Stephan, & Davis, 1979; Covington & Omelich, 1981b; Latta, 1976).

Thus it appears that we are not justified in deleting motivational constructs from our theories of achievement behavior. Are we then to assume that cognitive, attributional processes play no part in achievement dynamics? Certainly not. The more proper conclusion to be drawn here is that rational, cognitive determinants of achievement behavior were obscured in the full cognitive model as originally proposed. This is because attributions expressed retrospectively are more likely to be reactions to rather than causes of behavior. We know that in the case of retrospective reactions to failure, attributions are prone to reflect defensive, self-serving biases (Covington & Omelich, 1978; Miller, 1976; Snyder, Stephan, & Rosenfield, 1976; Stephan, Rosenfield, & Stephan, 1976) and thereby obscure their causal role as information-processing determinants of subsequent achievement behavior. An experiment by Weiner and Sierad (1975) illustrates how the introduction of self-serving excuses confound usual cognitive predictions. A drug (placebo) alleged to interfere with hand–eye coordination was administered to college students of high and low nAch prior to a learning task. Armed with an explanation for potentially poor performance other than inability, low nAch subjects were expected to perform better than usual, whereas high nAch subjects were expected to perform more poorly than usual owing to the presumed interference of the drug with ability. These predictions were born out. The authors correctly concluded that the experiment demonstrated the causal influence of cognitions on performance. But it illustrates something else as well. The presence of excuses, a factor overlooked by both traditional and cognitive theories of motivation, acted to confound the usual attributional linkages. A number of other similar so-called "misattribution" studies also illustrate this same point (Davison & Valins, 1969; Nisbett & Schachter, 1966).

If retrospective cognitions are beclouded by defensiveness, then relocating them as antecedent determinants might increase their causal impact on behavior to the extent that a predictive mode introduces elements of realistic appraisal not present retrospectively. To test this logic, Omelich and I (1981b) gathered additional data from our college samples described earlier in accordance with Heider's original model of causal action in which ability and effort variables ("can" and "try" in his terms) were considered antecedent determinants of behavior. The procedures and methodology were essentially identical to those we employed to test Weiner's model, with the exception that attributions were gathered in the form of predictive rather than retrospective elements. A path-analytic treatment of Heider's antecedent model revealed that 25% of the variance in subsequent test performance was accounted for by all predictor variables whereas in Weiner's retrospective model only 14% was explained. Moreover, *ability* when couched in an antecedent role ("How do you rate your ability to do well?") accounted for 83% of this greater proportion of explained variance whereas ability measured in a retrospective mode ("To what extent was your failure due to a lack of skill and ability?") accounted for only 4% of the variance in the original study.

Based on the evidence reviewed here, I conclude that it is counterproductive to view achievement behavior solely in terms of cognitions. Basically, cognitions appear to be influenced by the very motivational factors they have been invoked to explain. The stage has also been set for a more detailed consideration of the nature of these motivational states, and precisely how they gain expression through altered perceptions of causality. I have also anticipated a distinction that takes on considerable importance later when we turn to the instructional implications of motivated cognitions: the difference between attributions, such as effort and ability, as antecedent resources to be managed by individuals, and attributions as retrospective, defensively oriented explanations for one's behavior.

Motivated Cognitions

If both motivational and cognitive factors are important and their interaction influences achievement behavior in ways not predicted by either alone, how should we proceed to better understand these complexities? One possible answer lies in the direction implied by Weiner's (1977) perceptive observation that research should seek: "to specify the conditions under which individuals avoid feedback and information as a self-protecting, coping strategy [p. 8]". A recent formulation of achievement motivation, the *self-worth* theory (Beery, 1975; Covington & Beery, 1976), has sought to create a rapprochement between fear of failure dynamics, defensive motivation, and cognitive attribution theory. A major objective has been to investigate the conditions under which rational, coping mechanisms are subjected to distortion, to explore how such defensive processes are themselves limited by rational considerations, and to determine what makes failure experiences so devastating as to elicit broad defensive maneuvering. In this section I consider answers to these questions.

Our conclusions regarding the nature of the fear-evoking potential of achievement failure is not novel to self-worth theory. Actually, it is a point of common agreement among most students of the problem (see especially, Birney, Burdick, & Teevan, 1969). Briefly, failure evokes suspicions of inability. Given the pervasive tendency in our society to equate the ability to achieve with human value, one can readily see why failure or at least the implication of failure—that one lacks ability—is so actively avoided. Failure creates feelings of unworthiness and self-rejection. If one accepts the premise that human beings strive to create and maintain a sense of competency (Epstein, 1973), then failure is certainly sufficient cause for defensiveness. A truly remarkable variety of defensive techniques for avoiding failure, its implications, and subsequent negative affect have been investigated, ranging from cheating to setting one's academic goals to low as to comprise no risk at all. Although such tactics may gain the individual a short-term respite, they do not deal with the real issue and hence cannot sustain a sense of positive self-regard over the long term. For example, in the case of minimal goal setting, successes achieved at little or no risk of failure have negligible self-reinforcing value. Likewise, cheaters find little comfort in their ill-gotten gains because they know they cannot repeat such successes (Shelton & Hill, 1969). Whenever failure seems inevitable, still other self-serving tactics allow the individual to avoid the implications of failure. For instance, students may strive for unattainable goals that literally invite failure, but "failure with honor." Because so few are expected to succeed against these odds, such failure does not necessarily imply low ability.

Our research indicates that student effort is a central element in this defensive, self-serving drama. On the one hand, a combination of high effort/failure leads to suspicions of incompetency (Covington & Omelich, 1979b; Kun, 1977; Kun & Weiner, 1973), whereas, on the other hand, not trying minimizes information about one's ability in the face of failure. In attributional terms, inaction is an instance of Kelley's "discounting principle" (1967, 1973). A given cause of failure (e.g., low ability) is discounted and left vague and uncertain if other more plausible reasons (e.g., low effort) are available. However, the realities of classroom life make untenable such crude and obvious tactics as simply not trying. Teachers value effort; they reward success more and punish failure less when the student has tried hard (Rest, Nierenberg, Weiner, & Heckhausen, 1973; Weiner, 1972; Weiner & Kukla, 1970). Thus many students must thread their way between the threatening extremes of high effort and no effort at all. It is for this reason that effort has been characterized as a 'double-edged sword' (Covington & Omelich, 1979b). Excuses chiefly in the form of rationalizations and other forms of denial are the student's basic ally in achieving this precarious balance.

Attributionally, excuses function to externalize blame for failure away from the internal, stable element of ability.

One of our experiments (Covington & Omelich, 1979b) provides direct evidence on each of the major points made so far concerning: (1) the central role of ability demotion in triggering shame and a loss of self-esteem; (2) the conflict of teacher/student values over effort and ability; and (3) the self-serving benefits of excuses. College students were asked to estimate the ability level of hypothetical other students and to introspect their affective reactions to each of four test failures: little effort without excuse (E^-); little effort with excuse (E^-/x); high effort without excuse (E^+); and high effort with an excuse (E^+/x). The excuse accompanying high effort was that the instructor emphasized material on the test different from that studied by the student; little effort in failure was justified by reason of illness. The results of this study are presented in Fig. 6.2.

Students experienced the greatest loss of esteem under conditions of high effort and the least under low effort conditions. Additionally, shame was reduced when excuses were available to explain their inaction or why effort did not help. Degree of ability demotion was correlated with variations in shame reactions, thereby supporting our central argument that attributions to inability elicit the shame associated with failure. Stronger evidence of causality came from an analysis of the regression of affective ratings (shame) on ability estimates. This involved a path-analytic test of a two-variable causal model. The results indicated a substantial dependency of affect on estimates of ability (cognitions). Thus shame appears to follow from perceiving oneself as incompetent, and evidence of incompetency in turn depends on the conditions of failure, primarily effort level and the presence or absence of excuses.

The importance of the availability of excuses in this dynamic was recently demonstrated in an actual classroom context that featured a mastery learning paradigm (Covington & Omelich, 1981a). Students were allowed to take several parallel forms of a test with study interspersed until they reached their personal goals for grades. Students who repeatedly failed to achieve their grade aspirations experienced a crisis of defenses because externalizing excuses such as bad luck or not enough effort became less and less plausible as failure mounted. As a consequence, low ability explanations became, in Kelley's terms (1971, 1973), a "sufficient" reason for failure, which in turn triggered increasing shame and decreased estimates of the likelihood of future success.

Returning to the experiment portrayed in Fig. 6.2, we also asked our subjects to adopt the role of teachers and punish hypothetical students under the same four conditions of failure already described. These data were entirely consistent with previous findings regarding teacher punishment (Weiner, 1972, 1974). Teachers punished diligent students less than those who did not try. Effort was critical for students, too, but as we have seen in a different way. This incompatibility is best demonstrated by considering the superimposition of data for teacher punishment on that for students' self-estimates of ability and their affective reactions to

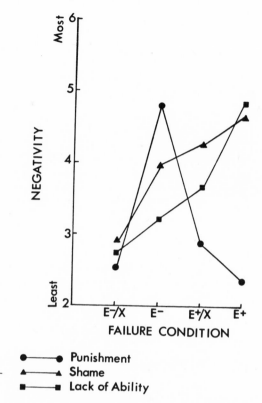

FIG. 6.2.   Student and teacher reactions to failure.

● ——— ● Punishment
▲ ——— ▲ Shame
■ ——— ■ Lack of Ability

failure. The implications of these juxtapositions are clear. The incompatibility of student and teacher reactions was most striking under conditions of failure with high effort (E^+). Although teachers punished students least under these circumstances, students felt most incompetent and experienced the greatest degree of personal dissatisfaction and shame. In contrast, although low effort (E^-) substantially reduced student discomfort, it did so at the cost of a considerable increase in teacher punishment. The data also suggested that excuses operated to maintain a balance between trying and not trying. For example, in Fig. 6.2 we see that teachers made allowance for low effort if the student had a plausible explanation for why he or she did not study (E^-/x). Without an excuse the same low effort was severely punished. At the same time, excuses acted to reduce student shame and feelings of worthlessness regardless of effort level. From this series of studies we can piece together the elements of a "safe strategy for students when risking failure designed to minimize teacher punishment and reduce, at least temporarily, the shame and humiliation that accompanies failure: Try, or at least appear to try, but not too energetically and with excuses always handy!

It must not be assumed, however, that individuals act only in a self-serving, opportunistic manner without concern for rational considerations even when they are threatened. Self-enhancing and self-denigrating tendencies are moderated, but by what mechanisms? A partial answer is suggested by the results of the previously cited experiment (Covington & Omelich, 1981a), in which students experienced repeated test failure under a mastery learning paradigm. In that study excuses were effective in sustaining a self-view of competency only while explanations remained plausible, or as Heider has put it (1958), only as long as they "fit the constraints of reason." This observation led us to construct a direct test of the conditions under which individuals create personal realities that either accurately reflect external circumstances or that encourage self-serving distortions (Covington & Omelich, 1978). We hypothesized that self-serving tendencies should prevail as long as the achievement situation is sufficiently ambiguous to permit multiple explanations for one's failure. Conversely, self-aggrandizing tendencies should be suspended temporarily when no plausible alternative explanations to low ability are available. The previously described excuse/effort conditions provided us with a convenient paradigm by which to test these assertions. Defensiveness was defined as the degree to which individuals attribute lower levels of ability to others than to themselves under identical circumstances of failure, a tendency referred to as *egotism* (Snyder et al., 1976). College students estimated their own level of ability and that of other hypothetical students under each of four combinations of failure. In an additional rating, the same students also estimated the extent to which they expected others to agree with their own self-perceptions of ability. This latter rating provided a measure of what Jones and Nisbett (1971) call *egocentricity,* after a similar use of the term by Heider (1958). This concept refers to the fact that success in maintaining an inflated view of one's ability depends on the expectation that others will also agree. If the person suspects that others do not share the same view, then doubts about one's credibility will likely arise, forcing a readjustment in egotistic tendencies.

Interestingly, the degree of egotism exhibited in this study depended on the sex of the subject and on the level of self-confidence of ability. Among males, both high and low in self-confidence, and for high self-confident females as well, egotistic tendencies emerged strongly in the three achievement circumstances where ability estimates remained vague and uncertain owing to plausible alternative explanations (i.e., E^-; E^-/x; E^+/x). In these situations self-deception was complete. These subjects also believed that others accepted their inflated self-image. In the fourth condition (E^+), where low ability is a sufficient and unambiguous explanation for failure, egotism did not occur for any of these three groups. Moreover, the absolute levels of ability self-estimates were depressed, and the subjects perceived others as being in substantial agreement with their own pessimistic judgments. This inhibition of egotism must be powerful, indeed, if we are to judge by its absence in males who by all accounts are particularly prone to defensiveness owing to societal pressures on them to maintain an image of competency (Snyder et al., 1976; Stephan et al., 1976; Streufert & Streufert, 1969; Wolosin, Sherman, & Till, 1973). Such pressure probably explains why even the low self-confident males aggrandized their ability whenever possible. In contrast, females low in self-confidence of ability acted in a manner entirely contrary to their male counterparts. These women underestimated their ability relative to others in *all* circumstances of failure and believed that others agreed with this negative appraisal. These women had apparently given up the struggle to maintain a positive self-image, and as a consequence denigrated their ability beyond what was rationally indicated by the information at hand.

Developmental Cognitions

Not only are self-serving tendencies moderated by rational considerations, but the relationship between cognitive and motivational elements has a developmental history as well. When Weiner's cognitive reinterpretation of achievement motivation was first proposed (Weiner, 1972, 1974), it was concluded that students would eventually internalize teacher reinforcement patterns and come to experience shame (self-punishment) for not trying hard. This is a reasonable expectation if one assumes, as was done at the time, that motivationlike states are synonymous with cognitions. But as has since been demonstrated, increased student effort is associated with more, not less shame (Covington & Omelich, 1979b; Covington, Spratt, & Omelich, 1980). This makes little sense until one recognizes the presence of motivational dynamics that override strictly cognitive considerations. It is now clear that the effort/affect linkage is an indirect one, mediated largely by attributions to inability that are subject to a variety of noncognitive influences. Interestingly, however, Weiner's original prediction concerning internalization has proven essentially correct in the case of young children. There is now considerable evidence that youngsters do internalize adult values (Brophy, 1977), and therefore should come to value effort. Yet it is also clear that for older people the preferred mode of achievement is via ability not effort (Covington & Omelich, 1979b, 1979c; Nicholls, 1976). Is it possible that young children attribute a different meaning to effort expenditure than do adults? To explore this possibility Oren Harari and I (Harari & Covington, 1981) conducted a developmental study employing a now familiar paradigm. Students from the first grade through the college level were asked to evaluate the achievement behavior of hypothetical students varying in effort expenditure, ability, and test outcome. All subjects evaluated the performance of each hypothetical pupil from the perspective of a teacher (pleased/displeased) and also judged the personal desirability of the same performances in their real-life role as students (preferred/not preferred). Finally, in a separate procedure all subjects estimated the ability level of yet other hypothetical students when furnished only with information about their effort level (high or low) and test outcome (good or poor).

Perceptions of teacher values were consistent over the entire age range investigated. For all age groups, effort and outcome were seen as highly salient cues for determining teacher reward and punishment with student ability level of little importance. In contrast to its minor role in determining teacher behavior, among students ability was highly valued at all age levels. Effort was also strongly valued, but only among younger students, a finding consistent with that of other investigators (Dweck, this volume; Nicholls, this volume). Changes in the direction of effort valuation occurred at the junior high school level, such that by high school and college a devaluation of effort had occurred. Apparently our younger students experienced none of the conflict regarding effort expenditure felt by the older students even though all groups valued ability equally. Why should this be? The puzzle was resolved by considering the data gathered on estimated ability level. Effort expenditure implied different levels of ability depending on age (Also see Dweck, this volume). Younger children perceived high effort as indicative of, if not synonymous with high ability. This occurred for two reasons. First, effort was considered a virtually infallible predictor of ability (first-grade student: "Smart people study; dumb ones don't."). Second, our young subjects repeatedly expressed the conviction that studying actually causes ability (second-grade student: "If you study, it helps the brain and you get smarter."). Thus for these youngsters there was no teacher/student conflict of values. By embracing effort they perceived themselves as *able* and *virtuous*, too, by reason of trying. However, in time this positive dependency on effort expenditure disappeared and was replaced by a view of ability as a stable entity, quite impervious to effort variations. Among older students, hard work was no longer seen as a guarantee of success. Instead, ability became a necessary condition for achievement, and in the view of some high school students, even a sufficient condition. By the high school years the inverse–compensatory relationship between ability and effort ascriptions was well established. Moreover, the self-serving aspects of effort variation were also quite apparent. Low effort in success was seen as assuring a reputation for brilliance while obscuring the causes of failure, should it occur. As we shall now see, this developmental divergence between ability and effort valuation is critical to instructional strategies.

The logic of a strict cognitive position argues for a restoration and/or strengthening of various attributional linkages in the teaching/learning process. This line of reasoning is best examplified by the classic attributional analysis of the phenomenon of learned helplessness. Learned helplessness has been described as a state of depression or loss of hope arising from a realization that the individual's responses are ineffectual in obtaining reinforcement (Abramson, Seligman, & Teasdale, 1978). In effect, demoralization is thought to follow from the fact that, try as one might, success continues to elude the individual. In order to demonstrate the importance of such a noncontingency mechanism, attribution theorists have manipulated experimentally the effort/outcome linkage. The result has been a series of attributional retraining experiments in which "motivationally deficient" youngsters were given repeated practice in verbalizing positive, uplifting interpretations of their failures typical of the explanations used by high nAch individuals. For example, Andrews and Debus (1978) administered insoluble laboratory tasks to first-grade students. Following failure the students were encouraged to attribute lack of success to insufficient effort and to verbalize this conclusion in their own words. Quite apart from theoretical implications, the results of this experiment and of other similar studies (Dweck, 1975; Dweck & Reppucci, 1973) are quite remarkable in their significance for educational practice. This simple treatment led to considerable improvements in the emotional reactions of helpless children to failure and to performances gains on achievement tasks quite different from those used in retraining.

Our previously cited study regarding the meaning of effort ascriptions among students of various ages (Harari & Covington, 1981) makes clear why these interventions are so effective despite their brevity and apparent artificiality. Among young populations, where the bulk of attribution-retraining research is concentrated, effort expenditure is self-reinforcing. Not only is trying hard consistent with adult values, but it is also associated in the child's mind with increasing skills and abilities. However, among older children, as we have seen, important changes occur in the valuation of effort. From this perspective, we can see how inappropriate an unqualified emphasis on effort may be whenever a combination of high effort/failure implies low ability to the learner. In such a circumstance, ironically, effort expenditure likely contributes to the very distress and demoralization that cognitive retraining is intended to overcome. Incidentally, our ability-focused interpretation of learned helplessness resolves an apparent contradiction within the cognitive paradigm (Abramson & Sackeim, 1977; Blaney, 1977; Rizley, 1978). These investigators wonder how it can be that individuals show despair at an event (failure) over which they believe they have no control. We now know that despair results not so much from unrewarded effort expenditure (noncontingency) as from a personal realization that low ability is the major cause of failure (Covington & Omelich, 1981a).

I do not intend to suggest that the attribution model is wholly inappropriate as an intervention paradigm. I only wish to argue that the model must accommodate additional realities, chiefly that inadequate effort/outcome linkages may be driven motivationally and are not simply the result of insufficient positive reinforcement or of developmental limitations. Two specific aspects of this reality involve: (1) the threat posed by success for some students; and (2) the quality of effort expenditure as contrasted to sheer amount of effort.

First, success does not automatically lead to an increased willingness to strive; quite to the contrary. Individuals of low self-esteem often reject success because they believe they will be obliged to repeat successful performances in the future, but feel that they cannot (Mettee, 1971). This lack of confidence is reflected in the tendency to ascribe success to external elements such as good luck or to the presumed benevolence of a teacher. Until the student is able to accept successes as caused by his or her own skilled effort, success will have little self-reinforcing value. Thus providing success per se is not sufficient to correct attributional deficiencies, and even worse may jeopardize the teacher's credibility because individuals often view their evaluators as untrustworthy if they feel the appraiser has been inaccurate (Gergen, 1971).

Second, it is probable that the critical difference between high and low nAch individuals lies in the quality of their effort expenditure. Research indicates that many low-achieving students actually persist longer in their studies than do high achievers (Goldman, Hudson, & Daharsh, 1973), but that additional effort may not pay off for these low achievers because nagging doubts about their ability interfere with their work (Wine, 1973). Yet despite such evidence, attribution theorists have until quite recently focused exclusively on effort level as the critical factor in motivational deficiency. Although, admittedly, the attribution-retaining studies cited previously were designed as demonstrations of the causal influence of cognitions on behavior and not as model instructional programs, their uniform stress on effort per se has caused some observers to conclude that such laboratory paradigms may be translated directly into classroom practice. If, as we have demonstrated, effort poses an increasing threat to the developing student, then perhaps less negative affect would be aroused by focusing on the *quality* of one's effort—its timing and appropriateness.

Attributions as Personal Resources

What seems called for is a reconceptualization of the instructional enterprise for the remediation of motivational deficiencies. I propose relocating cognitive attributions as antecedents of achievement behavior contrasted to their typical role as retrospective explanations for success and failure. We have already considered the confounding, defensive aspect of postdictive attributions and, as a consequence, their insufficiency as predictors of subsequent achievement behavior. Conversely, we have seen how attributions recast as antecedent resources account for considerable individual variation in achievement behavior. This is not to imply that the treatment of attributions as resources is bias-free. Self-serving explanations after the fact of, say, failure will undoubtedly precipitate further maneuvering when the individual once again confronts the same or a similar task. The point is, however, that despite the presence of self-serving bias, assessments made in a predictive mode will likely favor rational considerations to a greater degree than might otherwise occur. It is this element of realism that must be cultivated by the teacher.

I have spoken elsewhere of the management of personal and situational resources to achieve a desired goal as the capacity for *strategic thinking* (Covington, 1982). Such thinking involves formulating a problem or task in workable terms, establishing work priorities, and the capacity to alter tactics as unexpected obstacles or new information change the character of the task itself. In the present context of school achievement, strategic thinking involves the self-conscious planning, organizing, and orchestration of one's personal resources such as ability. Central here is a realistic recognition of one's strengths and limitations, and of the *time* and *energy* needed relative to both task demands and to one's own grade–goal aspirations. Students require instruction in developing a metacognitively sophisticated view of the factors that enter into successful achievement, how such factors interact, and how to offset deficiencies in one resource by the compensatory application of others (Brown & DeLoache, 1978; Flavell & Wellman, 1977).

Our understanding of such strategic self-management will be aided by an important distinction not sufficiently appreciated and frequently confused in the attribution literature. It involves the difference between attributions as *levels* and as *sources*. Attributional levels refers to the amount or degree of resources available to an individual for problem solving, such as the extent of one's ability or time available to study. In contrast, sources refers to the requirements for success at a given task. For example, assuming that outstanding ability is a key causal ingredient in success at solving a particular problem, does the person possess sufficient capacity to match the demands? This distinction between sources and levels and its significance is best conveyed by example. Tom has three tests in 2 days. Tom is bright and therefore will probably do reasonably well. But because Tom wants a straight ''A'' average he must divide his study time judiciously. To complicate things, Tom can devote only a few hours to his studies owing to the fact that he promised to substitute for a friend on his paper route. Tom's classmate, Richard, is less bright and struggles even for modest grades. Richard's math teacher is willing to give him a makeup test and has agreed to go over Richard's old test (that earned a failing grade) and explain the concepts once again. Richard is determined to do better this time and is free to study as much as necessary.

Thus an analysis of causal sources focuses on the question of what makes the task a problem in the first place. Such judgments involve task analysis and problem formulation: estimating the relative importance to success of various resources and gauging the severity of situational constraints to be overcome.

A level analysis concerns the degree of personal resources available to a person. For example, Tom has sufficient ability to cope successfully; what makes the task potentially difficult for him is insufficient time to study. For Richard, the culprit is low ability. But, most important, Richard is willing to study hard and by doing so will likely offset the usual causal contribution to success of one resource, namely ability, by increasing the level of another resource, effort.

This compensatory process lies at the heart of strategic self-management. Indeed, the key to successful management involves altering problem states so that a reasonable match is created between task difficulty and sufficiency of one's resources. In the simplest case, this may mean only studying a little more or in a different way so that, in effect, a difficult task is made easier. A proper match between resources and demands has long been known to be an essential ingredient in sustaining motivation. This point is well illustrated in an experiment by Woodson (1975), who created varying degrees of match and mismatch between student ability level and severity of performance standards required. Students who enjoyed a close match (e.g., high ability/demanding task) learned the most, and this was true at all ability levels. In contrast, a mismatch (e.g., low ability/difficult task) disrupted learning at all ability levels. This occurred because the less able students from whom much was demanded became demoralized, whereas able students who competed against easy standards became bored.

Naturally, levels and sources are not strictly independent constructs, and some circularity of definition is inevitable. For example, ultimately, one's ability can be defined only in terms of the kinds of tasks that can be mastered. However, in the ordinary course of daily events, individuals typically act and think in terms of an essential orthogonality of these factors, and it is at this level of a naive theory of action that the teacher must work.

As was mentioned earlier, the shift in emphasis on attributions from postdictive explanations (excuses) to antecedent resources and task demands represents a reaffirmation of Heider's original position. Yet to be of any real consequence, pedagogically, Heider's schema must be expanded to reflect the true complexities of the achievement dynamic. For one thing, other dimensions besides the classic sources of ability, task difficulty, effort and luck must be considered. A clear candidate is the factor of *time*, which represents both a personal resource to be managed and frequently an external constraint on the problem-solving process. Moreover, elaborations of already familiar factors must be undertaken. For example, effort involves more than sheer amount of study. It also involves, as already noted, the quality of such preparation. One or two examples will illustrate the variety of fruitful directions in which the effort dimension can be expanded. Consider the matter of the relevance of one's effort. The most effective recall of material occurs when learners correctly anticipate the form in which the information will later be needed and then rehearse it accordingly (Postman, 1975; Tulving & Thomson, 1973). I have found (Covington, 1980) that poor learners tend to rehearse information as a collection of isolated events, a strategy that may be sufficient for answering rote-type test items, but insufficient for the demands of the productive use of these facts. Another important consideration in the effective use of study time concerns the need for continual self-monitoring. Learners must periodically reassess whether or not what they now know is sufficient to the task at hand, and what yet remains to be learned in the time available (Brown, 1978; Markham, 1982). Without such vigilance, counterproductive distributions of learning time may occur with some material being overrehearsed to the relative neglect of other aspects of an assignment.

Another monolithic construct, that of ability, is also slowly giving way to a series of important differentiations. Perhaps the most critical development is the deemphasis on ability as a strictly psychometric concept with its traditional assumption of a stable, global, and immutable attribute. There is growing recognition of ability as a process that is by no means completely fixed or unchanging. Behind this trend lies a broad common agreement among contemporary cognitive psychologists that basic abilities are transformed into effective thought and action via intervening mediators in the form of knowledge acquisition strategies, learning-to-learn heuristics, and metacognitive skills such as question asking and problem identification (Perkins, 1982; Sternberg, 1982). Such plans, heuristics, and rules typically operate at an unconscious level during the problem-solving act, but can be made explicit and hence modifiable through direct skill training (Covington, Crutchfield, Davies, & Olton, 1974; Olton & Crutchfield, 1969). Such developments augur well for the notion of ability management.

Considerable motivational advantages derive from such a strategic, self-management approach to achievement. These benefits basically follow from an increased sense of personal control over one's learning. First, the task-analysis component discourages improper effort and focuses attention on the true obstacles of learning—the current limitations of the individual and the complexities of the task. Moreover, by altering task difficulty through compensatory actions, the individual can increase the odds for success without necessarily lowering his or her aspirations. Second, even in the wake of high effort, other interpretations of failure are now possible besides an automatic assumption of low ability: one's aspirations may have been set too high; a task may have been improperly analyzed; or the individual may have given up too soon. Such alternative explanations are not meant to evade recognition of the fact that we are constantly testing the limits of our ability and skills, but rather that we must focus equally on factors that are within our power to correct and overcome. In sum, proper task analysis and goal-setting reinforces a causal relationship between effort and outcome despite the intervening ability linkage. Third, regarding the tendency among some students to deny their successes, I have argued that the source of threat is their belief that they cannot reproduce their triumphs. But if students can bring their achievements under control through a combination of realistic goal setting, task analysis, and proper effort, then success *is* repeatable. Under these circumstances we can hope that students will not only accept credit for their accomplishment but will also express optimism about their chances for future success as well.

Assuming the benefits of skillful resource management, what do we know about the development of the individual's conception of attributions as resources? When does the child begin to appreciate the reciprocal, compensatory relationships among the various elements of the achievement matrix and when can the young child begin to act on such knowledge? At present few direct answers are available, although some speculation seems warranted. For instance, because effort is a major perceived cause of achievement success from an early age (Harari & Covington, 1981), trying harder is likely to be viewed as the main prescription for success management, and only in time will the unquestioned utility of effort be qualified by other factors such as ability level and task difficulty. As to the compensatory nature of achievement dynamics, it also seems clear that a fairly high degree of metacognitive sophistication must exist before individuals can invoke the kinds of defensively oriented explanations for failure documented earlier. For example, the self-serving tendency to underestimate study time following failure (Covington & Beery, 1976) implies a working knowledge of the inverse effort/ability schema. This relationship seems well in place for most children by the end of elementary school (Harari & Covington, 1981), a developmental finding also confirmed in the case of the child's view of the reciprocity between task difficulty and levels of ability needed to succeed (Nicholls, 1978, 1980).

In the most complete analysis of these questions to date, Alan Schnur, Carol Omelich, and I (Schnur, 1981) have shown that by the time children reach early adolescence (e.g., 12–14 years), they are generally as adept as adults at recognizing the causal importance of various resources and their compensatory interactions. We asked junior high students and their teachers to estimate the degree of success they believed hypothetical pupils would enjoy on a school test given various combinations of achievement factors. Not surprisingly teachers and students associated success with high ability, an easy task, high effort, and sufficient time to study. Effort and ability were by far the most salient cues for sucess in both groups with effort the more important, especially among students. This preoccupation with the "try" component of Heider's system among children was consistent with a previously demonstrated upsurge in work-ethic morality toward the end of the elementary school years (Harari & Covington, 1981; Weiner & Peter, 1973). Compensatory schemata are also well established by this age. Students, like teachers, perceived that the negative influences of low ability on performance can be partially offset by additional effort. As to the critical compensatory linkage between effort and task difficulty, students also appreciated the need for increasing effort in order to maintain a constant performance level as the task became more difficult.

From these data we concluded that young adolescents possess sufficient abstract capabilities to predict the results of compensatory achievement behavior, perhaps akin to Piaget's equilibrium balance task in the area of physical causality, where the same result can be achieved by different combinations of weight and distance of weight from a fulcrum (Piaget, 1950). Unfortunately, however, such metacognitive sophistication may reside only at an abstract level and in a recognition mode. When we asked these same youngsters to suggest ways that the hypothetical achievers might improve their chances of doing better on the test, the vast majority admonished pupils simply to work harder, even in those scenarios where effort level was already high. Moreover, there was little evidence that these children understood *how best* to work harder nor did they appear to possess a sense of the strategic possibilities for monitoring and controlling their effort.

The need for instruction in the strategic management of achievement resources is clearly apparent from these data. With this observation, I am reminded once again of the fully balanced interplay of motives and cognitions as lyrically described by Kahlil Gibran. Not only do motives and cognitions interact—the one driving and the other moderating behavior—but at yet another level, that of practical utility, we see that in order to overcome various motivational deficiencies, cognitive skill training is imperative.

Conclusions

In summary, I have argued that all cognitive activities—remembering, reasoning, and decision making—serve a larger, directed purpose and as such they are motivated. When legitimate human needs are being met, cognitions are the clarifier and servant of motives, and the handmaiden of further growth. Actually, under such positive, uplifting circumstances there is little need to invoke the explanatory concept of motivation, as the predictions and expectations of both cognitive and motivation theories are essentially identical at this point. However, cognitive theory alone cannot account adequately for those situations in which behavior defies strictly rational considerations. Indeed, cognitive theory is largely silent on the point of contrary, imprudent, and inconsistent behavior. It is when basic human motives are frustrated that cognitive organizations emerge that trade on excuses, fabrication, and denial, all wrapped in a cloak of credibility.

The practical implications of this subtle interplay between cognitions and affect revolve largely around the ability of teachers to detect the differences between developmentally immature cognitions, logically derived yet maladaptive cognitions, and cognitions that are defensively driven. To the extent that cognitions are defensive, we must first seek to identify the underlying pressures that initially trigger distortions and then build our curricula in response to these causes before cognitive skill training or remediation can hope to be effective.

Finally, it seems appropriate to wonder just how much more effective instructional strategies can be that start from the constructionistic premise of motivated cognitions rather than from a strictly cognitive view. At one level, at least, that of measuring benefits in terms of specific curricular objectives, there is reason to be optimistic. Surely the more we come to know about the processes of learning, coping, and adaptation, the better and more efficiently we can teach. But when we ask this question from the perspective of learning gains possible from all sources—curricular and otherwise—the verdict is decidedly less favorable. Simply put, improvements in instructional techniques can make only so much difference. The larger reality is that some of the most influential factors for student change lay outside the domain of curriculum and instruction as traditionally defined. For example, in the case of achievement deficiencies, the root problem is not the threatening nature of effort, although as an important consequence of the basic cause it must be dealt with. Rather the fundamental problem is that the individual defines his or her worth in terms of the ability to achieve competitively. To the extent that the evaluation process in schools promotes a scarcity of valued rewards and drives some children into self-defeating adjustment strategies, the problem remains. Even improved self-management skills are unlikely to offset fully the potentially devastating impact of realizing that one's own particular "strengths" are no greater than the "weaknesses" exhibited by some other students. Indeed, the very heart of an improved capacity for self-management is an increased, not a decreased sensitivity to the limits of one's personal resources. Gardner (1961) framed the larger problem of achievement deficiencies best when he asked: "How can we provide opportunities and rewards for individuals of every degree of ability so that individuals at every level will realize their full potentialities, perform at their best and harbor no resentment toward any other level? [p. 115]." Stated this way, the problem of achievement motivation transcends the traditional domains of instruction and curricular technology and calls for broad changes in society's view of the nature and mission of schools.

REFERENCES

Abramson, L. Y., & Sacheim, H. A. A paradox in depression: Uncontrollability and self-blame. *Psychological Bulletin*, 1977, *84*, 838–851.

Abramson, L. Y., Seligman, M. E. P., & Teasdale, J. D. Learned helplessness in humans: Critique and reformulation. *Journal of Abnormal Psychology*, 1978, *87*, 49–74.

Ames, C., & Felker, D. W. Effects of self-concept on children's causal attributions and self-reinforcement. *Journal of Educational Psychology*, 1979, *71*, 613–619.

Andrews, G. R., & Debus, R. L. Persistence and the causal perception of failure: Modifying cognitive attribution. *Journal of Educational Psychology*, 1978, *70*, 154–166.

Atkinson, J. W. Motivational determinants of risk-taking behavior. *Psychological Review*, 1957, *64*, 359–372.

Atkinson, J. W. *An introduction to motivation*. Princeton, N.J.: D. Van Nostrand Co., Inc., 1964.

Atkinson, J. W., & Raynor, J. D. *Personality, motivation and achievement*. New York: Hemisphere, 1977.

Beery, R. Fear of failure in the student experience. *Personnel and Guidance Journal*, 1975, *54*, 190–203.

Bernstein, W. M., Stephan, W. G., & Davis, M. H. Explaining attributions for achievement: A path analytic approach. *Journal of Personality and Social Psychology*, 1979, *37*, 1810–1821.

Birney, R. C., Burdick, H., & Teevan, R. *Fear of failure*. New York: Van Nostrand–Reinhold, 1969.

Blaney, P. H. Contemporary theories of depression: Critique and comparison. *Journal of Abnormal Psychology*, 1977, *86*, 203–223.

Brophy, J. *Child development and socialization*. Chicago: Science Research Associates, 1977.

Brown, A. L. Knowing when, where, and how to remember: A problem of metacognition. In R. Glaser (Ed.), *Advances in instructional psychology.* Hillsdale, N.J.: Lawrence Erlbaum Associates, 1978.

Brown, A. L., & DeLoache, J. S. Skills, plans and self-regulation. In R. Siegler (Ed.), *Children's thinking: What develops?* Hillsdale, N.J.: Lawrence Erlbaum Associates, 1978.

Covington, M. V. *Do slow learners deserve high grades? An analysis of individual differences in mastery learning.* Unpublished manuscript, Department of Psychology, University of California, Berkeley, 1980.

Covington, M. V. Strategic thinking and the fear of failure. In J. Segal, S. Chipman, & R. Glaser (Eds.), *Thinking and learning skills: Relating instruction to basic research.* Hillsdale, N.J.: Lawrence Earlbaum Associates, 1982.

Covington, M. W. Motivation for self-worth. In R. Ames & C. Ames (Eds.), *Research on motivation in education.* New York: Academic Press, Inc., in press.

Covington, M. V., & Beery, R. *Self-worth and school learning.* New York: Holt, Reinhart, & Winston, 1976.

Covington, M. V., Crutchfield, R. S., Davies, L. B., & Olton, R. M. *The productive thinking program: A course in learning to think.* Columbus, Ohio: Merrill, 1972, 1974.

Covington, M. V., & Omelich, C. L. *Sex differences in self-serving perceptions of ability.* Unpublished manuscript, Department of Psychology, University of California, Berkeley, 1978.

Covington, M. V., & Omelich, C. L. Are causal attributions causal? A path analysis of the cognitive model of achievement motivation. *Journal of Personality and Social Psychology,* 1979, *37,* 1487–1504. (a)

Covington, M. V., & Omelich, C. L. Effort: Double-edged sword in school achievement. *Journal of Educational Psychology,* 1979, *71,* 169–182. (b)

Covington, M. V., & Omelich, C. L. It's best to be able and virtuous too: Student and teacher evaluative responses to successful effort. *Journal of Educational Psychology,* 1979, *71,* 688–700. (c)

Covington, M. V., & Omelich, C. L. As failures mount: Affective and cognitive consequences of ability demotion in the classroom. *Journal of Educational Psychology,* 1981, *73,* 796–808. (a)

Covington, M. V., & Omelich, C. L. *A critical analysis of competing theories of achievement motivation: Cutting the Gordian knot.* Unpublished manuscript, University of California, Berkeley, 1981. (b)

Covington, M. V., Spratt, M. F., & Omelich, C. L. Is effort enough or does diligence count too? Student and teacher reactions to effort stability in failure. *Journal of Educational Psychology,* 1980, *72,* 717–729.

Davison, G. C., & Valins, S. Maintenance of self-attributed and drug-attributed behavior change. *Journal of Personality and Social Psychology,* 1969, *1,* 25–33.

deCharms, R. *Personal causation: The internal affective determinants of behavior.* New York: Academic Press, 1968.

Diggory, J. C. *Self-evaluation: Concepts and studies.* New York: John Wiley & Sons, 1966.

Dweck, C. S. The role of expectations and attributions in the alleviation of learned helplessness. *Journal of Personality and Social Psychology,* 1975, *31,* 674–685.

Dweck, C. S., & Reppucci, N. D. Learned helplessness and reinforcement responsibility in children. *Journal of Personality and Social Psychology,* 1973, *25,* 109–116.

Epstein, S. The self-concept revisited: Or a theory of a theory. *American Psychologist,* May 1973, 404–416.

Erikson, E. H. *Childhood and society.* New York: Norton, 1950.

Flavell, J. H., & Wellman, H. M. Metamemory. In R. V. Kail & J. W. Hagan (Eds.), *Perspectives on the development of memory and cognition.* Hillsdale, N.J.: Lawrence Erlbaum Associates, 1977.

Gardner, J. *Excellence: Can we be equal and excellent too?* New York: Harper & Row, 1961.

Gergen, K. J. *The concept of self.* New York: Holt, Rinehart, & Winston, 1971.

Gibran, K. *The Prophet.* New York: Knopf, 1957.

Goldman, R., Hudson, D., & Daharsh, B. Self-estimated task persistence as a nonlinear predictor of college success. *Journal of Educational Psychology,* 1973, *65,* 216–221.

Gould, R. An experimental analysis of "levels of aspiration." *Genetic Psychology Monograph,* 1939, *21,* 1–116.

Haan, N. *Coping and defending: Processes of self-environment organization.* New York: Academic Press, 1977.

Harari, O., & Covington, M. V. Reactions to achievement behavior from a teacher and student perspective: A development analysis. *American Educational Research Journal,* 1981, *19,* 15–28.

Heider, F. *The psychology of interpersonal relations.* New York: Wiley, 1958.

Jones, E. E., & Nisbett, R. E. The actor and the observer: Divergent perceptions of the causes of behavior. In E. E. Jones et al. (Eds.), *Attribution: Perceiving the causes of behavior.* Morristown, N.J.: General Learning Press, 1971.

Kelley, H. H. Attribution theory in social psychology. In D. Levine (Ed.), *Nebraska Symposium on Motivation* (Vol. 15). Lincoln: University of Nebraska Press, 1967.

Kelley, H. H. Causal schemata and the attribution process. In E. E. Jones et al. (Eds.), *Attribution: Perceiving the causes of behavior.* Morristown, N.J.: General Learning Press, 1971.

Kelley, H. H. The processes of causal attribution. *American Psychologist,* 1973, *28,* 107–128.

Kun, A. Development of the magnitude–covariation and compensation schemata in ability and effort attributions of performance. *Child Development,* 1977, *48,* 862–873.

Kun, A., & Weiner, B. Necessary versus sufficient causal schemata for success and failure. *Journal of Research in Personality,* 1973, *7,* 197–207.

Latta, R. M. Differential tests of two cognitive theories of performance: Weiner versus Kukla. *Journal of Personality and Social Psychology,* 1976, *34,* 295–304.

Lefcourt, H. The function of illusions of control and freedom. *American Psychologist,* 1973, *28*(3), 417–425.

Markham, E. M. Comprehension monitoring: Developmental and educational issues. In S. Chipman, J. Segal, & R. Glaser (Eds.), *Thinking and learning skills: Current research and open questions.* Hillsdale, N.J.: Lawrence Erlbaum Associates, 1982.

Mettee, D. R. Rejection of unexpected success as a function of the negative consequences of accepting success. *Journal of Personality and Social Psychology,* 1971, *17,* 332–341.

Miller, D. T. Ego involvement and attributions for success and failure. *Journal of Personality and Social Psychology,* 1976, *34,* 901–906.

Miller, D. T., & Ross, M. Self-serving biases in the attribution of causality: Fact or fiction? *Psychological Bulletin,* 1975, *82,* 213–225.

Nicholls, J. G. Effort is virtuous, but it's better to have ability: Evaluative responses to perceptions of effort and ability. *Journal of Research in Personality,* 1976, *10,* 305–315.

Nicholls, J. G. The development of the concepts of effort and ability, perception of academic attainment, and the understanding that difficult tasks require more ability. *Child Development,* 1978, *49,* 800–814.

Nicholls, J. G. The development of the concept of difficulty. *Merrill–Palmer Quarterly,* 1980, *26,* 271–281.

Nisbett, R. E., & Schachter, S. Cognitive manipulation of pain. *Journal of Experimental Social Psychology,* 1966, *2,* 227–236.

Olton, R. M., & Crutchfield, R. S. Developing the skills of productive thinking. In P. Mussen, J. Langer, & M. V. Covington (Eds.), *Trends and issues in developmental psychology.* New York: Holt, Rinehart, & Winston, 1969.

Perkins, D. N. General cognitive skills: Why not? In S. Chipman, J. Segal, & R. Glaser (Eds.),

Thinking and learning skills: Current research and open questions. Hillsdale, N.J.: Lawrence Erlbaum Associates, 1982.

Piaget, J. *The psychology of intelligence.* London: Routledge & Kegan Paul, 1950.

Postman, L. Test of the generality of the principle of encoding specificity. *Memory & Cognition,* 1975, *6,* 663–672.

Rest, S., Nierenberg, R., Weiner, B., & Heckhausen, H. Further evidence concerning the effects of perceptions of effort and ability on achievement evaluation. *Journal of Personality and Social Psychology,* 1973, *28,* 187–191.

Rizley, R. Depression and distortion in the attribution of causality. *Journal of Abnormal Psychology,* 1978, *87,* 32–48.

Schnur, A. E. *The assessment of academic self-management skills in adolescents.* Unpublished doctoral dissertation, University of California, Berkeley, 1981.

Shelton, J., & Hill, J. Effects on cheating of achievement anxiety and knowledge of peer performance. *Developmental Psychology,* 1969, *1,* 449–455.

Snyder, M. L., Stephan, W. G., & Rosenfield, D. Egotism and attribution. *Journal of Personality and Social Psychology,* 1976, *33,* 435–441.

Sohn, D. Affect–generating powers of effort and ability self-attributions of academic success and failure. *Journal of Educational Psychology,* 1977, *69,* 500–505.

Stephan, W. G., Rosenfield, D., & Stephan, C. Egotism in males and females. *Journal of Personality and Social Psychology,* 1976, *34,* 1161–1167.

Sternberg, R. J. Instrumental and componential approaches to the nature and training of intelligence. In S. Chipman, J. Segal, & R. Glaser (Eds.), *Thinking and learning skills: Current research and open questions.* Hillsdale, N.J.: Lawrence Erlbaum Associates, 1982.

Streufert, S., & Streufert, S. C. Effects of conceptual structure, failure, and success on attribution of causality and interpersonal attitudes. *Journal of Personality and Social Psychology,* 1969, *11,* 138–147.

Tulving, E., & Thomson, D. M. Encoding specificity and retrieval processes in episodic memory. *Psychological Review,* 1973, *80,* 352–373.

Weiner, B. *Theories of Motivation: From mechanism to cognition.* Chicago: Markham Publishing Co., 1972.

Weiner, B. (Ed.), *Achievement motivation and attribution theory.* Morristown, N.J.: General Learning Press, 1974.

Weiner, B. Psycho–social determinants of achievement evaluation. *UCLA Educator,* 1977, *19,* 5–9.

Weiner, B. A theory of motivation for some classroom experiences. *Journal of Educational Psychology,* 1979, *71,* 3–25.

Weiner, B., Frieze, I., Kukla, A., Reed, L., Rest, S., & Rosenbaum, R. Perceiving the causes of success and failure. In E. E. Jones et al. (Eds.), *Attribution: Perceiving the causes of behavior.* Morristown, N.J.: General Learning Press, 1971.

Weiner, B., & Kukla, A. An attributional analysis of achievement motivation. *Journal of Personality and Social Psychology,* 1970, *15,* 1–20.

Weiner, B., & Peter, N. A cognitive–developmental analysis of achievement and moral judgments. *Developmental Psychology,* 1973, *9,* 290–309.

Weiner, B., & Sierad, J. Misattribution for failure and enhancement of achievement strivings. *Journal of Personality and Social Psychology,* 1975, *31,* 415–421.

White, R. W. Motivation reconsidered: The concept of competence. *Psychological Review,* 1959, *66*(5), 297–333.

Wine, J. Cognitive–attentional approaches to test anxiety modification. In W. H. Holtzman (Chair), *Anxiety and instruction.* Symposium at the meeting of the American Psychological Association, Montreal, 1973.

Wolosin, R. J., Sherman, S. J., & Till, A. Effects of cooperation and competition on responsibility attribution after success and failure. *Journal of Experimental Social Psychology,* 1973, *9,* 220–235.

Woodson, C. E. *Motivational effects of two-stage testing.* Unpublished manuscript, Institute of Human Learning, University of California, Berkeley, 1975.

7
Some Thoughts about Feelings

Bernard Weiner
University of California, Los Angeles

In this chapter I consider feelings or emotions in the classroom. This is a neglected topic, but obviously one of great importance. Before launching into this discussion, I want to make some of my biases known. First of all, I am a cognitive psychologist. I believe that we feel the way we think. Let me give two examples illustrating this point. If someone intentionally harmed me, for example, purposively gave me the wrong homework assignment, then I would feel angry. But assume I later learn that this incorrect information was unintentionally given. The lender also did the wrong assignment and actually thought that he was giving me correct information. Then my anger might quickly subside, and could even give way to gratitude. Or assume that a young man calls a girl for a date and she says that she must stay in and study for an exam. He will feel disappointed. That evening, however, he sees her at the movies with someone else. His feelings will greatly change; he will perhaps feel "hurt," or angry. In these instances, a change in thinking gave rise to a change in feeling.

A second bias I have is that among the most important of the cognitions that influence feelings are what we call causal attributions—reasons why an event has or has not occurred. Studying for an examination is a reason for refusing a date. Another reason is that the girl already has a boyfriend, or dislikes her suitor's personality. Causal thoughts have far-reaching consequences for feelings. This is not to imply that they are the only determinants of feelings. That is not the case, for many factors influence affect.

Finally, I am an attribution theorist. Attribution theorists often assume that much information about psychology is already available to the layperson. My goal is to systematize and provide clarity to this information. Hence, the things that I write should strike a positive and responsive chord; they should not contradict your common sense. And anything that is written here about the feelings of pupils in a classroom also should apply to your life—how you feel on the job, your reactions to success and failure, and your feelings given interpersonal acceptance or rejection.

The chapter is organized in the following manner. First, attribution theory is briefly introduced, with special attention given to causal dimensions, or the underlying properties of causal inferences. Then relations between causal ascriptions and emotions are examined. Of particular interest from an attributional perspective are the emotions of pity, anger, and guilt. Finally, some of the implications of attributional research for teacher behavior are considered.

CAUSAL ATTRIBUTIONS

The guiding principle of attribution theory is that individuals search for understanding, seeking to discover why an event has occurred (Heider, 1958; Kelley, 1967; Weiner, 1980). Causal search is not confined to any single motivational domain. Individuals desire to know, for example, why they have been refused a date (an affiliative concern; Folkes, 1982), why their team has been defeated (an achievement concern; Lau & Russell, 1980), and why they have lost an election (a power concern; Kingdon, 1967). The number of perceived causes is virtually infinite, although the vast majority of answers to the foregoing questions are selected from a rather circumscribed array. In achievement situations, for example, success and failure typically are ascribed to ability (including both aptitude and learned skills), some aspect of motivation (such as short- or long-term effort expenditure, attention), others (friends, family), physiological factors (e.g., mood, maturity, health), the difficulty or the ease of the task, and luck (see Weiner, 1980). In an affiliative context, acceptance or rejection of a dating request often is ascribed to prior behavior (e.g., making a good impression, being too forward), physical appearance, and the desires or state of the potential date (wanting to go out, having a boyfriend or prior engagement; see Folkes, 1982).

Inasmuch as the potential list of causes is considerable within any motivational domain, and because the specific causes differ among domains, it is essential to create a classification scheme or a taxonomy of causes. In so doing, the underlying properties of the causes are ascertained and their similarities and differences can be determined. Causes that denotatively differ (e.g., intelligence as a cause of achievement success and physical beauty as a cause of affiliative success) may be connotatively quite similar (e.g., among other similarities, they refer to relatively enduring personal properties). The discovery of these bases for comparison, which are referred to here as causal dimensions, is an indispensable requirement for the construction of a relatively general attributional theory of emotion.

Causal Dimensions

Two methods of arriving at new knowledge, dialectic and demonstrative (following Rychlak, 1968), have been used to determine the basic dimensions of causality. The dialectic approach has involved a logical grouping of causes, discovery of an apparent contradiction in reasoning, and the emergence of a new dimension of causality to resolve the uncovered inconsistency. This logical and introspective examination within the attributional domain initiated with a differentiation between causes located within the person as opposed to causes external to the person (Heider, 1958; Rotter, 1966). Within the achievement domain, causes such as aptitude, effort, and health commonly are considered internal, whereas task difficulty, help from others, and luck are among the perceived environmental determinants of an outcome. Within the affiliative domain, causes such as physical beauty and personality are internal, whereas the availability of the desired dating partner is an external determinant of acceptance or rejection. The placement of a cause within a dimension is not necessarily invariant over time or between people. For example, rather than being an external cause, luck can be considered an attribute of a person ("He is lucky."). Given the focus of this chapter, the relative placement of a cause within a dimension is not important. Rather, what is important is that locus, for example, is perceived as a basic property of causes.

A shortcoming of this one-dimensional taxonomy became evident when it was discovered that disparate responses are displayed given causes with an identical locus classification. For example, in achievement-related contexts, failure perceived as due to lack of aptitude results in lower expectancies of success than failure believed to be caused by a lack of effort (see Weiner, Nierenberg, & Goldstein, 1976). This disparity shows that aptitude and effort differ in one or more respects, although both are considered properties of the person. A second dimension of causality therefore was postulated; it was labeled causal stability (see Heider, 1958; Weiner, 1979, 1980). The stability dimension differentiates causes on the basis of their endurance. For example, aptitude and physical beauty are perceived as relatively lasting, in contrast to mood and luck, which are temporary and can vary within short periods of time. Because aptitude is perceived as more enduring than effort, prior outcomes ascribed to aptitude are more predictive of the future than are outcomes ascribed to effort. This accounts for the expectancy differences produced by these two causal ascriptions.

In a similar manner, a third dimension of causality was proposed when it became evident that some causes identically classified on both the locus and stability dimensions yielded dissimilar reactions (see Litman-Adizes, 1978; Rosenbaum, 1972; Weiner, 1979). For example, failure attributed to lack of effort begets greater punishment than failure ascribed to ill health, although both may be conceived as internal and unstable causes. This indicates that yet another dimension of causality requires identification. Introspection suggested a third causal property, labeled controllability. The concept of control implies that the actor "could have done otherwise" (Hamilton, 1980). Effort is subject to volitional control; one is personally responsible for the expenditure of effort. On the other hand, one cannot typically control inherited characteristics or, in most cases, the onset of an illness. Within the achievement domain, effort is the most evident example of a controllable cause, although so-called traits such as patience or frustration tolerance also often are perceived by others as controllable.

At present, three dimensions of causality have been identified—locus, stability, and controllability (for a review of the experimental confirmation of these dimensions, see Weiner, 1982). In most instances, causes such as intelligence and physical beauty are perceived as internal, stable, and uncontrollable. This reveals a fundamental similarity between two denotatively different causes that often are invoked to explain positive and negative outcomes in the motivational domains of achievement and affiliation. I turn now from this brief introduction to attributional concepts and examine the influence of causal ascriptions on affective experiences, with particular attention paid to the union between causal dimensions and emotions.

AFFECTIVE REACTIONS TO CAUSAL ASCRIPTIONS

That we feel the way we think has often been advocated (Arnold, 1960; Beck, 1976; Ellis, 1974; Lazarus, 1966). Lazarus and his colleagues have been especially convincing in demonstrating that defensive thoughts, such as denial and intellectualization, can reduce fear. Yet there has not been a systematic mapping of what kinds of thoughts produce what kinds of feelings, and investigations of emotion have been virtually restricted to the negative states of fear and anxiety. An attributional approach suggests some specific relations between thoughts and affects, including the antecedents of positive feeling states.

In our initial study of the relations between causal ascriptions and feelings (Weiner, Russell, & Lerman, 1978), a dictionary list of approximately 250 potential affective reactions to success and failure was compiled, and the dominant causal attributions for achievement performance also were identified. A brief story was presented to the subjects that included a success or failure and the cause of that outcome. The participants rated the degree to which each of the 250 affects would be experienced in this situation. Responses were made on simple rating scales. A typical story was:

> Francis studied intensely for a test he took. It was very important for Francis to record a high score on this exam. He received an extremely high score on the test. He felt he received this high score because he studied so intensely [or, his high ability in this subject; he was lucky in which questions were selected; etc.] How do you think that Francis felt upon receiving this score? [p. 10].

It is not certain that such imaginative procedures capture what individuals experience in their own lives. Hence, in a follow-up investigation (Weiner, Russell, & Lerman, 1979), participants reported a "critical incident" in their lives in which they actually succeeded or failed for a particular reason, such as help from others or a lack of effort. They were then asked to report three affects that were experienced at that time.

Both investigations yielded similar, systematic findings. First, there was a set of outcome-dependent, attribution-independent affects that represent broad positive and negative reactions to success and failure, regardless of the "why" of the outcome. For example, given success, feelings of happiness were reported as equally experienced in disparate attributional conditions. When our favorite baseball team wins, we feel good whether we attribute the outcome to a poor decision by the umpire, to an error made by the other team, to the belief that we played well, or to luck. In a similar manner, given failure, being upset and frustrated were expressed in all the attributional conditions. These outcome-dependent affects for both success and failure were stated as being intensely experienced. I also believe they are of short duration.

There also were emotions discriminably related to particular attributions. Table 7.1 includes four dominant causal attributions (ability, long-term effort, others, and luck) and some specific emotions they gave rise to following success and failure. The linkages for success are: ability–competence and confidence; long-term effort–relaxation; others–gratitude; and luck–surprise. For failure, the attribution–affect associations are: ability–incompetence; effort–guilt and shame; others–anger; and luck–surprise.

At times, therefore, causal attributions yield opposing reactions to success and failure, as would be expected given contrasting outcomes (respectively, competence versus incompetence given an ability attribution; gratitude versus anger given attributions to others). At other times, the same emotion accompanies both positive and negative outcomes (surprise given a luck attribution, although it must be remembered that it is surprise plus happy given success and surprise plus frustration given failure). At still other times, such as when there

TABLE 7.1
Relations Between Causal
Attributions and Emotions

	Outcome	
Attribution	*Success*	*Failure*
Ability	Competence	Incompetence
Long-Term Effort	Relaxation	Guilt (Shame)
Others	Gratitude	Anger
Luck	Surprise	Surprise

are long-term effort attributions, the emotions that follow success (relaxation) are unrelated to the failure-tied affects (guilt and shame).

A third important source of feelings given success or failure were the causal dimensions discussed previously. It was found that feelings of pride and competence were more likely to be experienced when there were internal rather than external attributions for success. Affects associated with self-esteem require that the outcome be linked with the self. Pride, for example, is a self-reflective emotion. Thus, everyone at a party might feel joy about the good food, but only the cook can experience pride.

Causal stability, or the perceived duration of a cause, also influenced affective reactions. Affects such as depression, apathy, and resignation were expressed primarily when internal and stable attributions had been given for failure. For feelings of hopelessness to be generated, it must be perceived that not only is the present bad, but that things will not change. The emotional consequences of the third dimension of causality, controllability, were not examined in these studies but are discussed in detail in the remainder of this chapter.

In summary, emotions are partly responses to achievement-related outcomes, causal ascriptions, and the dimensions of causality. There is a clear mapping between causal thoughts and both positive and negative feelings. In a prior publication (Weiner et al., 1979), it was speculated that:

> In achievement-related contexts the actor might progress through various cognition-emotion scenarios, such as (a) "I just received a 'D' on the exam. That is a very low grade." (This generates intense but relatively fleeting feelings of being frustrated and upset). "I received this grade because I never try sufficiently hard." (This is followed by feelings of guilt.) "There really is something lacking in me." (This is ensued by low self-esteem or lack of worth.) "What I lack I probably always will lack." (This produces helplessness.)
>
> Alternatively, there is (b) "I just received an 'A' on the exam. That is a very high grade." (This generates happiness.) "I received this grade because I worked very hard during the entire school year." (This produces contentment and relaxation.) "I really do have some positive qualities that will persist in the future." (This is followed by high self-esteem, feelings of self-worth, and optimism.) [p. 1218].

PITY, ANGER, AND GUILT

I now want to shift focus and concentrate on three specific emotions in greater detail, for they are of great importance in the classroom. These emotions are pity, anger, and guilt. When our research program was initiated in the affective domain, these three affects had not been selected for special attention. But as our research in emotion began to concentrate on the controllability dimension of causality, these affects repeatedly emerged as associates of this causal perception. In the following pages I make the following arguments regarding these affects:

1. One feels pity for others who are in need of aid or in a negative state due to uncontrollable conditions. Another's loss of a loved one because of an accident or illness, or failure by another because of a physical handicap, are prototypical situations that elicit pity.

2. Anger is experienced given an attribution for a personally relevant negative outcome or negative event to factors controllable by others. For example, anger is aroused when a person is prevented from studying due to a noisy roommate. In addition, anger is elicited when a negative state or outcome of another is perceived as under personal control of that person. A pupil failing because of a lack of effort therefore tends to elicit anger from a teacher.

3. Guilt is suffered when one has brought about a negative consequence for a personally controllable cause. Thus, for example, failure because of insufficient effort often engenders guilt within the actor.

Let me repeat these thoughts and offer some comparisons between the affects of pity, anger, and guilt. I suggest that pity is associated with uncontrollable causes, with the cause residing either within the target of the emotion or within his or her environment. For example, one may pity another because he or she is blind (internal causation) or lives in a dark cave (external causation). On the other hand, anger will often be exhibited given controllable causes. Hence, the distinction between a controllable versus an uncontrollable cause may determine whether we experience anger or pity toward one another. This fact is surely known by the layperson. Thus, when late for an appointment, the tardy individual will offer an account that implicates an uncontrollable cause (my car could not start; the traffic was unusually heavy; etc.). If accepted, such an excuse should minimize the anger that might be generated by the belief that the lateness was due to mere negligence.

Guilt, just as anger, is experienced given a controllable cause. The emotional target for anger is another individual, whereas guilt is self-directed. Thus, anger and guilt differ from one another in terms of the locus of the cause—another versus oneself. Given a controllable cause, the distinction between other-blame versus self-blame therefore determines whether one will experience anger or guilt.

These ideas have been substantiated empirically. In a study with college students, Weiner, Graham, and Chandler (1982) simply read the following instructions:

> We want you to recall and write a very brief description of times that you experienced certain feelings. We hope that you will be as honest and truthful as possible

and remember the situations as best as you can. It makes no difference when the event happened, where, etc. Just try to think of situations that primarily aroused the particular emotion that we ask about.

The participants then described two instances each in which the emotions of pity, anger, and guilt were experienced. Following this, they also rated the causes of the incidents on the three dimensions of locus, stability, and controllability.

There was relatively high similarity among the situations that were recounted. Stories involving pity most often made reference to a physical disability (24%), victimization by environmental circumstances such as poverty (22%), or a catastrophic event (20%). Two typical stories were:

1. A guy on campus is terribly deformed. I pity him because it would be so hard to look so different and have people stare at you.
2. I felt great pity for friends of our family when they were suffering the loss of their son in a car accident.

Incidents associated with anger most often involved conflicts with parents and/or siblings (47%), the disloyalty of a dating partner (15%), or something a roommate had done (13%). For example:

1. My roommate brought her dog into our "no pets" apartment without asking me first. When I got home she wasn't there, but the barking dog was. . . . As well, the dog relieved itself in the middle of the entry.
2. I felt angry toward my boyfriend for lying to me about something he did. All he had to do was to tell me the truth.

Finally, the most frequent guilt-related situations involved lying to parents (17%), stealing (17%), cheating on an exam (15%), or being disloyal to a dating partner (13%). Two typical stories were:

1. One situation in which I felt guilt was in lying to my mother about having a certain guest in my apartment. She thought he was staying somewhere else, but he was really staying with me.
2. When I got caught cheating on a math final in high school, I had extreme guilt feelings. I learned my lesson but I always will feel guilty about the situation.

Classification of the causes of the emotional event revealed clearly that the cause of pity was uncontrollable and stable, and equally apportioned as either internal to the target of pity or as residing in his or her environment. For both anger and guilt, the cause was perceived as controllable and internal to the target of the emotion. For example, participants felt angry when lied to by a friend, but guilty when they lied to a friend.

AFFECTS AS CUES GUIDING SELF-PERCEPTION

I now turn to some of the practical implications and potential applications of the relations between attributions and emotions. Some of the most interesting areas of relevance regard communications from teachers to their pupils.

Certain types of attributional information rarely are directly communicated. It is quite atypical, for example, to refuse a dating request by responding: "You are not physically attractive," or "You have a terrible personality," even when these are the true reasons for rejection. Rather, a rejector is more likely to reply: "I have to study tonight," or "I already have an engagement." These reasons are external to the requester and therefore the person seeking the data does not have his or her "feelings hurt" (Folkes, 1982). Recall that earlier it was contended that self-esteem is related to the locus of an attribution, with internal causes for success or failure maximum influences on self-esteem.

But information that is emotionally upsetting and lowers the recipient's self-esteem may be subtly and unknowingly conveyed, in spite of the good intentions of the communicator. This appears to be particularly true when an observer perceives that the actor is low in ability. One anecdote illustrating this point concerns a Little League baseball coach. Looking over the players on the bench, he said: "Johnny, you go in now. The rules are that everyone has to play." Johnny is then put in a playing position, such as right field, where balls rarely are hit.

In a similar manner, private attributions concerning the low ability of a student are not publicly expressed by a teacher. However, a number of indirect cues transmit low ability messages. For example, Brophy and Good (1974) have documented that teachers infrequently call on students perceived as low in ability and give them only a short amount of time to complete an answer when they falter. Consistent with the findings reported in this paper, Brophy and Good (1974) state: "The determinants of this behavior could include an excessive sympathy for the student [p. 331]." In a related analysis, Weinstein and Middlestadt (1979) suggest that the extra attention given to low achievers indicates their low ability to them. Other, less evident cues related to ability have been uncovered by Meyer, Bachmann, Biermann, Hemplemann, Plöger, and Spiller (1979). These investigators documented that praise for success and the absence of criticism for failure at easy tasks imply to the receiver of such feedback that he or she is low in ability. Although extra praise and withholding of punishment from those believed to be low in ability are attempts to raise their self-esteem, the attributional message being conveyed may undermine this laudable goal.

Might not emotional feedback also convey ability messages to their recipient? What are students likely to think about themselves when feedback from their teacher conveys pity, or anger, or guilt? My colleagues and I (Weiner, Graham, Stern, & Lawson, 1982) have undertaken a series of investigations to demonstrate that affects from others have important attributional consequences. In one experiment, the participating subjects were given scenarios such as:

> A student failed a test and the teacher became angry (or displayed pity, or was sad, etc.). Why did the teacher think that the student failed?

Five affects were manipulated: anger, guilt, surprise, pity, and sadness. The attributions included as possible responses or reasons for the affective display were low ability, insufficient effort, the teacher made the task too difficult, and bad luck.

In Fig. 7.1, the attributional ratings are plotted as a function of the affect that was presented. Each of the affects is associated with a particular causal attribution. Given an expression of anger, the implication is that the student has not tried sufficiently hard. Anger is an "ought" emotion and often indicates a moral evaluation. Pity, on the other hand, is expressed when lack of ability is thought to be the perceived cause. This also is true, but to a much lesser extent, when the affect is sadness. Sadness is known to be more strongly associated with outcome

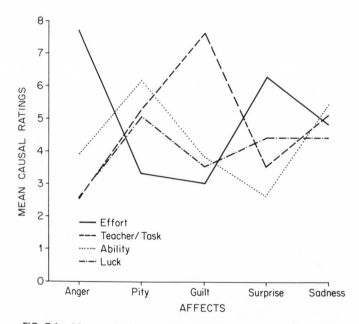

FIG. 7.1. Mean attributional ratings as a function of the described affect.

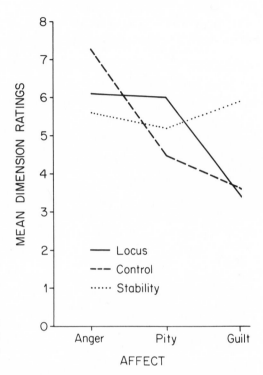

FIG. 7.2. Mean dimensional ratings as a function of the described affect (high ratings indicate internal, unstable, and controllable causation).

than with the attribution for the outcome. In addition, guilt is associated with teacher blame, whereas surprise is relatively weakly associated with a lack of effort.

In this investigation, we also asked the participants to rate the teachers' perceptions of the dimensions or properties of causality. For example, we asked:

> If the teacher feels angry, is the cause of the student failure perceived as internal or external to the student, stable or unstable, and controllable or not controllable by the student?

Figure 7.2 shows some of these data. Of most interest for the present discussion is the finding that, if the teacher is feeling anger or pity, the cause of failure is perceived as internal to the student. If the reaction is anger, the cause is perceived as controllable, whereas the cause is deemed to be uncontrollable if the reaction is pity or guilt.

We also have examined the development of perceived affect–causal ascription linkages. In one pertinent investigation (Weiner, Graham, Stern, & Lawson, 1982), participants ranging in age from 5–9 were told that a teacher felt anger or pity when a student failed; they were then asked to infer whether the perceived

TABLE 7.2
Percentage of Choice of Effort Given the Anger Cue and Ability
Given the Pity Cue, as a Function of Age (From Weiner, Graham,
Stern, & Lawson, 1982.)

Linkage	Age Nine (N = 36)	Seven (N = 37)	Five (N = 30)
Anger–Effort	100%	89	77
Pity–Ability	72	62	50

cause of the pupil failure was low ability or a lack of effort. The percentage of correct responses (where 50% is the chance rate) revealed that, for all age groups, anger–lack of effort was a stronger association than pity–lack of ability (Table 7.2). Furthermore, the linkages grew progressively stronger with increasing age. Note that among the 5-year-olds, the perceived relation between expressions of pity and low ability inferences is at the level of chance.

Does this demonstrate that 5-year-olds do not understand and/or experience the emotion of pity? We think not. Other data have revealed that even children of this age "feel sorry for" people with physical handicaps and others who are in uncontrollable plights. Hence, it appears that these younger children have a different conception of ability than do adults, perceiving ability as much more fluctuating and controllable.

Implications for Self-Concept and Teacher Behavior

One might reason that affective displays of, for example, pity and anger are used by students, particularly the older students, to infer why they failed: whether they are deficient in effort or ability. This process assumes that the pupil attends to and decodes the affective communications from the teacher. This leads them to infer why the teacher believes that they failed. This information is then used along with other cues and determines the pupil's own attribution for his or her failure. As implied previously, it is unlikely that a teacher will tell students publicly that they are not able. Such private beliefs may nonetheless become public through the interpretation of affective displays.

One might speculate that sympathy and pity for failure, rather than anger, are expressed toward the handicapped, ethnic minorities, and females. There are some data, although yet equivocal, that support these contentions. Regarding sex differences, it at times has been reported that boys are criticized for failure more often than girls, especially for behavioral problems and nonintellectual aspects of their performance (Dweck, Davidson, Nelson, & Enna, 1978). Some educational specialists also have noted the prevalence of sympathetic reactions, and their negative consequences, toward minority group members (see, for example, Kleinfeld, 1975). Of course, sympathy need not always reduce self-esteem, nor need anger enhance it. This depends, in part, on the total emotional and informational context in which these emotions are displayed.

Social Cognition in the Classroom

The more general message in the preceding pages is that social cognitions and social understanding have important consequences for self-attribution, self-esteem, and, in turn, achievement strivings. There is now a growing field in psychology with the label of social cognition. This area differs from some other fields within psychology because of its emphasis on cognitive processes. Whereas other areas within psychology might specify reinforcement principles or motivational processes as determinants of behavior, practitioners of social cognition argue that much of our behavior can be understood by comprehension of how the world is cognitively represented: our impressions, inferences, and causal attributions. This emphasis leads, among other things, to a fuller consideration of how teacher and pupil both form and alter constructions of each other and the educational context in which learning occurs. It is assumed that there is an active construction of social reality, that this process is engaged in by children as well as adults, and that thinking, feeling, and behaving form a constellation. These assumptions, I feel, find support in the work presented in this chapter.

ACKNOWLEDGMENT

This chapter was written while the author was supported by a grant from the Spencer Foundation. Reprint requests should be addressed to Bernard Weiner, Department of Psychology, University of California, Los Angeles, California 90024.

REFERENCES

Arnold, M. *Emotions and personality* (Vol. 1). New York: Columbia Press, 1960.

Beck, A. T. *Cognitive therapy and the emotional disorders*. New York: International University Press, 1976.

Brophy, J. E., & Good, T. L. *Teacher–student relationships: Causes and consequences*. New York: Holt, 1974.

Dweck, C. S., Davidson, W., Nelson, S., & Enna, B. Sex differences in learned helplessness: II. The contingencies of evaluative feedback in the classroom and III. An experimental analysis. *Developmental Psychology,* 1978, *14,* 268–276.

Ellis, A. Rational emotive therapy. In A. Burton (Ed.), *Operational theories of personality*. New York: Brunner/Mazel, 1974.

Folkes, V. S. Communicating the reasons for social rejection. *Journal of Experimental Social Psychology,* 1982, *18,* 235–252.

Hamilton, V. L. Intuitive psychologist or intuitive lawyer? Alternative models of the attribution process. *Journal of Personality and Social Psychology*, 1980, *39*, 767–772.

Heider, F. *The psychology of interpersonal relations*. New York: Wiley, 1958.

Kelley, H. H. Attribution theory in social psychology. In D. Levine (Ed.), *Nebraska Symposium on Motivation* (Vol. 15). Lincoln: University of Nebraska Press, 1967.

Kingdon, J. W. Politicians' beliefs about voters. *American Political Science Review*, 1967, *61*, 137–145.

Kleinfeld, J. Effective teachers of Eskimo and Indian students. *School Review*, 1975, *83*, 301–344.

Lau, R. R., & Russell, D. Attributions in the sports pages: A field test of some current hypotheses in attribution research. *Journal of Personality and Social Psychology*, 1980, *39*, 29–38.

Lazarus, R. S. *Psychological stress and the coping process*. New York: McGraw-Hill, 1966.

Litman-Adizes, T. *An attributional model of depression*. Unpublished doctoral dissertation, University of California, Los Angeles, 1978.

Meyer, W. U., Bachmann, M., Biermann, U., Hempelmann, M., Plöger, F. O., & Spiller, H. The informational value of evaluative behavior: Influence of praise and blame on perceptions of ability. *Journal of Educational Psychology*, 1979, *71*, 259–268.

Rosenbaum, R. M. *A dimensional analysis of the perceived causes of success and failure*. Unpublished doctoral dissertation, University of California, Los Angeles, 1972.

Rotter, J. B. Generalized expectancies for internal versus external control of reinforcement. *Psychological Monographs*, 1966, *80*(1, Whole No. 609).

Rychlak, J. F. *A philosophy of science for personality theory*. New York: Houghton Mifflin, 1968.

Weiner, B. A theory of motivation for some classroom experiences. *Journal of Educational Psychology*, 1979, *71*, 3–25.

Weiner, B. *Human motivation*. New York: Holt, Rinehart, & Winston, 1980.

Weiner, B. The emotional consequences of causal ascriptions. In M. S. Clark & S. T. Fiske (Eds.), *Affect and cognition: The 17th annual Carnegie symposium on cognition*. Hillsdale, N.J.: Lawrence Erlbaum Associates, 1982.

Weiner, B. Graham, S., & Chandler, C. Causal antecedents of pity, anger, and guilt. *Personality and Social Psychology Bulletin* 1982, *8*, 226–232.

Weiner, B., Graham, S., Stern, P., & Lawson, M. E. Using affective cues to infer causal thoughts. *Developmental Psychology*, 1982, *18*, 278–286.

Weiner, B., Nierenberg, R., & Goldstein, M. Social learning (locus of control) versus attributional (causal stability) interpretations of expectancy of success. *Journal of Personality*, 1976, *44*, 52–68.

Weiner, B., Russell, D., & Lerman, D. Affective consequences of causal ascriptions. In J. H. Harvey, W. J. Ickes, & R. F. Kidd (Eds.), *New directions in attribution research* (Vol. 2). Hillsdale, N.J.: Lawrence Erlbaum Associates, 1978.

Weiner, B., Russell, D., & Lerman, D. The cognition–emotion process in achievement-related contexts. *Journal of Personality and Social Psychology*, 1979, *37*, 1211–1220.

Weinstein, R. S., & Middlestadt, S. E. Student perceptions of teacher interactions with male high and low achievers. *Journal of Educational Psychology*, 1979, *71*, 421–431.

8 On Doing Well in Science: Why Johnny No Longer Excels; Why Sarah Never Did

Martin L. Maehr
University of Illinois at Urbana–Champaign

Because public education is an enterprise in which almost everyone at one time or another participates, it is also a focal point of discussion, argument, and controversy. More often than not, the claim is made that the schools are failing; school *success* does not seem to be equally newsworthy. Recently, the popular media as well as the professional community have focused on minimal competence in basic skill areas (Glass, 1978; Hill, 1980). The common assertion is that Johnny and Sarah, and perhaps their teacher, are no longer learning to read, write, and compute at the most basic levels. With this new (or renewed) focus on the basic skills, there is some reason to believe that the presumably nonbasic domains may be overlooked. Thus, a recent survey of science education in the United States (Stake & Easley, 1978) suggests that teachers all too readily turn toward the security of teaching the basics and away from what may be a kind of uncertainty, the creative teaching of science. Whether or not that is indeed happening, there is justifiable concern regarding the level of science achievement exhibited by students in the public schools. Not only is there a concern with overall levels of science achievement, there is also a special concern that, in spite of recent efforts to encourage females and minorities, science remains the virtually exclusive province of the white male.

Regarding an overall deterioration in science achievement, two basic conclusions seem warranted. There does not in fact seem to have been a systematic deterioration in science achievement in the case of college-bound students. However, a marked deterioration in science achievement across all students apparently has occurred. Figure 8.1 presents a summary of College Board ATP (Admissions Testing Program) data in support of the first conclusion, and Fig. 8.2

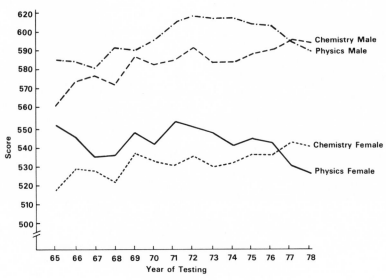

FIG. 8.1.   Mean scores of ATP chemistry and physics candidates for years 1965–1978.[1]

presents NAEP (National Assessment of Educational Progress) data in support of the second (See also Ahmann, Crane, Searls, & Larson, 1975).

Inevitably, science achievement is a national concern and cross-national comparisons are sought. Particularly as industrial productivity remains an obsession (cf. Ouchi, 1981), questions about the future of the United States as a leader in science become paramount. However, putting the results of Fig. 8.1 and 8.2 in the context of other advanced technological societies is difficult. There is some suggestion here and there that the Japanese have already passed us, certainly in math (Harnisch, in press; Husen, 1967), and that the Russians may have done the same (Wirzup, 1980, 1981). In any event, there is a fact or two on which the perception that "Johnny no longer excels" can fixate.

That "Sarah never did excel" likewise has its line of support. A clear pattern of small but consistent differences between male and female science achievement is evident in Fig. 8.1. Adding a second line of evidence to this picture suggests the severity of the problem. In spite of intensive efforts, it does not seem that we will soon increase the proportionate number of women Nobel laureates. Table 8.1 presents a summary of doctorates awarded to women from 1920 to 1964 and 1972. The change has not been dramatic. Indeed, we seem to have difficulty catching up with where we were in the 1920s.

---

[1]Information taken from an unpublished source of the College Board Admissions Testing Program and furnished by Educational Testing Service, Princeton, New Jersey.

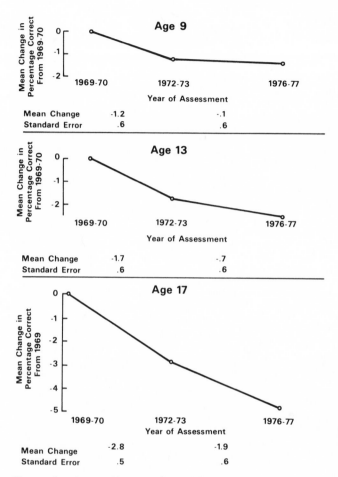

FIG. 8.2.   Changes in science achievement from 1969–70 to 1972–73 and from 1972–73 to 1976–77 for 9-, 13-, and 17-year-olds.[2]

But aside from such interesting objective data on the ups and downs of science achievement, there is a more fundamental point. Achievement in science is certainly a high priority in our society. Not only do we need a scientific elite, we need a scientifically oriented citizenry. As Atkin (1981) points out, science is not altogether unlike sports in this regard. One can have a lively system of professional and interscholastic sports competition only if there are fans to support it.

---

[2]*Three national assessments of science: Changes in achievement, 1969–77.* Science Report No. 08–S–00, National Assessment of Educational Progress. National Center for Education Statistics, U.S. Department of Health, Education, and Welfare.

TABLE 8.1
Percentage of All Doctorates Awarded to Women, 1920–64, 1972 As
Compiled and Organized by Cole (1979)

Five-Year Period	Physical[a] Sciences	Biological Sciences	Social Sciences	Arts Professions	Education
1920–1924	7.6	15.4	20.2	21.4	15.2
1930–1934	6.8	15.5	15.8	22.6	17.6
1940–1944	4.1	11.3	15.7	21.7	23.3
1950–1954	2.8	9.2	9.7	14.7	17.0
1960–1964	2.8	9.4	12.9	17.3	19.6
1972	4.4	18.4	18.7[b]	24.4	23.2

[a] Includes engineering
[b] Includes history
Sources: National Academy of Sciences–National Research Council, *Doctorate Production in United States Universities, 1920–1962*, publication 1142 (Washington, D.C.: NAS–NRS, 1963), pp. 52–63; National Research Council, Office of Scientific Personnel, *Doctorate Recipients from United States Universities*, Summary Report (Washington, D.C.: NRC, 1972), Table 2.

The few high achievers in science are not enough. Therefore, it is every bit as disturbing, if not more so, that the population as a whole is exhibiting a deterioration in science achievement even if a deterioration is not especially noteworthy among the elite.

Finally, anyone who has spent some time in classrooms can observe that there is room for improvement in science instruction. Most teachers at the elementary level have only limited training in science and science teaching. What is more, this situation seems to be getting worse rather than better. With fewer and fewer National Science Foundation programs aimed at upgrading science education at elementary and secondary levels, it is doubtful that great improvements will be seen in the near future. Indeed, the recent creationist controversy may suggest that a significant portion of the public does not feel altogether comfortable with having science taught in the schools at all (Skow, 1981).

TWO QUICK SOLUTIONS

There are at least two quick solutions whenever problems like these are posed. They represent typical, almost reflexive responses. They are, however, inadequate and simply will not suffice.

Offer More Science

A first solution to the problem is—give the students more science! A sophisticated version of this can be found in recent writings of a distinguished scholar, Professor Isaac Wirzup of the University of Chicago. In an earlier article

(Wirzup, 1980) and a later address (Wirzup, 1981), Professor Wirzup carefully outlined new developments in Soviet science education. These developments seem to consist, in the main, of an increased number of hours of instruction devoted to mathematics and science. Professor Wirzup was alarmed by his comparisons with this country and attempted to alarm others: The United States was falling behind again! Certainly, in examining achievement test scores, one finds little basis for arguing against that basic assertion; one could only hope that it would be heard on Capitol Hill. But it is Professor Wirzup's solution that is problematic. That solution seems to be little more than "Give them more geometry."

As one who has spent considerable time working with educational systems in developing countries, I have my own reasons for skepticism in this regard. For example, I was much impressed with the science/math curriculum in Iran. Not only did it look good on paper, students in the high school years seemed to spend an extraordinary amount of time studying. Then, I taught at the University of Tehran for a year and observed the contrast between Iranian high school and university students. What I thought was concern with academic excellence at the high school level turned into blatant disinterest at the university level.

Such informal observations were further supported by systematic research comparing motivation and achievement in the United States and Iran (Fyans & Maehr, 1982). Clearly, "Give them more geometry," chemistry or whatever was not succeeding in creating more scientists or more fans of science. That prompted me and my colleagues to enter the high school classroom again and probe more deeply into what was going on. A teacher's response to one of our questions says it all. When asked to evaluate the new chemistry curriculum, this teacher responded with uninhibited enthusiasm. She even volunteered that she especially liked the lab manual and the place given for experiments in the curriculum. "Why" she continued "just yesterday I performed one of the experiments for the class and they actually applauded." We did not have the heart to tell her that the students—not the teachers—were to be the experimenters. Her idea of teaching science did not include having students *do* science (Maehr, 1974). The time spent on science learning in that classroom may not have been wasted but it is hard to believe that it was especially fruitful when the students were seldom engaged in experiencing discovery for themselves.[3]

Demand More—Control Better

Certainly, education in the United States cannot fall into such simple traps. Maybe. With the increased interest in educational productivity (Walberg, 1980, 1981), one particular correlation has been repeatedly touted as an important, if

---

[3]I am particularly indebted in this regard to Professors Mahtash Esfandiari and Farideh Salili.

not final solution: the correlation between "time on task" and achievement (Rosenshine & Berliner, 1978).

One can hardly argue against the notion that attention to the task at hand is a critical antecedent to achievement at that task. Thus, it is not all that surprising to learn that there is a rather consistent correlation between time on task and achievement. What is bothersome are the deductions that are made from such findings, not always directly, but often by implication. "Offer more science, math, or whatever" is perhaps the least problematic. "Make the kids attend to the tasks through greater teacher control" is more questionable. Although recognizing that a disorderly, disorganized, and undisciplined classroom does not facilitate achievement, it is questionable whether putting learning primarily in the hands of the teacher is the solution. How often do we have to be taught the lesson of Dewey and others that it is the student who learns? It is student participation in the learning act that eventuates in long-term growth. In this regard, the classic study of Lewin and his colleagues (Lewin, Lippitt, & White, 1939; White & Lippitt, 1968) on leadership styles nicely established the relevant issues. Although the study itself is not above criticism, the actual results have in fact worn rather well with time (see, e.g., Maehr & Willig, 1982).

The study involved a comparison of the effects of three leadership styles on group morale and productivity. The groups were composed of 10-year-old boys who were members of afterschool "hobby clubs." In each group, the adult leader played one of three different roles: (1) an autocrat, who controlled virtually every facet of the activity; (2) a laissez-faire leader who more or less let the children do as they pleased; and (3) a democratic leader who, while taking an active role in the group's activity, encouraged participation and decision making on the part of the children. The laissez-faire condition proved to be the least conducive to morale and productivity. Equally interesting, perhaps, is that the boys in the autocratic and democratic groups were equally productive when the leader was present. The most intriguing result, however, concerned the behavior of the children when the leader was absent. Children in the democratic group were little affected by the absence of the leader. They seemed to work in about the same manner whether or not he was present. In contrast, the behavior of the children in the autocratic group seemed to be dependent on the presence of the leader. When he was absent, the productivity not only decreased significantly, but the general decorum of the group was rather dramatically affected. The autocratic leader apparently did not allow for, or encourage, the development of reasons in the students themselves for performing the tasks. The development of individual initiative and responsibility in the children was apparently sacrificed in the course of retaining a tight rein. Reflecting on these and other results, Maehr and Willig (1982) emphasized the point that autocratic teaching styles have their most important and negative effects on the development of "continuing motivation" (Fyans, Kremer, Salili, & Maehr, 1981; Maehr, 1976; Salili, Maehr, Sorensen, & Fyans, 1976). Participation in a project or learning experience under autocratic teaching does not encourage the development of an independent interest in the task. When the teacher is no longer present, neither is student interest. An emphasis on external control in the course of learning may achieve immediate positive effects on performance but at the price of inhibiting the development of an interest in working on the task on one's own initiative for one's own reasons.

In sum, one cannot simply talk about attention. One must talk about optimum attention, about the quality of attention—or perhaps more importantly, about the *reasons* for attention. One should not have to say this, particularly to sophisticated scholars. Yet, it is a fact of life that the stress on correlations between time on task and achievement has led to the strong contention that directed learning is the answer to diminished achievement in U.S. schools. The point is that, insofar as directed learning diminishes the participation of the learner in the learning process, it will in the long run reduce achievement. Further, it might be hypothesized that the problems with directed learning are likely to be most severe in the areas of science education where, above all else, the intent is to create an independent achiever. Finally, although these two solutions may, in part, suggest why Johnny no longer excels, they do not offer much that is helpful in determining why Sarah never did.

A THIRD SOLUTION

There are a variety of other solutions that could be suggested. Many of them, such as improving science materials, have been tried and deserve to be a continuing part of the solution. But I wish to turn to what is, surprisingly enough, a seldom considered possibility. More directly, the point I wish to make is that decreased science achievement is a motivational problem as much as it may be a social, economic, cognitive, or instructional problem. Motivation theory can provide a useful perspective on why Johnny no longer excels and explain why Sarah never did.

Some may quibble with my priorities here. Probably few would deny that motivational factors play some role, perhaps a critical one. Indeed, my assertion regarding the importance of a motivational perspective may be taken as simplistic or trivial. It is interesting, however, that motivation theory has not to date been applied in a pervasive and systematic way to the realm of science education or science achievement. Although the earlier work of Roe (1953, Roe & Siegelman, 1964), Terman (1954), and others (Cattell & Drevdahl, 1955; Cooley, 1963) stressed the role of motivation in science achievement, this was not based on or followed by an intensive program of research. Moreover, there are few studies that attempt to apply motivation theory in any systematic way to the study of achievement in science.

Recently, Marjorie Steinkamp and I conducted an extensive search of the science achievement literature preparatory to conducting a series of meta-analyses relating to gender differences in science achievement (Maehr & Steinkamp, 1981). First, I can report that we are dismayed with the lack of integrating theory in the area of science education and science achievement. In particular, the research in science education that we have reviewed tends to be ad hoc in nature, not guided by any agreed-upon concepts, hypotheses, or assumptions. There are few integrating principles that generalize across the many and varied studies. It is, in short, close to a "hodgepodge"—a factor that makes research syntheses especially difficult. Second, the only operative theory in the domain is Piagetian theory. Whereas we have managed to identify numerous studies employing Piagetian theory in explaining issues of relevance to science achievement, we found no studies applying any currently accepted form of achievement theory to teaching—learning in science. It should be noted that we confined our search to studies dealing with the substantive areas of science (biology, physics, etc.) and specifically excluded mathematics. Thus, the small but growing number of studies on women, motivation, and mathematics (see, e.g., Parsons, Heller, & Kaczalla, 1980) would be outside the domain of my example.

Whether or not one is as surprised or as dismayed as I regarding the state of affairs in science education, it may at least be admitted that the area is wide open for considering science achievement from a motivational perspective. Science achievement is a fitting object for motivation research. Possibly the serious application of motivation theory to science may suggest how the talents of both Johnny and Sarah can be actualized.

A BROAD FRAMEWORK FOR STUDYING MOTIVATION AND ACHIEVEMENT IN SCIENCE

There are at least three approaches that one might take in studying motivation and achievement in science and I herein attempt to add a fourth. The first approach focuses on the individual. In specific regard to motivation, three basic questions are asked: (1) What enduring orientations characterize the person? (2) What are the sources of these traits? (3) How do they relate to achievement and science? This approach suggests that we consider certain personality characteristics that might be associated with science achievement. For example, this might include some version of the personality trait of achievement motivation (see, e.g., Lipman-Blumen, Leavitt, Patterson, Bies, & Handley-Isaksen, 1980; Steinkamp, in press), or perhaps notions relating to locus of control (Lefcourt, 1976) or attributional style (Fyans & Maehr, 1979). In any event, the focus is on the proposition that the individual has acquired an orientation through the course of socialization experiences and that this is the predominant motivation of science achievement—or at least one on which attention should be focused.

A second approach focuses on the social context that happens to exist for the person at any given moment in which achievement is likely to occur. Considering Johnny and Sarah again, what differential role expectations exist for these two at this point in time? What alternatives are available? Aside from experiences in the past or possibilities in the future, what are the social and structural contingencies that impinge on these two individuals *now*?

This type of question is typically posed by the sociologist and the social psychologist (cf. Cole, 1979). It is increasingly posed also by the developmental psychologist who takes a life-span perspective (cf. Maehr & Kleiber, 1980, 1981). It is also a question that must be kept firmly in mind by the motivational psychologist, especially in attempting to understand gender differences in achievement. For example, Lesser (1973) reviewed evidence on age-related changes in achieving orientation that, although in no sense definitive, perhaps should have been attended to more than it has been. Briefly, the data reported by Lesser suggested differential waxing and waning of achievement motivation (nAch) in the case of males and females. Moreover, such waxing and waning seemed to parallel changing stations in life experienced by the sexes separately. Generally, women at a time when their children were becoming independent were increasingly exhibiting higher nAch. Parallel in time the nAch of men was leveling off or decreasing. It seems evident that social context rather than early socialization was the primary factor; a new set of possibilities had begun to emerge for the women, role demands and social expectations had shifted. Contrastingly, males were experiencing a leveling off of their career with lessening expectations for achievement. In any event, one might surmise that motivation to achieve might vary throughout the life-span depending on situations, contexts, and expectancies that impinge on the individual (Maehr & Kleiber, 1981).

To some extent, this point seems to be implicit also in Cole's (1979) extensive study of science achievement. In this particular volume, Cole argues that there is little overall gender discrimination in the academic marketplace so far as the elite research-oriented science departments are concerned. Productive men and women scientists seem to be equally hired and rewarded. However, a significant difference occurs in the area of promotion, with women taking longer to gain promotion, possibly because of endeavoring to meet family-related expectations and concerns (see especially p. 74).

Focusing at earlier ages, specifically on science achievement in schools, Haertel, Walberg, Junker, and Pascarella (1981) have noted the development of differential motivational patterns in regard to science achievement on the part of boys and girls around the age of 13. It is at this stage that girls' interests show a marked shift away from science, a shift that may later be reversed, but one that may have detrimental effects so far as pursuing a career in science is concerned.

Social and contextual factors likely influence achievement motivation (cf. for example, Maehr, 1978). In reference to gender differences three points are especially relevant. First, the context is often different for boys and girls. Second, that context varies across the life-span. Third, one can surmise that social and structural factors may predispose women to be more or less motivated to achieve in science (or for that matter in any other domain) at any given point in time. The lack of synchronization with what is *thought* to be the optimum pattern may prove hazardous so far as science achievement is concerned.

The third approach is the logical combination of the first two. It seems reasonable that individual differences and situational factors should not only be considered separately, but also in combination, focusing particularly on how they may interact. There are at least two lines of research suggested by this general approach.

The first line of research involves the problem of matching personal dispositions with appropriate social psychological environments (Hunt, 1971). Specific to the present case: What instructional conditions allow for the actualization of science-oriented predispositions? Assuming, for example, that budding scientists have an independent intellectual orientation, the degree of freedom granted them in a learning setting may mediate actual creative achievement. The effect of differing learning environments on different types of persons has been the object of considerable research (Endler & Magnusson, 1976; McKeachie, 1961; McKeachie & Lin, 1971; Miller, 1981). However, this research has not as often been specifically and systematically directed toward understanding variations in science achievement.

A second tack is equally obvious but perhaps less frequently discussed. That tack involves considering how individuals select themselves into certain facilitating environments. A study conducted by Fyans and Maehr (1979) is illustrative. The essential question of the study was: How will individuals who characteristically attribute success to ability differ in "open-field" task selections from those who characteristically attribute success either to effort or to luck? The findings were interesting and, I think, of considerable importance for science educators. Those who characteristically attribute success in their academic tasks to ability were, when given the opportunity, likely to choose to perform tasks that challenged and further enhanced their actual ability. Parallel to this, those who attributed success to effort chose tasks where success was a function of effort and those who attributed success to luck chose tasks that were not likely to be intellectually self-enhancing. There are some disturbing aspects to this finding, including the implication that attributional styles, already evident in the fourth grade, were associated with tendencies for students to select tasks that clearly varied in their potential for intellectual enhancement. Aside from this, and more germane to science achievement, is the point that potential scientists may think of themselves in a certain way and select experiences accordingly at a very early age. Those who think of themselves as competent (attribute success to ability) are not only more than likely to become scientists but also more than likely to be males. To put a different gloss on this, the fact that females characteristically retain an effort orientation in school tasks (Maehr & Nicholls, 1980) may be associated with selection patterns that enhance skills other than those required in science. Persistence may do it all in the early grades, but confronting the challenging problem becomes increasingly important as one tackles serious science in high school.

A Fourth Approach

Each of the three approaches has a place in the study of science achievement from a motivational perspective. Each approach represents a useful perspective on the multivariate problems that exist in this domain. There is, however, a fourth approach, which both integrates the concern of the previous three and suggests new directions for the search. That fourth approach begins with the meaning of achievement to the achiever and views any demonstrated achievement as a direct function of such meaning. Whether a given person will demonstrate what is customarily labeled achievement motivation in any given situation (Maehr, 1974) depends on what I call the "experiential gestalt" of the moment—that is, on how he or she happens to construct the situation in terms of available information as well as in terms of personal goals and beliefs. It is the meaning of achievement in that situation that determines achievement behavior. The nature and utility of this "fourth perspective" in understanding motivation and achievement, particularly in science, is the focus of the rest of this chapter.

ON THE MEANING OF ACHIEVEMENT

The Importance of Meaning

During the past 20 years, I have spent a considerable amount of time discussing research and theory related to achievement. As I have covered the major theoretical approaches to the question of *why* the Johnnys and Sarahs of the world do or do not achieve, several reactions have become almost standard.

When I happen to be addressing a group that is especially concerned with social influences on achievement, there is always someone who will question the cross-cultural validity of much of achievement theory. Often, though not always, it will be a student from Japan and she or he will immediately take issue with the emphasis on individualistic striving. Inevitably also, my black and Chicano students will question the relevance of much of achievement theory so far as their respective cultures are concerned. In short, a first criticism that emerges in thinking through the perspectives that have been followed in the study of achievement motivation is that they are ethnocentric.

A second reaction is similar. There is usually also a woman or two or more who will question why the findings with males have not been consistently replicated with females. Pursuing this question highlights the importance of social role in determining achievement motivation (Klinger & McNelley, 1969). Further, the possibility exists that much of achievement motivation theory may be specific to the role of white, middle-class males (Maehr, 1974).

A third reaction is increasingly voiced as we become a nation of older persons (Maehr & Kleiber, 1980, 1981): Are the concepts of achievement motivation perhaps agecentric as well? Earlier models of achievement motivation were based on the young and forward-looking. According to some of the standards implicit in these models, aging means the loss of achievement motivation. But perhaps it is simply that achievement takes on different meanings at different ages and is exhibited in different forms and in different places.

In sum, there is a subjective side to achievement. The response to an achievement task will depend on the meaning applied to the situation by the person. It is that meaning that will mediate and determine the persistence, choice patterns, and performance variations that we take as evidence of achievement motivation. The point is not that objective assessments of personality and situation are irrelevant to the study of achievement. Indeed, they are in many cases remarkably predictive. However, it is, finally, the subjective construction of the situation by the individual that is of critical importance.

The Nature of the Meaning of Achievement

It is one thing to propose the importance of the meaning of achievement and quite another to define what the essence of that meaning might be. During the last several years, our research group has been exploring these questions in a variety of ways. We have analyzed the meaning of achievement in more than 30 cultural–linguistic groups, using semantic differential data (Fyans, Salili, Maehr, & Desai, in press). We have conducted extensive interviews with various cultural groups (Duda, 1980) and with people of differing ages (Maehr & Kleiber, 1981). We have also constructed questionnaires in which we elicit individual definitions of achievement: what it is, where it occurs, and why (cf. Ewing, 1981). Although we have not as yet come up with a truly saisfactory system that fully captures variation in the meaning of achievement, we have arrived at an outline of factors that might be considered in the pursuit of this elusive quarry.

On the basis of our work thus far, it appears reasonable to assume that the meaning of achievement will involve a number of different, but interrelated facets, including:

1. Judgments about one's competence to perform.
2. Judgments about one's role in initiating and controlling the performance.
3. Projected goals in performing.
4. Perceived ways in which these goals can and should be reached.

Although recognizing the importance of each of these facets, I focus in this chapter primarily on only one: achievement-related goals.

A FOCUS ON GOALS

Nature and Function of Goals

There is much that could be said about *goal* as an achievement construct. The use of the term itself implies interesting questions about the nature of human nature. It suggests an intentional psychology (Klinger, 1977) in which the organism makes plans (Miller, Galanter, & Pribram, 1960) and lives the present in terms of the future as much as in terms of the past (Allport, 1955). However, rather than to delve into these varied aspects of employing a construct such as goal, I wish merely to sketch out several facets of goals and to describe certain functions that may determine achievement behavior. This sketch takes the form of four basic assertions. These assertions not only define goals in operational terms, they also suggest a set of predictions regarding how goals affect behavior.

1. Goals are Essentially Associated with an Individual's Perception of Personal Success (or Failure)

For all practical purposes, goals may be viewed as synonymous with ''subjective success'' (Frieze, 1980; Frieze, Shomo, & Francis, 1979; Spink & Roberts, 1980). Defining goals in this way leads readily to procedures for assessing them. Specifically implicit in this definition is the suggestion that the assessment of goals properly involves eliciting examples and definitions of successes or failures that the individual has had in the past and asking him or her to define further why these events are viewed as successful or unsuccessful. Several approaches can be and have been followed in this regard (Duda, 1980, 1981; Farmer, 1980b; Maehr & Nicholls, 1980). One example should, however, suffice to make the procedure explicit.

Table 8.2 suggests the form that the questionnaire might take. There are three characteristics of the format presented here that merit special comment. First, the questionnaire is addressed to a specific content area. Of course, this content area can be varied and may be more or less abstract in nature. Conceivably, the nature and number of goals could vary depending on the domain in question. Second, a kind of retrospective critical incident technique is employed in which the student identifies a success (or failure) event in his or her experience. Although the critical incident technique does not exhaust the measurement possibilities, it does provide an example of how goals can be assessed in terms of life events with which the person is readily familiar. Indeed, it suggests, further, the commonplace nature of goals. It is not that individuals necessarily spend large amounts of time thinking about their goals and how to attain them. Yet, in a very

TABLE 8.2
Example of Item Format Employed in Eliciting Subjective Definitions
of Success/Failure

List three *successes* you have had in school science classes. Take time to think about these. It may take you five to ten minutes to finish this page.

A. _____
B. _____
C. _____

Please enter the main words for your three successes in the spaces at A, B, and C below. What were the things that made you feel successful? For each statement, circle the number representing the degree to which you agree or disagree.

1–Strongly disagree; 2–Disagree; 3–Neutral; 4–Agree; 5–Strongly agree

A. _____

I felt successful because

[a]1. I did better than anyone in the class.	1	2	3	4	5
2. I pleased people important to me.	1	2	3	4	5
3. I showed I was more intelligent than others.	1	2	3	4	5
4. I experienced adventure/novelty.	1	2	3	4	5
5. I got paid for my efforts.	1	2	3	4	5
6. I made other people happy.	1	2	3	4	5
7. I understood something important to me.	1	2	3	4	5
8. My performance/behavior earned me an increase in my allowance.	1	2	3	4	5
9. Other (write in) _____.	1	2	3	4	5

B. _____

I felt successful because

1. . . .	1	2	3	4	5
2. . . .	1	2	3	4	5
.	1	2	3	4	5
.	1	2	3	4	5

[a] Limited item set for illustration purposes

basic way they have a feeling about what a situation yields for them and act accordingly. Third, the student is asked to define the reasons why the activity was listed as a success or failure. The reasons are taken from common statements made in such situations but probably tend to reflect a certain theoretical bias about the kinds of goals that exist in any given achievement situation (Maehr & Nicholls, 1980). It is assumed that the reasons given will reflect goals that an individual may hold with reference to a specific situation.

2. Four Goals of Prime Importance Are Regularly Associated With School Achievement

One might imagine that goals defined as subjective success could be of an unlimited number. At least for reasons of convenience, it is desirable to narrow the possibilities. A review of the literature (Maehr & Nicholls, 1980) and recent factor analytic work (Ewing, 1981) suggest that such narrowing is possible and perhaps also justifiable, at least for the limited conditions of school-related achievement. Specifically, I would propose that one can reasonably limit one's consideration to the following four goals or goal categories. Following Nicholls (1980, this volume), the first two categories are designated *task* and *ego* goals. The second two categories may be labeled somewhat arbitrarily as *social solidarity* and *extrinsic rewards*. The term goal *category* is perhaps preferable in view of the variety of possibilities associated with each goal, the somewhat arbitrary manner of designating these goals, and the limited available research specifically directed toward goal analysis. Further, these goals may be thought of as existing more or less along an intrinsic/extrinsic rewards continuum, as suggested in Table 8.3. Although Table 8.3 briefly defines these goals in terms of the specific questionnaire items listed in Table 8.2, an additional word or two about each is in order.

Task Goals.   This category is comprised of at least two different types of goals often suggested in theoretical writings but difficult to distinguish in practice. First, there is a performance situation described by Csikszentmihalyi (1975, 1978), in which the individual is totally absorbed in the task and where social comparisons of performance are remote. Second, there is the competence motivation situation initially described by White (1959, 1960) and currently the object of an extensive program of research conducted by Harter (1980, 1982; Harter & Connell, in press). Compared to the "flow experience" described by Csikszentmihalyi, the competence situation may be somewhat less task-bound and more affected by social definitions of success and failure. However, in spite of these and perhaps other differences it seems justifiable to assume one goal category that embraces both "flow" and "competence motivation" patterns.

Ego Goals.   Under ego goal conditions, the individual's intentions revolve around doing better than some socially defined standard, especially a standard inherent in the performance of others. Whereas task-oriented goals are at most self-competitive, ego goals are socially competitive (Maehr & Sjogren, 1971). Achieving the goal involves "beating" someone, doing better than another, winning, being the best.

Social Solidarity Goals.   The goals comprised in this category are not always thought of as achievement goals. Yet, any serious consideration of achievement in the classroom can hardly ignore the fact that pleasing significant others is apparently a critical factor in many instances. Thus, in interaction with the teacher, the student may wish to demonstrate that he or she has good intentions, means well, tries hard, and in this sense is a good boy or girl. To those with social solidarity goals, faithfulness is more important than simply doing the task for its own sake; faithfulness is also more important than doing the task to show that one is better than someone else. In conducting cross-cultural research in Iran

TABLE 8.3

Goal Categories with Associated Item Indicators

	Intrinsic Goals		Extrinsic Goals	
Task	Ego	Social Solidarity	Extrinsic Rewards	
[a](4) Venture/Novelty	(1) Did better than others	(2) Pleased others	(5) Got paid	
(7) Understood something	(3) Showed more intelligence	(6) Made other people happy	(8) Increased allowance/privileges	

[a] Numbers refer to items listed in questionnaire presented in Table 8.2.

(Salili, Maehr, & Gillmore, 1976), I was initially struck by a particular kind of conflict that I, as an American, had with uneducated Iranian laborers. When I would hold back payment to a repairman because of the quality of his work, he would counter that this was unfair, as he had worked so hard and thus was quite deserving of payment. I was thinking outcome; he was thinking effort. Clearly, demonstrating good intentions is an acceptable means of gaining social approval, not only in various areas of life but most specifically in classrooms. It is that means of gaining social approval that is especially designated by the category, social solidarity.

Extrinsic Rewards.   The final category refers to a class of goals that are often symbolized by tangible rewards such as money and are often characteristically associated with the definition of work. Presumably, these rewards are essentially alien to the task and/or to the individual's personal reasons for performing the task. Perhaps it is more appropriate to view goals in this category, not as ends in themselves, but as means to other ends. They are subgoals, the attaining of which facilitates the attainment of other goals. In any event, recent work on the social psychology of intrinsic motivation (Deci, 1975, 1980) has made it quite clear that any comprehensive understanding of achievement must consider the role that external rewards play in controlling achievement, not only in the world of work but also at school.

3. Goals Vary With the Situation as Well as With the Individual

On the one hand, a person brings a certain package of meanings into a given situation as a result of previous experience, membership in certain social systems, and developmental level. The item examples given in Table 8.2 are primarily designed to tap goals that an individual might bring into any given situation. For example, the person who cited "I pleased people important to me" as a major reason for the success experience he or she listed, might be expected to try to please the teacher in the science class.

On the other hand, situational factors also affect goals. When, for example, the teacher announces that he or she is going to give a test to determine who is the best at fractions, one might surmise that this will affect the meaning of success held by the students. More generally, conditions implying competition, intrinsic rewards, personal fulfillment, or intrinsic satisfaction doubtless have differential effects on behavior (Maehr, 1976, 1978; Maehr & Nicholls, 1980; Nicholls, 1979); it is proposed here that they do so by affecting purposes and goals held by the performer.

4. As Goals Vary, So Does Behavior

A major question associated with goal analysis is—how does holding one or another goal affect behavior? The answer, in broad outline, is that when a person holds a certain goal he or she will orient her or his behavior so that the goal is attained. Fine and well; but what, more precisely, might this mean? I do not attempt here to exhaust all the ramifications of this basic, essentially viable, but rather general assertion. Instead, I suggest how paths will vary in attractiveness depending on the goals held. As Fyans and Maehr (1979) point out, such preferences have continuing and pervasive effects on the development of abilities and skills.

Task Goals.   Individuals who hold a task goal such as mastery or competence ''spontaneously select'' tasks that challenge their ability and, incidentally, are also likely to further enhance their competence. More specifically, this means that they will choose tasks that tend to possess the following characteristics: they are responsible for the outcome; performance of the task can be evaluated as successful or unsuccessful (i.e., a standard of excellence is applicable); and the outcome is uncertain. Another way of putting this is to suggest that they demonstrate the behavioral patterns characteristically attributed to persons high in achievement motivation, as defined and set forth by McClelland, Atkinson, and others (cf., for example, Atkinson & Feather, 1966; Atkinson & Raynor, 1974; McClelland, 1961).

Ego Goals.   Ego goals are unlike task goals in at least one important respect. The intention in this case is not just to accomplish something, but to do better than someone else. Thus, whereas a standard of excellence is applicable in both cases, in the ego goal condition, the standard of excellence is clearly social. The goal is to do better than someone else. We, of course, have considerable information on how competition affects behavior and likewise know a great deal about how competition affects achievement. Briefly summarized, social competition affects different individuals differently. Earlier work on achievement motivation (Atkinson, 1957; Atkinson & Feather, 1966) called specific attention to this as has more recent work on test anxiety (Hill, 1980) and attribution theory (Kukla, 1978; Nicholls, 1980, this volume). It is more compatible with the theoretical approach outlined in this chapter to follow Kukla and Nicholls and propose that the critical modifying variable is the person's perception of his or her competence on such tasks in comparison to referent others.

Particularly in considering the ego goal condition one cannot ignore the role that general self-related meaning systems play. Limiting the present discussion to the analysis of subjectively held goals rules out an extensive discussion of such self-related meanings. However, several points can be made in this regard. First, it is assumed that a person brings to each situation a general sense of how competent he or she is in reference to selected others in performing tasks of the nature presented. Second, ego goal conditions make such a general sense of competence especially salient. The individual is, as it were, forced to think about whether he or she is good or bad at tasks like this. Reflecting on one's ability in this way is likely to have important modifying effects on motivation. Those who come to the situation with low perceived competence are not likely to risk failure. Either they will choose tasks on which they can most certainly succeed or they will opt for tasks on which they have virtually no chance at all of succeeding. In either case, their behavior may be interpreted as avoiding any direct confrontation with how competent they are for they are fearful of the answer. In contrast, persons with a high sense of competence are more likely to risk failure and confront challenge.

Focusing on goal analysis, the important part to be stressed is this: Whereas persons who are confident of their ability operate similarly in both task and ego goal conditions, persons lacking in confidence are likely to show a drastic difference in behavior in the two conditions.

Social Solidarity.   In contrast to both the task and ego goal conditions, the social solidarity condition minimizes such challenge-seeking behavior and prompts faithful conformity to the expectation of others. Holding a social solidarity goal might encourage faithful effort in performing a boring and tedious task, a task requiring much effort but little ability; persons holding either task or ego goals would tend to avoid tasks requiring primarily effort. One can demonstrate good intentions and often obtain social approval for such faithfulness, but one cannot readily demonstrate competence or superior ability on such tasks. Carrying out extensive learning exercises and tedious homework assignments are compatible with a social solidarity goal. Pursuing the unusual path or engaging in intellectual risk taking would not be.

Extrinsic Rewards.   Recently a considerable literature has evolved that focuses on how extrinsic rewards may modify motivation in performing a task (Deci, 1975, 1980; Maehr, 1976, 1977).

Apparently, the introduction of extrinsic rewards redefines the goal of the behavior for the person. Thus, when the behavior is contracted and paid for, it is "work" and the rules of work obtain (Maehr, 1978). For the present purposes, two such rules seem to have relevance. First, one does not work without pay. Motivation is not controlled by the factors inherent in the task but by an "add-on" such as a monetary reward. The second rule is that, if an extrinsic reward is the goal of behavior, then one typically does not experiment with means, manners, and styles. The surest route to success is preferred, and risk taking is eschewed. The greater the degree of success, the higher the motivation. In the task goal situation, an individual may be attracted by challenge and by a moderate amount of uncertainty in outcome. However, in the extrinsic reward condition, behavior patterns are proposed to be quite different (Maehr, 1978).

Goals and Challenge.   It will be noted that this sketch of the possible effects of goals on behavior tends to stress the responses to challenge. Although discussions of achievement behavior should not be limited to this particular situation, a tradition begun by Atkinson (1957) makes this almost inevitable. In any event, one way of summing up the essential predictions comprised under each goal category is to construct four graphs that describe level of motivation in relationship to a subjective probability of success (P_s). These four graphs are presented in Fig. 8.3. Clearly, they represent idealized curves and just as clearly they represent hypotheses for which there is certainly varying degree of support. However, such a picture may not only summarize the thrust of my argument but may also lay it open to attack. Hesitant as I am to be so specific with so limited a body of data, such specificity is the only route to progress.

Considering Fig. 8.3, it will be noted that Graph 1 essentially suggests that all will exhibit the choice–performance pattern as described by Atkinson under task goal conditions. Graph 2 represents the basic patterns proposed by Atkinson, but with Kukla (1978) and Nicholls (1980, this volume), I am proposing that perceived competence, rather than Resultant Achievement Motivation, is the more appropriate moderating variable. Graph 3 suggests that P_s is essentially unimpor-

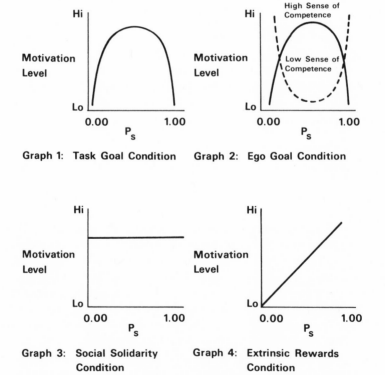

FIG. 8.3.   Hypothesized risk-challenge-seeking patterns under four goal conditions.

tant in the social solidarity condition. Although the level of motivation may be generally high, it does not vary with P_s. Graph 4 also represents the more or less intuitively plausible situation associated with arguments made earlier. The essential point is that the surest route to obtaining extrinsic reward is preferred. Given a choice between an assured path to obtaining the extrinsic reward and a less certain one, a person chooses the more certain one.

Again, I would stress the tentative character of these projections. Graph 3 in particular is as much a function of intuition as it is a summary of empirical observations. Moreover, each is an idealized curve designed to illustrate in a general way how goals might modify preference for challenge. Be that all as it may, these graphs possibly serve as a heuristic summary of how goals may affect behavior.

APPLICATIONS TO SCIENCE ACHIEVEMENT

My assumption is that the theoretical perspectives outlined in the preceding section have specific implications for understanding the role of motivation in science achievement. In this regard, there are a number of different questions that might profitably be pursued. There are three that I pursue, and I do not presume to present an exhaustive discussion of these. Rather, the intent is to suggest how this theorizing might be applied in certain instances. First, the discussion focuses on persons who excel in science and become practicing scientists. What motivational characteristics are implicated in this pattern of achievement? Second, consideration is given to interpreting gender differences in achievement. How might one understand gender-related issues in terms of the motivational perspectives reviewed earlier? Third and finally, how might one improve science instruction to improve science achievement overall?

On Becoming a Scientist

Research on the characteristics of scientists (Cattell & Drevdahl, 1955; Cooley, 1963; Roe, 1953; Roe & Siegelman, 1964; Terman, 1954) has generally indicated two important things so far as motivational patterns are concerned. First, those who excel are in fact very confident of their abilities. They do not tend to be obsessed with self-doubts. Second, they possess a certain orientation toward life and work. Interpreting this orientation in terms of the four goals outlined earlier, it can be suggested that neither social solidarity nor extrinsic rewards seem to be particularly prominent in guiding their behavior. There are several interesting and not altogether obvious implications of such findings when interpreted in the light of the theoretical analysis presented earlier. Generally, one might surmise that successful scientists might do equally well in operating under both task and ego goal conditions. Indeed, two recent studies indicate that success in science demands the ability to operate under both of these conditions. Somewhat surprisingly, successful scientists often show a strong preference for social competition.

The first study was conducted by Segal, Busse, and Mansfield (1980). This study was important and interesting from a number of respects, not the least of which was in regard to how early experiences affected science achievement. What was particularly intriguing was the fact that the extracurricular high school activity that was most closely related to later science achievement was participation in interscholastic sports. I was frankly surprised by these results, as I believe the authors were also. Yet neither I nor the authors should have been so naive as to expect that scientists simply pursue truth for its own sake. Robert Merton (1973) should have put this idea to rest long ago. Moreover, there is a popular literature extant (Hunt, 1981; McKean, 1981; Wade, 1982) that repeatedly reminds us that, for good and sometimes for ill, science is a very competitive enterprise.

The second study is quite different in design and execution. This study (Fowler, Braskamp, & Ory, 1981), was directed broadly at career development of faculty at large research institutions. The specific focus, however, was on motivation patterns at various career stages, using faculty of a small liberal arts college as a comparison group. Because the faculty at the research institution was largely devoted to science, this study holds interest in the present context. Not surprisingly, assistant professors were caught up in what only could be described as a socially competitive enterprise. Whatever science they were doing, was done in reference to salient social norms and in light of ever present external evaluation. Their goal in concrete form was simple: Do better than others and get promoted. Professors, further along with their career, were not as obsessed or controlled by this competitiveness but they remained quite concerned with recognition. As a consultant to the project, I had predicted a progression from more extrinsic goals to more intrinsic concerns as these individuals progressed in their careers (following theoretical formulations proposed by Maehr & Kleiber, 1980, 1981). However, this sample of senior scholars seemed to retain a kind of competitive orientation. In summary, then, the Braskamp et al. study reinforces the first study in stressing the socially competitive nature of scientific endeavor. A single-minded, independent, and intrinsic task orientation was by no means a dominant theme. Indeed, it was hardly, if ever expressed.

These two studies, as well as others cited, suggest that becoming a scientist involves being able to perform effectively under both task and ego goal conditions. A person who will excel must be a special kind of person motivationally. It is not simply that a scientist is highly motivated. The present analysis suggests that it is perceived competence that is of primary significance. Confidence in one's ability is not an incidental characteristic of the successful scientist. As far as motivation is concerned, it is the *sine qua non*.

Gender Differences in Science Achievement

Apparently, it takes a special kind of person to excel in science. More accurately, certain goal orientations and a sense of competence seem to form a critical motivational component. One possible reason why girls are less likely to excel in science than boys is that they simply do not possess the same combination of goal orientations and sense of competence as boys in regard to science.

Gender differences in achievement motivation are, of course, an old story (Alper, 1979; Farmer, 1976, 1980a; Horner, 1968; Mednick, Tangri, & Hoffman, 1977; Stein & Bailey, 1973). The present analysis, however, suggests a new perspective on this question. First, it does not assume that boys are generally more motivated to achieve in a general sense than girls. The motivational differences that are observed may vary from task to task (Maehr & Nicholls, 1980) and change at different age levels (Lesser, 1973). Given such variation, one might suggest that gender differences may appropriately be attributed to the basic meanings that girls or boys may have in reference to a particular task.

A recent analysis by Maehr and Nicholls (1980) suggests that boys and girls typically do hold quite different achievement goals. Briefly summarized, girls are more inclined to demonstrate that they are well-intentioned ''good girls'' than to demonstrate that they are competent or superior. At least this seems to be true in most classroom-related studies. Focusing particularly on science achievement, Steinkamp (in press) has recently argued that it is the development of a ''compliant style'' in academic settings that may, in fact, be detrimental to science achievement in girls. She has also suggested that, although this style may change at different life stages, its presence at certain critical stages may be overwhelmingly inhibiting. Thus, if this style is the accepted pattern in the early adolescent period, it may be detrimental to long-term career choices that will not be changed easily by later experiences. Steinkamp's description of compliant style may be interpreted as similar to the goal orientations attributed to girls by Maehr and Nicholls (1980). And, in general, it seems plausible that gender differences in achievement that have been found on a variety of achievement tasks are associated with such different goal orientations.

The evidence also suggests that girls are likely to differ in the degree to which they will orient themselves to task and ego goals when the situation imposes these on them. This stems from their lower sense of competence as they approach the learning of science. Like earlier work on achievement motivation, recent work stemming from cognitive theories of motivation shows somewhat disturbing gender differences. Thus, following an attribution theory approach to achievement, the research evidence repeatedly indicates that females are less likely to attribute success to high ability and more likely to attribute failure to poor ability than are males (Frieze, 1980). Possibly, this line of evidence, along with other such evidence indicates that girls do indeed have lower perceived competence than boys, perhaps in the academic realm generally, but in science in particular. Given the fact that science often has to be done under ego goal conditions, one might wonder whether such gender-related differences in perceived competence eventuate in gender differences in the confrontation of challenge that affects science achievement.

Science and the Schools

The third question is in many ways the most important one: What can schools do to facilitate motivation and achievement in science?

It may seem self-evident that educational experiences critically influence science achievement. Yet, the point bears repeating and some degree of elaboration. We live in an era in which education is still stunned by the Coleman (1966) report and various follow-ups (Jencks, Smith, Acland, Bane, Cohen, Gintis, Heyne, & Michelson, 1973; Mosteller & Moynihan, 1972); stunned by the apparent finding that schools, schooling, and varying classroom experiences do not really seem to make a difference. Of course, they do—as studies that focus more specifically on school-related achievement indicate (Shea, 1976). But of special relevance in the present case is that the school's effects are likely to be especially evident in science achievement, as pointed out by Comber and Keeves (1973). Of course, the essential question is *what* can schools do? Specifically, what is it that the schools can do to facilitate motivation in science? There is much that should and can be done, of course, but I limit myself to one specific suggestion: In the main, *science should be taught under task goal conditions.*

Achievement in the science classroom probably occurs under each of the four goal conditions set forth earlier and scientists achieve for a variety of intrinsic and extrinsic reasons. Focusing, however, on creating the kind of classroom that is most likely to foster continuing achievement in science for most of the students most of the time, the emphasis has to be placed on creating task goal conditions. This general piece of advice breaks down into four more specific suggestions. Although each suggestion boasts a measure of research support, each also should be viewed as a hypothesis to be subjected to further testing.

1. External Evaluation Should Be Minimized. Evaluation is basic to the instructional process. However, it may have unintended effects on the motivation, achievement, and continuing interest of the student in learning. A growing number of studies (Fyans et al., 1981; Maehr, 1976; Maehr & Stallings, 1972; Salili et al., 1976) has indicated that placing stress on tests and on the teacher's evaluation of performance can have essentially negative effects. Although an emphasis on such external evaluation may momentarily enhance the performance of some students it also has negative effects on "continuing motivation" (Maehr, 1976). That is, students are less likely to continue working on the task on their own, seeking new challenges and opportunities in this regard. In other words, they may perform for the evaluator or when the implied reward/

punishment of the evaluation is present. Remove this, however, and their motivation decidedly wanes.

In terms of the theory sketched earlier, the evaluation conditions affect the individual's definition of the task at hand. Specifically, external evaluation tends to rule out the establishment of more intrinsic, task-related goals; therewith, either ego goals or perhaps extrinsic rewards increase in salience. This change in goal condition from the intrinsic to the more extrinsic has two possible effects. Insofar as external evaluation connotes extrinsic rewards, students are likely to be responsive only when these extrinsic rewards are operative. Assuming that a major goal of science instruction is to foster a continuing and independent interest in the subject matter, it is clearly desirable to foster a task orientation. Reducing the emphasis on external evaluation serves this purpose.

An emphasis on external evaluation may also serve to establish ego goal conditions. That is, it may foster social competition and encourage the student to become especially sensitive about his or her ability. This will not negatively affect the elite few who see themselves as highly competent. However, it will have a definite negative effect on individuals who are lacking in a sense of competence. In the area of science, this would probably include the majority of girls as well as most boys.

2. Choice and Freedom of Movement Must Be Fostered.   In many respects, this second assertion is parallel, similar, and complementary to the first one. Both assertions are concerned with freedom and independence in learning. The former is concerned with freedom from external evaluation. The present assertion is concerned with the freedom of the student to select what will be learned and how. Both relate to the issue of allowing students to take independent initiative in the learning process.

A study conducted by Wang and Stiles (1976; see also Wang, 1981) is of interest in this respect. They conducted an investigation in which the effects of student selection and teacher selection of school work schedules were compared. Results indicated that students were more likely to complete assignments under the former than under the latter condition. In many ways, the most dramatic case of experimenting with the effects of freedom on learning is presented by de-Charms (1976). One of the major manipulated variables in this major intervention study was choice. Motivation of his inner city subjects was enhanced as they participated in educational planning and decisions—and as they could exercise some reasonable degree of choice over what they could do in the classroom.

In more general terms, it was "open education" that ideally presented the opportunities for such choice, freedom, and independence. And interestingly, in spite of all the negative things that have been said about "open education" there is evidence that it may not be all that bad after all. Thus, Horowitz's (1979) extensive review indicates basically two things of importance in this regard: (1) Although "open education" has not been shown to be superior in terms of standard measures of classroom achievement, neither has it been shown to be inferior. (2) "Open education" does seem to emerge as superior in the creation of affective outcomes that might logically be expected to have an enduring effect on achievement patterns that reach beyond the classroom experience or the school as such.

A recent and extensive study (Pascarella, Walberg, Junker, & Haertel, 1981) underscores the importance of freedom and learning in the area of science. This investigation made a special point of examining the classroom environment correlates of continuing motivation in science, using data gathered in the National Assessment of Educational Progress. Although teacher control was found to be positively associated with science achievement for both early and later adolescent boys and girls, it was negatively associated with a measure of continuing motivation in science. Apparently, educational conditions that emphasize control of student behavior in the classroom may attain desirable effects of an immediate and short-term nature. Simultaneously, however, they may discourage the behavior that we have come to call continuing motivation.

In summary, encouraging independence in learning can be shown to have important positive effects, particularly so far as developing a continuing interest in the subject matter is concerned. This may be no more true in science than in other areas. However, it certainly seems important to consider whether instruction in science comes increasingly under the definition of the teacher and scientific authority and decreasingly an area in which the student experiments, discovers, and creates. Freedom is basic to the doing of science. It would be ironic to learn that authoritarianism dominates the teaching of science.

3. Social Competition Must Be Minimized.   Earlier, the point was made that those who excel in science seem to be able to operate effectively under both self-competitive and socially competitive conditions. The most devastating problem with social competition may well be found most prominently in the case of those who are not on the road to becoming scientists—and indeed social competition does appear to have negative effects that must be considered to be of critical importance in most educational situations (cf. Johnson & Johnson, 1978).

Given the evidence of the negative effects of social competition now available to us, two assertions about science achievement are relevant. First, it may be suggested that establishing a competitive atmosphere is not facilitative. Although it may not prevent the elites from emerging, it probably reduces the number of fans available to cheer science on. That is the least that it can do. There is, secondly, the possibility that still more can be done. It is too soon to close the door on the possibility that socially competitive conditions in training the scientist may not be optimal. As is well known from the popular media (cf. for example, Hunt, 1981; McKean, 1981; Wade, 1982), competition in science has eventuated in cheating and other base forms of behavior. It possibly reduces the interest of girls in science as well as many others who could make creative contributions. It may cause others to focus too quickly on a narrow range of problems of immediate—but not long-term—significance. In any event, there is sufficient reason to wonder about the effects of social competition in the training of scientists.

4. Task Goals and Science: A Conclusion. The embryonic theory of motivation outlined in this chapter appears to have direct applicability to teaching science in the schools. The foregoing discussion hopefully illustrates this. Indeed, there is already considerable evidence regarding how classrooms might be structured to further science achievement. In the main, task goals should prevail. Yet, having said this, there is a nagging thought that persists regarding the predominantly task goal-oriented classroom. Although there seems to be little question but that task goal conditions should facilitate science achievement in most students most of the time, one might wonder about special cases. Of special importance is the question of the elite few who are on the way to becoming scientists. The challenge-seeking patterns of these individuals may not, for example, vary under task or ego conditions. However, will these elite few possibly benefit somehow from competitive (ego goal) classroom experience? They might. After all, science as now practiced is a competitive enterprise and, apparently, those who succeed as scientists must be able to survive competitive situations. A task-oriented classroom may not fully prepare future scientists for the competitive world they will face. For that matter, the ego-oriented classroom that is not homogeneously grouped in terms of ability would not provide experience in coping with competition either. Unfortunately, this line of questioning must be treated as a mere aside. It underlines the tentativeness with which we counsel classroom teachers on the basis of the present or any other psychological theory.

CONCLUSION

I will end this chapter as I began. There is an increasingly pervasive perception that "Johnny no longer excels and that Sarah never did." Although the perception is not totally valid, it is sufficiently valid overall to provide a cause for concern. Something does need to be done about how science is handled in the schools, but the most often suggested solutions are wrong. If indeed there has been a decrease in science achievement, there is no logical reason to assume that lack of teacher control over the educational process is at fault. Indeed, it seems more logical to argue that it has been the schools' tendency to respond to public outcry and demand about educational outcomes by exerting greater control over achievement that is at fault. This control may or may not increase the numbers who manage to pass minimal competence tests. There is strong reason to believe that when such control is generalized across all areas, especially when it includes science instruction, it may be distinctively counterproductive.

It seems that the perception that "Sarah never did" is reasonably accurate. Motivational factors are again implicated. But one cannot readily understand this phenomenon unless a broad perspective on science and achievement is considered. Initial socialization apparently plays its role in creating goals for girls that are not systematically challenged by the schools. But persistent and pervasive societal expectations and opportunities are also important.

Whether this line of argumentation is correct is, of course, a fitting subject for future research. Hopefully, this chapter has increased the probability that such research will be conducted.

ACKNOWLEDGMENTS

The author is indebted to many colleagues, particularly to John Nicholls and Marjorie Steinkamp. This chapter has evolved out of work conducted under support from a grant from NSF, "A Synthesis of Findings on Sex Differences in Science Education Research," NSF–SED 80–07857.

REFERENCES

Ahmann, J. S., Crane, R., Searls, D., & Larson, R. Science achievement: The trend is down. *The Science Teacher,* 1975, *42,* 23–35.

Allport, G. W. *Becoming: Basic considerations for a psychology of personality.* New Haven, Conn.: Yale University Press, 1955.

Alper, T. G. Achievement motivation in college women: A now-you-see-it-now-you-don't phenomenon. *American Psychologist,* 1979, *29,* 194–203.

Atkin, J. M. *Discussant's comments.* AERA Symposium, Los Angeles, Calif., April 1981.

Atkinson, J. W. Motivational determinants of risk-taking behavior. *Psychological Review,* 1957, *64,* 359–372.

Atkinson, J. W., & Feather, N. T. (Eds.). *A theory of achievement motivation.* New York: John Wiley & Sons, 1966.

Atkinson, J. W., & Raynor, J. O. (Eds.). *Motivation and achievement.* New York: John Wiley & Sons, 1974.

Cattell, R. B., & Drevdahl, J. E. A comparison of the personality profile (16 P.F.) of eminent researchers with that of eminent teachers and administrators, and of the general population. *British Journal of Psychology,* 1955, *46,* 248–261.

Cole, J. *Fair science.* New York: The Free Press, 1979.

Coleman, J. S., & Associates. *Equality of educational opportunity.* U.S. Department of Health, Education, and Welfare, Washington, D.C.: U.S. Government Printing Office, 1966.

Comber, L. C., & Keeves, J. P. *Science education in nineteen countries: International studies in evaluation I.* New York: John Wiley & Sons, 1973.

Cooley, W. W. *Career development of scientists: An overlapping longitudinal study.* Cambridge, Mass.: Harvard University, 1963.

Csikszentmihalyi, M. *Beyond boredom and anxiety.* San Francisco: Jossey-Bass, 1975.

Csikszentmihalyi, M. Intrinsic rewards and emergent motivation. In M. R. Lepper & D. Green (Eds.), *The hidden costs of reward.* Hillsdale, N.J.: Lawrence Erlbaum Associates, 1978.

de Charms, R. *Enhancing motivation: Change in the classroom.* New York: Irvington Publishers, 1976.

Deci, E. L. *Intrinsic motivation.* New York: Plenum, 1975.

Deci, E. L. *The psychology of self-determination.* Lexington, Mass.: D. C. Heath & Co., 1980.

Duda, J. Achievement motivation among Navajo students: A conceptual analysis with preliminary data. *Ethos,* 1980, *8–4,* 316–337.

Duda, J. *A cross-cultural analysis of achievement motivation in sport and the classroom.* Unpublished doctoral dissertation, University of Illinois at Urbana–Champaign, 1981.

Endler, N. S., & Magnusson, D. Toward an interactional psychology of personality. *Psychological Bulletin,* 1976, *83,* 956–974.

Ewing, M. E. *Achievement orientations and sport behavior of males and females.* Unpublished doctoral dissertation, University of Illinois at Urbana-Champaign, 1981.

Farmer, H. S. What inhibits achievement and career motivation in women? *The Counseling Psychologist,* 1976, *6,* 12–14.

Farmer, H. S. Environmental, background, and psychological variables related to optimizing achievement and career motivation for high school girls. *Journal of Vocational Behavior,* 1980, *17,* 58–70. (a)

Farmer, H. *Why women contribute less to the arts, sciences and humanities.* Research in progress under NIE Grant 679–0022, University of Illinois, Urbana–Champaign, 1980. (b)

Fowler, D. A., Braskamp, L. A., & Ory, J. C. *Faculty development and achievement: A faculty's view.* Manuscript submitted for publication, 1981.

Frieze, I. H. Beliefs about success and failure in the classroom. In J. H. McMillen (Ed.), *The social psychology of school learning.* New York: Academic Press, 1980.

Frieze, I. H., Shomo, K. H., & Francis, W. D. *Determinants of subjective feelings of success.* Unpublished paper presented at the LRDC Conference, Teacher and Student Perceptions of Success and Failure: Implications for Learning. Pittsburg, Pa., October 25–26, 1979.

Fyans, L. J., Jr., Kremer, B., Salili, F., & Maehr, M. L. The effects of evaluation conditions on continuing motivation: A study of the cultural, personological, and situational antecedents of a motivational pattern. *International Journal of Intercultural Relations,* 1981, *5,* 1–22.

Fyans, L. J., Jr., & Maehr, M. L. Attributional style, task selection and achievement. *Journal of Educational Psychology,* 1979, *71,* 499–507.

Fyans, L. J., Jr., & Maehr, M. L. A comparison of sex differences in career and achievement in Iran and the U.S. *International Journal of Instructional Relations,* 1982, *6,* 355–367.

Fyans, L. J., Jr., Salili, F., Maehr, M. L., & Desai, K. A. *A cross-cultural exploration into the meaning of achievement.* Journal of Personality and Social Psychology, in press.

Glass, G. V. Minimum competence and incompetence in Florida. *Phi Delta Kappan,* 1978, *59,* 602–605.

Haertel, G. D., Walberg, H. J., Junker, L., & Pascarella, E. T. Early adolescent sex differences in science learning: Evidence from the National Assessment of Educational Progress. *American Educational Research Journal,* 1981, *18,* 329–341.

Harnisch, D. Women and mathematics: A cross-national perspective. In M. Steinkamp & M. L. Maehr (Eds.), *Women in science.* Greenwich, Conn.: JAI Press, in press.

Harter, S. A model of intrinsic mastery motivation in children: Individual differences and developmental change. In W. A. Collins (Ed.), *Minnesota Symposium in Child Psychology (Vol. 14).* Hillsdale, N.J.: Lawrence Erlbaum Associates, 1980.

Harter, S. Developmental perspectives in the self-system. In M. Hetherington (Ed.), *Carmichael's manual of child psychology: Volume on social and personality development.* New York: Wiley, 1982.

Harter, S., & Connell, J. P. A structural model of the relationships among children's academic achievement and their self-perceptions of competence, control, and motivational orientation in the cognitive domain. In J. Nicholls (Ed.), *The development of achievement motivation*. Greenwich, Conn.: JAI Press, in press.

Hill, K. T. Motivation, evaluation, and testing policy. In L. J. Fyans, Jr. (Ed.), *Achievement motivation: Recent trends in theory and research*. New York: Plenum Press, 1980.

Horner, M. S. *Sex differences in achievement motivation and performance in competitive and noncompetitive situations*. Unpublished doctoral dissertation, University of Michigan, 1968.

Horowitz, R. A. Psychological effects of the "open-classroom." *Review of Educational Research*, 1979, *49*, 71–86.

Hunt, D. E. *Matching models in education*. Toronto: Ontario Institute for Studies in Education, 1971.

Hunt, M. A fraud that shook the world of science. *New York Times Magazine*, November 1, 1981, Section 6, pp. 42–58; 68–75.

Husen, T. (Ed.). *International study of achievement in mathematics*. Stockholm: Almquist & Wiksell, 1967.

Jencks, C., Smith, M., Acland, H., Bane, M. J., Cohen, D., Gintis, H., Heyne, B., & Michelson, S. *Inequality: A reassessment of the effect of family and schooling in America*. New York: Harper & Row, 1973.

Johnson, D. W., & Johnson, R. T. (Eds.). Social interdependence in the classroom: Cooperation, competition, and individualism. *Journal of Research and Development in Education*, 1978, *12*(1).

Klinger, E. *Meaning and void: Inner experience and the incentives in people's lives*. Minneapolis, University of Minnesota Press, 1977.

Klinger, E., & McNelley, F. W. Fantasy need achievement and performance: A role analysis. *Psychological Review*, 1969, *76*, 574–591.

Kukla, A. An attributional theory of choice. In L. Berkowitz (Ed.), *Advances in social psychology* (Vol. 11). New York: Academic Press, 1978.

Lefcourt, H. M. *Locus of control: Current trends in theory and research*. Hillsdale, N.J.: Lawrence Erlbaum Associates, 1976.

Lesser, G. S. Achievement motivation in women. In D. C. McClelland & R. S. Steel (Eds.), *Human motivation*. Morristown, N.J.: General Learning Press, 1973.

Lewin, K., Lippitt, R., & White, R. K. Patterns of aggressive behavior in experimentally created "social climates." *Journal of Social Psychology*, 1939, *10*, 271–299.

Lipman-Blumen, J., Leavitt, H. J., Patterson, K. J., Bies, R. J., & Handley-Isaksen, A. A model of direct and relational achieving styles. In L. J. Fyans, Jr. (Ed.), *Achievement motivation: Recent trends in theory and research*. New York: Plenum, 1980.

Maehr, M. L. Culture and achievement motivation. *American Psychologist, 1974, 29*, 887–896.

Maehr, M. L. Continuing motivation: An analysis of a seldom considered educational outcome. *Review of Educational Research, 1976, 46*, 443–462.

Maehr, M. L. Turning the fun of school into the drudgery of work: The negative effects of certain grading practices on motivation. *UCLA Educator, 1977, 19*, 10–14.

Maehr, M. L. Sociocultural origins of achievement. In D. Bar-Tal & L. Saxe (Eds.), *Social psychology of education: Theory and research*. New York: Wiley, 1978.

Maehr, M. L., & Kleiber, D. A. The graying of America: Implications for achievement motivation theory and research. In L. J. Fyans, Jr. (Ed.), *Achievement motivation: Recent trends in theory and research*. New York: Plenum Press, 1980.

Maehr, M. L., & Kleiber, D. A. The graying of achievement motivation. *American Psychologist, 1981, 36*, 787–793.

Maehr, M. L., & Nicholls, J. G. Culture and achievement motivation: A second look. In N. Warren (Ed.), *Studies in cross-cultural psychology* (Vol. 3). New York: Academic Press, 1980.

Maehr, M. L., & Sjogren, D. Atkinson's theory of achievement motivation: First step toward a theory of academic motivation? *Review of Educational Research, 1971, 41*, 143–161.

Maehr, M. L., & Stallings, W. M. Freedom from external evaluation. *Child Development,* 1972, *43,* 177–185.

Maehr, M. L., & Steinkamp, M. *A synthesis of findings on sex differences in science education research.* First year summary report, NSF project NSF–SED 80–07857, June 1981.

Maehr, M. L., & Willig, A. C. Expecting too much or too little: Student freedom and responsibility in the classroom. In H. Walberg & R. Luckie (Eds.), *Improving educational productivity: The research basis of school standards.* Chicago: NSSE Series in Contemporary Issues in Education, 1982.

McClelland, D. C. *The achieving society.* New York: The Free Press, 1961.

McKeachie, W. J. Motivation, teaching methods, and college learning. In M. R. Jones (Ed.), *Nebraska Symposium on Motivation.* Lincoln: University of Nebraska Press, 1961.

McKeachie, W. J., & Lin, Yi-Guang. Sex differences in student responses to college teachers: Teacher warmth and teacher sex. *American Educational Research Journal,* 1971, *8,* 221–226.

McKean, K. A scandal in the laboratory. *Discovery,* 1981, *2,* 18–20,23.

Mednick, M. S., Tangri, S. S., & Hoffman, L. W. (Eds.). *Women and achievement: Social and motivational analyses.* New York: Halsted Press, 1977.

Merton, R. K. *The sociology of science.* Edited and with an introduction by N. W. Storer. Chicago: University of Chicago Press, 1973.

Miller, A. Conceptual matching models and interactional research in education. *Review of Educational Research,* 1981, *51,* 33–84.

Miller, G. A., Galanter, E., & Pribram, K. H. *Plans and the structure of behavior.* New York: Holt, Rinehart, & Winston, 1960.

Mosteller, F., & Moynihan, D. P. *On equality of educational opportunity.* New York: Random House, 1972.

Nicholls, J. G. Creativity in the person who will never produce anything original and useful: The concept of creativity as a normally distributed trait. *American Psychologist,* 1972, *27,* 717–727.

Nicholls, J. G. Quality and equality in intellectual development: The role of motivation in education. *American Psychologist,* 1979, 1071–1084.

Nicholls, J. G. Striving to demonstrate and develop ability: A theory of achievement motivation. In W-U. Meyer & B. Weiner (Chair), *Attributional approaches to human motivation.* A symposium held at the Center for Interdisciplinary Research, University of Bielefeld, West Germany, July 1980.

Ouchi, W. *Theory Z corporations: How American business can meet the Japanese challenge.* Reading, Mass.: Addison–Worley, 1981.

Parsons, J. E., Heller, K. A., & Kaczalla, C. The effects of teachers' expectancies and attributions on students' expectations for success in mathematics. In D. McGorgan (Ed.), *Women's lives: New theory, research, and policy.* Ann Arbor, Mich.: Center for Continuing Education of Women, 1980.

Pascarella, E. T., Walberg, H. J., Junker, L. K., & Haertel, G. D. Continuing motivation in science for early and late adolescents. *American Educational Research Journal,* 1981, *18,* 439–452.

Roe, A. *The making of a scientist.* New York: Dodd, Mead & Co., 1953.

Roe, A., & Siegelman, M. *The origin of interests.* Washington, D.C.: American Personnel and Guidance Association, 1964.

Rosenshine, B. V., & Berliner, D. C. Academic engaged time. *British Journal of Teacher Education,* 1978, *4,* 3–16.

Salili, F., Maehr, M. L., & Gillmore, G. Achievement and morality: A cross-cultural analysis of causal attribution and evaluation. *Journal of Personality and Social Psychology,* 1976, *33,* 327–337.

Salili, F., Maehr, M. L., Sorensen, R. L., & Fyans, L. J., Jr. A further consideration of the effects of evaluation on motivation. *American Educational Research Journal,* 1976, *13,* 85–102.

Segal, S. M., Busse, T. V., & Mansfield, R. S. The relationship of scientific creativity in the biological sciences to predoctoral accomplishments and experiences. *American Educational Research Journal*, 1980, *17*, 491–502.

Shea, B. M. Schooling and its antecedents: Substantive and methodological issues in the status attainment process. *Review of Educational Research*, 1976, *46*, 463–526.

Skow, J. Creationism as social movement: The genesis of equal time. *Science 81*, 1981, *2*, 54, 57–60.

Spink, K. S., & Roberts, G. C. Ambiguity of outcome and causal attributions. *Journal of Sport Psychology*, 1980, *2*, 237–244.

Stake, R. E., & Easley, J. A. *Case studies in science education. A project for the National Science Foundation*. Center for Instructional Research and Curriculum Evaluation and Committee on Culture and Cognition, University of Illinois, Urbana–Champaign, January 1978.

Stein, A. H., & Bailey, M. M. The socialization of achievement orientation in females. *Psychological Bulletin*, 1973, *80*, 345–366.

Steinkamp, M. Motivational style as a mediator of adult achievement in science. In M. Steinkamp & M. L. Maehr (Eds.), *Women in science* (Recent advances in motivation and achievement, Vol. 1). Greenwich, Conn.: JAI Press, in press.

Terman, L. M. Scientists and nonscientists in a group of 800 gifted men. *Psychological Monographs: General and Applied*, 1954, *68*(7, Whole No. 378).

Wade, N. *The Nobel duel: Two scientists' 21-year race to win the world's most coveted research prize*. New York: Anchor/Doubleday, 1982.

Walberg, H. J. A psychological theory of educational productivity. In F. H. Farley & N. Gordon (Eds.), *Perspectives on educational psychology*. Chicago and Berkeley, Calif.: National Society for the Study of Education and McCutchan Publishing Co., 1980.

Walberg, H. J. *Educational productivity: Theory, evidence, and prospects*. Paper presented at an AERA Symposium, Los Angeles, Calif., April 1981.

Wang, M. C. Development and consequences of students' sense of personal control. In J. Levine & M. C. Wang (Eds.), *Teacher and student perceptions: Implications for learning*. Hillsdale, N.J.: Lawrence Erlbaum Associates, 1981.

Wang, M. C., & Stiles, B. An investigation of children's concept of self-responsibility for their school learning. *American Educational Research Journal*, 1976, *13*, 159–179.

White, R. W. Motivation reconsidered: The concept of competence. *Psychological Review*, 1959, *66*, 297–333.

White, R. W. Competence and the psychosexual stages of development. In M. R. Jones (Ed.), *Nebraska Symposium on Motivation* (Vol. 8). Lincoln: University of Nebraska Press, 1960.

White, R., & Lippitt, R. Leader behavior and member reaction in three "social climates." In D. Cartwright & A. Zander (Eds.), *Group dynamics: Research and theory*. New York: Harper & Row, 1968.

Wirzup, I. Soviet mathematics education. *University of Chicago Magazine*, 1980, *8*, 27–31.

Wirzup, I. *Meeting the new Soviet challenge in science education*. Remarks given at the meeting of the NSF–SEDR Project Directors, Washington, D.C., February 1981.

9
Conceptions of Ability and Achievement Motivation: A Theory and its Implications for Education

John G. Nicholls
Purdue University

Philip Jackson (1968) found that competent elementary school teachers judge their success by observing student interest or involvement in learning. There are good reasons for believing that these teachers are right to adopt involvement in learning as a working goal. As is shown later, there is evidence to support the view that, if teachers create and sustain the right motivation, many other educational problems will solve themselves. For example, students will themselves select material of an appropriate difficulty level and attend to it in a fashion that will most effectively foster their intellectual growth. It is simply beyond the resources of a teacher to assess constantly every student's understanding of every topic, to explain everything they must do to learn, to direct them to the most appropriate material, and to check that they spend the appropriate time and effort on each task. Fortunately, if the right motivation is maintained, children will select tasks of a suitable difficulty level and work on them in a productive manner.

What, then, is the optimum form of motivation for intellectual development? This question is addressed in the first half of this chapter, where an informal outline of an integrative theory of achievement motivation is presented. (For a derivation of the theory and more details, see Nicholls, 1980; submitted, 1982a). In the second half of the chapter, I consider the problem of maintaining optimum motivation in schools.

CONCEPTIONS OF ABILITY AND TASK- VERSUS EGO-INVOLVEMENT

Achievement behavior is distinguished from other forms of behavior by its purpose, which is the development or demonstration of competence rather than incompetence (Maehr & Nicholls, 1980; Nicholls, 1980). As one of the major functions of schools is to develop competence, one might leap to the conclusion that this would be best achieved by encouraging a strong desire for competence in students. But competence, or ability, has more than one meaning. There can also be different reasons for wanting to develop one's competence. There is, therefore, no unitary state of achievement motivation. Each individual's states of achievement motivation can vary in quality or type as well as in strength. Solution of the problems of motivation in education depends, it is argued, on maintenance of the right type, not just the right level of motivation. Three types or states of motivation can be distinguished: task-involvement, ego-involvement, and extrinsic involvement (Crutchfield, 1962; Nicholls, 1979). Normally, these will not exist as pure states. For the sake of economy, however, I write as if they do. This theory deals primarily with the first two, so let us first dispose of extrinsic involvement and then focus on task- and ego-involvement.

In extrinsic involvement, learning is seen or experienced as a means to an end. If children are learning to please a teacher, to gain a token, or to get out of school early, they are described as extrinsically involved. Learning is, for them, a means to these ends rather than an end in itself. It has been well established that extrinsic involvement is relatively ineffective in sustaining continuing motivation for learning (Condry & Chambers, 1978; Lepper & Greene, 1978; Maehr, 1976). It may also impair learning by focusing student attention on task completion and extrinsic incentives at the expense of the task (Condry & Chambers, 1978).

Task- and ego-involvement can more truly be called forms of achievement motivation because, in these states, the individual's purpose is to develop or demonstrate high rather than low ability. Nevertheless, task- and ego-involvement are very different psychological states and each individual's behavior changes when one rather than the other state is induced.

John Holt's (1964) book, *How Children Fail*, contains many descriptions of ego-involvement. For example:

> This child *must* be right. . . . When she is told to do something, she does it quickly and fearfully, hands it to some higher authority and awaits the magic words, "right," or "wrong." If the word is "right" she does not have to think about that problem any more; if the word is "wrong," she does not want to, cannot bring herself to think about it. . . . This fear leads her to other strategies. . . . The question arose the other day, "What is half of forty-eight?" Her hand was up; in the tiniest whisper she said, "Twenty-four." I asked her to repeat it. She said loudly, "I said," then whispered "twenty-four." I asked her to repeat it again, because many couldn't hear her. Her face showing tension, she said, very loudly, "I said that one-half of forty-eight is . . ." and then, very softly, "twenty-four." Still, not many of the students heard. She said, indignantly, "OK, I'll shout." I said that would be fine. She shouted in a self-righteous tone, "The question is, what is half of forty-eight. Right?" I agreed. And once again, in a voice scarcely above a whisper, she said, "Twenty-four." I could not convince her that she had shouted the question but not the answer [p. 33–34].

This illustrates two aspects of ego-involvement. First, the child is preoccupied with herself—with avoiding looking stupid—rather than with learning, understanding, or finding out. The second aspect of ego-involvement illustrated here is that learning, as such, is not valued. Learning is not an end in itself. Whether she was "right" or "wrong," that is the finish of the matter for her. She has little desire to go on learning. At best, learning is a means of avoiding looking stupid.

The essence of task-involvement is exemplified by Holt's (p. 67) question: "Are there any of them who are so busy with the world and with living that they just don't bother to think about themselves? Perhaps Betty." Compare Betty's approach to schoolwork with that of the previous girl. When other children in her class were trying to remember rules for adding fractions:

> Betty said, "$\frac{2}{4} + \frac{3}{5}$ is 1 or more. You need two more fifths to make 1 and $\frac{2}{4}$ is more than $\frac{2}{5}$ so the answer is bigger than 1." A remarkable kid. And yet, in a conventional school she might have been considered a "slow" pupil, and might have become one. She *likes* to look at things from several angles, to consider the meaning, or meanings of what she is doing before she does it. But on the whole, this is not the way to get ahead in school. [p. 114].

Betty illustrates two features of task-involvement: First a focus on the task rather than the self. Second, learning or understanding is, for her, an end in itself. Learning or understanding rather than looking smart or not looking stupid is her goal.

Task- and ego-involvement also differ in a third respect that is less clearly evident in the preceding examples: The basis for feelings of competence or incompetence is different in each state. In other words, individuals "use" different conceptions of ability when task-involved and when ego-involved (Nicholls, 1980). The conception of ability "employed" when individuals are task-involved is simpler than that employed in ego-involvement. At the simpler level, ability can be judged with reference to one's previous levels of performance. Learning is seen as dependent on effort, and more effort is seen as leading to more learning or greater ability. When we are task-involved, feelings of competence result if we gain a new insight or if we improve our performance: Ability is equivalent to learning. This is the conception of ability normally employed by children below about 6 years of age (Nicholls, 1978; Nicholls & Miller, in press-a).

There are, especially for adults and older children, times when a new insight or a gain in performance will not lead to feelings of competence. If we realize that others have achieved the same gain more quickly or with less effort, we may feel incompetent. In this instance, ability is judged high or low by comparison with others and is conceived as capacity. We judge IQ by comparing children's test scores with those of a normative reference group. We also require evidence of optimum effort if we are to judge an IQ score as valid. Such judgments indicate that we are thinking of ability as capacity relative to that of others—as something that sets a limit on the effects of effort. When ego-involved, individuals employ this more differentiated conception of ability.

Effort and learning have quite different meanings in task- and ego-involvement. With both conceptions of ability, it is assumed that more effort leads to more learning. When task-involved and employing the simpler conception of ability, individuals feel more competent if they master something with more effort. Learning is an end in itself and learning implies ability. When individuals are ego-involved, however, learning through effort only implies high ability if others need more effort for the same learning or if others learn less with the same effort. In other words, ego-involved students will not always expect learning through effort to lead to feelings of competence. Even when they expect to look able, ego-involved students will experience effort and learning as means to the end of demonstrating high ability.

To summarize, it is argued that it is useful to distinguish the psychological states of ego- and task-involvement. In task-involvement, learning is more inherently valuable, meaningful, or satisfying, and attention is focused on the task and the strategies needed to master it rather than on the self. In ego-involvement, on the other hand, learning is a means to the end of looking smart or avoiding looking stupid and attention is focused on the self. These differences between ego- and task-involvement are linked to different conceptions of ability. In task-involvement, learning or improvements in mastery imply competence. In ego-involvement, however, ability is conceived as capacity relative to that of others. The contrast between task- and ego-involvement is perhaps best encapsulated by visualizing task-involved individuals as asking themselves, "How does this work?" or "How can I learn this?" and ego-involved individuals as asking, "What can I do to look smart (compared to others) rather than stupid?" (Nicholls, 1979).

Evidence: The States of Task- and Ego-Involvement

A variety of forms of evidence support the distinction between task- and ego-involvement. Diener and Srull (1979), for example, found that when self-awareness was induced satisfaction depended on surpassing the performance of others. Peer norms, however, had little effect when self-awareness was not induced. In this case, satisfaction depended on improvement in performance. Peer performance norms, though available, had little impact. In other words, self-awareness led students to apply the conception of ability associated with ego-involvement—ability relative to that of others. Similar findings were obtained in two studies by Carver and Scheier (1980). They found that self-awareness was associated with a heightened concern about the performance of others.

When tasks are presented as measures of intelligence that will be used to evaluate individuals, the personal importance of performance is emphasized and the conception of ability as capacity is implied. Test anxiety researchers have repeatedly employed this manipulation. Results consistently indicate it produces both the increased self-focus and the concern to meet normative standards that characterize ego-involvement (Wine, 1971).

The subjective states of people who become absorbed in tasks such as rock climbing and surgery have been analyzed by Csikszentmihalyi (1977). He describes a flow experience involving self-forgetfullness. This: "does not mean, however, that a person loses touch with his own physical reality. In some flow activities, one becomes intensely aware of internal processes. . . . What is usually lost in flow is not the awareness of one's functions, but only the self-construct [p. 42]." This is an excellent description of a high level of task-involvement.

Csikszentmihalyi reports two other aspects of these task-involved states that are consistent with predictions for task-involvement. First, activities where this state occurs are seen as satisfying for reasons such as "enjoyment of the experience" and "use of skills." They are seen as ends in themselves. Ego-enhancing reasons such as: "prestige, rank, glamor or competition, measuring self against others," were more often given for competitive activities [p. 17]. This supports the link between task-involvement and perception of learning as an end in itself. This link is also supported by Diener and Srull's (1979) finding that self-awareness produced diminished feelings of freedom about the reward students could give themselves for performance. This applied even to self-aware individuals who surpassed group norms and improved on their own record.

A second feature of the flow states described by Csikszentmihalyi was that they depended on performance opportunities that were perceived as offering a reasonable challenge. As the concept of task-involvement implies, tasks presenting too small or too great a challenge in relation to the individual's own level of skill would not be seen as providing a chance to develop competence. The performance of others was not important in these states.

Finally, in a role-playing experiment, Jagacinski and Nicholls (1982) asked students to anticipate their feelings of competence on passing an Italian language test after high versus low effort. All subjects expected higher effort to lead to greater gains in competence. However, when a highly competitive (ego-involving) situation was simulated, students anticipated feeling less able when effort was high. This implies that they employed the differentiated conception where the "fact" that effort improves mastery conflicts with the "fact" that lower capacity is implied if higher effort is needed. No such conflict was apparent when a noncompetitive, learning for learning's sake situation was simulated. These results support the view that competitive rather than learning-oriented conditions engage the more differentiated conception of ability.

All in all, evidence from diverse types of study supports the distinction between task- and ego-involvement. Ego-involvement is likely to predominate over task-involvement when conditions, such as competition, induce self-focus or self-evaluation. Ego-involvement more than task-involvement implies evaluation of one's capacity compared to that of others, self-awareness, and perception of learning as a means to an end. These differences between task- and ego-involvement take on added significance for education when it is seen that the two states may have different effects on learning and performance.

Performance Attributions

The preceding discussion implies that individuals will interpret their performance differently in task- and ego-involvement. In task-involvement, for example, failure is likely to stimulate individuals to ask, "What must I do differently to succeed?" In ego-involvement, failure is more likely to occasion the question, "Am I stupid?" Success is also likely to be seen differently. In task-involvement, more effort implies greater gains in competence. Individuals would, therefore, tend to focus on what they learn through effort, and experience a greater sense of accomplishment, if they feel they have learned by trying hard. In ego-involvement, however, effort and learning are not sufficient to imply competence—effort or learning are but a means of beating others. Thus, effort should be emphasized less and ability more.

Carole Ames and her associates (Ames, 1978, 1981; Ames & Ames, 1978; Ames, Ames, & Felker, 1977) have conducted a series of studies comparing children's attributions in competitive (ego-involving) and noncompetitive conditions. These studies have shown that, in competitive conditions, children emphasize ability and (perhaps defensively) luck when interpreting their performance. In noncompetitive conditions, on the other hand, effort attributions are more salient. In noncompetitive situations students also feel more satisfied when they believe they have tried harder (Ames et al., 1977). Competitive conditions, however, minimize the association between satisfaction and perception of high effort and make beating others more important.

This research on performance attributions supports the view that ego-involvement is less likely to foster learning, especially in students who believe they lack ability. When ego-involved, such students would focus on their low ability and gain little satisfaction from trying hard. Task-involvement, by focusing attention on what is (or might be) accomplished through effort, should support continued learning and satisfaction with learning. This hypothesis is more directly supported by evidence on the effects of task- versus ego-involving conditions on task choice and performance on intellectual tasks.

Task Choice and Performance

When task-involved, individuals want to learn or understand and they feel competent when they feel they have learned. Thus, when task-involved, students are predicted to behave so as to maximize their chances of learning. They should choose tasks offering the best chances for learning. They should not choose impossibly difficult or trivially easy tasks because these offer little opportunity for improving one's skills. Instead they should choose tasks offering a realistic level of challenge. And, if presented with tasks on which they expect to be able to improve, they should set about doing this and experience satisfaction when they sense they are increasing their mastery.

The picture is quite different when individuals are ego-involved. In this state, learning is a means to the end of demonstrating higher rather than lower capacity than that of others. Thus, when ego-involved, individuals are only likely to make effective attempts to learn when they believe their attempts will show they have superior ability. Children with high perceived ability will generally expect to be able to look competent. Accordingly, they should generally behave adaptively: They should select tasks offering a reasonable challenge and work effectively with the expectancy of being able to demonstrate high ability.

Children who believe their ability is low relative to that of others, however, face a serious problem. They will generally not expect to be able to appear smart. Their self-preoccupation and expectation of looking stupid may produce anxiety that will impair their performance (Sarason, 1975). Such children will also prefer impossibly difficult tasks. Even though they will expect to fail on those tasks, they will at least avoid feeling stupid: No one can be expected to succeed on excessively difficult tasks.

The strain of expecting to look stupid can also lead to giving up. The term learned helpless (Abramson, Seligman, & Teasdale, 1978; Dweck & Goetz, 1978) appears best applied to such children—those who have given up any real commitment to avoiding looking stupid (as well as hope of looking smart). These children will choose very easy tasks where they are sure of success (Nicholls, submitted). They will also avoid learning unless coerced or bribed.

In summary, whether they are highly anxious about looking stupid or have given up hope of looking smart rather than stupid, children who perceive their ability (compared to that of others) as unacceptably low are not likely to learn effectively when they are ego-involved. When, on the other hand, children are task-involved, their capacity relative to that of others is not a concern. Instead they will focus their attention on the business of learning. Accordingly, their learning will not be impaired.

There is evidence to support the foregoing predictions (Nicholls, 1980, submitted, 1982a). Many studies show that individuals with low perceived ability perform better in task-involving than in ego-involving conditions and at a similar level to those with high perceived ability. Those with high perceived ability perform at similar levels in both states (Brockner, 1979; Brockner & Hulton, 1978; Ganzer, 1968; Gjesme, 1974; Paul & Eriksen, 1964; Perez, 1973; Sarason, 1959; Sarason & Palola, 1960; Shrauger, 1972).[1] Even on the short-term

---

[1]In these studies, measures of resultant achievement motivation, test anxiety, and self-esteem rather than measures of perceived ability are used. The rationale for considering the above as indices of perceived ability is given in Nicholls (1980, submitted).

tasks employed in this experimental research, task-involvement produces more effective performance in students with low perceived ability than does ego-involvement. Students with high perceived ability perform similarly in task- and ego-involvement.

The evidence on task difficulty preferences, though less abundant, also supports the foregoing predictions. Most important, ego-involving conditions induce low perceived ability individuals to choose tasks at which either success or failure is highly probable (DeCharms & Carpenter, 1968; Sears, 1940). In task-involvement, their choices are more realistic and thus more likely to enable skill development (Raynor & Smith, 1966; Schneider 1973).

A fairly common response to the suggestion that schools should not emphasize competition is the claim that children have to learn to be realistic about their abilities. Competition is often seen both as a means of rewarding excellence and as a means of helping children to assess their abilities realistically (Tuchman, 1980). People who advance this view overlook the paradox that competitive conditions produce unrealistic levels of aspiration and maladaptive levels of anxiety and helplessness. Realistic goalsetting and optimum performance are favored by task-involvement. The theory and data on performance and task choice, therefore, support the view that induction and maintenance of task-involvement should be a major educational goal.

Help Seeking

Readiness to acknowledge a lack of understanding and to seek help seems a rational strategy if one's goal is to improve one's understanding. Holt (1964) suggests that: "The good student may be one who often says that he does not understand, simply because he keeps a constant check on his understanding [p. 28]."

Russell Ames (in press) has proposed that ego-involving conditions are likely to make asking for help seem like an admission of low ability and, thereby, to reduce the likelihood that students who doubt their competence will seek help. His review of the evidence on asking for assistance supports this proposal. Almost all the studies of help seeking were conducted in evaluative situations that would be likely to induce ego-involvement. Ames and Lau (in press), for example, found that help seeking after low exam scores was most common among students who believed they had high general ability and believed that effort and acquisition of specific skills would overcome learning difficulties. In this and other studies reviewed by Ames, students with low perceived ability were less likely to seek assistance. Thus, it seems that ego-involvement will reduce the likelihood that students with doubts about their ability will take advantage of teachers' offers to assist them.

Ames also proposes that task-involvement will minimize this problem because, when task-involved, individuals are concerned with learning rather than with avoiding appearing incompetent. This thesis receives support from a study of peer tutoring (Bierman & Furman, 1981). When it was implied that learners were assigned to the learner role because of a lack of competence, they showed reluctance to seek assistance from the tutor. When differential ability was not implied, however, tutees were more receptive to help. There is, therefore, reason to believe that task-involving conditions will increase learning by increasing students' readiness to seek help when they need it.

Piaget and Intellectual Development

The case for task-involvement is consistent with the Piagetian view of intellectual development. Piaget's concept of equilibration implies that intellectual development occurs when children sense inadequacies in their knowledge. This sense of inadequacy is not, however, a sense of personal inadequacy. Disequilibrium implies "epistemic shock" (Coie, 1973) rather than personal shock. It is more a matter of "What's going on here?" than of "Wrong again" or "I must be stupid." A sense of inadequacy or disequilibrium state is resolved by development of more adequate knowledge or new states of equilibrium. Techniques designed to induce disequilibrium or a sense of contradiction in the child's own knowledge have been found to stimulate the development of logical thought (Kuhn, 1972; Smedslund, 1968) and more mature problem solving (Coie, 1973).

In the Piagetian view (Elkind, 1976; Kohlberg & Mayer, 1972), sound intellectual development requires that children reorganize their own physical and social worlds because these reorganizations make these worlds more meaningful. If children's purpose in learning is to gain their teacher's approval, to demonstrate that they are smarter than their peers, or if they have any goal other than improved understanding, understanding and the learning process itself will, in this view, suffer. It would, however, be a mistake to conclude that the Piagetian view implies that teachers should not play an active role in the development of logical thought. The teacher's role is to stimulate, guide, and encourage rather than to instruct.[2] Fostering the development of logical thinking "involves the Socratic method and is exciting and challenging for both teacher and learner [Elkind, 1976, p. 230]." In short, the Piagetian view is that intellectual development will be fostered by a focus on understanding rather than on the self or on extrinsic inducements: by task-involvement rather than ego- or extrinsic involvement.

---

[2]Direct instruction does have a place, for example, in the memorization of arithmetic tables. It does not, however, have a place in the development of understanding of the logic behind the arithmetic tables (Elkind, 1976).

Creative Achievement and Task-Involvement

T. S. Kuhn (1968) has noted a parallel between Piaget's view of the mechanism of the development of logical thinking in children and the development of the sciences. In Kuhn's view, scientific revolutions are precipitated by perception of an anomaly or anomalies in accepted scientific positions. This is analogous to the sense of contradiction to which Piaget refers. In science, new theories or approaches result from attempts to resolve such perceived anomalies just as new levels of logical thinking in children are responses to a sense of contradiction. Kuhn implies that creative scientists may differ from less creative scientists in their sensitivity to such anomalies. This implies that creative scientists would be distinguished from others by a stronger desire to understand the world or to make sure theories "make sense": that is, by higher levels of task-involvement rather than ego- or extrinsic involvement.

In fact, research evidence gives some support to the notion that outstanding creative achievement in science and the arts is fostered by high levels of task-involvement (Nicholls, 1972, 1979). This adds weight to the argument that conditions that facilitate this form of motivation might indeed foster children's intellectual development and performance. Crutchfield (1962) has suggested that creative people are resistant to social pressure because of a stronger orientation to task requirements. McCurdy (1960) concluded that the childhood pattern of genius involves early finding of pleasure in the world of ideas. He also contended that eminent people are highly independent by virtue of reliance on and commitment to their own ideas. Roe (1952) reported a similar pattern in physical and biological scientists. Creative architects studied by MacKinnon (1965) were inclined to strive where independent activity was called for and were guided by self-generated standards of excellence, whereas less creative architects achieved through conformity to professional standards. A similar pattern was also found with mathematicians (Helson, 1971; Helson & Crutchfield, 1970). Taylor and Ellison (1967) and Chambers (1964) reported self-initiated, task-oriented striving as a distinguishing characteristic of creative scientists. Thus, creative individuals do appear to be more task-involved.

Helmreich and Spence (1977) found that productivity in science and grades at university were higher for people who showed a preference for challenging tasks, internal standards of excellence, hard work, and keeping busy. The desire to outperform others was not a distinguishing characteristic of high achievers. This also suggests that task-involvement rather than ego-involvement may provide the basis of favorable intellectual achievement in children. Cecil Day-Lewis's (1969) advice to poets could also apply to children and scientists. "Each poet must (he says) go on writing as best he may, learning to stop worrying about his stature, his rank in the hierarchy . . . and to become ever more fully absorbed in the task [p. v]."

It should be noted that outstanding achievements are generally made in the context of a relatively competitive society (Maehr, this volume). The theory and experimental evidence previously reviewed indicates that, in a competitive context, it may be necessary to be assured of one's ability to perform well compared to others before one can follow Day-Lewis's advice to forget about one's rank in the hierarchy and focus on the requirements of the task. The admittedly competitive nature of the sciences and the arts might lead one to speculate that a tendency to ego-involvement would lead to high achievement. The evidence reviewed here does not indicate that creative adults are devoid of competitive tendencies. But, it is not consistent with the view that such tendencies distinguish them from their less creative peers.

The desire to win has almost certainly played a role in many valuable achievements (e.g., Watson, 1968). However, it also seems to have produced plenty of cheating. For example, Cyril Burt's slide into dubious scientific practices, according to Hearnshaw (1979), appears partly due to the fact that: "he gradually became more and more jealous of any rivals to his own pre-eminence in his chosen field. [p. 269]." "He could not tolerate any challenge . . . 'he had to win' . . . [p. 269–270]." As the balance between task-involvement and ego-involvement swung toward the latter, his contributions to psychology, which had been of the highest order, became increasingly spurious (Hearnshaw, 1979).

Even though some elements of interpersonal competition will probably always be present in the sciences and the arts, there are not good grounds for advocating more of it. Task-involvement, on the other hand, appears to be a major contributor to significant creative work as well as to optimum learning in children.

Ethical Considerations

The case for task-involvement as a working educational objective is supported by a variety of forms of empirical evidence. But, even if task-involvement produced slower learning than ego- or extrinsic involvement, there would be ethical grounds for favoring task involvement. Would not something be wrong if children believed that the world is round or that $2 + 2 = 4$ simply because "the teacher says it is" or because they get higher grades by learning such things more quickly than others?

The case for task-involvement is consistent with the progressive approach to education. As stated by Kohlberg and Mayer (1972): "Intellectual education in the progressive view is not merely a transmission of information and intellectual skills, it is the communication of patterns and methods of scientific reflection and inquiry [p. 475]." A "scientific" orientation resists indoctrination and frees the individual from dependence on arbitrary external authority. It does not substitute idiosyncratic impulse or unexamined notions for the imperatives of arbitrary authority. It fosters an open-mindedness that is disciplined by facts and rational reflection and renewed by novel hypotheses. No discipline is more severe or more liberating. The progressive view is not merely that intellectual development *is* best fostered by the concern to understand that is exemplified by a scientific approach to the world. Progressives also hold that intellectual development *ought* to be fostered in this way (Dewey, 1938; Kohlberg & Mayer, 1972). In other words, even if learning could be fostered by encouraging dependence on external authority or the desire to beat others, it should not be.

As Piaget (1964) argued, we need people who: "can be critical, can verify, and not accept everything they are offered. The great danger today is of slogans, collective opinions, ready-made trends of thought. . . . So we need pupils who are active, who learn early to find out by themselves . . . who learn early to tell what is verifiable and what is simply the first idea to come to them [p. 5]."

Other Achievement Theories

The present theory incorporates distinctions and insights from many others. (For a formal derivation of the present version, see Nicholls, submitted, 1982a.) My purpose, in this section, is to note the major predecessors of and contributors to the present theory and to show how they contrast with it.

Perhaps the most important difference between this and many other approaches to achievement motivation is that others do not explicitly recognize that competence can be construed in different ways. Consequently, many other theorists do not make a distinction equivalent to that between task- and ego-involvement. Atkinson's theory (Atkinson & Raynor, 1974), for example, applies best to the state of ego-involvement. Its predictions are similar to those made here for ego-involvement. Atkinson's theory, however, does not encompass task-involvement. Like the present theory, Kukla's position gives perceived ability an important role in the mediation of behavior. Kukla does not, however, distinguish the two conceptions of ability. His predictions apply in some cases to task-involvement (1972) and in others (1978) to a state midway between task- and ego-involvement. Learned helplessness theory (Abramson et al., 1978; Dweck & Goetz, 1978) implicitly employs the conception of ability as capacity. It, therefore, applies better to ego-involved states. Bandura (1977) also fails to distinguish the different conceptions of competence. At times he appears to refer to both task- and ego-involved states, but the distinction is blurred.

Attribution theory (Weiner, 1972) implicitly employs the more differentiated conception of ability as capacity. It distinguishes the concepts of effort, difficulty, and ability. These can only be distinguished from one another when ability is conceived as capacity relative to that of others (Nicholls, submitted, 1982a; Nicholls & Miller, in press-a). Thus, it might appear that attribution theory is more applicable to ego- than task-involvement. In practice, however, attribution theory proves very flexible. As shown previously, attribution theory-generated research (Ames et al., 1977) can help illuminate the nature of both task- and ego-involvement.

Other theorists have separately made the three distinctions that are integrated here under the rubric of task- versus ego-involvement. First, Carver and Scheier (1981) distinguish self-aware and non-self-aware states and apply this distinction to the phenomena of achievement behavior. Second, Kruglanski (1975) distinguishes endogenously and exogenously attributed actions. That is, respectively, actions seen as ends in themselves and actions seen as means to an end. This is similar to the distinction between intrinsic and extrinsic motivation (Lepper & Greene, 1978). These theorists do not, however, make the three-way distinction between task-, ego-, and extrinsic involvement. Third, Covington and Beery (1976) point out that a sense of personal worth can be achieved either through striving toward individual excellence or through beating others. This implies the present distinction between the two conceptions of ability. Consequently, Covington and Berry's suggestions for education are similar to and complement those presented in the following section. Maehr (this volume) also makes similar and further distinctions and educational suggestions.

Finally, I should not overlook Holt's (1964) observations, which were not intended as theory, but which capture what I have tried to describe and quite a bit more.

SUSTAINING TASK-INVOLVEMENT

Many problems of academic motivation appear to result from the ego-involving properties of classrooms (Nicholls, 1979). Teaching, grading, and feedback practices that focus student attention on comparisons of their performance with the performance of others appear widespread and have been well documented (Bloom, 1976; Brophy & Good, 1974; Covington & Beery, 1976; Good, 1980; Heckhausen & Krug, 1982; Weinstein, 1976). Weinstein, for example, has observed teachers emphasizing ability differences between reading groups. If ego-involvement is induced by such practices, this would explain why children with low attainment and low perceived ability typically behave in ways that impair their learning. Rather than trying to determine how to understand material or learn the relevant procedures, these children appear to spend much of their energy trying to avoid looking stupid (Covington & Beery, 1976; Good, 1980; Holt, 1964). Even if they are not actively wasting effort in this maladaptive pursuit, their learning is, as the preceding review reveals, likely to suffer.

In classes that foster ego-involvement, techniques that improve one child's perceived ability are likely to diminish that of others. Miller, Brickman, and Bolen (1975), for example, found that teacher statements implying that randomly selected students were able led to lowered perceived ability in students who observed but did not receive this feedback. There appears to be no way of resolving this dilemma if ego-involvement—concern about how one's ability compares to that of others—is maintained. Ego-involved students are concerned about looking smart compared to their peers and someone will always have to be below average. Even extra teacher assistance for low achievers is likely to be taken as evidence that they lack ability (Weinstein & Middlestadt, 1979). Thus as Ames (in press) shows, they will avoid seeking help. And, even if they receive assistance, it may be self-defeating.

The problems associated with ego-involvement become more serious with age. Young children conceive of ability as learning through effort. The conception of ability as capacity develops gradually over the elementary and junior high school years (Nicholls, 1978; Nicholls & Miller, in press-a, in press-b). This means that older children are more likely to become concerned about how their ability compares with that of others. It also means that perception of low ability is more serious for older children. Perception of lack of capacity has serious personal consequences (Nicholls & Miller, in press a), and only older children conceive of ability as capacity. These developmental trends are paralleled by increases in the frequency of ego-involving teaching practices (e.g., public and socially comparative grading) as children progress through the grades (Eccles, Midgley, & Adler, in press). Though the problem becomes less tractable with age, it is by no means absent even in the first grade (Weinstein, 1976).

Invaluable though they are for our understanding of classrooms, the many studies of the ways teachers influence student expectancies or perceived ability (Bar-Tal, 1979) do not help solve the problems associated with ego-involvement. Such studies do not show how low self-concepts can be prevented or suggest how optimum motivation and learning can be fostered in children who know they are at the bottom of their class. Someone has to be at the bottom. It would be rash to deny this or to lie about it. But even the child at the bottom will improve if task-involvement can be sustained.

It is not necessary for teachers to know a student's intellectual potential to establish whether that student is fulfilling his or her potential. Evidence of task-involvement will indicate that optimum learning is occurring. Paradoxically, teachers who are preoccupied with estimating children's potential in the classroom may create conditions that will reduce their chances of fulfilling that potential (Heckhausen & Krug, 1982). If a teacher is trying to judge whether Jane should be performing at third-grade level, the teacher is concerned about how Jane's reading compares with that of others. If this concern is communicated to her, it is likely to make her ego-involved. Research on the processes whereby teachers form and communicate general performance expectancies is useful for explaining how low self-concepts of ability are formed. It is, however, not directly applicable to the teacher's central task. As competent teachers realize (Jackson, 1968), their major task is to create and sustain task-involvement and to minimize children's preoccupation with task-extrinsic incentives or with how their ability compares with that of others. If we can sustain task-involvement, students will be more likely to focus their attention on methods of mastering tasks and to gain a sense of competence from gains in mastery. They will find learning meaningful. They will choose tasks of suitable difficulty levels, perform on them effectively, ask for help when they need it, and have a continuing interest in learning. What then are methods that will sustain task-involvement?

Characteristics of classroom materials and teachers' methods of introducing and explaining content must surely contribute to task-involvement. I focus here, however, on three categories of social and personal factors that might sustain task-involvement: first, the value framework of teaching or the wider goals school is seen as serving; second, the organizational strategies that can be adopted to facilitate learning and motivation; and finally, specific feedback from teachers to children. The following suggestions are not all as soundly grounded in research evidence as one might wish. These suggestions are, therefore, intended to stimulate thought about the problem rather than to announce definitive solutions.

Reasons for Schooling

Educational psychologists at times appear prone to view educational problems as technological rather than ethical or value problems. But if our values contribute to our problems, the technological approach is unlikely to solve them. Rather we will have to reexamine our values. What might be the role of values in achievement motivation?

Values and Ego-Involvement.   Informal observations suggest that children who ask, "Why do we have to learn math (or any other subject)?" are often told it is important to do well in schoolwork to get a good job. This rationale invokes self-interest and is, at best, only likely to appeal to those who believe they have high ability. It also presents school learning as a means rather than an end. As Dewey (1938) put it, "The ideal of using the present simply to prepare for the future contradicts itself. It omits, and even shuts out the very conditions by which a person can be prepared for his future [p. 49]."

Interviews of third graders (Nicholls, unpublished data, University of Illinois, 1979) confirmed that they understood that the purpose of school was to prepare them for occupations. But this fact had already been noted by others. Kahl (1953) reported that among bright working-class boys:

> School and the possibility of college were viewed . . . solely as steps to jobs. None was interested in learning for the subtle pleasures it can offer; none craved intellectual understanding for its own sake. The most common phrase in the entire body of interviews was "nowadays you need a high school diploma (or a college degree) to get a good job." . . . the boys wanted the parchment, not the learning [p. 196].

This theme is supported by Friedenberg's (1963) observations. For example, when high school students or PTA members discussed dropouts: "Nobody suggested that they might be missing anything in school that was worthwhile for its own sake or that might enrich their later life aesthetically or conceptually." "They spoke only of the trouble the dropouts were going to have getting and keeping jobs . . . and a satisfactory level of social status [p. 165]."

When schooling is seen as a means to occupational status, learning is not of inherent value. It is a means to an end and success is defined in terms of the competitive status ranking of occupations. Views such as those already expressed, of the purposes of schooling are, therefore, likely to induce ego-involvement. This may make learning (and even life itself) less meaningful even for those who expect to make it to the top. It is, however, likely to be especially serious for those who believe their capacity is below average. Ego-involvement produces markedly impaired performance in such students. When the long shadow of work falls across the schoolroom, inequality in the motivation necessary to develop intelligence seems sure to follow (Bowles & Gintis, 1976). "Fair" competition for status and wealth becomes inherently unfair because it produces inequalities in motivation. Intervention attempts that do not substitute a more benign ethic seem bound for limited success.

Individualized learning or mastery learning programs, for example, have been proposed as techniques that allow children to gain satisfaction from progressing at their own rate (Bloom, 1976). However, I and others (Crockenberg & Bryant, 1978) have observed such programs turning into races. Instead of serving as individualized goals, the various steps of these programs can become important for students as evidence of their place in the race. If task-involving reasons for learning can be substituted, such programs might function more effectively.

Values and Task-Involvement. Though education is often conceived as a race for occupational status, there are other views that provide a value context that appears more likely to facilitate task-involvement. For example, according to Friedenberg (1963): "The highest function of education . . . is to help people understand the meaning of their lives, and become more sensitive to the meaning of other people's lives and relate to them more fully [p. 221]." If one's purpose is to gain understanding, then a very wide range of learning activities can, in and of themselves, achieve this purpose—such learning can be an end in itself.

Such statements may appear unrealistically idealistic. Yet, Adelson and O'Neil (1966) found that older adolescents held a similar view of the purpose of education. These students saw competence and general understanding on the part of citizens as essential for the vitality of society and the well-being of individuals within it. There is also evidence that at least some adolescents personally adopt such altruistic purposes (Hoyt & Hebeler, 1974). Learning that increases one's understanding is itself justified within this value context. We might, therefore, attempt to articulate such altruistic reasons in schools and make our choice of subjects and methods of teaching more consistent with them. This strategy is supported by a study by Wiesieltier with university students (cited by Kruglanski, 1978). She found that perceptions of altruistic goals of others increased perception of others' intrinsic involvement in learning. Someone who studied medicine to gain a high income was seen as less intrinsically interested in learning than someone whose goal was to help cure cancer patients. For the second type of person, more than the first, the study of medicine itself was seen to be inherently worthwhile—an end in itself. A recent study with junior high and high school students (Nicholls, 1982b) produced the same result.

There are many ways such goals might be expressed in the classroom. For example, if a class were discussing Abraham Lincoln, teachers might suggest or elicit the possibility that his concern for and understanding of people, law, and justice make us respect him. The mere fact that he made it from log cabin to White House did not make him memorable. Others who made a similar change of lodgings are more forgettable. Similar opportunities might be used if teachers were looking for them.

Recent interviews I have conducted (Nicholls, 1982b) indicate that children believe that schooling does not merely serve to get them employment. They also realize that increased understanding of the world is of value in its own right and that learning is more meaningful if it is to serve others. Schooling might more effectively engage this altruism and desire to learn if we treated it less like a race for status. We might do well to reflect more fully on the ways we talk about education to our children. However, sensitive discussion of the purposes of schooling is unlikely to be sufficient to maintain task-involvement. In addition, we should consider the more down-to-earth matter of organizing classroom learning in ways that are consistent with the view that the purpose of education is to increase understanding and contribute to society rather than simply to select and prepare students for their place in the occupational status hierarchy.

The Organization of Learning

Task-involvement can often be transformed to extrinsic involvement by the introduction of rewards or surveillance (Lepper & Green, 1978). Presence of an obvious reason for learning, such as a prize or the possibility of pleasing a teacher, can reduce interest in the task itself. Learning that is felt to be an end in itself can thereby be transformed to a means. Research on such effects is useful in that it suggests the dangers of techniques that imply, for children, either coercion or bribery. More relevant, however, are studies that suggest positive actions teachers might take to induce and maintain task-involvement.

First, Maehr and Stallings (1972) and Salili, Maehr, Sorenson, and Fyans (1976) compared the effects of student evaluation of their own performance with normative evaluation by teachers. Teacher evaluation (where test performance was assessed by the teacher and would contribute to grades) is a plausible task-extrinsic reason for learning. This would be likely to make learning a means rather than an end. Children would feel they are learning to "look good" or to gain approval. Personal evaluation should make learning more an end in itself—children appear more likely to feel they are doing the work to master it. In fact, personal evaluation did produce greater continuing interest in the learning material.

Another technique that can help induce task-involvement is student scheduling of classroom learning. Though learning remains required, as it normally is, students are systematically given and encouraged to take considerable responsibility for organizing their own learning schedules. This should help make learning an end in itself. In the more usual system, where work is assigned by the teacher, endogenous reasons for learning, like interest, are likely to be discounted because teacher assignment is a plausible alternative reason. In accord with this prediction, Wang and Stiles (1976) found assignments were completed more frequently with self-scheduling than teacher scheduling of schoolwork. Similarly, high school science students showed more care and involvement in laboratory work when encouraged to organize their own experiments than when given detailed instructions and direction (Rainey, 1965; see also Thomas, 1980).

Naturally occurring differences among classrooms produce comparable results. Elementary school teachers who encourage student autonomy rather than emphasize direct teacher control produce higher levels of task-involvement and a higher sense of competence (Deci, Schwartz, Sheinman, & Ryan, 1981). Similarly, in high school science classrooms where students had greater control over learning, there was more evidence of interest in science (Pascarella, Walberg, Junker, & Haertel, 1981).

In the aforementioned studies, students were given only slightly more personal control over learning than is traditional. Nevertheless, the results support Dewey's (1938) view that: "There is, I think, no point in the philosophy of progressive education which is sounder than its emphasis upon the importance of the participation of the learner in the formation of the purposes which direct his activities in the learning process [p. 65]." When schools do follow Dewey's advice more fully, they appear to enhance dramatically the development of higher levels of knowledge (Clinchy, Lief, & Young, 1977).

Cooperative learning methods not only serve to minimize competition and to give students more responsibility for learning. They are also consistent with the view that learning can enable us to make a contribution to the lives of others rather than serve as a means of triumphing over them. One of the more ingenious cooperative methods is the jigsaw learning method (Aronson, Stephan, Sikes, Blaney, & Snapp, 1978). In this method, material for a lesson (in, for example, social studies) is presented in sections. Students in small groups each learn one section of the lesson. They prepare to teach their section to students who, at the same time, are learning other sections. When each group has mastered its section, new groups are formed. In these, each member has learned and must teach a unique part of the whole lesson. Each student must also learn, from the others, what the others have learned. Thus, the children are interdependent. Compared to traditional methods, the jigsaw method reduces derogation of other students and improves self-esteem, attitudes to learning, and achievement in low achievers. (Effects for more able students are slight.) A variety of other methods of inducing student collaboration rather than competition have been shown to have similar positive effects (e.g., Sharan, 1980).

A cooperative climate appears to make students more inclined to learn from others. Conflict of ideas, rather than being a threat to one's self-concept of ability, can be seen as a source of greater understanding (Johnson, Johnson, & Scott, 1978; Smith, Johnson, & Johnson, 1981). Thus, cooperative methods may both reduce ego-involvement and foster task-involvement—a concern to learn and understand without an emphasis on whether one has thereby demonstrated higher or lower capacity than that of others.

Finally, we should expect that, provided a competitive atmosphere is avoided, task-involvement will be maintained best by teachers who assign or allow students to choose materials of an appropriate difficulty level for each child. Rheinberg (1982; Heckhausen & Krug, 1982) developed a test that distinguishes teachers who evaluate student performance in terms of each individual's learning history from those who emphasize comparison of students. Those who adopt the perspective of the individual's own progress strive to provide each student with tasks that present a moderate challenge and offer praise or blame on the basis of improvement or its absence. Teachers who compare students with others generally assign the same tasks to all students and praise those who perform better than others. Children were found to be aware of these differences in teaching styles. Further, the students of teachers who individualized instruction had less academic anxiety, were less likely to attribute failure to low ability, and felt they improved more. These effects were most marked with low-achieving students—those who suffer the worst effects in ego-involvement and stand to gain most in well-being and learning in task-involvement (Heckhausen & Krug, 1982).

The different approaches to organizing learning discussed in the foregoing section have normally been considered as separate topics. But, each approach is related to one or another aspect of task involvement. The techniques that encourage increased student responsibility for their own learning make learning more an end than a means. Likewise, cooperative learning techniques transfer responsibility for learning to students. Cooperative methods also directly counter the competitive ethos that would foster ego-involvement and would, thereby, make others' knowledge a threat rather than an interest. Individualized learning allows students to progress without preoccupation with the progress of others. As noted earlier, however, individualized learning alone may fail to achieve this objective. (See also Heckhausen & Krug, 1982). The application of any one method may not, in itself, guarantee task-involvement. In any event, the method as such is probably not the crucial focus for teachers. Methods will have to be used, with appropriate rationales for learning, in whatever combinations are necessary to achieve task-involvement with each student and each class.

Teacher Feedback

If a teacher has managed to establish a climate of task-involvement, feedback on the correctness of responses or on procedures for solving problems seems likely to serve its purpose. Students are likely to use such feedback to improve their understanding or mastery. If, on the other hand, ego-involvement predominates, the same feedback may present a threat to student self-esteem—it may imply low capacity. In other words, the effect of teacher feedback may often depend on the climate of the classroom. If this is so, establishment of a task-involving climate would be the first order of business. There may, however, be forms of feedback teachers could give to individual students and to the entire class that would help sustain a climate of task-involvement.

One possibility is teacher attribution—to individual students or the entire class—of interest or desire for understanding. The effectiveness of attribution (or labeling) has been demonstrated by Miller, Brickman, and Bolen (1975) in a pair of studies (already noted above) conducted in intact classrooms. In these studies, teachers attributed desired qualities to their children. They simply told the children they had certain characteristics. In one study, teachers repeatedly but in diverse ways told their classes they were very litter conscious. These statements were directed at the entire class. In the other study, teachers told randomly selected students they were hard workers or high in ability at math. Though children did not immediately accept the labels applied to them, they began to behave in ways consistent with these labels—they became litter conscious and showed stable increases in math performance.

When some children are labeled smart, others are, by implication, labeled low in ability. This may be less of a problem with attributions of interest or of a desire to understand. Interest is a quality that all children could have. One child's interest need not imply another's lack of it. Such attributions can also be made to a whole class as were the attributions of litter consciousness (e.g., "Well, you people certainly really think about this." "It's great to see everyone wanting to understand this properly." "My word, you sure are interested in. . . ."). Attributions of this type could help maintain task-involvement and, thereby, optimum learning.

Labeling should be distinguished from persuasion and reward or praise. Persuasion usually labels the student as deficient in desired qualities (e.g., "You should work harder" implies "You don't work hard."). Reward avoids this problem, but can only be used when the student has already done the right thing.

Labeling of students with desired characteristics may not be the technique most of us would think of first, but it proved more effective than reward or persuasion in Miller et al's (1975) studies. Labeling students as interested, therefore, seems worth trying as a supplement to the other strategies for fostering task-involvement.

CONCLUDING CAUTIONS

We should have no illusions about the problems of creating task-involvement in every classroom. Two related obstacles loom particularly large. First is the schools' function of separating those students who will enter high status occupations from those who will not and the associated student view that the purpose of learning is to gain a high status occupation. When schools emphasize this function, they appear bound to induce ego-involvement and thereby impair intellectual development—especially in those students who realistically or erroneously come to conclude that they lack intellectual capacity. Technological or methodological fixes can be expected to have limited impact as long as schooling is seen as a race for status. Educational reform movements that do not deal with this problem of values (rather than merely of psychology) are likely to be subverted.

In Bowles and Gintis' (1976) view, the fruit of Dewey's progressive educational theory withered because: "his central thesis as to the economic value of an educational system devoted to fostering personal growth is untrue in capitalist society. Dewey's view requires that work be a natural extension of intrinsically motivated activity. The alienated work of corporate life is inimical to intrinsic motivation [p. 46]." It does not follow that teachers who set out to increase task-involvement are doomed to fail. As the preceding review indicates, there are teachers who make impressive strides in this direction. Their task might be more manageable if occupational life were less autocratic, alienating, and status oriented.

The second problem is that ability to teach so as to maintain task-involvement appears to require a high level of maturity. Harvey, Hunt, and Schroder (1961) have distinguished four levels of cognitive style. The most mature style is termed abstract and the least mature, concrete. Abstract teachers, who appear to be a minority, have been observed to teach in ways that are more likely to sustain task-involvement. They are less overtly controlling, encourage individual responsibility more, are more resourceful in presenting learning activities, and encourage more student theorizing and search behavior (Harvey, Prather, White, & Hoffmeister, 1968; Harvey, White, Prather, Alter, & Hoffmeister, 1966; Murphy & White, 1970). Concrete teachers appear to see knowledge as something that they as authorities must transmit to students with no need for student initiative or self-direction. (See also Sarason, Davidson, and Blatt, 1962.)

Cohen, Emrich, and DeCharms (1976) sought to train a group of teachers to adopt the strategies employed by abstract teachers. But, they report: "We trained the teachers to understand our concepts; we assumed that teachers would want to apply our training inputs and would know how to do so. Apparently these assumptions were unwarranted [p. 38]." It seems, therefore, that the most effective strategy may not be to explain or show what is necessary to maintain task-involvement. On the other hand, teacher education programs that foster personal and cognitive development (Sprinthall & Thies-Sprinthall, 1982) may thereby educate teachers who will themselves seek out or devise methods like or much better than those suggested here.

This concluding note may seem unduly negative. However, the important question is, is it realistic? The problems of education must be as old as history (Candland, 1980). They inevitably involve societal and ethical as well as psychological problems (Kohlberg & Mayer, 1972). If we see these problems purely as technical and psychological problems in isolation from the functions of schools in our society and the personal development of educators, I submit that we will underestimate the difficulty of the task.

The problem may be that we have not been pessimistic enough. Even though Dewey overlooked the obstacles to progressive education noted by Bowles and Gintis (1976), he believed that: "the road of the new education is not an easier one to follow than the old road but a more strenuous and difficult one. . . . The greatest danger that attends its future is . . . the idea that it is an easy way to follow, so easy that its course may be improvised [Dewey, 1938, p. 90]." Dewey feared that his arguments would be taken as support for laissez-faire romanticism—as favoring abdication of responsibility on the part of teachers rather than increased teacher responsibility for making students more responsible for their own learning. As the evidence gathered by Harvey and associates indicates, teaching so as to encourage task-involvement demands more, not less, of teachers.

Unrealistic aspirations are increased by ego-involvement. Perhaps I am trying to avoid the accusation of ego-involvement by ending on a rather bleakly realistic note. But it seems that one should recognize the difficulties teachers must face when they seek to teach as if "The most important attitude that can be formed is that of desire to go on learning [Dewey, 1938, p. 48]."

ACKNOWLEDGMENTS

Preparation of this paper was supported in part by NSF Grant 7914252, University of Illinois subcontract. I am grateful to Carol Dweck and Martin Maehr for discussions that contributed to the ideas presented here. Many graduate students in New Zealand and the United States have, over the years, seen fit to argue with me on many of the matters discussed here. They were often right. I may forget some names so I will not mention any. But, wherever they are, thanks.

REFERENCES

Abramson, L. Y., Seligman, M. E. P., & Teasdale, J. D. Learned helplessness in humans: Critique and reformulation. *Journal of Abnormal Psychology*, 1978, *87*, 49–74.

Adelson, J., & O'Neil, R. The development of political thought in adolescence: The sense of community. *Journal of Personality and Social Psychology*, 1966, *4*, 295–306.

Ames, C. Children's achievement attributions and self-reinforcement: Effects of self-concept and competitive reward structure. *Journal of Educational Psychology*, 1978, *70*, 345–355.

Ames, C. Competitive versus cooperative reward structures: The influence of individual and group performance factors on achievement attributions and affect. *American Educational Research Journal*, 1981, *18*, 273–287.

Ames, C., & Ames, R. Thrill of victory and agony of defeat: Children's self and interpersonal evaluations in competitive and non-competitive learning environments. *Journal of Research and Development in Education*, 1978, *12*(1), 79–81.

Ames, C., Ames, R., & Felker, D. W. Effects of competitive reward structure and valence of outcome on children's achievement attributions. *Journal of Educational Psychology*, 1977, *69*, 1–8.

Ames, R. Help-seeking and achievement orientation: Perspectives from attribution theory. In De-Paulo, Nadler, & Fisher (Eds.), *New directions in helping*, in press.

Ames, R. & Lau, S. An attributional analysis of help-seeking in academic settings. *Journal of Educational Psychology*, in press.

Aronson, E., Stephan, C., Sikes, J., Blaney, N., & Snapp, M. *The jigsaw classroom*, Beverly Hills, Calif.: Sage, 1978.

Atkinson, J. W., & Raynor, J. E. (Eds.). *Motivation and achievement*. New York: V. H. Winston, 1974.

Bandura, A. Self-efficacy: Toward a unifying theory of behavioral change. *Psychological Review*, 1977, *84*, 191–215.

Bar-Tal, D. Perceptions and behaviors of pupils and teachers: An attribution of analysis. In I. H. Frieze, D. Bar-Tal, & J. S. Carroll, (Eds.), *Attribution theory: Applications to social problems*, San Francisco: Jossey–Bass, 1979.

Bierman, K. L., & Furman, W. Effects of role and assignment rationale on attitudes formed during peer tutoring. *Journal of Educational Psychology*, 1981, *73*, 33–40.

Bloom, B. S. *Human characteristics and school learning*. New York: McGraw–Hill, 1976.

Bowles, S., & Gintis, H. *Schooling in capitalist America*. New York: Basic Books, 1976.

Brockner, J. Self-esteem, self-consciousness, and task performance: Replications, extensions, and possible explanations. *Journal of Personality and Social Psychology*, 1979, *37*, 447–461.

Brockner, J., & Hulton, A. J. B. How to reverse the vicious cycle of low self-esteem: The importance of attentional focus. *Journal of Experimental Social Psychology*, 1978, *14*, 564–578.

Brophy, J. E., & Good, T. L. *Teacher–student realtionships: Causes and consequences*. New York: Holt, Rinehart, & Winston, 1974.

Candland, D. K. Speaking words and doing deeds. *American Psychologist*, 1980, *35*, 191–198.

Carver, C. S., & Scheier, M. F. *Attention and self-regulation: A control-theory approach to human behavior*. New York: Springer–Verlag, 1981.

Chambers, J. A. Relating personality and biographical factors to scientific creativity. *Psychological Monographs*, 1964, *78*(7, Whole No. 584).

Clinchy, B., Lief, J., & Young, P. Epistemological and moral development in girls from a traditional and a progressive high school. *Journal of Educational Psychology*, 1977, *69*, 337–343.

Cohen, M. W., Emrich, A. M., & DeCharms, R. Training teachers to enhance personal causation in students. *Interchange*, 1976, *7*(1), 34–38.

Coie, J. D. The motivation of exploration strategies in young children. *Genetic Psychology Monographs*, 1973, *87*, 177–196.

Condry, J. D., & Chambers, J. Intrinsic motivation and the process of learning. In M. R. Lepper & D. Greene (Eds.), *The hidden costs of reward: New perspectives on the psychology of human motivation.* Hillsdale, N.J.: Lawrence Erlbaum Associates, 1978.

Covington, M. V., & Beery, R. G. *Self-worth and school learning.* New York: Holt, Rinehart, & Winston, 1976.

Covington, M. V., & Omelich, C. L. Effort: The double-edged sword in school achievement. *Journal of Educational Psychology*, 1979, *71*, 169–182.

Crockenberg, S., & Bryant, B. Socialization: The "implicit curriculum" of learning environments. *Journal of Research and Development in Education.* 1978, *12*, 69–77.

Crutchfield, R. S. Conformity and creative thinking. In H. E. Gruber, G. Terrell, & M. Wertheimer (Eds.), *Contemporary approaches to creative thinking.* New York: Prentice–Hall, 1962.

Csikszentmihalyi, M. *Beyond boredom and anxiety.* San Francisco: Jossey–Bass, 1977.

Day-Lewis, C. *Selected poems.* Harmondsworth, Eng.: Penguin, 1969.

DeCharms, R., & Carpenter, V. Measuring motivation in culturally disadvantaged school children. In J. J. Klausmeier & G. T. O'Hearn (Eds.), *Research and development toward the improvement of education.* Madison: Dembar Education Services, 1968.

Deci, E. L., Schwartz, A. J., Sheinman, L., & Ryan, R. M. An instrument to assess adults' orientations toward control versus autonomy with children: Reflections on intrinsic motivation and perceived competence. *Journal of Educational Psychology*, 1981, *73*, 642–650.

Dewey, J. *Experience and education.* Kappa Delta Pi: 1938.

Diener, E., & Srull, T. K. Self-awareness, psychological perspective, and self-reinforcement in relation to personal and social standards. *Journal of Personality and Social Psychology*, 1979, *37*, 413–423.

Dweck, C. S., & Goetz, T. E. Attributions and learned helplessness. In J. H. Harvey, W. Ickes, & R. F. Kidd (Eds.), *New directions in attribution research* (Vol. 2). Hillsdale, N.J.: Lawrence Erlbaum Associates, 1978.

Eccles (Parsons), J. E., Midgley, C. & Adler, T. Age-related changes in the school environment: Effects on achievement motivation. In J. G. Nicholls (Ed.), *The development of achievement motivation.* Greenwich, Conn.: JAI Press, in press.

Elkind, D. *Child development and education: A Piagetian perspective.* New York: Oxford University Press, 1976.

Friedenberg, E. Z. *Coming of age in America.* New York: Vintage Books, 1963.

Ganzer, V. J. Effects of audience presence and test anxiety on learning and retention in a serial learning situation. *Journal of Personality and Social Psychology*, 1968, *8*, 194–199.

Gjesme, T. Goal distance in time and its effects on the relations between achievement motives and performance. *Journal of Research in Personality*, 1974, *8*, 161–171.

Good, T. L. *Teacher expectations, teacher behavior, student perceptions, and student behavior: A decade of research.* Invited address presented at the meeting of the American Educational Research Association, Boston, 1980.

Harvey, O. J., Hunt, D. E., & Schroder, H. M. *Conceptual systems and personality organization.* New York: Wiley, 1961.

Harvey, O. J., Prather, M., White, B. J., Hoffmeister, J. K. Teachers' beliefs, classroom atmosphere, and student behavior. *American Educational Research Journal*, 1968, *5*, 151–165.

Harvey, O. J., White, B. J., Prather, M., Alter, R. D., & Hoffmeister, J. K. "Teachers" belief systems and preschool atmospheres. *Journal of Educational Psychology*, 1966, *57*, 373–381.

Hearnshaw, L. S. *Cyril Burt: Psychologist.* New York: Cornell University Press, 1979.

Heckhausen, H., & Krug, S. Motive modification. In A. Steward (Ed.), *Motivation and society: Essays in honor of David C. McClelland.* San Francisco: Jossey–Bass, 1982.

Helmreich, R. L., & Spence, J. T. The secret of success. *Discovery: Research and Scholarship at the University of Texas at Austin*, 1977, *11*(2), 4–7.

Helson, R. Women mathematicians and the creative personality. *Journal of Consulting and Clinical Psychology*, 1971, *36*, 210–220.

Helson, R., & Crutchfield, R. S. Mathematicians: The creative researcher and the average PhD. *Journal of Consulting and Clinical Psychology*, 1970, *34*, 250–257.

Holt, J. *How children fail*. New York: Dell, 1964.

Hoyt, K. B., & Hebeler, J. R. *Career education for gifted and talented students*. Salt Lake City: Olympus, 1974.

Jackson, P. W. *Life in classrooms*. New York: Holt, Rinehart, & Winston, 1968.

Jagacinski, C., & Nicholls, J. G. *Conceptions of ability*. Paper presented at the meeting of the American Educational Research Association, New York, 1982.

Johnson, D. W., Johnson, R., & Scott, L. The effects of cooperative and individualized instruction on student attitudes and achievement. *Journal of Social Psychology*, 1978, *104*, 207–216.

Kahl, J. A. Educational and occupational aspirations of "common man" boys. *Harvard Educational Review*, 1953, *23*, 186–203.

Klinger, E. Consequences of commitment to and disengagement from incentives. *Psychological Review*, 1975, *82*, 1–25.

Kohlberg, L., & Mayer, R. Development as the aim of education. *Harvard Educational Review*, 1972, *42*, 449–496.

Kruglanski, A. W. The endogenous–exogenous partition in attribution theory. *Psychological Review*, 1975, *82*, 387–406.

Kruglanski, A. W. Endogenous attribution and intrinsic motivation. In M. R. Lepper & D. Greene (Eds.), *The hidden costs of reward: New perspectives on the psychology of human motivation*. Hillsdale, N.J.: Lawrence Erlbaum Associates, 1978.

Kuhn, D. Mechanisms of change in the development of cognitive structures. *Child Development*, 1972, *43*, 833–844.

Kuhn, T. S. A function for thought experiments. *Ontario Journal of Educational Research*, 1968, *10*, 211–231.

Kukla, A. Foundations of an attributional theory of performance. *Psychological Review*, 1972, *79*, 454–470.

Kukla, A. An attributional theory of choice. In L. Berkowitz (Ed.), *Advances in social psychology* (Vol. 11). New York: Academic Press, 1978.

Lepper, M. R., & Greene, D. (Eds.). *The hidden costs of reward: New perspectives on the psychology of human motivation*. Hillsdale, N.J.: Lawrence Erlbaum Associates, 1978.

MacKinnon, D. W. Personality and the realization of creative potential. *American Psychologist*, 1965, *20*, 273–281.

Maehr, M. L. Continuing motivation: An analysis of a seldom considered educational outcome. *Review of Educational Research*, 1976, *46*, 443–462.

Maehr, M. L., & Nicholls, J. G. Culture and achievement motivation: A second look. In N. Warren (Eds.), *Studies in cross-cultural psychology* (Vol. 2). New York: Academic Press, 1980.

Maehr, M. L., & Stallings, W. M. Freedom from external evaluation. *Child Development*, 1972, *43*, 177–185.

McCurdy, H. G. The childhood pattern of genius. *Horizon*, 1960, *2*, 33–38.

Miller, R. L., Brickman, P., & Bolen, D. Attribution versus persuasion as a means for modifying behavior. *Journal of Personality and Social Psychology*, 1975, *31*, 430–441.

Murphy, P. D., & White, M. M. Conceptual systems and teaching styles. *American Educational Research Journal*, 1970, *7*, 529–520.

Nicholls, J. G. Creativity in the person who will never produce anything original and useful: The concept of creativity as a normally distributed trait. *American Psychologist*, 1972, *27*, 717–727.

Nicholls, J. G. The development of the concepts of effort and ability, perception of own attainment, and the understanding that difficult tasks require more ability. *Child Development*, 1978, *49*, 800–814.

Nicholls, J. G. Quality and equality in intellectual development: The role of motivation in education. *American Psychologist*, 1979, *34*, 1071–1084.

Nicholls, J. G. Striving to develop and demonstrate ability: A theory of achievement motivation.

Paper presented in W.-U. Meyer & B. Weiner (Chair), *Symposium on Human Motivation*, Center for Interdisciplinary Studies, University of Bielefeld, West Germany, August 1980.

Nicholls, J. G. *Achievement motivation: Conceptions of ability, subjective experience, task choice, and performance*. Manuscript submitted for publication, 1982. (a)

Nicholls, J. G. Reasons for schooling. Paper presented in J. Parsons (Chair), *Defining the meaning of success and achievement*. Symposium presented at the meeting of the American Educational Research Association, New York, 1982. (b)

Nicholls, J. G., & Miller, A. T. Development and its discontents: The differentiation of the concept of ability. In J. G. Nicholls (Eds.), *The development of achievement motivation*. Greenwich, Conn.: JAI Press, in press. (a)

Nicholls, J. G., & Miller, A. T. The differentiation of the concepts of ability and difficulty. *Child Development*, in press. (b)

Pascarella, E. T., Walberg, H. J., Junker, L. K., & Haertel, G. D. Continuing motivation in science for early and late adolescents. *American Educational Research Journal*, 1981, *18*, 439–452.

Paul, G. L., & Eriksen, C. W. Effects of test anxiety on "real-life" examination. *Journal of Personality*, 1964, *32*, 480–494.

Perez, R. C. The effect of experimentally induced failure, self-esteem, and sex on cognitive differentiation. *Journal of Abnormal Psychology*, 1973, *81*, 74–79.

Piaget, J. Development and learning. In R. E. Ripple & V. N. Rockcastle (Eds.), *Piaget rediscovered*. Ithaca, N.Y.: Cornell University, 1964.

Rainey, R. G. The effects of directed vs. non-directed laboratory work on high-school chemistry achievement. *Journal of Research in Science Teaching*, 1965, *3*, 286–292.

Raynor, J. O., & Smith, C. P. Achievement-related motives and risk-taking in games of skill and chance. *Journal of Personality*, 1966, *34*, 176–198.

Rheinberg, F. *Achievement motivation and its application to educational psychology*. Paper presented at the meeting of the American Educational Research Association, New York, 1982.

Roe, A. *The making of a scientist*. New York: Dodd, Mead, 1952.

Salili, F., Maehr, M. L., Soresen, R. L., & Fyans, L. J. A further consideration of the effects of evaluation on motivation. *American Educational Research Journal*, 1976, *13*, 85–102.

Sarason, I. G. Relationships of measures of anxiety and experimental instructions to word association test performance. *Journal of Abnormal and Social Psychology*, 1959, *59*, 37–42.

Sarason, I. G. Anxiety and self-preoccupation. In I. G. Sarason & C. D. Spielberger, (Eds.), *Stress and anxiety* (Vol. 2). Washington, D.C.: Wiley–Hemisphere, 1975.

Sarason, S. B., Davidson, K. S., & Blatt, B. *The prepration of teachers: An unstudied problem*. New York: Wiley, 1962.

Sarason, I. G., & Palola, E. G. The relationship of test and general anxiety, difficulty of task, and experimental instructions to performance. *Journal of Experimental Psychology*, 1960, *59*, 185–191.

Schneider, K. *Motivation under Erfolgsriskia*. Gottingen: Hogrefe, 1973.

Sears, P. S. Levels of aspiration in academically successful and unsuccessful children. *Journal of Abnormal and Social Psychology*, 1940, *35*, 498–536.

Sharan, S. Cooperative learning in small groups: Recent methods and effects on achievement, attitudes, and ethnic relations. *Review of Educational Research*, 1980, *50*, 241–271.

Scheier, M. F., & Carver, C. S. *Self-directed attention and the comparison of self with standards*. Unpublished manuscript, Carnegie–Mellon University, 1980.

Shrauger, J. S. Self-esteem and reactions to being observed by others. *Journal of Personality and Social Psychology*, 1972, *23*, 192–200.

Smith, K., Johnson, D. W., & Johnson, R. T. Can conflict be constructive? Controversy versus concurrence seeking in learning groups. *Journal of Educational Psychology*, 1981, *73*, 651–663.

Sprinthall, N. A., & Thies-Sprinthall, L. Career development of teachers: A cognitive developmental perspective. In H. Mitzel (Ed.), *Encyclopedia of Educational Research,* Riverside, N.J.: MacMillan, 1982.

Taylor, C. W., & Ellison, R. L. Biographical predictors of scientific performance. *Science,* 1967, *155,* 1075–1080.

Thomas, J. W. Agency and achievement: Self-management and self-regard. *Review of Educational Research,* 1980, *50,* 213–240.

Tuchman, B. The decline of quality. *New York Times Magazine.* November 2, 1980, pp. 38–41; 104.

Wang, M. C., & Stiles, B. An investigation of children's concept of self-responsibility for their school learning. *American Educational Research Journal,* 1976, *13,* 159–179.

Watson, J. D. *The double Helix: A personal account of the discovery of the structure of DNA.* New York: Atheneum, 1968.

Weiner, B. *Theories of motivation: From mechanism to cognition.* Chicago: Markham, 1972.

Weinstein, R. Reading group membership in first grade: Teacher behaviors and pupil experience over time. *Journal of Educational Psychology,* 1976, *68,* 103–116.

Weinstein, R. S., & Middlestadt, S. E. Student perceptions of teacher interactions with male high and low achievers. *Journal of Educational Psychology,* 1979, *71,* 421–431.

Wine, J. Test anxiety and direction of attention. *Psychological Bulletin,* 1971, *76,* 92–104.

10 Children's Theories of Intelligence: Consequences for Learning

Carol S. Dweck
Janine Bempechat
Harvard University

Motivational factors can have pronounced and far-reaching effects on children's learning and performance. They determine such critical things as whether children seek or avoid challenges and whether they persist in the face of obstacles—in short, whether children actually pursue and master the skills they value and are capable of mastering. Interestingly, facilitating and debilitating motivational tendencies are often independent of actual ability, as measured either by prior performance on a given task, school grades, or standardized intellectual assessments, such as IQ tests (Crandall, 1969; Dweck & Licht, 1980; Weiner, 1972). This implies that even among the most highly capable students are those who are apt to show impairment in the face of challenge. It also means that among children who are not particularly proficient are those who thrive on challenge. Why might this happen?

In this chapter we examine beliefs about intelligence that are unrelated to measures of intelligence but that appear to promote or interfere with learning. Specifically, we focus on children's theories of intelligence and show how the different theories may dictate children's choice of achievement goals and may determine their success in reaching those goals.

We begin by describing our past research on the patterns of cognition, affect, and behavior that appear to facilitate or impair performance in achievement situations. Following this, we show how these patterns may stem from different theories of intelligence—intelligence as an "entity" or trait that is judged vs. intelligence as a dynamic repertoire of skills that is increased through one's efforts. We suggest that the view of intelligence as a judgeable entity orients children toward competence judgments (toward looking smart, or, "performance" goals), whereas the view of intelligence as a quality that grows orients

239

children toward competence building (toward getting smarter, or, "learning" goals). Further, we suggest it is the former view that renders children vulnerable to debilitation in the face of obstacles, and the latter view that spurs persistence even when children believe themselves to be unskilled at the task at hand. We then describe a series of recent studies that provides evidence that children's beliefs about the nature of intelligence do in fact predict the goals they choose to pursue (learning or performance) and the achievement patterns they display (facilitating or debilitating).

Finally, we explore the educational implications of these findings: What practices might foster the different theories of intelligence, and how might teachers' own theories dictate these practices? For example, what strategies (e.g., types of tasks or feedback regimes) would teachers holding different theories employ to make children feel smart? How might some of these strategies produce effects that are virtually the opposite of what was intended?

We turn now to the patterns that we have repeatedly observed in achievement situations.

PATTERNS OF PERFORMANCE IN ACHIEVEMENT SITUATIONS

In a variety of studies in classrooms and laboratory settings in which children have been asked either to master new academic materials (e.g., certain principles of psychology), learn novel skills, or perform already demonstrated skills, we have repeatedly observed coherent, organized patterns of behavior that come into play and appear to either facilitate or impair performance. These patterns become particularly pronounced in the face of obstacles. That is, under conditions in which difficulty is experienced, some children become incapable of performing effectively, even on problems they had previously solved with relative ease. In contrast, other children bring to bear on the task new levels of concentration and effort. These pronounced individual differences, although experimentally manipulable (Dweck, Davidson, Nelson, & Enna, 1978), emerge reliably in the absence of clear cues (Diener & Dweck, 1978, 1980; Dweck, 1975; Dweck & Reppucci, 1973; Licht & Dweck, 1981). Moreover, it has been a continual source of interest to us that the tendency to display the facilitating or debilitating pattern in the face of difficulty appears to be virtually independent of the child's level of ability—either as assessed by such standardized measures as IQ or achievement tests or by measures of task performance prior to encountering obstacles.

These affect-cognition-behavior patterns were examined in detail in a series of studies conducted by Diener and Dweck (1978, 1980), and this research serves as the basis for the discussion that follows. Briefly, fifth and sixth graders were trained to perform a three-dimension, two-choice visual discrimination task. The stimuli were systematically varied so that each child's hypothesis-testing strategy could be inferred from his or her choices, classified according to level of sophistication, and tracked for changes in sophistication over all problems (cf. Gholson, Levine, & Phillips, 1972). Children were given a total of twelve problem sets. All children, with training, succeeded in solving the first eight problems (success trials), but failed to reach solution on the next four problems (failure trials). In order to tap salient moment-to-moment cognition and affect, children were instructed, following the seventh problem set, to verbalize aloud as they performed.

Table 10.1 presents these verbalization results. However, before continuing, two points should be addressed. First, children were divided into two groups prior to the individual sessions on the basis of their responses to an attribution questionnaire (The Intellectual Achievement Responsibility (IAR) scale of Crandall, Katkovsky & Crandall, 1965.) Although these responses are extremely reliable predictors of reactions to failure, as we will see they are likely to be reflective of even more basic, underlying beliefs. Second, we are very sensitive to the issue of confronting children with such difficult tasks, and have perfected procedures involving mastery experiences that ensure that each child leaves the situation feeling his or her performance was highly commendable. Indeed, this mastery procedure is similar to ones that have been shown to have beneficial effects on children's subsequent persistence in the face of failure (e.g., Dweck, 1975).

To return to our data, two distinct patterns emerged. As we will see, one pattern appears to be organized around evaluations of ability and the other appears to be organized around the acquisition of ability. The first, the "learned

TABLE 10.1
Number of Helpless and Mastery-Oriented Children with
Verbalizations in Each Category

Category of verbalizations	Group Helpless	Mastery-oriented	x^2 $(df = 1)$	p
Ineffectual task strategy	14	2	12.27	.001
Attributions to lack of ability	11	0	13.46	.001
Self-instructions	0	12	15.00	.001
Self-monitoring	0	25	42.86	.001
Statements of positive affect	2	10	6.00	.025
Statements of negative affect	20	1	26.46	.001
Statements of positive prognosis	0	19	27.8	.001
Solution-irrelevant statements	22	0	34.74	.001

Adapted from Diener, C.I., & Dweck, C.S., 1978. An analysis of learned helplessness: Continuous changes in performance, strategy, and achievement cognitions following failure. *Journal of Personality and Social Psychology*, 1978, *36*, p. 459. Copyright 1978 by the American Psychological Association. Adapted by permission.

helpless" pattern (cf. Seligman, Maier & Solomon, 1971) is accompanied by marked debilitation in the face of obstacles. Despite their prior successes, children who displayed this pattern tended to react to difficulties as though they were insurmountable: They very quickly began to interpret their errors as indicative of insufficient ability and as predictive of future failure. That is, they began to make attributions for their errors to a lack of ability (e.g., "I never did have a good 'rememory'") and for many of them, errors were readily viewed as implying some rather permanent and generalized incompetence (e.g., "I'm not smart enough") (see Weiner, 1972, 1974). This type of self-denigration occurred even though, moments before, their performance had been quite excellent, and even though they had not really attempted very much in the way of alternative strategies or increased effort.

Nevertheless, in line with their attributions to lack of ability, these children showed increased impairment of their problem-solving strategies, increased negative affect, and negative prognosis for subsequent outcomes. Whereas by the end of training, all children were using effective strategies and a sizable proportion were using the top level strategy employed by children their age, by the fourth trial 60 to 70% had lapsed into stereotypical or perseverative choice patterns, ones that could never yield solution. Furthermore, when children were asked whether they thought they could now solve one of the problems they had solved before if it were to be readministered, 100% of the "mastery-oriented" children replied in the affirmative, whereas only 65% of the helpless children did so.

It is also interesting to note the striking differences between the helpless children and their mastery-oriented counterparts in recall for success and failure. As depicted in Table 10.2, helpless children recalled having successfully solved significantly fewer problems and having failed to solve significantly more problems than the mastery-oriented children. In short, helpless children rapidly question their ability in the face of obstacles, perceiving past successes to be few and irrelevant, and perceive future effort to be futile.

The second pattern, called "mastery oriented," is characterized by intensified effort in the face of difficulty. Children who displayed this pattern seemed to focus at once on how to overcome their errors. Indeed, they did not tend to

TABLE 10.2
Recall of Successes and Failures by Helpless and Mastery-Oriented
Children

Type of Problem and Actual Number	Helpless	Mastery-Oriented	p Value of Difference
Success (=8)	5.14	7.51	p < .01
Failure (=4)	6.14	3.71	p < .01

leap to or even seek attributions for failure, and much of their behavior indicated that they did not really consider themselves to be failing. Specifically, their verbalizations consisted primarily of self-instructions and self-monitoring designed to aid performance (e.g., "OK, now I really need to concentrate," "I should slow down and try and figure this out"). In addition, these "mastery-oriented" children maintained positive affect and a positive prognosis about task outcomes. Some expressed what appeared to verge on delight at the chance to confront a challenge or gain new skills. Furthermore, many children not only maintained but improved their problem-solving strategies over the "failure" trials: They taught themselves new and more sophisticated strategies in their attempt to master the task. In sharp contrast to the helpless children, who were no longer using the top level strategy by the end of the failure trials, an additional 25% of the mastery-oriented children had begun to use this strategy by the end of these trials. Interestingly, some proportion of the mastery-oriented children lapsed temporarily into ineffective patterns, but then climbed out and began to strategize anew. In short, these children appeared to view the skill required by the task as one that they could acquire by applying themselves. Moreover, they appeared to give themselves the time and the leeway to do so.

Thus, although both groups of children received identical problems and feedback, the evidence suggests that they were structuring the situation quite differently—either as a *performance* situation that involved evluations of competence, a display or demonstration of that competence, or as a *learning* situation that provided an opportunity to increase competence.

What might underlie these different ways of structuring achievement situations? These different views imply an emphasis on very different conceptions of competence: competence as a stable, general, "judgeable" entity or as a repertoire of dynamic, acquirable skills. And, indeed, our current research is suggesting that children's conceptions of intellectual competence—their personal theories of intelligence, play an important role in these achievement patterns.

CHILDREN'S THEORIES OF INTELLIGENCE

Our research has indicated that children hold two functional or operating theories of intelligence. The one they tend to emphasize is the one that appears to guide their behavior in novel achievement settings. We propose that these implicit theories are beliefs around which achievement behavior, affect, and cognitions are organized.

The first theory, which we have called an "entity" theory, involves the belief that intelligence is a rather stable, global trait. Children favoring this theory tend to subscribe to the idea that they possess a specific, fixed amount of intelligence, that this intelligence is displayed through performance, and that the outcomes or judgments indicate whether they are or are not intelligent. The second theory, which we call an "instrumental-incremental" theory, involves the belief that intelligence consists of an ever-expanding repertoire of skills and knowledge, one that is increased through one's own instrumental behavior. By middle to late grade school, children understand aspects of both theories, but tend to focus on one in thinking about intelligence. (For related observations see Harari & Covington, 1981; Marshall, Weinstein, Middlestadt, & Brattesani, 1980; Surber, 1982. For treatment of conceptions of mind and intelligence from a more "cognitive" point of view see Goodnow, 1980; Sternberg, Conway, Ketron, & Bernstein, 1981; Wellman, 1981.) That is, although instrumental theorists realize that individuals may differ in the rate at which they acquire skills, they focus on the idea that anyone can become smarter (more skillful and more knowledgeable) by investing effort. Entity theorists also realize that virtually everyone can increase their skills or knowledge, but they do not believe that people can become smarter. It is important to note that some children may act in accordance with different theories in different skill areas (e.g., physical vs. intellectual skills). In addition, situational factors may create strong tendencies to adopt one theory over the other. For example, a critical exam may make entity considerations highly salient. Yet, in the absence of strong cues, we find striking individual differences in which theory children tend to endorse and use as a guide for their behavior (M. Bandura & Dweck, 1981).

We have assessed these differences by presenting children with several pairs of contrasting notions about the meaning of smartness. Each pair of ideas pits an essential component of the entity view against an essential component of the incremental view of intelligence. The extent to which children endorse one of the two perspectives is taken to indicate their favored theory of intelligence. For example, inherent in the entity view is the belief that intelligence is essentially static, whereas the incremental theory implies that intelligence can be increased by one's own actions. Thus, one item poses the choice: "You can learn new things, but how smart you are stays pretty much the same" vs. "Smartness is something you can increase as much as you want to."

Essentially, then, children with an entity theory are those who tend to view intelligence as an attribute they possess that is relatively global and stable, that can be judged as adequate or inadequate, and that is both limited and limiting. In contrast, children with an incremental theory tend to view intelligence as something they produce—something with great potential to be increased through their efforts.[1]

---

[1]An intriguing issue, and one we are investigating, concerns the extent to which entity and incremental theories may serve as the basis for conceptualizing other major domains. That is, are these two theories alternative ways of viewing a variety of personal attributes, not simply intelligence? Indeed, most of the attributes that are generally considered to constitute basic qualities of the "self" are amenable to these alternative conceptualizations (e.g., artistic or physical competence, physical appearance, or morality). That is, they may be seen as rather fixed traits that can be judged to be adequate or inadequate or as dynamic qualities that can be cultivated by actions or increased through effort.

Predictions

When one considers the differences inherent in the two definitions of intelligence, one is led to predict that entity and incremental theorists would adopt different goals in achievement situations. That is, the tendency to conceive of intelligence as a judgeable entity would seem likely to incline one towards seeking positive judgments and/or avoiding negative ones, toward goals that involve "looking smart"—*performance* goals. In contrast, the tendency to conceive of intelligence as a body of skills that grows through one's efforts would seem likely to incline one toward seeking to increase one's skills, toward the goal of "becoming smarter"—*learning* goals (see Dweck & Elliott, 1983 and Nicholls, 1981 for an extensive discussion of achievement goals).

It is important to note that these various goals need not be mutually exclusive and, indeed, may often be held simultaneously. Some situations allow one both to learn and to perform well. Therefore, we are not suggesting that entity theorists do not wish to develop skills or increase their knowledge, or that incremental theorists are always unconcerned with global judgments that others might make. We are proposing, however, that the two theories of intelligence create a differential likelihood of adopting one goal over others, particularly when they come into conflict. And they do, because the same tasks that maximize learning are often poor tasks for looking smart and vice versa. Tasks most suitable for learning are often ones that are difficult, involve errors, confusion, or revelations of ignorance, and require a lengthy presolution period. In contrast, tasks that are often best-suited for performance goals are ones that appear to be difficult or are difficult for others, but are relatively easy for the individual—tasks that yield rapid solutions with little effort, or at least tasks on which one is fairly certain one can outperform others.

Thus, entity theorists should adopt goals that tend to involve positive judgments of their intelligence or avoid negative judgments of their intelligence. If they feel confident of their ability, this should lead them to aim toward the former and, under these conditions, to display mastery-oriented behavior. Low confidence should make them aim toward the latter, to attempt to conceal their perceived lack of ability from an evaluator, and to be vulnerable to the helpless pattern in the face of failure. In contrast, incremental theorists should be more likely to choose goals that involve learning. Unlike entity theorists, who focus on the documentation of competence, children with an incremental view should focus on the acquisition of competence. Because within a learning framework, encountering obstacles does not signify lack of ability, these children should display the mastery-oriented pattern in the pursuit of their goals.

Therefore, we would actually predict *two* facilitating (mastery-oriented) patterns: a performance-oriented one and a learning-oriented one. When might these two types of mastery-oriented children differ? One would predict this to occur when the different goals come into conflict, that is, when a choice must be made between learning and performing. For example, if the acquisition of some valued skill or knowledge involved a likely display of errors or confusion, mastery-oriented entity theorists might be more likely than incrementalists to sacrifice that opportunity, particularly if a less "risky" option were available. Indeed, our findings suggest that this distinction between the two types of mastery-orientation is in fact a useful one.

In the following section, we present research evidence for the hypothesis that children's theories of intelligence predict their choice of achievement goals, and that their achievement goals predict their achievement patterns.

Research Evidence

Table 10.3 both summarizes the foregoing discussion and provides the structure within which we will place our research findings. Let us look first at the second column, labeled "performance goal expectancy." This refers to the child's subjective probability of obtaining positive and avoiding negative competence judgments, and, in conjunction with the third column "goal choice" is intended to represent the idea that this estimate will be a determining factor in goal choice within an entity theory, but not within an incremental theory.

We assume that performance goal expectancies are the result of a series of judgments on the part of the child. For example, the child may make some assessment of his or her present skill or aptitude, may consider this in relation to such factors as the perceived task requirements, may use this information to predict some level of performance, may then ask whether the predicted performance will reach his or her standards, and so on (see Dweck & Elliott, 1983). Although we will not scrutinize this process, it is important to note that actual competence, however defined, does not necessarily translate directly into performance goal expectancies. In fact, for girls, a *negative* relationship is sometimes

TABLE 10.3
Theories of Intelligence, Choice of Achievement Goals, and Type of
Achievement Pattern

Theory of Intelligence	Performance Goal Expectancy		Achievement Goal Choice		Achievement Pattern
			Performance Goals:		
Entity Theory	High	→	Obtaining a Favorable Competence Judgment	→	Mastery-oriented
	Low	→	Avoiding a Negative Competence Judgment	→	Helpless
			Learning Goal:		
Incremental Theory	High Low	⇉	Increasing Competence	→	Mastery Oriented

Note. See Dweck & Elliott (1983) for a more complete discussion of the distinction between the two performance goals, and of the conditions under which the goal of avoiding a negative judgment would spur approach *vs* avoidance behavior.

found between measures of actual skill and measures of expectancies. In the face of unfamiliar tasks, the more able girls may be the ones who are most likely to underestimate their skills, overestimate task difficulty, and adopt excessively high performance standards (see Crandall, 1969; Dweck, Goetz & Strauss, 1980; Frieze, Fisher, Hanusa, McHugh, & Valle, 1978; Lenney, 1977; Montanelli & Hill, 1969; McMahan, 1972; Nicholls, 1975; Parsons, 1982; Small, Nakamura & Ruble, 1973; Stipek & Hoffman, 1980).

To continue, the child's perceptions of present competence and his or her performance expectancies should figure very differently in the two types of theories and goals. As noted, we propose these factors to play a critical role in determining task choice and achievement pattern within the context of an entity theory. That is, high expectancies will predict choice of tasks that will enable the child to look smart and will predict a mastery-oriented pattern in the face of obstacles. Low expectancies will predict choice of tasks that will allow the child to avoid looking incompetent (if this choice is provided), and will predict debilitation in the face of obstacles. In either case, children with entity theories will tend to avoid difficult learning tasks that involve the risk of appearing incompetent.

However, when children have an incremental theory and are oriented toward learning goals, perceived skill and performance expectancy should play a less important role. For these children, such factors do not preclude the possibility of satisfactory gains. That is, even what might be considered poor performance by normative standards may well involve some noteworthy skill acquisition. Although we are not suggesting that these children would tend to embark on unrealistic ventures, we do predict that those who favor an incremental theory and learning goals would, regardless of perceived skill, tend to choose challenging tasks that maximize acquisition and to pursue them in a mastery-oriented manner.

In a study by Bandura and Dweck (1981), entity and incremental theorists were identified (on the basis of their responses to the contrasting notions of ability described earlier) and were presented with stimulus discrimination problems similar to those used in the Diener and Dweck research. Prior to working on the problems, however, they were asked a series of questions relating to their performance expectancies and their goals and concerns in the situation, as well as to how they would react to different outcomes. Thus, although all children were confronted with "objectively" the same situation, entity and incremental theorists were expected to structure the situation in terms of different goals.

As predicted, there were clear differences in their goal choices. Children were presented with the stem "I hope these problems are . . . ," and were given learning versus performance goals to rank order. In line with our analysis, the learning option ("hard, new, and different so I can try to learn from them") was ranked significantly higher by the incremental theorists (regardless of performance expectancies) than by the entity theorists. In order to assess further their differing goals in the situation, six different achievement goals or concerns were described. Entity and incremental theorists again differed, as predicted, in the degree to which they endorsed four of the six goals. Specifically, entity theorists showed significantly more concern than incremental theorists with "not making mistakes," as well as with "how smart a teacher (or adult) who saw your work thinks you are." In contrast, incremental theorists were significantly more likely to focus on "how much you feel you'll learn from the problems," and to be concerned that "the problems might be too easy for me." In short, there appears to be a difference between entity and incremental theorists in the achievement goals they emphasize: Incremental theorists are more concerned than entity theorists with meeting challenges and increasing competence (becoming smarter) as opposed to obtaining positive judgments of competence and avoiding negative ones (looking smart). This relationship between children's theories of intelligence and their goals and concerns has been replicated with a large sample of Junior High School children as well.

This differential focus on learning versus evaluation is further illustrated by differences in reported affect (Bandura & Dweck, 1981). For example, children were asked:

> Now think about how you'd feel if you solved these problems right away without having to try much at all. Here are some of the ways other kids say they'd feel if the problems were real easy for them. Some kids say they'd feel kind of proud they solved them so fast, some say they'd feel relieved that the problems weren't too hard, some say they'd feel disappointed that they weren't harder, and others say they'd probably feel bored. Think about how you'd feel if the problems were easy for you.

Incremental theorists reported significantly more often than entity theorists that they would be *disappointed* or *bored* as opposed to *relieved* or *proud* if the problems were easy and required little effort.

The different emphases of the two types of theorists is perhaps most strikingly illustrated by their responses to the following question about the problems they were about to attempt:

> Kids say different things about what would make them feel smartest. Some kids say they'd feel smartest if these problems were easy for them but hard for other kids. Some kids say they'd feel smartest if they worked hard on the problems and make a lot of mistakes, but learned something. Which thing would make you feel smartest?

Some children tended to find only one of the options plausible—but they differed in which one it happened to be. Incremental theorists were more likely than the entity theorists to feel smartest when they confront a challenging task and learn something new. Children with an entity view feel smartest when the task allows them to appear more competent than others. Or, considering these free responses from another study (with E. Elliott) in which we asked children:

Question: Sometimes kids feel smart in school, sometimes not. When do you feel smart?

Incremental: When I don't know how to do it and it's pretty hard and I figure it out without anybody telling me.

When I'm doing school work because I want to learn how to get smart.

When I'm reading a hard book.

Entity: When I don't do mistakes.

When I turn in my papers first.

When I get easy work.

As can be seen, quite disparate, even opposite, experiences appear to make entity and incremental theorists feel smart.

The proposed conceptualization is also receiving support from our experimental work relating achievement goals to the achievement patterns children display. Using the Deiner and Dweck paradigm, Elliott and Dweck (1981) differentially oriented children toward the achievement goals of increasing competence *vs* obtaining positive judgments of competence or avoiding negative judgments of competence by (1) highlighting either the learning or the performance aspects of the situation (i.e., value of the skill vs. degree of external evaluation), and by (2) simultaneously manipulating children's confidence of performing well (via feedback on a pretest said to be predictive of future performance). Children's goal choices (learning *vs* performance) and task performance were then assessed.

For all children, the "performance" task was presented basically in the following manner:

In this box we have problems of different levels. Some are hard, some are easier. If you pick this box, although you won't learn new things, it will really show me what kids can do. [Children were also given a choice of difficulty levels: moderately easy, moderate, or moderately difficult].

The "learning" task was depicted as follows:

If you pick the task in this box you'll probably learn a lot of new things. But you'll probably make a bunch of mistakes, get a little confused, maybe feel a little dumb at times—but eventually you'll learn some useful things.

Following their task choices, children were all given the same series of discrimination problems to solve. (For those who chose performance tasks, the task actually administered was described as being of moderate difficulty and as being consonant with their choice. So that this could be done, children had been asked to make two selections in choosing among the three difficulty levels. Thus, moderately difficult tasks always represented either one of their actual choices or the average of their two choices.) They were requested to verbalize as they worked on the problems; strategies and verbalizations were monitored and scored as in the Diener and Dweck research.

The results showed the predicted relationships. When children were oriented toward skill acquisition, their "performance" expectancy was largely irrelevant: They adopted the learning goal and displayed a mastery-oriented pattern. That is, children in this condition were more concerned with acquiring new skills than with exhibiting or concealing their present ones. In contrast, when children were oriented toward evaluation, the goal they adopted (seeking positive judgments or avoiding negative ones) and the achievement pattern they displayed (mastery-oriented or helpless) were highly dependent on their expectation of performing well or poorly. Indeed, the great majority of children in the evaluation-oriented condition sacrificed altogether the opportunity for new learning that involved a display of errors or confusion. Instead, depending on their expectancy, they selected performance tasks that would allow them to obtain judgments of competence (by succeeding on difficult tasks) or to avoid judgments of incompetence (by succeeding on easier tasks).

What was most striking was the degree to which the manipulations created the entire constellation of performance, cognition, and affect characteristic of the naturally occurring achievement patterns. For example, children who were given an evaluation orientation and a low performance expectancy showed the same strategy deterioration, negative ability attributions, and negative affect that characterized the helpless children in our earlier studies (Diener & Dweck, 1978; 1980).

We have just completed a study (Dweck, Tenney, & Dinces, 1982) in which children's theories of intelligence were manipulated by means of a reading passage about intelligence (embedded in a series of passages), in which the accomplishments of notable individuals (Albert Einstein, Helen Keller, and the child Rubik's Cube champion) were presented in either an entity or incremental context. The structure, content, tone, and inerest value of the two passages were highly similar, except that they presented and illustrated different definitions of smartness. Great care was taken to avoid attaching any goals to the theories, that is, to avoid any mention or implication of learning vs performance goals. Yet, when the children were asked, as a separate task, to select the type of problems they wished to work on when the experimenter returned, our preliminary analyses suggest that their choices reflected the theory to which they had been exposed.

In summary, our research to date has provided encouraging support for the notion that children's implicit theories of intelligence influence the goals they seek to pursue and the persistence they display in pursuit of those goals. If it is true that children's theories play a major role in achievement strivings, it becomes important to examine the conditions that foster the different conceptions of intelligence. For example, how do teachers convey what it means to be smart?

How might teachers' own theories of intelligence lead to differential teaching and feedback practices?

Practices that May Foster Different Theories of Intelligence

How do children get messages about the meaning of smartness? We propose that teachers themselves have implicit theories of intelligence, and that these theories may guide their practices, such as feedback techniques or selection and assignment of tasks.

We assume that most teachers would wish their students to feel intelligent (or not feel unintelligent) and to learn effectively. In the discussion that follows, we examine how entity and incremental perspectives might dictate very different teaching regimes designed to accomplish these aims—how different teaching strategies flow ''intuitively'' from the two views. We also use available research evidence to judge what consequences these practices actually have for children's beliefs about their abilities, and thus whether the practices would in fact foster what teachers intend them to foster.

Teachers who define intelligence as a quality or trait that a child possesses are likely to categorize students, for example, as smart, average, or not smart. They may nonetheless wish all children to feel smart, to have confidence in their abilities. Within this ''entity'' orientation, what would teachers do to accomplish this end? A likely strategy would be to fill children with success and shield them from errors. For example, such teachers might give each child tasks that could be performed with a minimum of struggle and confusion resulting in a maximum of praise. The implicit belief here would be that the accumulation of successes untarnished by failures would lead children to conclude they are intelligent. This inference would then arm them against debilitation when setbacks might occur.

Yet it is precisely this regime of programmed success that has been shown to be ineffective in promoting persistence, and to foster, if anything, greater debilitation in the face of obstacles (Dweck, 1975). In such an environment, or in other environments that do not protect them, these children would be likely to interpret setbacks as failure. Some children (the ''less bright'' ones) may even begin to label themselves as failures simply because they are consistently assigned easy work, may be praised for work that does not seem particularly noteworthy (Meyer, Bachman, Biermann, Hempelmann, Ploger, & Spiller, 1979), or may even receive praise for intellectually-irrelevant aspects of their work when the intellectual content is questionable (cf. Dweck, Davidson, Nelson, & Enna, 1978; Eisenberger, Kaplan, & Singer, 1974; Paris & Cairns, 1972). It may also be the case that when these children do encounter obstacles or commit errors, teachers are apt to gloss over the errors or supply the answer in a well-meant attempt to prevent discomfort. However, this means that the teacher fails to convey to the children that they can overcome obstacles, and fails to model the strategies for doing so (see Bandura, 1980; Brophy & Good, 1974).

What about the "smart" children—i.e., the ones who perform the tasks quickly and easily, who finish first? These are the very conditions under which entity theorists say they feel smartest; however, as our research has suggested, to the extent that children become dependent on such conditions in order to feel smart, this regime may lead them to avoid challenges and may increase susceptibility to self-doubts and impaired performance when obstacles are encountered. Thus, quite contrary to teacher's intentions, practices designed to make children feel smart within an entity framework may render children more vulnerable to maladaptive patterns.

In contrast, teachers who view a child's intelligence as an ever-growing quality that is increased through the child's own efforts would likely provide for all children challenging, long-term tasks that require planning and persistence in search of resolution. Children may not always be sure exactly where they are, where they are going, or when they will get there, but coping with uncertainly becomes intriguing rather than threatening, a direct source of competence feelings rather than self-doubt. These, "incremental," teachers would be available as models and guides in the process of learning, rather than judges of the products of performance (see Bruner, 1961, 1965; Covington, 1980; Nicholls, 1981). In fact, it might be the less proficient children who would receive the most instruction in how to strategize in the face of obstacles. Research evidence suggests that when errors are capitalized upon as vehicles for teaching children how to deal with failure, they tend to react to difficulty with renewed effort (Andrews & Debus, 1978; Chapin & Dyck, 1976; Dweck, 1975). Indeed, "incremental" teachers might show a reverse teacher expectancy effect, with the less proficient children receiving more attention and showing greater gains [Brophy and Good (1974) report that some teachers show a facilitating pattern of interaction (more explanations, encouragement, etc.) with "brighter" children and some with "less bright" children. It would be most interesting to determine whether these teachers differed in their theories of intelligence].[2]

In sum, teachers' beliefs about children's intelligence may lead them to adopt different teaching practices. We have suggested that for teachers with an entity perspective, the consequences of their practices may be quite discrepant with the intended consequences. For as long as we can remember it has been fashionable to criticize educators for undermining children's confidence in their abilities by exposing them to failures, criticism, negative social comparison and the like. And, it is clear that such practices often warrant criticism. However, we are led to the hypothesis that seemingly positive experiences may also have deleterious

---

[2]Indeed, a series of studies has been designed to examine how teachers' theories might influence their practices, and whether these practices (when programmed in an experimental situation) do in fact foster the predicted beliefs and behavior in children.

effects—that certain practices designed to make children feel smart in the short run may prevent them from becoming smarter in the long run.

Entity vs. Incremental Theory: What is Adaptive?

Although our research findings and the earlier discussion may give the impression that it is good to have an incremental orientation and bad to have an entity orientation, it is clear that what is good or bad (i.e., adaptive, maladaptive) depends very much on the environment in which the child is asked to perform. Indeed, many grade school classrooms may foster and favor entity theories. In such an "entity" environment, where the emphasis is on performance and judgment, the child may be provided with little other justification for engaging in school tasks. Lessons are to be learned not for their own value or interest, but as a means of gaining the teacher's approval of one's work and, ultimately, oneself. An incremental child may indeed not be as "good" a child in such an environment. Lacking a more profound justification for learning, and being less interested in attaining positive judgments than in acquiring skills, he or she may put little effort into school tasks and may come to be viewed as an "underachiever." Under such circumstances, it may be considered to be more adaptive to have an entity orientation. That is, the best way to be successful in such an environment—the best way to continually obtain a teacher's positive judgment—may be not to question the validity of assignments and to perform well when asked to do so.

If this type of environment were typical of the ones children would confront in the future, then perhaps in some ways an entity theory might represent good training for that future. However, in many cases, this orientation may be adaptive only in the short run, and may render a child less suited for later pursuits, particularly ones that call for independent choice, long-term planning, perseverance, and the maintenence of confidence in the face of unclear outcomes or actual setbacks. Children with entity views will be at a sharp disadvantage when faced with these circumstances. Indeed, as the school environment changes to include more difficult courses and to afford a greater degree of latitude in course choice, one would expect differential challenge-seeking from entity and incremental theorists. Similarly, when career choices are perceived to differ in the degree of risk for failures or negative evaluation, one would predict differential choice as a function of theory. An incremental orientation, it would seem, would lead children to generate a larger set of options, to make decisions based on interests or values, not fear of failure, and to pursue the chosen goal with greater vigor.

ACKNOWLEDGMENT

The authors acknowledge the support of Grant BNS 79–14252 from the National Science Foundation, Grant MH 31667 from the National Institute of Mental Health, and a Research Scientist Development Award from the National Institute of Mental Health to the first author, as well as Doctoral Fellowships 453–81–0178 and 452–82–8178 from the Social Sciences and Humanities Research Council of Canada to the second author.

REFERENCES

Andrews, G. R., & Debus, R. L. Persistence and the causal perception of failure: Modifying cognitive attributions. *Journal of Educational Psychology*, 1978, *70*, 154–166.

Bandura, A. The self and mechanisms of agency. In J. Suls (Ed.), *Social psychological perspectives on the self*. Hillsdale, N.J.: Lawrence Erlbaum Associates, 1980.

Bandura, M., & Dweck, C. S. *Children's theories of intelligence as predictors of achievement goals*. Unpublished manuscript, Harvard University, 1981.

Brophy, J. E., & Good, T. *Teacher-student relationships: Causes and consequences*. New York: Holt, Rinehart & Winston, 1974.

Bruner, J. S. The act of discovery. *Harvard Educational Review*, 1961, *31*, 21–32.

Bruner, J. S. The growth of mind. *American Psychologist*, 1965, *20*, 1007–1017.

Chapin, M., & Dyck, D. G. Persistence in children's reading behavior as a function of n length and attribution retraining. *Journal of Abnormal Psychology*, 1976, *85*, 511–515.

Covington, M. V. Strategic thinking and fear of failure. Chapter for *NIE-LRDC Proceedings*, October 1980.

Crandall, V. C. Sex differences in expectancy of intellectual and academic reinforcement. In C. P. Smith (Ed.), *Achievement-related motives in children*, New York: Russell Sage, 1969.

Crandall, V. C., Katkovsky, W., & Crandall, V. J. Children's beliefs in their own control of reinforcements in intellectual-academic situations. *Child Development*, 1965, *36*, 91–109.

Diener, C. I., & Dweck, C. S. An analysis of learned helplessness: Continuous changes in performance, strategy, and achievement cognitions following failure. *Journal of Personality and Social Psychology*, 1978, *36*, 451–462.

Diener, C. I., & Dweck, C. S. An analysis of learned helplessness: II. The processing of success. *Journal of Personality and Social Psychology*, 1980, *39*, 940–952.

Dweck, C. S. The role of expectations and attributions in the alleviation of learned helplessness. *Journal of Personality and Social Psychology*, 1975, *31*, 674–685.

Dweck, C. S., Davidson, W., Nelson, S., & Enna, B. Sex differences in learned helplessness: II. The contingencies of evaluative feedback in the classroom and III. An experimental analysis. *Developmental Psychology*, 1978, *14*, 268–276.

Dweck, C. S., & Elliott, E. S. Achievement motivation. In P. Mussen (gen. Ed.), and E. M. Hetherington (vol. Ed.), *Carmichael's manual of child psychology: Social and personality development*. New York: Wiley, 1983.

Dweck, C. S., Goetz, T. E., & Strauss, N. L. Sex differences in learned helplessness: IV. An experimental and naturalistic study of failure generalization and its mediators. *Journal of Personality and Social Psychology*, 1980, *38*, 441–452.

Dweck, C. S., & Licht, B. G. Learned helplessness and intellectual achievement. In J. Garber & M. E. P. Seligman (Eds.), *Human helplessness: Theory and applications*. New York: Academic Press, 1980.

Dweck, C. S., & Reppucci, N. D. Learned helplessness and reinforcement responsibility in children. *Journal of Personality and Social Psychology*, 1973, *25*, 109–116.

Dweck, C. S., Tenney, Y., & Dinces, N. *Unpublished data*, Harvard University, 1982.

Eisenberger, R., Kaplan, R. M., & Singer, R. D. Decremental and nondecremental effects of noncontingent social approval. *Journal of Personality and Social Psychology*, 1974, *30*, 716–722.

Elliott, E. S., & Dweck, C. S. *Children's achievement goals as determinants of learned helpless and mastery-oriented achievement patterns: An experimental analysis.* Unpublished manuscript, Harvard University, 1981.

Frieze, I. H., Fisher, J., Hanusa, B., McHugh, M. C., & Valle, V. A. Attributions of the causes of success and failure as internal and external barriers to achievement in women. In J. Sherman & F. Denmark (Eds.), *Psychology of women: Future directions for research.* New York: Psychological Dimensions, 1978.

Gholson, B., Levine, M., & Phillips, S. Hypotheses, strategies, and stereotypes in discrimination learning. *Journal of Experimental Child Psychology,* 1972, *13,* 423–446.

Goodnow, J. J. Concepts of intelligence and its development. In N. Warren (Ed.), *Studies in cross-cultural psychology,* Vol. 2, London: Pergamon, 1980.

Harari, O., & Covington, M. V. Reactions to achievement behavior from a teacher and student perspective: A developmental analysis. *American Educational Research Journal,* 1981, *18,* 15–28.

Lenney, E. Women's self confidence in achievement settings. *Psychological Bulletin,* 1977, *84,* 1–13.

Licht, B. G., & Dweck, C. S. *Determinants of academic achievement: The interaction of children's achievement orientations with skill area.* Manuscript submitted for publication, 1981.

Marshall, H. H., Weinstein, R. S., Middlestadt, S. & Brattesani, K. A. *"Everyone's smart in our class," Relationship between classroom characteristics and perceived differential teacher treatment.* Paper presented at the American Educational Research Association, Boston, April 1980.

McMahan, I. D. *Sex differences in expectancy of success as a function of task.* Paper presented at The Eastern Psychological Association, Boston, April 1972.

Meyer, W., Bachmann, M., Biermann, U., Hempelmann, M., Ploger, F., & Spiller, H. *The informational value of evaluative behavior: Influences of praise and blame on perceptions of ability.* Unpublished manuscript, University of Bielefeld, 1979.

Montanelli, D. S., & Hill, K. T. Children's achievement expectations as a function of two consecutive, reinforcement experiences, sex of subject, and sex of experimenter. *Journal of Personality and Social Psychology,* 1969, *13,* 115–128.

Nicholls, J. G. Causal attributions and other achievement related cognitions. Effects of task outcome, attainment value, and sex. *Journal of Personality and Social Psychology,* 1975, *31,* 379–389.

Nicholls, J. G. Quality and equality in intellectual development. *American Psychologist,* 1979, *34,* 1071–1084.

Nicholls, J. G. *Striving to demonstrate and develop ability: A theory of achievement motivation.* Unpublished manuscript, Purdue University, 1981.

Paris, S. G., & Cairns, R. B. An experimental and ethological analysis of social reinforcement with retarded children. *Child Development,* 1972, *43,* 717–729.

Parsons, J. E. Expectancies, values, and academic behaviors. In J. T. Spence (Ed.), *Assessing achievement.* San Francisco: W. H. Freeman, 1982.

Seligman, M. E. P., Maier, S. F., & Solomon, R. L. Unpredictable and uncontrollable aversive events. In F. R. Brush (Ed.), *Aversive conditioning and learning.* New York: Academic Press, 1971.

Small, A., Nakamura, C. Y., & Ruble, D. N. *Sex differences in children's outer directedness and self-perceptions in a problem-solving situation.* Unpublished manuscript, University of California at Los Angeles, 1973.

Sternberg, R., Conway, B. E., Ketron, J. L., & Bernstein, M. People's conceptions of intelligence. *Journal of Personality and Social Psychology,* 1981, *41,* 37–55.

Stipek, D. J., & Hoffman, J. M. Children's achievement related expectancies as a function of academic performance histories and sex. *Journal of Educational Psychology,* 1980, *72,* 861–865.

Surber, C. F. The development of achievement-related judgment processes. In J. Nicholls (Ed.), *The development of achievement motivation*. Greenwich, Conn.: JAI Press, 1982.

Weiner, B. (Ed.).*Theories of motivation: From mechanism to cognition*. Chicago: Markham, 1972.

Weiner, B. (Ed.). *Achievement motivation and attribution theory*. Morristown, N.J.: General Learning Corporation, 1974.

Wellman, H. M. The child's theory of mind: The development of conceptions of cognition. In S. R. Yussen (Ed.), *The growth of insight in the child*. New York: Academic Press, 1981.

III EDUCATION AND PUBLIC POLICY

The authors of the last three chapters are concerned with ways in which behavioral research can be applied to practical problems. There could have been many more chapters in this section, for the past decade has been a particularly fertile period for the production of such research. During this period psychologists and educators have also created new domains of studies and filled in details of traditional areas that bear directly on policy issues in education. To represent this research, the next section includes chapters on the education of mathematically talented children, the management of elementary school classrooms, and the development of social policies.

Julian Stanley and Camilla Benbow, psychologists at Johns Hopkins University, have attracted national attention through their program for young, intellectually talented students. Special emphasis has been placed in their program on the identification and education of children who do exceptionally well in mathematics. In a chapter describing this program, the authors delineate many of the characteristics of these precocious children and offer recommendations about how their education can be improved.

It is surprising that until quite recently little was known about the characteristics of effective teachers. Teaching is partly an art, but fortunately many of the variables that enter into effective teaching can be isolated, observed, and quantified. From studies of teachers' behavior, ways can be described for enhancing students' learning. Jere Brophy, one of the leading researchers on teachers and classrooms, has summarized some of these characteristics in a chapter dealing with effective teaching and the theoretical considerations that underlie current research on teaching.

The volume ends with a chapter on social policy. Financial support for research is provided from public funds, not simply because citizens believe that such research will advance knowledge, but because they expect the information gained from research eventually will be useful in improving people's everyday lives. This can happen when research is used as a basis for creating wise social policies. In his chapter on social science and social policy, Morton Weir argues that social scientists are less effective than they should be in relating their research to the development of policies and in getting their research into the hands of policy makers. Universities also can do a better job, he believes, in meeting this important need, and a way is suggested for doing this.

11 Intellectually Talented Students: The Key is Curricular Flexibility

Julian C. Stanley
Camilla P. Benbow
The Johns Hopkins University

> What is particularly striking here is how little that is distinctly psychological seems involved in the Study of Mathematically Precocious Youth (SMPY), and yet how very fruitful SMPY appears to be. It is as if trying to be psychological throws us off the course and into a mire of abstract dispositions that help little in facilitating students' demonstrable talents. What seems most successful for helping students is what stays closest to the competencies one directly cares about: in the case of SMPY, for example, finding students who are very good at math and arranging the environment to help them learn it as well as possible. One would expect analogous prescriptions to be of benefit for fostering talent at writing, music, art, and any other competencies that can be specified in product or performance terms. But all this in fact is not unpsychological; it simply is different psychology [Wallach, 1978, p. 617].

The pace of educational programs must be adapted to the capacities and knowledge of individual children (Robinson, in press). The rationale behind this position is based on three principles derived from findings in developmental psychology. The first principle is that learning is a sequential and developmental process (Hilgard & Bower, 1974). The second is that there are large differences in learning status among individuals at any given age. In other words, although the acquisition of knowledge and the development of patterns of organization follow predictable sequences, the rates with which children progress through these sequences vary considerably (Bayley, 1955, 1970; George, Cohn, & Stanley, 1979; Keating, 1976; Keating & Stanley, 1972; Robinson & Robinson, 1976).

A final principle is that effective teaching involves assessing the student's status in the learning process and posing problems that slightly exceed the level already mastered. Work that is too easy produces boredom; work that is too

259

difficult cannot be understood. This has been referred to, according to Hunt (1961), as "the problem of the match," which is based on the premise that learning occurs only when there is "an appropriate match between the circumstances that a child encounters and the schemata that he has already assimilated into his reportoire [p. 268]." Hunt notes that "the principle is only another statement of the educator's adage that 'teaching must start where the learner is' [p. 268]."

These three principles have important implications for working with intellectually talented students. Clearly, gifted students are not at the same levels academically as their average-ability classmates. It can thus be deduced that in order for gifted children to learn effectively, they need to be advanced to levels slightly beyond those they have already mastered. Certainly, what is offered in the regular classroom for all children cannot possibly begin to meet this requirement. Thus, the curriculum must be adapted to match the gifted child's developmental stage. Parallel to the development of appropriate curricula, however, is the need to identify the students for whom the curriculum must be adapted.

This chapter focuses on means to identify and facilitate the education of gifted children, especially those who reason extremely well mathematically. It emphasizes programs developed at Johns Hopkins by the Study of Mathematically Precocious Youth (SMPY) and the Office of Talent Identification and Development (OTID), now called the Center for the Advancement of Academically Talented Youth (CTY). These programs cover the Middle Atlantic region (Delaware, District of Columbia, Maryland, New Jersey, Pennsylvania, Virginia, and West Virginia). As of September, 1982, they are also extending into the Northeast, all the way to northern Maine. Moreover, the SMPY model is being replicated on a large scale in the South, Midwest, and West. Duke University conducts a program based on the SMPY model in 16 states: Alabama, Arkansas, Florida, Georgia, Iowa, Kansas, Kentucky, Louisiana, Mississippi, Missouri, Nebraska, North Carolina, Oklahoma, South Carolina, Tennessee, and Texas. At Arizona State University, Professor Sanford J. Cohn is conducting a program similar to the Hopkins one and is extending it into nearby states, especially California, Oregon, and Washington, and also into Hawaii and some Canadian provinces.

Origins of SMPY

The early 1970s, when SMPY began, was a ripe time to start a program focusing on intellectually brilliant students. In the 1970s, renewed interest in the gifted became apparent. According to Tannenbaum (1979): "While as late as 1973 fewer than four percent of the nation's gifted children were receiving satisfactory attention at school, and most of the fortunate ones were concentrated in ten states, by 1977 every state in the union demonstrated at least some interest in the ablest [p. 22].'' This thrust in activity for the gifted was, however, mostly programmatic and promotional. Little emphasis was given to research.

The Study of Mathematically Precocious Youth (SMPY), founded by Professor Julian C. Stanley at Johns Hopkins in September of 1971, was and is an exception to the current programmatic and promotional trend in the field of gifted children. It is modeled after the Terman study as described in his *Genetic Studies of Genius* (Burks, Jensen, & Terman, 1947; Cox, 1926; Terman, 1925; Terman & Oden, 1947, 1959) and several more recent publications (Oden, 1968; Sears, 1977; Sears & Barbee, 1977), but with certain differences. It is research-oriented, as Terman's was, but SMPY is a longitudinal study of students who reason exceptionally well mathematically, rather than of students high in overall ability. Furthermore, SMPY tries to understand (cognitively and affectively) each mathematically precocious adolescent, so that it will be possible to facilitate the education of every such individual (Stanley, 1977). The SMPY model is also based strongly on work by Hollingworth (1942) and Pressey (1949).

The philosophy behind SMPY can be stated succinctly in pseudochemical fashion—MT : D_4P_3. MT stands for Mathematical Talent. The four D's are Discovery, Description, Development, and Dissemination. The three P's, which implement D_4, are Principles, Practices, and Programs. Certainly, this acronym illustrates that discovery, description, and development lead to the ultimate goal of SMPY, research and dissemination of its findings. A more thorough discussion of the rationale behind SMPY can be found in Stanley (1977).

Identification

In order to identify mathematically talented students, SMPY developed the concept of an annual talent search and conducted six separate searches. These were carried out in 1972, 1973, 1974, 1976, 1978, and 1979. In the first three searches, seventh and eighth graders, as well as a few accelerated ninth and tenth graders, were eligible, whereas the last three involved only seventh graders and a few accelerated students of seventh-grade age. In addition, in the 1976, 1978, and 1979 searches the students had to be in the upper 3% in mathematical ability as judged by a standardized in-grade achievement test. The criterion in 1972 was the upper 5%, and in 1973 and 1974 the upper 2%. Thus, participants were selected by high criteria for mathematical ability. Girls comprised 43% of the participants.

In each talent search the students took one or more parts of the College Board's Scholastic Aptitude Test (SAT), i.e., the mathematics [SAT–M] sections every time, the verbal [SAT–V] sections except in 1972 and 1974, and the newly introduced Test of Standard Written English [TSWE] in 1978 and 1979. The SAT is designed for able 11th and 12th graders; on the average, these students are 4 to 5 years older than the students in the talent searches. The test is

TABLE 11.1
Performance of Students in the Study of Mathematically Precocious Youth in Each of the
First Six Talent Searches (N = 9927)

Test Date	Grade	Number		SAT–M Scores[a]				SAT–V Scores[b]			
		Boys	Girls	Boys		Girls		Boys		Girls	
				Mean	S.D.	Mean	S.D.	Mean	S.D.	Mean	S.D.
March 1972	7	90	77	460	104	423	75				
	8+	133	96	528	105	458	88				
January 1973	7	135	88	495	85	440	66	385	71	374	74
	8+	286	158	551	85	511	63	431	89	442	83
January 1974	7	372	222	473	85	440	68				
	8+	556	369	540	82	503	72				
December 1976	7	495	356	455	84	421	64	370	73	368	70
	8[c]	12	10	598	126	482	83	487	129	390	61
January 1978	7 and 8[c]	1549	1249	448	87	413	71	375	80	372	78
January 1979	7 and 8[c]	2046	1628	436	87	404	77	370	76	370	77

[a] Mean score for a random sample of high school juniors and seniors was 416 for males and 390 for females.
[b] Mean score for a random sample of high school juniors and seniors was 368 for males and females.
[c] These rare 8th graders were accelerated at least 1 year in school grade placement.

particularly designed to measure mathematical and verbal *reasoning* ability (Angoff, 1971; Messick & Jungeblut, 1981). SMPY's primary criterion for mathematical aptitude has been a high score on the mathematical part of the SAT. Obviously, SMPY searches for mathematical aptitude that even by age 11 or 12 is already well developed.

Results from SMPY's six talent searches are shown in Table 11.1. Most students scored rather high on both SAT–M and SAT–V. On SAT–V the boys and girls performed equally well, except for accelerated eighth graders in 1976, where the 12 such boys performed better ($p < .05$). The overall performance of seventh-grade students on SAT–V was at or above the average for a national sample of high school students, whose mean score is 368 (ATP, 1982), or at about the 30th percentile of college-bound seniors. The eighth graders, regular or accelerated, scored at about the 52nd percentile of college-bound seniors.

On the SAT–M, however, a large sex difference favoring boys occurred in every talent search. The smallest mean difference was 32 points in 1979. The largest mean difference (excluding the 22 accelerated eighth graders in 1976) was 70 points, in 1972. Benbow and Stanley (1980b, 1981) discuss this point further. Although a consistent sex difference was found on SAT–M, it can still be concluded that the SMPY students of both sexes were very able mathematically. The seventh-grade girls scored at about the 40th percentile of college-bound 12th-grade females on SAT–M, and the eighth-grade girls at about the 68th percentile. The seventh-grade boys scored at about the 36th percentile of college-bound 12th-grade males on SAT–M, and the eighth-grade boys at about the 62nd percentile.

In conclusion, we can state that SMPY identified a group of mathematically precocious students. Furthermore, mathematically precocious students also tend to be highly able verbally. As we had expected from knowledge about statistical regression to the mean, the verbal ability of these groups was somewhat lower than the mathematical ability. Moreover, our tests were better finders of great math talent than teachers were (Stanley, 1976b).

The first six talent searches (1972–1979) were conducted to seek young people who reason extremely well mathematically. This was, however, primarily a means to the end of finding suitable students on whom to develop educational principles, practices, and techniques that schools could then adapt to their own needs. As of the seventh talent search, conducted in January 1980, SMPY relinquished that important service function to a newly created agency under the Provost at Johns Hopkins, the Center for the Advancement of Academically Talented Youth (CTY). CTY, however, does not search only for mathematically talented students. It has adapted the talent search model to discover verbally and/ or generally talented students also. The effectiveness of this approach for these areas has been proven thus far in three massive talent searches involving about 40,000 students. The criterion for being verbally talented is high SAT–V and/or

TSWE scores. A generally talented seventh grader is one who scores highly on both of those and also SAT–M, e.g., at least 500M, 430V, and 43TSWE.

Description

The foregoing discussion can be said to describe SMPY's discovery phase and part of its description phase. The description phase also includes analyses of other cognitive abilities, backgrounds, and attitudes of talent search participants (Benbow & Stanley, 1980a, 1982a; Keating, 1974). Students who score extremely well in the talent searches are brought back for further testing. In 1976, for example, the top third of the talent search participants were given a day of further testing (Cohn, 1977), followed by another day of more testing for the top 97 males (Cohn, 1980). In 1978 approximately the top 10% (Benbow, 1978) and in 1979 the top 1% of students ever identified and their parents returned for further cognitive testing (Benbow, Stanley, Zonderman, & Kirk, in press b; Benbow, Zonderman, & Stanley, in press c). The cognitive tests that we employed assessed specific cognitive abilities, such as mechanical comprehension, abstract reasoning, and spatial relations. The student's knowledge about science and mathematics was also determined. The values and interests of students were evaluated by the Allport, Vernon, and Lindzey *Study of Values,* the *Holland Occupational Checklist,* and the *Strong–Campbell Interest Inventory.*

Cohn (1977, 1980), Benbow (1978), and Benbow et al. (in press b) found that the mathematically precocious students are also advanced in their specific abilities and in their knowledge of science and mathematics. Weiss, Haier, and Keating (1974) and Haier and Denham (1976) concluded that students of exceptional mathematical ability are more interpersonally effective and socially mature than their nongifted peers and thus are more likely to face successfully the social and emotional challenges that may arise from their talents. Furthermore, they were found to be solid, competent individuals who seem to be successful in handling their extraordinary talents. These conclusions were based on testing results from the *California Psychological Inventory,* the *Eysenck Personality Inventory,* the *Study of Values, Holland's Vocational Preference Inventory,* and the *Adjective Checklist.* With regard to the mathematically precocious student's values and career interests, it was found that such students tended to have high theoretical but low religious orientation and prefer investigative careers (Cohn, 1980; Fox & Denham, 1974; Haier & Denham, 1976).

The SMPY students tend to come from larger than average families with well-educated parents who pursued careers with high occupational status (Benbow & Stanley, 1980a; Keating, 1974). Student SAT scores relate positively to their parents' educational level and fathers' occupational status (Benbow & Stanley, 1980a), but not to the number of siblings in the family or the sibling position (Benbow & Stanley, 1980a; Keating, 1974).

SMPY students' educational attitudes, experiences, interests, and values in the seventh grade are remarkably homogeneous in spite of the wide range in SAT scores. In most affective respects the rare seventh grader with an SAT–M score of 700 seems to differ little from the relatively more common one with a score of 500. Most participants exhibit a strong liking for and do well in school, mathematics, and science. They perceive science as important for their future careers. Only slight differences were seen between the girls and boys in their liking for mathematics, chemistry, and physics (Benbow & Stanley, 1982a). Keating (1974) found that even though the talent search participants had an overall liking for school, there was a trend in which the students with the highest aptitude liked it less than students with less high aptitude.

Development

Further testing provides rich profiles of students' specific cognitive abilities and knowledge of science and mathematics, as well as of their attitudes, values, interests, and backgrounds. This leads to the prime focus of SMPY, the development phase. During it the identified youths are continually helped and encouraged. Each is offered a broad variety of educationally accelerative opportunities (Benbow, 1979; Fox, 1974a; Stanley, 1978a) from which he or she may choose whatever combination, or nothing, that best suits their individual interests and needs. Some of the options are as follows: skipping grades, graduating a year early from high school, entering a course a year or more early, completing 2 or more years of a subject in 1 year, being tutored via SMPY's diagnostic testing followed by prescriptive instruction procedure (Stanley, 1978b, 1979), taking regular college courses on a part-time basis while still enrolled in a secondary school (Benbow & George, 1979; Solano & George, 1976), credit through examination (Benbow & Stanley, 1978), and earning the master's degree concurrently with the bachelor's. Thus, SMPY utilizes already available educational programs but adapts them to meet the needs of talented students.

The chief exception to the approach is the fast-paced mathematics classes pioneered by SMPY in which several years of mathematics are completed in 1 year or a summer (Bartkovich & George, 1980; Bartkovich & Mezynski, 1981; Fox, 1974b; George & Denham, 1976; Stanley, 1976a; Mezynski & Stanley, 1980). A special class was even formed to cater to the special social needs of girls (Fox, 1976). The special fast-paced approach was recently adapted to the study of chemistry and physics (Mezynski, McCoart, & Stanley, in press), as well as for the verbal area (Durden, 1980).

We work with the individually talented youth and his or her parents and teachers. No attempt is made to change the schools' programs. Curriculum revision would take far more time and resources than SMPY could possibly muster. At best, too, it would probably benefit the intellectually talented youth's younger siblings or perhaps his or her children, rather than the talented person. Programmatic efforts by others are essential, but the staff of SMPY is content with the results secured thus far for individuals eager to move ahead faster and better than the usual school curricula permit. As a consequence, precedents are established so that special facilitation becomes easier for the next qualified youth. The effectiveness of this approach is illustrated through the numerous school systems that have adopted and modified some of SMPY's procedures (see, for example, Lunny, in press; Van Tassel-Baska, in press).

Early Admission to College

One of the first approaches utilized to facilitate the education of some of the extremely precocious students identified by SMPY was to have them enter college early. What are these individuals like? The personal descriptions that follow provide some insight through biographical sketches. (Names have been changed.)

Craig, born in 1959, is the only son in a family of four children. His father, a college graduate, is a sales manager; his mother, a high school graduate, is an executive secretary. Both are bright as judged from standardized testing. As an accelerated eighth grader in SMPY's January–February 1973 Talent Search, Craig scored 750 on SAT–M and also extremely high on SAT–V. Through SMPY's first fast-paced mathematics class, which began when he had just finished the sixth grade, Craig learned 4½ years of precalculus mathematics chiefly on Saturdays, in 14 months. He skipped grades 7, 9, 10, and 12 and entered Johns Hopkins with sophomore standing through Advanced Placement Program (AP) course work and college credits earned while attending the 8th and 11th grades. In high school he was on the wrestling and TV quiz teams and participated in student government. At barely 17 years of age, Craig finished his work for the BA degree in quantitative studies at Johns Hopkins at the end of the first semester of the academic year 1976–77 after only five semesters (Stanley & Benbow, 1982b). During his undergraduate years, he was on the Hopkins varsity golf team and was described by a journalist as an "all-rounder" (Nevin, 1977). Craig held a variety of jobs while in college, including summer work as an associate editor of a weekly newspaper. His hobbies include skiing, tennis, golf, horseracing, and writing. Several letters written during graduate school reflect not only the substance but also the style of a student well into his twenties. In September 1977, while still 17 years old, Craig became a graduate student at the University of Chicago. He remained there, earning his MBA degree at 19 and completing all work for the PhD degree in finance before age 22. While still 21 years old and with several research publications already to his credit, he became an assistant professor of management in a major Midwestern university and a consultant to businesses.

Chin is also among the brightest students identified by SMPY. In December 1975, a month after his 10th birthday, he took the SAT and scored 600 on the

Verbal and 680 on the Mathematical parts. In SMPY's December 1976 Talent Search he raised these scores to 710 and 750, respectively. A variety of intelligence test scores indicated an IQ of at least 200. A Chinese–American youngster whose father is a professor of physics and whose mother has a master's degree in psychology, Chin has two younger simblings who are also extremely able. Because of his father's persistent efforts he was able to have special educational opportunities in a private school. Through diagnostic testing it was discovered that, even though Chin had taken only first-year high school algebra in the fifth grade, by age 11 he knew Algebra II, Algebra III, and plane geometry. Trigonometry and analytic geometry were taught to him in a few weeks. By age 12 Chin had completed his work for a diploma from an excellent public school while simultaneously taking university calculus courses. In the fall of 1978, when still 12 years old, Chin entered Johns Hopkins with sophomore standing. He had been accepted at Harvard and Cal Tech as well. In May of 1981 he received his baccalaureate at age 15, with a major in physics, general and departmental honors, the award in physics, a scholarship for a year at a major English university, and a 3-year National Science Foundation Graduate Fellowship to work toward his doctorate in physics at the California Institute of Technology after returning from England.

A third example is a girl who entered Johns Hopkins 1 year early with sophomore standing. In May 1980, near the end of the 11th grade, Nola, from a small town in Oklahoma, took five AP examinations in one week and scored four 5s and a 4. Thereby, she earned a full year of college credits. As a tenth-grader she had won the state high school piano competition. Not only is Nola an academic and musical prodigy, she also shows leadership potential, as evidenced by having been elected governor of the high school political assembly, Girls' State, in Oklahoma. In September 1980, with a National Merit Scholarship and sophomore class standing, Nola became a full-time student at Johns Hopkins, choosing the University both for its accelerated mathematics program and for the opportunity to pursue piano studies at the Peabody Conservatory. At Hopkins she played the flute and violin, was a member of the women's varsity fencing team, and participated in a biology research project. In a total of four semesters she completed her BA degree in mathematics with high honors, including election to Phi Beta Kappa, at age 18. She was one of the youngest Americans ever to win a Rhodes Scholarship, which provides 2 years of study at Oxford University. She is studying mathematics and science there. In addition, Nola won a Churchill Scholarship to Cambridge University for a year. Faced with this choice, she accepted the Rhodes.

There are numerous examples of students who entered college quite early or (like Nola) greatly accelerated their education in other ways. For example, a student entered Brooklyn College from the sixth grade in 1973 at age 11½ and started mathematics with Calculus III. He was graduated in 1977 summa cum laude, having majored in mathematics, at age 15 years and 3 months. Two years later he received a master's degree in mathematics from a famous Ivy League university and continued there toward a PhD in the same field.* A second student entered the same Ivy League university at 13. A boy completed the first semester at a fine New England college at age 12 with all A's. A youth who had earned 64 college credits part-time while still in high school came to Johns Hopkins at age 14 as a junior and received a BA degree in biology at age 16 (Stanley & Benbow, 1982b). Our earliest protégé, whose identification in 1969 antedates the founding of SMPY, took his PhD in computer science at Cornell University 10 years later at age 23. During the 1980–81 school year, six of SMPY's ablest students were in the fourth year of graduate work toward the PhD degree (see Nevin, 1977). Another was an outstanding third-year medical student and researcher at Columbia University. During recent years, eight students graduated successfully from John Hopkins at ages 15–17 (see Stanley & Benbow, 1982b). Only four others are known to have earned their baccalaureates that young in the entire history of the university, 1876–1982.

Acceleration

The preceding discussion illustrates that SMPY's educational facilitation of the ablest students it identifies relies heavily on acceleration. Much concern continues to be expressed about the presumed dangers of acceleration, especially with respect to social and emotional development. This myth concerning acceleration persists despite the strong research base that supports positive effects of acceleration (Gallagher, 1975). It has led to one of the most unfortunate dichotomies in the field of education—the enrichment versus acceleration conflict (George et al., 1979). The single experimental study that has compared enrichment and acceleration found that a combination of the two provided the best educational benefit for the gifted (Goldberg, Passow, Camm, & Neill, 1966).

Some of the usual reasons stated for an age-graded educational system are outlined in the following section. The most frequently proposed is that advancing students according to their demonstrated mastery of subject areas fails to take into account the level of their social competencies and their emotional strengths and weaknesses (Hildreth, 1966; Hollingsworth, 1929). Social and emotional maturity is thought to correspond rather specifically to chronological age (Gold, 1965; Rothman & Levine, 1963). It is argued that intellectual and academic accomplishments indicate very little about social and emotional development and that to accelerate a student on the basis of progress in one domain may jeopardize healthy progress in other areas (Congdon, 1979). Another contention is that skipping grades produces gaps in knowledge (Hildreth, 1966). Moreover, it is believed that valuable nonacademic experiences will be eliminated through the use of acceleration (Rothman & Levine, 1963).

*He received it at age 20.

Although acceleration has received only minimal acceptance among educational practitioners, it has achieved maximal support from the results of experimental and quasi-experimental studies. Terman and Oden (1947) recommended that students with an IQ greater than 135 be accelerated at least 1 year. This was based on their longitudinal findings. Furthermore, they showed that the risk of maladjustment resulting from acceleration is much less than commonly believed, and the disadvantages of acceleration mentioned by the Terman gifted group were usually temporary. In contrast, Terman and Oden (1947) pointed out the danger of *not* accelerating an academically highly able child. Lack of acceleration resulted in a considerable proportion of the Terman group's languishing in idleness through the elementary grades and high school and thus failing to develop the ambition or work habits necessary to make them successful in college.

Pressey (1949) also found only advantages in the acceleration of the rate of completing the undergraduate degree. The accelerated students in college were found to have better academic accomplishments and to have participated in more extracurricular activities. They were also found to have superior all-around development compared to students completing their degrees in normal or longer than normal time.

The Fund for the Advancement of Education (1957) concluded that the results from experiments in allowing bright students to enter college early were impressive at all 12 colleges where it was tested. Again, concern was expressed about the dangers of not allowing bright students to accelerate. The ambition and creativity needed for college work might be "educated" out of the bright student unless he or she is accelerated.

Hobson (1963, 1979) concluded that "the scholastic superiority in elementary school of underage children, originally admitted to school on the basis of physical and psychological examinations, is continued and somewhat increased through high school [p. 167]." Furthermore, the underage students participated in a higher number of extracurricular activities in a variety of areas and won more awards and honors in high school than did regular students. Hobson believed he had shown that early admission to school is an excellent way to provide for individual differences in intellectual ability.

Robinson (in press) reviewed over 200 articles that examined the experiences of accelerated students. His conclusion was that "not one of these studies lends credence to the notion that such practices lead to major difficulties for the students involved. It is, indeed, much easier from the available evidence to make the case that students who are allowed to move ahead according to their competencies are benefited in their social and emotional development than it is to make the case that they are harmed [p. 5]."

In his review of the literature on the enrichment versus acceleration controversy, Daurio (1979) reached the following conclusions: (1) academic enrichment may be worthwhile for all students, and not specifically for the gifted; (2) results have not been found to show that enrichment is superior to acceleration; (3) much of the resistance toward acceleration is based on preconceived notions and irrational grounds, rather than on examinations of the research evidence; (4) accelerated students are shown to perform at least as well as if not better than nonaccelerated students on both academic and nonacademic measures; and (5) acceleration appears to be the more feasible method for meeting the needs of gifted students.

Other reviewers who have examined this issue have come to the same conclusions as Robinson (in press) and Daurio (1979) (e.g., Gallagher, 1975; Newland, 1976). Thus, Keating (1979) concluded: "as for the socioemotional concerns, it seems time to abandon them unless and until some solid reliable evidence is forthcoming that indicates real dangers in well-run programs [p. 218]." With regard to the concern that grade skipping can cause gaps in knowledge, there is no evidence to support the position that gifted students who do skip grades appropriately are afflicted with substantial lacunae in their knowledge base (Benbow, Perkins, & Stanley, in press; Keating, 1976; Stanley, Keating, & Fox, 1974). In summary, various forms of educational acceleration do provide needed advantages for the special needs of gifted students.

Subject Matter Acceleration

Acceleration does not mean only skipping grades. Subject-matter acceleration is another alternative investigated by SMPY through fast-paced mathematics, chemistry, and physics classes. As the name indicates, subject matter in these classes is presented at a rapid pace geared to the ablest members of the class. The content of SMPY's and CTY's fast-paced mathematics is the regular precalculus curriculum taught in junior and senior high school (Algebra I and II, geometry, college algebra, trigonometry, and analytic geometry). The first such class, designated Wolfson I in honor of its splendid teacher, Joseph R. Wolfson, met from 24 June 1972 until 11 August 1973. Although the goals for its students were impressive, they were successfully met (see Fox, 1974b). In 12 to 14 months, mainly on Saturdays, eight students completed 4½ years of mathematics, two completed 3½ years, and the remaining six completed 2 years.

This group has been studied intensively (Benbow et al., in press; Fox, 1974b; Stanley, 1976a, pp. 156–159). The success of the 10 top students of the 22 enrolled for some appreciable part of the time is striking. Nine of them accelerated their education by at least a year. One was Craig, mentioned previously. Two others from the Wolfson I class received their bachelor's degrees at age 18 and two at age 19. One of the latter also received a master's degree concurrently with the baccalaureate. Although the seven boys in that group tended to move considerably faster educationally than the three girls, the latter also did splendidly; one received the bachelor's degree in computer engineering from the University of Michigan a year ahead of her age group, another the bachelor's degree in Russian Studies from the University of Virginia a year early, and the third a bachelor's degree in architecture from Princeton University.

The top group has been compared with three reference groups: those who dropped out of the class at the end of the summer of 1972, those who remained in the class but were provided a different instructor who could move them at a slower rate, and those who declined to join the class. Although the students in the comparison groups were highly able and made above-average college records, the students in the top group were outstanding even relative to them. The great difference in educational acceleration between the top 10 and the others was perhaps the most impressive finding thus far (see Benbow et al., in press). It seems likely, too, that the extent and quality of their graduate work will differentiate the groups even more.

In the summer of 1973 a second fast-paced precalculus class was also conducted. Students who enrolled were mainly those who had completed the eighth grade and already taken a year of algebra (see George & Denham, 1976). Follow-up results for this group are less impressive thus far than for Wolfson I, but nevertheless the participants in this class appear to have made vastly better progress educationally than their equally able nonparticipants (Benbow et al., in press). Thus, students in the first class, who were younger, tended to attain levels and rates of achievement somewhat higher than the students in the second class, most of whom were older. We believe it is desirable, therefore, to intervene before the first year of algebra occurs on behalf of youths who reason exceptionally well mathematically at that time. The slow-paced yearlong course of Algebra I in a regular school class is stifling for this type of student. As a result, those classes tend to establish poor attitudes toward mathematics and improper study habits. Thus, SMPY's precalculus mathematics programs have been mainly directed at students not yet into the eighth grade.

Hypotheses

Several hypotheses about extreme acceleration in mathematics, in related areas, and in overall grade placement have emerged from the outcome of these initial fast-paced mathematics classes and their many successors. These need to be validated through more research. The staff of SMPY has tried to develop hypotheses initially for cognitive variables and then to supplement them for affective variables. We have done this because assessing affective variables is more subject to situational and motivational influences than testing cognitive variables. Some of the tentative findings, based on our observations, are as follows:

1. High scores at age 10–13 on the mathematical part of the College Board's Scholastic Aptitude Test, which is a difficult test of mathematical *reasoning* ability designed for above-average 11th and 12th graders, strongly predict students' abilities to progress well in speeded-up mathematics classes paced by the student's intellectual peers and insightful mentors.

2. The SAT–M score scale has excellent validity from just above a chance score (about 270) to the top reported score, 800, *if* the critical activities are difficult enough and paced fast enough to challenge students appropriately. For example, other things being equal, a youth who scores 600 will tend to outdistance and outperform one who scores 500, even though the average college-bound male 12th grader scores less than 500. We therefore hypothesize that the higher the SAT–M score, the better the learning of mathematics, all other variables being equal.

3. Youngsters who score considerably higher on SAT–M than on SAT–V tend to be interested in mathematics and preoccupied with it, compared to their participation in such verbal activities as general reading.[1]

4. The converse also seems to be true, that youths who score considerably higher on SAT–V than on SAT–M tend to be oriented verbally more than mathematically.

5. For excellent performance in fast-paced mathematics classes and on standardized tests of knowledge of mathematics covered quickly, a substantial IQ is desirable. SAT–V seems to serve as a "proxy" for IQ. For example, poor performers on the standardized test of Algebra I after only 18 hours of instruction in SMPY's first fast-paced mathematics class tended to be those students who had not scored in the top percentile on a word-meaning test before the course began (Fox, 1974b).

Most youths who *reason* extremely well mathematically have rather high IQs, but the range is great. For example, among the 20 people, 19 of whom were 12 years old and the other barely 13, who scored 700–800 on SAT–M in the January of 1980 talent search, the SAT–V score range was from 370–760—that is, a 100-point SAT–M range produced a 390-point SAT–V range.[2] Although the average verbal score of these young groups was high, the variability was great. One would hardly expect a 760M–310V scorer to keep up with a 760M–700V scorer's optimum pace as the mathematics become more abstract.[3] We may hypothesize that for a given SAT–M score, success in fast-paced pre-calculus mathematics at age 12 will tend to be a curvilinear function of SAT–V score, optimum at some fairly high value such as 550.

---

[1]One must avoid the layman's fallacy of thinking that "verbal" in this context means "oral." The SAT–V sections explicitly test reading comprehension, verbal analogical ability, the ability to complete incomplete sentences logically and grammatically, knowledge of antonyms, and the like, not oral expression or skill in writing.

[2]Of the 20, two were first-generation U.S. citizens of Chinese parentage. One of these scored the 370 and the other the 760.

[3]The average SAT–M score of college-bound male 12th graders is 493. Their average SAT–V score is 431. Therefore, the intrinsic difference in the meaning of the two scales is about 60 points for such males. This makes 760–M essentially the same as 700–V; that student is about as well developed verbally as mathematically. Each is 10 score points above the 99th percentile.

6. When mathematics becomes more abstract, such as courses in analysis, higher algebra, number theory, topology, college geometry, and mathematical logic, the predictive value of SAT–M scores seems to decline considerably. Part of this is probably due to the great ability of the other students who take such courses. Many mathematicians say, however, that high verbal ability is crucial for success in "pure" mathematics. Also, evaluative attitudes become important. As MacKinnon (1978) and others showed, a theoretical–investigative orientation, combined with high aesthetic sensitivity, characterizes eminently creative mathematicians. Strongly practical orientations, particularly the craving for power and control, tend to turn even the ablest students away from theoretical concerns.[4] We are led to hypothesize that SAT–M will lose much of its predictive value for such courses, whereas the predictive value of SAT–V will increase.

7. Youths who reason extremely well mathematically seem to behave more "reasonably" in educational situations than do those who score far higher on SAT–V than on SAT–M. Perhaps this is because the mathematical, physical, and engineering sciences seek unique, correct solutions to problems in rational, analytical ways. That approach puts a premium on convergent thinking.[5] High verbal young students, however, may tend more toward divergent thinking about a problem for which no unique solution exists, as in art, literature, or sociology. This may make a considerable percentage of them appear refractory and contentious, because often they reject the conventional educational approach.

What the high-V student lacks in mathematical aptitude and interest is compensated for by greater verbal brightness. What the high-M student lacks in verbal brightness is compensated for by greater mathematical aptitude and interest. This type of thinking led the staff of SMPY to devise formulas that allow SAT–M to compensate for lower verbal skills, point for point, and allow SAT–V to compensate for lower mathematical skills beyond a certain minimum score. This composite-criterion approach is illustrated by SMPY's definition of the "mathematics prime group" as those students who, before reaching their 13th birthday, score as follows:

$$(SAT-M \geq 500) + SAT-V + 5 (TSWE) \geq 1150.$$

---

[4]There is some confounding of evaluative attitude with ability. For example, Cohn (1980) found that the Allport–Vernon–Lindzey "Study of Values" theoretical scores of 188 highly able male seventh graders correlated positively with their scores on each of eight cognitive variables, whereas the political scores correlated negatively with each of the eight.

[5]Some educationalists seem to think that convergent thinking cannot be "creative." They overlook the creativity that goes on in the process of searching for new truths (Michael, in press). For instance, mathematicians prize what they call "elegant" solutions to problems, as contrasted with unimaginative ones.

The SAT–M score must be at least 500; as noted earlier, the average college-bound 12th grade male scores 493. Youths who score the 500 minimum required for SAT–M will make the 1150 cutoff if, for example, they also score 430 on SAT–V and 44 on SAT's Test of Standard Written English. On V, 431 is the average of college-bound male 12th graders. (For each of the three scores the arithmetic mean of the higher-scoring sex was used as the criterion: e.g., a score of 44 on TSWE is the 49th percentile of college-bound female 12th graders, but the 53rd percentile of such males.)[6]

Of the 9040 participants in the January of 1980 talent search, all of whom were of upper-3% ability among their agemates verbally, mathematically, or overall, 568 boys (13%) and 348 girls (8%) attained the aforementioned criterion. Though the ratio of boys to girls was 1.63, a large number of each sex qualified for the mathematics prime group. Overall, the percentage qualifying was almost exactly 10. If one considers the talent search participants to be the ablest 5% of their agemates nationally, the 1/10 times 1/20 reveals that a student reaching the composite-score criterion is the ablest one in approximately 200 of his or her age group. In CTY's January of 1981 talent search, about 1400 boys and girls of nearly 15,000 met this criterion.

Of course, other prime groups can be constructed readily—e.g., using 75th or 90th percentile, rather than average performance. We hypothesize that for a fixed SAT–M level, therefore, there appears to be an optimal, intermediate, level of V + 5 (TSWE) for learning mathematics quickly.

8. Attitudes and effectiveness of parents in dealing with school personnel seem extremely important for the suitable utilization of mathematical reasoning ability. This may be especially true with respect to educational acceleration, particularly of girls. We hypothesize that parents' attitudes toward fast progress in mathematics and science relate strongly to their children's attitudes and success in the special classes.

9. Deleterious effects on social and emotional development resulting from educational acceleration have not been found. From our experience thus far it seems that students who score extremely high on SAT–M and rather high on SAT–V benefit greatly from accelerating their educational progress in various, individualized ways. This is especially true if they are eager to succeed, are reasonably well adjusted initially, and have cooperative, effective (but not neces-

---

[6]The formula appears to weight TSWE scores five times as heavily as SAT–M or SAT–V scores, but actually it half-weights them. This occurs because the TSWE score scale has only two digits, compared with three for SAT–M and SAT–V. One first multiplies the TSWE score by 10 to add a digit and then divides by 2 to half-weight the score; 10/2 produces the 5 coefficient. The mechanics of English writing are known to predict success in various school courses, including mathematics, rather well—perhaps because the student who writes carefully also exercises care in other scholastic contexts. The TSWE score scale goes only to 60; that is the equivalent of 600 on SAT–V (which can go up to 800). Inasmuch as TSWE is a short, screening test, it yields scores not as reliable as the two major parts of the SAT. Therefore, full weighting would seem inappropriate.

sarily brilliant) parents. On the other hand, many of the highly able students who accelerate little or none tend to lose their academic motivation and not achieve well enough in college to utilize their intellectual abilities effectively. It is hypothesized, therefore, that the short- and long-term social and emotional adjustment of highly able youths eager to accelerate educationally will be enhanced by their being allowed and helped to do so.

These nine hypotheses were formed on the basis of informal and formal observations made by the staff of SMPY over an 11-year period. One of the main trends of SMPY in the 1980s is to test and confirm them on a national group of highly able students. These are students who scored at least 700 on SAT–M before their 13th birthday. Only 5% of college-bound male 12th graders score that well.

Sex Differences

A final area to be mentioned is sex differences. The staff of SMPY can identify mathematically talented students, but has found that far fewer girls than boys score at the high levels of mathematical reasoning ability measured by the SAT–M (Benbow & Stanley, 1980b, 1981). For example, at the 500-SAT–M level (the 51st percentile of college-bound 12th-grade males) the ratio of SMPY males to SMPY females is about two to one. At 600 it is four to one, and at 700 it is 14 to one. This difference cannot be accounted for by the previously held belief that boys have superior mathematical reasoning ability because they tend to take more high school mathematics than girls do. Certain socialization explanations for the differences were also rendered implausible (Benbow & Stanley, 1980b, 1981, 1982a). Moreover, Fox, Brody, and Tobin (1982) found "few differences in the attitudes and experiences of these students and the attitudes or behaviors of their parents or teachers that suggest some of the social processes that may influence the development of interest in pursuing scientific careers or accelerating the learning of mathematics at home or school [p. 168]."

The consequences and development of this sex difference in high school are of interest. Does the sex difference make a difference in learning mathematics and related subjects? Benbow and Stanley (1982b) investigated this and found that the abilities of SMPY males developed more rapidly than those of SMPY females. Moreover, sex differences in high school favoring males were found in participation in mathematics, performance on the SAT–M, and taking of and performance on mathematics achievement and Advanced Placement Program examinations. In contrast, SMPY females received better grades in their mathematics courses than the SMPY males did, and few significant sex differences were found in attitudes toward mathematics. Indications of a relationship between the sex difference on SAT–M in the seventh grade and some later sex differences in mathematics achievement were found. It appears that in the area of mathematics there seem to be sex differences in level of action but not in level of expressed attitudes.

Because of the many sex differences in ability and achievement in mathematics among its participants, SMPY has attempted to devise suitable ameliorative strategies. Fox (1976) describes one such program. Moderately gifted seventh-grade SMPY girls in Baltimore County were invited to an accelerated mathematics program in algebra during the summer of 1973. In addition to providing accelerated and condensed algebra, this program catered to the social needs of girls. It offered interaction with female role models who had careers in the mathematical sciences as well as encouragement to study more advanced mathematics. The girls who successfully completed the program (i.e., those who were placed in Algebra II that fall) did take more advanced mathematics in high school and college (Fox, Benbow, & Perkins, in press). That was, however, the only major difference between this group of girls and an equally able group of girls not invited to attend the program. No effects were found for the girls who attended the accelerated algebra program but were not successful. Clearly, an early intervention strategy can improve the participation of girls in higher level mathematics, but only if the girls are able to succeed in such a program. Unfortunately, several of the girls in this study may not have reasoned well enough mathematically to benefit much from the speeded-up special training.

It was also of interest to see what effects the sex difference in mathematical reasoning ability might have had for achievement in high school science (Benbow & Stanley, in press a). It was found that mathematically precocious youths, whether male or female, tended to have favorable attitudes toward science and high levels of participation in science. Many sex differences were discovered, however. Far more SMPY males than females took a physics course in high school, took the high school and college level achievement tests in science, and planned to major in physics and engineering in college. In addition, SMPY males performed better than SMPY females on achievement tests measuring knowledge and understanding of biology, chemistry, or physics. Some of this sex difference in the taking of and performance on these tests could be accounted for by the females' lower mathematical reasoning ability in the seventh or eighth grade. In contrast, no pervasive sex differences in attitudes toward science were detected. The only areas in which there were large sex differences in attitudes and participation were physics and engineering.

Clearly, we have found a large set of sex differences in science and mathematics achievement that seem related to the sex difference in mathematical reasoning. A major challenge to any theory of educational acceleration in mathematics and related subjects such as physics, computer science, and chemistry is to find variables that apply equally well to both sexes. It would seem desirable to consider many cognitive and basic affective variables before invoking differential treatment of the sexes with respect to mathematics as "the" explanation of the differences in aptitude and interest. We hypothesize that performance of girls enrolled in fast-paced precalculus can be explained better by cognitive and affective variables than by societal pressures, although the three used together explain more than any one of them alone.

Conclusions

A major conclusion is that academically advanced students need to be identified early and, through curricular flexibility, helped educationally in major ways. Rather than providing special programs within regular schools, it is better to allow students to advance to a level of the curriculum that is at their intellectual level. Thus, instead of having teachers of the gifted, we need educational coordinators for the gifted. These coordinators would plan with each student his or her educational program, using available opportunities. Stanley (1980) has also proposed longitudinal teaching teams in each subject area. Thereby students could advance at their own pace within each subject.

It is apparent that SMPY has encouraged acceleration for gifted students (see Stanley & Benbow, 1982a). Readers may wonder, "Why hurry?" One part of the answer is that boredom stifles interest, liking for these subjects, and sharpness of thinking in them. Moreover, accelerated youths who reason extremely well mathematically will tend to go much further educationally, in more difficult fields and at more demanding universities, than if they were left age-in-grade (see Nevin, 1977; *Time,* 1977). They will tend to stay more directly in the mathematical, engineering, and physical sciences and earn outstanding doctorates, master's degrees, or baccalaureates before entering the job market at an early age. This enables them to be fully functioning professionals during their peak mental and physical years (see Lehman, 1953), when most of their equally able agemates are still students. Instead of receiving the doctorate at around 30 years of age, they will have it in the early 20s or even the late teens. Both creative contributions and those of the "normal scientist" (Kuhn, 1970) are likely to be enhanced greatly by the better base laid earlier and by the in-depth pursuit of important special fields.

Finally, Zuckerman (1977) found that a common thread among Nobel laureates was their systematic, long-term accumulation of educational advantage. Accelerating a student's education would be one such advantage. In SMPY we have already shown how acceleration is an advantage that accumulates. Thus, our most salient finding from working with 35,000 gifted young students over an 11-year period is that school systems need far more curricular flexibility than most of them yet have. SMPY has extensively tried out practicable, cost-effective ways to gain such flexibility. An excellent beginning seems to have been made, but of course much more research is needed.

ACKNOWLEDGMENT

We thank Lola L. Minor and Barbara S. K. Stanley for editorial assistance and the editors for valuable suggestions.

REFERENCES

Angoff, W. (Ed.). *The College Board Admissions Testing Program.* Princeton, N.J.: College Entrance Examination Board, 1971.

ATP. *National report, college-bound seniors,* 1982. Princeton, N.J.: Educational Testing Service, 1982.

Bartkovich, K. G., & George, W. C. *Teaching the gifted and talented in the mathematics classroom.* Washington, D.C.: National Education Association, 1980.

Bartkovich, K. G., & Mezynski, K. Fast-paced precalculus mathematics for talented junior high students: Two recent SMPY programs. *Gifted Child Quarterly,* 1981, *25*(2), 73–80.

Bayley, N. On the growth of intelligence. *American Psychologist,* 1955, *10*, 805–818.

Bayley, N. Development of mental abilities. In P. H. Mussen (Ed.), *Carmichael's manual of child psychology* (3rd ed.) (Vol. 1). New York: Wiley, 1970.

Benbow, C. P. Further testing of the high scorers from SMPY's 1978 talent search. *ITYB* (Intellectually Talented Youth Bulletin), 1978, *5*(4), 1–2.

Benbow, C. P. The components of SMPY's smorgasbord of accelerative options. *ITYB,* 1979, *5*(10), 21–23.

Benbow, C. P., & George, W. C. Creating bridges between high school and college. *ITYB,* 1979, *5*(5), 2–3.

Benbow, C. P., Perkins, S., & Stanley, J. C. Mathematics taught at a fast pace: A longitudinal evaluation of the first class. In C. P. Benbow & J. C. Stanley (Eds.), *Academic precocity: Aspects of its development.* Baltimore, Md.: The Johns Hopkins University Press, in press.

Benbow, C. P., & Stanley, J. C. It is never too early to start thinking about AP. *ITYB,* 1978, *4*(10), 4–6.

Benbow, C. P., & Stanley, J. C. Intellectually talented students: Family profiles. *Gifted Child Quarterly,* 1980, *24*, 119–122. (a)

Benbow, C. P., & Stanley, J. C. Sex differences in mathematical ability: Fact or artifact? *Science,* 1980, *210*, 1262–1264. (b)

Benbow, C. P., & Stanley, J. C. Mathematical ability: Is sex a factor? *Science,* 1981, *212*, 118; 121.

Benbow, C. P., & Stanley, J. C. Intellectually talented boys and girls: Educational profiles. *Gifted Child Quarterly,* 1982, *26*, 82–88. (a)

Benbow, C. P., & Stanley, J. C. Consequences in high school and college of sex differences in mathematical reasoning ability: A longitudinal perspective. *American Educational Research Journal,* 1982, *19*, 598–622. (b)

Benbow, C. P., & Stanley, J. C. Gender and the science major. In M. L. Maehr and M. W. Steinkamp (Eds.), *Women in science.* Greenwich, Conn.: JAI Press, in press. (a)

Benbow, C. P., Stanley, J. C., Kirk, M. K., & Zonderman, A. B. Structure of intelligence in intellectually precocious children and in their parents. *Intelligence,* in press. (b)

Benbow, C. P., Zonderman, A. B., & Stanley, J. C. Assortative marriage and the familiality of cognitive abilities in families of extremely gifted students. *Intelligence,* in press. (c)

Burks, B. S., Jensen, D. W., & Terman, L. M. The promise of youth: Follow-up studies of a thousand gifted children. *Genetic studies of genius* (Vol. 3). Stanford, Calif.: Stanford University Press, 1947.

Cohn, S. J. Cognitive characteristics of the top-scoring participants in SMPY's 1976 talent search. *Gifted Child Quarterly,* 1977, *22*(3), 416–421.

Cohn, S. J. *Two components of the Study of Mathematically Precocious Youth's intervention studies of educational facilitation and longitudinal follow-up.* Unpublished dissertation. Baltimore, Md.: The Johns Hopkins University, 1980.

Congdon, P. J. Helping parents of gifted children. In J. J. Gallagher (Ed.), *Gifted children: Reaching their potential.* Jerusalem: Kollek and Son, 1979.

Cox, C. M. The early mental traits of three hundred geniuses. *Genetic studies of genius* (Vol. 2). Stanford, Calif.: Stanford University Press, 1926.

Daurio, S. P. Educational enrichment versus acceleration: A review of the literature. In W. C. George, S. J. Cohn, & J. C. Stanley (Eds.), *Educating the gifted: Acceleration and enrichment.* Baltimore, Md.: The Johns Hopkins University Press, 1979.

Durden, W. G. The Johns Hopkins program for verbally gifted youth. *Roeper Review,* 1980, *2*(3), 34–37.

Fox, L. H. Factilitating educational development of mathematically precocious youth. In J. C. Stanley, D. P. Keating, & L. H. Fox (Eds.), *Mathematical talent: Discovery, description, and development.* Baltimore, Md.: The Johns Hopkins University Press, 1974. (a)

Fox, L. H. A mathematics program for fostering precocious achievement. In J. C. Stanley, D. P. Keating, & L. H. Fox (Eds.), *Mathematical talent: Discovery, description, and development.* Baltimore, Md.: The Johns Hopkins University Press, 1974, 101–125. (b)

Fox, L. H. Sex differences in mathematical precocity: Bridging the gap. In D. P. Keating (Ed.), *Intellectual talent: Research and development.* Baltimore, Md.: The Johns Hopkins University Press, 1976.

Fox, L. H., Benbow, C. P., & Perkins, S. An accelerated mathematics program for girls: A longitudinal evaluation. In C. P. Benbow & J. C. Stanley (Eds.), *Academic precocity: Aspects of its development.* Baltimore, Md.: The Johns Hopkins University Press, in press.

Fox, L. H., Brody, L., & Tobin, D. *The study of social processes that inhibit or enhance the development of competence and interest in mathematics among highly able young women.* Report to the National Institute of Education, Washington, D.C., January 1982.

Fox, L. H., & Denham, S. A. Values and career interests of mathematically and scientifically precocious youth. In J. C. Stanley, D. P. Keating, & L. H. Fox (Eds.), *Mathematical talent: Discovery, description, and development.* Baltimore, Md.: The Johns Hopkins University Press, 1974.

Fund for the Advancement of Education. *They went to college early* (Evaluation report #2). New York: The Ford Foundation, 1957.

Gallagher, J. J. *Teaching the gifted child* (2nd ed.). Boston: Allyn & Bacon, 1975.

George, W. C., Cohn, S. J., & Stanley, J. C. (Eds.). *Educating the gifted: Acceleration and enrichment.* Baltimore, Md.: The Johns Hopkins University Press, 1979.

George, W. C., & Denham, S. A. Curriculum experimentation for the mathematically talented. In D. P. Keating (Ed.), *Intellectual talent: Research and development.* Baltimore, Md.: The Johns Hopkins University Press, 1976.

Gold, M. J. *Education of the intellectually gifted.* Columbus, Oh.: Charles E. Merrill, 1965.

Goldberg, M. L., Passow, A. H., Camm, D. S., & Neill, R. D. *A comparison of mathematics programs for able junior high school students* (Vol. 1—final report). Washington, D.C.: U.S. Office of Education, Bureau of Research, 1966.

Haier, R. J., & Denham, S. A. A summary profile of the non-intellectual correlates of mathematical precocity in boys and girls. In D. P. Keating (Ed.), *Intellectual talent: Research and development.* Baltimore, Md.: The Johns Hopkins University Press, 1976.

Hildreth, G. H. *Introduction to the gifted.* New York: McGraw–Hill, 1966.

Hilgard, E. R., & Bower, G. H. *Theories of learning* (4th ed.). Englewood Cliffs, N.J.: Prentice–Hall, 1974.

Hobson, J. R. High school performance of underage pupils initially admitted to kindergarten on the basis of physical and psychological examinations. *Educational and Psychological Measurement,* 1963, *33*(1), 159–170. Reprinted in W. C. George, S. J. Cohn, & J. C. Stanley (Eds.), *Educating the gifted: Acceleration and enrichment.* Baltimore, Md.: The Johns Hopkins University Press, 1979.

Hollingworth, L. S. *Gifted children: Their nature and nurture.* New York: Macmillan, 1929.

Hollingworth, L. S. *Children above 180 IQ Stanford–Binet: Origin and development.* Yonkers-on-Hudson, N.Y.: World Book Co., 1942.

Hunt, J. M. *Intelligence and experience*. New York: Ronald Press, 1961.

Keating, D. P. The study of mathematically precocious youth. In J. C. Stanley, D. P. Keating, & L. H. Fox (Eds.), *Mathematical talent: Discovery, description, and development*. Baltimore, Md.: The Johns Hopkins University Press, 1974.

Keating, D. P. (Ed.). *Intellectual talent: Research and development*. Baltimore, Md.: The Johns Hopkins University Press, 1976.

Keating, D. P. The acceleration/enrichment debate: Basic issues. In W. C. George, S. J. Cohn, & J. C. Stanley (Eds.), *Educating the gifted: Acceleration and enrichment*. Baltimore, Md.: The Johns Hopkins University Press, 1979.

Keating, D. P., & Stanley, J. C. Extreme measures for the exceptionally gifted in mathematics and science. *Educational Researcher*, 1972, *1*(9), 3–7.

Kuhn, T. S. *The structure of scientific revolutions* (2nd ed.). (International encyclopedia of unified science, Vol. 2, No. 2). Chicago, Ill.: University of Chicago Press, 1970.

Lehman, H. C. *Age and achievement*. Princeton, N.J.: Princeton University Press, 1953.

Lunny, J. F. Fast-paced mathematics class for a rural county. In C. P. Benbow & J. C. Stanley (Eds.), *Academic precocity: Aspects of its development*. Baltimore, Md.: The Johns Hopkins University Press, in press.

MacKinnon, D. W. *In search of human effectiveness*. Buffalo, N.Y.: Creative Education Foundation, 1978.

Messick, S., & Jungeblut, A. Time and method in coaching for the SAT. *Psychological Bulletin*, 1981, *89*(2), 191–216.

Mezynski, K., McCoart, R. F., & Stanley, J. C. How SMPY's AP-oriented calculus, chemistry, and physics classes helped youths. In C. P. Benbow & J. C. Stanley (Eds.), *Academic precocity: Aspects of its development*. Baltimore, Md.: The Johns Hopkins University Press, in press.

Mezynski, K., & Stanley, J. C. Advanced placement oriented calculus for high school students. *Journal for Research in Mathematics Education*, 1980, *11*, 347–355.

Michael, W. B. The manifestation of creative behaviors by maturing participants in the Study of Mathematically Precocious Youth (SMPY). In C. P. Benbow & J. C. Stanley (Eds.), *Academic precocity: Aspects of its development*. Baltimore, Md.: The Johns Hopkins University Press, in press.

Nevin, D. Young prodigies take off under special program. *Smithsonian*, 1977, *8*(7), 76–82; 160.

Newland, T. E. *The gifted in socioeducational perspective*. Englewood Cliffs, N.J.: Prentice–Hall, 1976.

Oden, M. H. The fulfillment of promise: 40-year follow-up of the Terman gifted group. *Genetic Psychology Monograph*, 1968, *77*, 3–93.

Pressey, S. L. *Educational acceleration: Appraisal and basic problems*. Bureau of Educational Research, College of Education, the Ohio State University, 1949.

Robinson, H. B. A case for radical acceleration: Programs of The Johns Hopkins University and The University of Washington. In C. P. Benbow & J. C. Stanley (Eds.), *Academic precocity: Aspects of its development*. Baltimore, Md.: The Johns Hopkins University Press, in press.

Robinson, N. M., & Robinson, H. B. *The mentally retarded child* (2nd ed.). New York: McGraw–Hill, 1976.

Rothman, E., & Levine, M. From Little League to Ivy League. *Educational Forum*, 1963, *28*, 29–34.

Sears, P. S., & Barbee, A. H. Career and life satisfaction among Terman's gifted women. In J. C. Stanley, W. C. George, & C. H. Solano (Eds.), *The gifted and creative: A fifty-year perspective*. Baltimore, Md.: The Johns Hopkins University Press, 1977.

Sears, R. R. Sources of life satisfaction of the Terman gifted men. *American Psychologist*, 1977, *32*, 119–128.

Solano, C. H., & George, W. C. College courses for the gifted. *Gifted Child Quarterly*, 1976, *20*(3), 274–285.

Stanley, J. C. Special fast mathematics classes taught by college professors to fourth- through fifth-graders. In D. P. Keating (Ed.), *Intellectual talent: Research and development*. Baltimore, Md.: The Johns Hopkins University Press, 1976. (a)

Stanley, J. C. Test better finder of great math talent than teachers are. *American Psychologist*, 1976, *31*(4), 313–314. (b)

Stanley, J. C. Rationale of the Study of Mathematically Precocious Youth (SMPY) during its first five years of promoting educational acceleration. In J. C. Stanley, W. C. George, & C. H. Solano (Eds.), *The gifted and the creative: A fifty-year perspective*. Baltimore, Md.: The Johns Hopkins University Press, 1977.

Stanley, J. C. Educational non-acceleration: An international tragedy. *G/C/T* (Gifted/Creative/Talented), 1978, May–June, Issue No. 3. 2–5; 53–57; 60–64. (a)

Stanley, J. C. SMPY's DT → PI model: Diagnostic testing followed by prescriptive instruction. *ITYB*, 1978, *4*(10), 7–8. (b)

Stanley, J. C. How to use a fast-pacing math mentor. *ITYB*, 1979, *5*(6), 1–2.

Stanley, J. C. On educating the gifted. *Educational Researcher*, 1980, *9*(3), 8–12.

Stanley, J. C., & Benbow, C. P. Educating mathematically precocious youths: Twelve policy recommendations. *Educational Researcher*, 1982, *11*(5), 4–9. (a)

Stanley, J. C., & Benbow, C. P. Using the SAT to find intellectually talented seventh-graders. *College Board Review*, 1982, *122*, 2–7; 26–27. (b)

Stanley, J. C., Keating, D. P., & Fox, L. H. (Eds.). *Mathematical talent: Discovery, description, and development*. Baltimore, Md.: The Johns Hopkins University Press, 1974.

Tannenbaum, A. J. Pre-Sputnik to post-Watergate concern about the gifted. In A. H. Passow (Ed.), The gifted and the talented: Their education and development. *Seventy-eighth year-book of the National Society for the Study of Education*. Chicago: University of Chicago Press, 1979.

Terman, L. M. Mental and physical traits of a thousand gifted children. *Genetic Studies of Genius* (Vol. 1). Stanford, Calif.: Stanford University Press, 1925.

Terman, L. M., & Oden, M. H. The gifted child grows up: Twenty-five years' follow-up of a superior group. *Genetic Studies of Genius* (Vol. 4). Stanford, Calif.: Stanford University Press, 1947.

Terman, L. M., & Oden, M. H. The gifted group at mid-life: Thirty-five years' follow-up of the superior child. *Genetic studies of genius* (Vol. 5). Stanford, Calif.: Stanford University Press, 1959.

Time. Smorgasbord for an IQ of 150. 1977, *109*(23), 64.

Van Tassel-Baska, J. Illinois' state-wide replication of the Johns Hopkins' Study of Mathematically Precocious Youth. In C. P. Benbow & J. C. Stanley (Eds.), *Academic precocity: Aspects of its development*. Baltimore, Md.: The Johns Hopkins University Press, in press.

Wallach, M. A. Care and feeding of the gifted. *Contemporary Psychology*, 1978, *23*(9), 616–617.

Weiss, D. S., Haier, R. J., & Keating, D. P. Personality characteristics of mathematically precocious boys. In J. C. Stanley, D. P. Keating, & L. H. Fox (Eds.), *Mathematical talent: Discovery, description, and development*. Baltimore, Md.: The Johns Hopkins University Press, 1974.

Zuckerman, H. *Scientific elite: Nobel laureates in the United States*. New York: Free Press, 1977.

12 Fostering Student Learning and Motivation in the Elementary School Classroom

Jere E. Brophy
Michigan State University

A great deal of classroom research is now available to inform teachers' decision making about promoting student learning and motivation. Research findings do not translate directly into classroom practice, however. The latter involves decisions about how to manage the trade-offs involved in allocating limited teacher attention and classroom time to competing goals (e.g., basic skill mastery, citizenship preparation, group dynamics). Consequently, practitioners considering implications for teaching will differ in the data they consider relevant and sometimes even in the implications drawn from research.

I approach the task as a developmental and clinical psychologist interested in how individual teachers and students construe and cope with their roles in the classroom. This orients me toward the classroom, the teacher's interactions with the class, and especially individual students. I focus in this chapter on elementary school, especially the early grades. This is partly because much of the available research has concentrated there, but also because I believe that effective instruction in the early grades when students are mastering basic skills differs in important respects from effective instruction at higher grades when students are using these tool skills to master other content. In general, I believe that essentially the same principles for effective teaching and learning apply across levels of schooling ranging from fourth grade through graduate school but that many of these principles are inappropriate at the early grades.

I also concentrate on the traditional public school setting in which individual teachers work with classes of 20–40 students at a given grade level. Although not ideal, this arrangement works better than it is usually given credit for. Furthermore, economic and other practical constraints make it likely that it will continue to be the dominant form of education. Thus, I concentrate on research suggesting how typical teachers working with typical students in typical schools during everyday activities can improve student learning and motivation.

TEACHER BEHAVIOR AND STUDENT LEARNING

The 1970s were a decade of great excitement and progress in research on teaching. For the first time, researchers concentrated on the individual teacher as the unit of analysis rather than masking individual teachers' effects by aggregating data from all teachers working at a given school or using a given curriculum. They collected data based on sustained observation of teacher behavior rather than pencil and paper measures of teachers' status characteristics, attitudes, or personalities. They also began to focus on inservice rather than preservice teachers, which allowed them to study teaching under more naturalistic conditions and to compare groups who had established contrasting "track records" of relative success in producing student learning gains on standardized tests. Comparability of data from different teachers was enhanced by exercising control over the contexts within which instruction was observed (grade level, subject matter, student status characteristics, time of year) or by observing teachers often and long enough to build up a reliable sample of their behavior. Sophisticated, multivariate classroom observation systems were introduced that combine high inference ratings with low inference coding of specific behaviors and allow for separate coding and analysis of behavior that occurs in separate contexts. They express classroom process measures not merely as frequencies per unit of time but as percentages of the total number of times that the behavior in question might be observed or expected.

These and other methodological improvements (Berliner, 1977; Brophy, 1979b; Doyle, 1977) were used initially in several large-scale correlational studies (Brophy & Evertson, 1976; Evertson, Anderson, Anderson, & Brophy, 1980; Good & Grouws, 1977; McDonald & Elias, 1976; Soar & Soar, 1972; Stallings & Kaskowitz, 1974; Tikunoff, Berliner, & Rist, 1975), and later in several large experimental studies (Anderson, Evertson, & Brophy, 1979; Good & Grouws, 1979, 1981; Program on Teaching Effectiveness, 1978; Stallings, Cory, Fairweather, & Needels, 1978; Stallings, Needels, & Stayrook, 1979). As revealed in several reviews (Brophy, 1979a, 1980; Good, 1979; Medley, 1979; Peterson & Walberg, 1979; Rosenshine, 1979), this work has yielded a reasonably coherent body of data linking teachers' characteristics and behaviors to students' learning of basic skills.

Teachers Make a Difference

Common sense tells us that some teachers will teach more effectively than others. Yet in the late 1960s, writers like Stephens (1967) asserted that learning depends almost entirely on events occurring spontaneously within students, so that the behavior of the teacher is almost irrelevant. Data from the Coleman report (Coleman, Campbell, Hobson, McPartland, Mood, Weinfield, & York, 1966) seemed to support this. However, 1970s research focusing on the teacher as the unit of analysis revealed that experienced teachers differ in relative effectiveness in producing student learning gains. Correlations of class mean residual gain scores from one year to the next are not high, averaging about .30 (Acland, 1976; Veldman & Brophy, 1974), but they do indicate stable individual differences in teacher effectiveness despite changes in class size and composition, cohort effects unique to specific classes, and teacher health and welfare factors that vary from year to year. Let us consider some of the major factors that recent research has shown to be linked to teacher effectiveness in producing student learning gains.

Teacher Expectations/Role Definitions/Sense of Efficacy

A congruent set of expectations and attitudes underlies the specific behaviors of effective teachers. These teachers accept the responsibility for teaching their students, believe that the students are capable of learning, and believe that they (the teachers) are capable of teaching them successfully. If existing curricula, instructional methods, or evaluation devices do not work with the students, these teachers find some that will (Brophy & Evertson, 1976). If something is not learned the first time through, they teach it again. In general, they treat student failure as a challenge and a responsibility and do not write off certain students as unteachable. These attitudes are characteristic of effective teachers in any setting but they are especially vital for teachers working in schools serving students from low socioeconomic status families.

Academic Focus/Time Allocation

Effective teachers allocate and use most available classroom time for instruction and academic activities. They are businesslike, task-oriented teachers who structure their classrooms as learning environments. Most of their time is spent actively instructing the students, supervising them, and giving them feedback as they work independently. Most of the students' time is allocated to academic activities directly related to the formal curriculum (Fisher, Berliner, Filby, Marliave, Cahen, & Dishaw, 1980; Rosenshine, 1979; Rosenshine & Berliner, 1978).

This academic focus is realized, however, within the context of a pleasant, friendly classroom. Although highly effective teachers stress cognitive over affective objectives, they are not perceived as slave drivers and their classrooms do not resemble sweatshops. They maintain high standards and demand that students do their best (Brophy & Evertson, 1976), but they are not punitive or hypercritical. They are perceived as enthusiastic, thorough, and effective instructors, and their classrooms are perceived as friendly and convivial (Tikunoff et al., 1975).

Classroom Management/Student-Engaged Time

Effective teachers not only allocate most of their time for instruction, but actually spend most of that time actively instructing the students or supervising their work on assignments. They minimize the time devoted to transitions and other purely procedural matters, and especially the time devoted to dealing with classroom disruptions. In part, they accomplish this by displaying signal continuity, "withitness," "overlappingness," challenge and variety in assignments, and the other principles of effective group organization and management identified by Kounin (1970). These techniques allow the teacher to minimize disruption and off-task behavior through prevention. Students are likely to remain attentive and engaged when their teacher presents an appropriate activity for them to focus on, keeps it moving at a good pace, and monitors their responsiveness to it.

These effective teachers' classrooms often seem to "run themselves," but a good deal of preparation early in the year and maintenance throughout the year is required. Evertson and Anderson (1979) have shown that effective classroom managers prepare their classrooms as efficient learning environments by arranging the physical space and seating patterns to complement their instructional objectives and methods. They instruct their students in expected classroom procedures and routines and follow through with reminders and periodic reviews as needed. In the early grades it may be necessary for the teacher to begin the year by giving detailed instructions, with opportunities for practice and feedback, to teach students when and how to make smooth transitions between activities (e.g., how to sharpen pencils, obtain equipment, get help with an assignment, or check their work). Older students usually require less actual instruction in how to carry out procedures and routines but they do require clarity about teacher expectations and consistent follow-through. In general, effective teachers make sure that their students know what they are supposed to do, understand how to do it, and realize that they will be held accountable for meeting these expectations.

Student Opportunity to Learn

By allocating most of their available time to instruction, and by organizing and managing the classroom to insure that most of the allocated time is in fact spent on instruction, effective teachers cause their students to spend more hours per year in contact with academic subject matter, sometimes several hundred hours more (Fisher et al., 1980). Consequently, their students have more opportunity to learn the material. Thus, one reason that the students of effective teachers learn more is that they are exposed to more in the first place.

Brisk Pacing/Easy Tasks

Task engagement is not enough by itself. Students must be engaged in meaningful tasks if they are going to learn efficiently. Although variety and a degree of challenge are important, the key here seems to be pacing: Students learn the most when they proceed rapidly but in very small steps. If they are consistently given work that is too difficult, they can be expected to give up and eventually become "motivation problems."

This general principle is well known, but recent research on teaching makes a contribution by showing that students require a *very* high success rate in order to progress efficiently. Theoretical sources vary on this point. The achievement motivation literature suggests that a 50% success rate is optimal for maximizing achievement motivation, at least for individuals who do not fear failure (Crawford, 1978), and this finding has sometimes been inappropriately generalized and transformed into the notion that classroom questions and assignments should be geared to a 50% success rate. Similarly, writers who believe that higher level or "thought" questions are more valuable than lower level or "fact" questions frequently imply that learning that is "too easy" is likely to be repetitive, boring, or pointless. On the other hand, mastery learning advocates usually demand at least 80% success on assignments and tasks, and programmed learning advocates expect to approach 100%. Classroom data support the latter position, indicating that teachers who program for 90–100% success rates on student assignments produce more learning than teachers who tolerate higher failure rates (Fisher et al., 1980). In fact, Fisher et al. defined their concept of "academic learning time" as the time students spend engaged in academic tasks with high success rates.

Very high success rates are especially important in seatwork assignments on which students are expected to work independently without frequent monitoring by and opportunity to get help from the teacher. Somewhat lower success rates are appropriate in situations where the teacher is able to monitor responses and provide immediate feedback, such as when asking the students questions during a group lesson. Even here, though, effective teachers get 70–80% correct answers (Brophy & Evertson, 1976).

Thus, even though the students of more effective teachers are exposed to and progress through more material than other students, and even though the pacing of classroom activities and of progress through the curriculum in general is brisk, they move along in small steps, experiencing consistent success all along the way. Because so much of the curriculum in the early grades is cumulative, and because students are expected to work independently for much of the time, this approach probably is not only effective but necessary.

Active Teaching

Effective teachers are not mere instructional managers who distribute assignments and correct completed work. They actively teach the students in whole class and small group lessons, demonstrating skills, explaining concepts, conducting recitations and other activities that allow participation and practice, explaining how assignments are to be done before releasing students to do them, and reviewing. If they are first-grade teachers working in reading groups, they do not merely mention new words but show them and point out important phonetic features, and they spend much of their time explaining and questioning the students about word analysis and story comprehension in addition to merely listening to the students read (Anderson et al., 1979). If they are teaching mathematics to fourth graders, they spend time explaining and interacting with the class to develop key concepts or skills being introduced in the day's lesson, making sure that these are thoroughly understood before releasing the students to work independently (Good & Grouws, 1979).

In general, students taught with structured curricula do better than those taught with more individualized or discovery learning approaches, and those who receive much of their instruction directly from the teacher do better than those expected to learn on their own or from one another (Brophy & Evertson, 1976; Gage, 1978; Good, 1979; Good & Grouws, 1977; McDonald & Elias, 1976; Rosenshine, 1976; Stallings et al., 1978; Stallings & Kaskowitz, 1974; Wright, 1975: Zimmerman & Jaffe, 1977). It is difficult to imagine how it could be otherwise, despite the appeal and occasional elegance of humanistic and discovery learning theories.

To learn independently, students must be able to read, understand, and follow directions, identify key concepts, and correct their own errors. Furthermore, they must be willing and able to sustain sufficient levels of concentration and effort. This combination of skills and self-sustaining motivation does not exist at all among students in the early grades, and probably exists in only a minority of older students. Yet, the emphasis in the 1960s and early 1970s was on teacher-proof curricula and individualized learning packages that changed the teacher's role from instructor to instructional manager. This, coupled with the notion that there is too much "teacher talk" and not enough "student talk," has displaced many teachers from their traditional instructional leadership role. The research of the 1970s suggests that this has been a mistake.

Teaching to Mastery

One reason that the students of effective teachers consistently experience high success rates is that their teachers see that sequences of knowledge and skills are mastered to the point of overlearning at each step along the way. Because basic skills are taught in hierarchically sequenced strands, success at any given level usually requires application of skills mastered at earlier levels. Typically, students are not able to retain and apply skills unless they have been mastered to the point of overlearning. However, it is vital to teach to this level of mastery consistently if consistent success is to be reasonably expected.

Teachers are often criticized, especially by curriculum theorists, for placing too much emphasis on "low level" objectives. Such criticism has a misleading face validity to it, because the very term "low level objectives" implies that such objectives are trivial in importance and easily mastered. Neither is true. National and state assessment data regularly reveal that vast numbers of individual students, and often the majority of students in given schools, have not mastered even fundamental objectives in basic skills areas. Furthermore, everything we know about learning complex and hierarchically organized skills tells us that higher level objectives will not be well comprehended, let alone mastered, until lower level objectives are not only mastered but overlearned to the point that they can be combined and applied to the learning of more complex material. Thus, it should not be surprising to learn that effective teachers spend much of their time asking factual questions and supervising practice of basic skills (Rosenshine, 1979). There appear to be no shortcuts to efficient performance on higher level objectives.

Context-Dependent Relationships

Some teacher behaviors foster student learning only in certain contexts. Contexts can include student individual differences and status characteristics (e.g., age, sex, race, ethnicity, social class, intelligence, cognitive stye), subject matter, group structure (e.g., individual versus small group versus whole class), task structure (e.g., lecture, discussion, recitation, drill, seatwork), instructional goals (e.g., introduce new material versus apply new material versus review versus generalize to new situations), and even time of year. When investigators build such context factors into their research designs, they almost invariably report significant differences in what constitutes effective teaching in the different contexts studied (Brophy & Evertson, 1978).

There are few if any generic teaching competencies that apply in all situations but many that are important for the teacher to be able to do well in relevant contexts. Clarity in giving explanations is one example. Whenever the teacher must explain something, it will be important to do so clearly (Land & Smith, 1979). However, in many teaching situations the key variables are not explanatory abilities but abilities to conduct fast-paced drills or to lead discussions. Here, clarity of explanation and other skills important for didactic teaching are inappropriate or irrelevant.

Group and individual differences among students are among the more important context variables that determine what constitutes effective teaching behavior. Three of these are considered here.

Student Age/Grade Level.   Students in the early grades require a lot of one-to-one dyadic interaction with the teacher, who provides them with opportunities for overt practice with feedback. Most of this dyadic interaction occurs during group settings but it is dyadic interaction nevertheless. In reading groups, for example, teachers who call on students to read or recite in a predetermined patterned order tend to be more successful than teachers who call on students "randomly" (Anderson et al., 1979; Brophy & Evertson, 1976). In part, this is because the pattern method provides structure to students who may need it and cuts down on distractions caused by students trying to coax the teacher to call on them. Perhaps more importantly, the method insures that all students participate regularly and equally. Earlier research on communication of teacher expectations to students (reviewed by Brophy & Good, 1974) showed that most teachers who use the "random" method do not actually call on students randomly. Instead, they call on high-achieving and assertive students more often than low-achieving or shy students, resulting in unequal opportunities for practice and feedback.

At higher grade levels, the need for dyadic interactions between the teacher and each individual student gives way to the need for more briskly paced lessons in which most teacher communications are directed to the group or the class as a whole. Whole class presentations become the usual setting for introducing new material, with small group activities being used more for remedial work. Most students are now able to learn by attending to teachers' presentations to the whole class (supplemented by dyadic interactions with a few individuals) without requiring overt practice in the form of dyadic interaction with the teacher. In fact, at the higher grade levels, it is often counterproductive for teachers to interrupt large group activities for any length of time in order to deal with concerns specific to an individual student because this may lead to loss of lesson momentum and student attention. It remains important even at these higher grade levels, however, for teachers to monitor students' independent work closely and provide needed assistance and feedback. Students left on their own too long are likely to get distracted or "lost," and likely to develop misconceptions about the content even if they remain engaged in their tasks and are able to produce correct answers (Erlwanger, 1975).

Student Intelligence/Achievement Level.   Within a given grade level, students who are less intelligent or less far along in mastering key objectives of the curriculum will require: more structured learning experiences; more detailed and redundant explanations; more frequent and individualized interaction with the teacher; more opportunities to respond overtly to questions and performance demands; more individualized feedback; shorter and more closely monitored assignments; and, in general, more continuous direction and supervision from the teacher. Brighter or more skilled students can assume more of the burden for managing their own learning, especially once they make the transition from learning the tool skills as ends in themselves to using them as means to learn other things. Within the limits of their attention spans, development of metaknowledge, and self-monitoring skills, these students can be expected to work longer and more independently on a greater variety of assignments, to identify and correct their own errors, to check their own answers, and, in general, to know whether or not they understand the task and how to do it. Even so, however, active teaching by the teacher remains important. Even skilled adult learners will learn more efficiently when guided externally (Larkin & Reif, 1976; Tennyson, 1980).

Student Confidence/Assertiveness/Field Independence. A cluster of student personality dimensions including confidence–inhibition, assertiveness–shyness, and field independence–field dependence interact with the teacher behavior dimensions of demandingness–supportiveness and a businesslike, impersonal style versus an emphasis on warmth and personalized interactions. Confident, assertive students, especially if they also tend toward a field-independent cognitive style, tend to prefer and to achieve more when taught by teachers who are oriented more toward subject matter than toward individuals, and who are intellectually stimulating but also demanding of their students (Witkin, Moore, Goodenough, & Cox, 1977). Such teachers challenge their students to stretch themselves intellectually and put forth their best efforts. Often they are sparing in their praise but detailed in their criticism, although both the praise and the criticism tend to be impersonal and concentrated on the quality of academic performance. By demanding the most from students who are capable and desirous of fulfilling those demands, such teachers tend to get the most from such students.

At the same time, however, they tend to terrorize or alienate students who lack (or think they lack) the ability to meet their high standards, especially those who are anxious, insecure, or field dependent in cognitive style. These students respond better to support and encouragement from teachers who get to know them personally and establish themselves as concerned helpers rather than distant authority figures. Teachers get maximum performance from these students not by demanding it (with implied rejection or punishment for failure to deliver), but by fostering it gradually through parise, encouragement, expression of appreciation for effort, and so on. Such teaching is important for anxious and insecure students of any kind in any setting, but especially when the students' racial/ethnic group or social class membership makes them part of a minority group attending a school dominated by a majority from which they are (or feel) excluded (Brophy & Evertson, 1976; Kleinfeld, 1975; Peterson, 1977; Solomon & Kendall, 1979; St John, 1971; Witkin et al., 1977).

It is important for teachers to recognize and respond appropriately to such individual needs and preferences. This does not necessarily mean teaching these students at all times in the ways that they prefer, because this may reduce their achievement even though it enhances their attitudes (Dorsel, 1975; Peterson, 1977; Peterson & Janicki, 1979). Furthermore, although they should receive sensitivity and understanding, students with narrow, rigid preferences probably will be better off in the long run if they are gradually weaned away from these preferences toward a more flexible and differentiated ability to handle a broad variety of situations and people (Brophy, 1978). Thus, ideally, teachers would be supportive of anxious or dependent students, but at the same time would look for opportunities to help them become more independent and assertive. These considerations lead us from the topic of student learning to our other major topic, student motivation to learn.

TEACHER BEHAVIOR AND STUDENT MOTIVATION TO LEARN

There seems to be less research-based information available about how teachers can optimize student motivation to learn than there is about how teachers can maximize student learning. In part, this is because motivation theorists traditionally have concentrated on describing and predicting individual differences and not on methods of developing particular motives and related behaviors. Yet teachers need prescriptions for how to change students, not just concepts to help them understand why students are the way they are.

Early motivation concepts were developed from research on (mostly) subhuman organisms motivated by deprivation of tissue needs. These had little application to the classroom, which is concerned with higher cognitive activities in students whose purely biological needs are usually satisfied. More recently developed concepts involving the operation of need hierarchies, equilibration, or the arousal and satiation of curiosity seem more applicable. Still, like most other concepts of motivation, they were developed to describe behavior in free-choice situations. Yet, few teachers are teaching students who are in school by choice and who have selected the course on their own initiative because they perceive it as relevant to their own needs and goals. Thus, school is a *work setting* in which individuals cope with compulsory activities under some kind of accountability system, not a play setting offering free choice according to personal preferences. This and several other features of classrooms need to be considered in attempting to draw implications for teachers from research on motivation.

Need Theory

Information about individuals' need hierarchies is helpful in anticipating their interests and concerns, and in predicting their free-choice behaviors. Need for achievement is especially relevant to the classroom. Useful ideas exist for developing students' needs for achievement by teaching them to set goals based on internal standards and to reinforce themselves for success in meeting these goals.

Not all findings from research on achievement motivation generalize directly to the classroom, however. For example, motivation research done mostly in play settings suggests that a 50% success rate is optimal for maximizing achievement motivation, at least for individuals who do not fear failure (Crawford, 1978). However, school is a work setting where failure has serious social and personal consequences and where many students are much more concerned about avoiding failure than about seeking success. Even for those oriented toward success, excessive demands become counterproductive. Harter (1978) has shown that the key variable affecting students' motivation is not the degree of success that can be achieved with sustained maximal effort, but the degree that can be achieved with what the student sees as *reasonable* effort.

Furthermore, school learning involves cognitive activities, in which a 50% failure rate not only does not promote motivation, but is discouraging to the point of extinguishing further effort for most students. The level of cognitive strain associated with tasks on which only a 50% success rate can be achieved is such as to make efficient learning impossible for many students and extremely difficult for the rest. As noted earlier, efficient progress occurs in the classroom when success rates of 70–80% are achieved when the teacher is available to provide immediate feedback, and when success rates of 90–100% occur in independent seatwork.

A second potential problem with fostering need for achievement in the classroom is that it can be overemphasized. Too much of it may induce a tendency to be rigidly and overly competitive with self or others. Perhaps there should be less emphasis on building a *need* for achievement and more on developing a *value* or *appreciation* for achievement. Students can learn to enjoy the processes that go into achievement and not merely the outcomes represented by success or task completion.

The third potential problem with need for achievement, especially rigid and powerful need for achievement, is that it may detract from the intrinsic motivation that can be derived from academic tasks. When people attribute their own task involvement to factors external to the task itself, this may interfere with the quality of their task performance (Kruglanski, 1978). Rigid or powerful achievement motivation could constitute such an external factor, even though it comes from within the person, because it acts as a force driving and controlling the person just as an external force would. Various needs in addition to the need for achievement also provide useful clues to motivating students. Information about the need for affiliation, for example, is useful in deciding whether students will work better in a group or alone. In general, however, these other needs are still needs, and are subject to the same limitations as need for achievement if used as a basis for motivating students.

Reinforcement Theory

It is clear that relatively neutral behaviors can be shaped through systematic application of sufficiently powerful reinforcers. This principle is well established, but its application value for teachers has perhaps been oversold. There are limits to what teachers can accomplish with reinforcement in the classroom, and even where reinforcement can be used, its use must be limited and qualified if undesirable side effects are to be avoided.

Availability.   A great many reinforcers are available to teachers, but none of these are very powerful. Token systems driven by powerful reinforcers are used in prisons and mental hospitals, but these cannot be applied by teachers (even if this were considered desirable) because teachers do not have sufficient control over their students' lives. Furthermore, the kinds of reinforcers available to the typical teacher are most effective with students who *least* need external motivation or control, and least effective with students who present the biggest problems (Walker, 1979).

Applicability.   Reinforcement is easier to apply to overt behavior than to internal thoughts, desires, or attributions; easier to apply to quantity than quality of achievement; and easier to apply to frequency or rate of performance of already acquired skills than to efficient acquisition of these skills. Yet, the biggest problems facing teachers usually involve eliciting given levels of performance in the first place, not reinforcing repetition of this performance later. Thus, reinforcement may be useful for motivating persistence in repetitious drill and practice, but it is difficult to apply (and may be counterproductive) when the goal is to motivate students to concentrate on and absorb new learning (McGraw, 1978).

Feasibility.   Traditional forms of reinforcement call for rewarding each successive approximation to a goal and maintaining desired rates of behavior using reinforcement schedules determined to be effective for the individual and the behavior in question. This simply cannot be done in the classroom. One teacher cannot even keep track of, let alone consistently reinforce all the relevant behaviors of all the students in the class (Emery & Marholin, 1977). At best, the teacher can concentrate on a few behaviors for most of the class and deal with a few individual students more intensively. Therefore, so long as teachers must deal with classes of 20 to 40 students, attempts to maintain all relevant behaviors at desirable levels through efficient reinforcement will remain practically unfeasible, even if theoretically possible.

Side Effects.   Attribution theorists have shown that extrinsic rewards (or in fact any extrinsic reason for doing a task—competition, time deadlines, etc.) will decrease intrinsic task motivation (at least where such motivation has existed previously). Once you start paying people for doing a task or offering them rewards for doing it, they will be less likely to do it voluntarily in the future (Lepper & Greene, 1978). What is more, introduction of these extrinsic considerations tends to reduce the quality of task engagement. People become more concerned about the rewards they are expecting than about the content of the task they are doing to get the rewards, and more concerned about completing the task (at minimal levels of acceptability) than about doing the task well or thoroughly (Condry & Chambers, 1978). They develop a piecework mentality rather than a pride in craftmanship.

Many of these problems with traditional reinforcement applications to the classroom are reduced with newer techniques often called cognitive behavior modification (Meichenbaum, 1977). Here there is an emphasis on goal setting, self-monitoring of behavior, self-recording of behavior, self-reinforcement for meeting goals, and the like. Such techniques can be especially effective if combined with teacher modeling of what students should say to themselves at key points in task engagement. These techniques are more applicable to internal events occurring during acquisition of knowledge and skills than traditional reinforcement is, and more feasible because they can be used independently by students. Side effects can be minimized if the emphasis is placed on noticing and taking pride in accomplishment rather than on extrinsic reinforcement for success.

Tie School Activities to Life Goals

One often recommended approach to classroom motivation, which draws upon both need theory and reinforcement theory, is to attempt to present academic activities as instrumental to success in life. Students are exhorted to work hard and master academic skills because they can use them to meet their own goals in the present or will need them to succeed in the future. This is probably a good idea in theory, but observations in classrooms suggest that it is not done nearly as often as it could be, and when it is done, it is often done in self-defeating ways. Rather than stress the positive by indicating the present or future application value of what is being learned, some teachers tend to stress personal embarrassment ("You don't want people to think that you are ignorant") or future educational or occupational disasters ("You'll never get through sixth grade," "How are you going to get a job if you can't do basic math?"). Other well-meaning motivational attempts cast the student in a more positive light but portray society as a hostile environment (e.g., learn to count so storekeepers don't cheat you; learn to read so you don't get taken when signing a contract). Rather than stir up needless fear or anxiety, teachers would do better to help students to recognize and appreciate developing knowledge and skills, and to come to value these for their own sake in addition to whatever application value they may have.

There are other problems in trying to portray present school tasks as applicable to future goals. For one thing, this can work only when students see the future goals as attainable and believe that they are making progress toward them. Students who do not buy into these goals or who believe that they are out of reach will only be discouraged by such attempts to motivate. Also, unless handled carefully, stress on a present task's instrumental value for future activities can have the effect of devaluing the task itself, by making it seem to be just a hurdle in one's path rather than an intrinsically worthwhile activity.

Applications of Attribution Theory

Weiner (1979) and others have shown that people's engagement, persistence, and ultimate success in achievement-related activities are affected by their attributions for success or failure outcomes. Dweck (1975) and others have shown that attribution-retraining procedures can alleviate learned helplessness. These and other classroom applications of attribution theory are discussed in detail in other presentations in this volume. I will not review them here, but will make a few brief comments.

First, I believe that attribution theory has made and will continue to make important contributions to the development of a systematic approach to motivating students in the classroom. It focuses attention on the relatively neglected cognitive side of motivation, and it helps us to understand individual differences in response to classroom events. In particular, it complements reinforcement approaches nicely by helping us to understand why ostensible "success experiences" are not always rewarding or motivating, and why ostensible "failures" are not always debilitating. These and the various other contributions detailed in other chapters of this volume underscore the value of the attribution theory approach and it is within this context that I offer the qualifications and criticisms that follow.

I am impressed with the breadth and consistency of experimental data on attributions, but I believe that attributions occur less frequently and have less predictable effects in everyday settings (including classrooms) than the experimental data seem to imply. First, although one can stimulate people to make attributions by questioning them, there is little evidence that they spontaneously make such attributions with regularity. Much behavior consists of conditioned habits that are responsive to situational contingencies and played out with little or no conscious monitoring, let alone analysis of the reasons for outcomes. This is especially true of young children, who ordinarily do not engage in much self-analysis and, when they do, are likely to reach false conclusions due to their egocentrism and immature social cognition. Thus, people in general and young children in particular probably engage in relatively little attributional thinking.

Furthermore, the attributional thinking that does occur often involves attributing outcomes to causes other than ability, effort, task difficulty, and luck (Frieze & Snyder, 1980). Again, this is a problem especially with young children, whose attributional responses do not always relate to other variables in the ways that would be predicted from a rational model of intellect. As I have argued elsewhere (Brophy, 1977) in discussing the limited application of cognitive dissonance theory to young children, cognitively based personality theories developed from research on adults usually assume that everyone has "become operational" in the Piagetian sense, so that the contents of the mind have been organized into an integrated cognitive structure that apprehends not only facts but the relationships between them. This level of cognitive development and organization must be present before cognitive inconsistencies will begin to be recognized regularly and to motivate efforts at resolution. It will also be necessary before we can expect to see systematic linkages among perceptions of success or failure, attributions of these outcomes to causes, and effects on self-concept, future preferences for or persistence in similar tasks, etc. Thus, attribution theory may have less systematic application to preoperational children than it does to those who have become operational, even where attributional thinking does occur spontaneously (Nicholls, 1979; Surber, 1980).

My final concern is that attribution theorists may have overemphasized effort and underemphasized ability, particularly in attribution-retraining programs. Although it is clear that "helpless" students have learned to become frustrated quickly and to attribute failure to lack of ability, successful or mastery-oriented students do not typically show a parallel tendency to turn their attention from the task to self-congratulation. Instead, they concentrate on the processes of the task at hand when they are succeeding smoothly, and on problem-solving efforts when they are not. Attributional thinking occurs only at the end of the task, if at all. With the exception of "helpless" students, students' engagement in academic tasks might be improved more by programs that increased their enjoyment of the actual processes of task engagement and their abilities to tolerate frustration and cope with failure than by programs directed at their attributional thinking. Cognitive behavior modification approaches involving modeling with verbalized self-instruction seem especially applicable here.

Also, when successful or mastery-oriented children do make attributions concerning their task outcomes, they stress ability at least as much as effort, especially when talking about success. I believe that attribution-retraining programs should have this same emphasis, at least in programming success attributions. Recall Harter's (1978) finding that success achieved with what is perceived as reasonable effort is motivating, but success achieved only with sustained maximal effort is discouraging. Consider also Covington and Omelich's (1979) findings that students prefer to be seen as both able and motivated over being seen merely as well motivated. Such data indicate that the motivational value of successes will be maximized when students learn to interpret those successes in part as evidence of ability, not just effort.

Attributing failures to low effort must be handled carefully. It is essential that tasks be carefully matched to individual students so that attribution of failure to effort becomes a credible, factual statement. If the task is such that the student is bound to fail with even sustained maximal effort, attribution of that failure to effort is not only incorrect but insulting and discouraging. Therefore, teachers should be cautioned about the importance of appropriate task difficulty and of

TABLE 12.1
Guidelines for Effective Praise[a]

Effective Praise.

1. Is delivered contingently.
2. Specifies the particulars of the accomplishment.
3. Shows spontaneity, variety, and other signs of credibility; suggests clear attention to the student's accomplishment.
4. Rewards attainment of specified performance criteria (which can include effort criteria, however).
5. Provides information to students about their competence or the value of their accomplishments.
6. Orients students toward better appreciation of their own task-related behavior and thinking about problem solving.
7. Uses students' own prior accomplishments as the context for describing present accomplishments.
8. Is given in recognition of noteworthy effort or success at difficult (for *this* student) tasks.
9. Attributes success to effort and ability, implying that similar successes can be expected in the future.
10. Fosters endogenous attributions (students believe that they expend effort on the task because they enjoy the task and/or want to develop task-relevant skills).
11. Focuses students' attention on their own task-relevant behavior.
12. Fosters appreciation of, and desirable attributions about, task-relevant behavior after the process is completed.

Ineffective Praise:

1. Is delivered randomly or unsystematically.
2. Is restricted to global positive reactions.
3. Shows a bland uniformity that suggests a conditioned response made with minimal attention.
4. Rewards mere participation, without consideration of performance processes or outcomes.
5. Provides no information at all or gives students information about their status.
6. Orients students toward comparing themselves with others and thinking about competing.
7. Uses the accomplishments of peers as the context for describing students' present accomplishments.
8. Is given without regard to the effort expended or the meaning of the accomplishment (for *this* student).
9. Attributes success to ability alone or to external factors such as luck or (easy) task difficulty.
10. Fosters exogenous attributions (students believe that they expend effort on the task for external reasons—to please the teacher, win a competition or reward, etc.)
11. Focuses students' attention on the teacher as an external authority figure who is manipulating them.
12. Intrudes into the ongoing process, distracting attention from task-relevant behavior.

[a] From Brophy, Jere E., "Teacher Praise: A Functional Analysis." *Review of Educational Research,* Spring 1981, pp. 5–32. Copyright 1981, American Educational Research Association, Washington, D.C.

insuring that attributions of failure to low effort are factually accurate when applying attribution-retraining procedures, or the approach may backfire.

Even when done correctly, though, there is a limit to what can be gained by systematically attributing failure to low effort. Realities of individual differences and limits on the degree to which schooling can be truly individualized make it certain that some students will not be able to do what some of their peers do, even with maximum time and effort. To me, this suggests that a complete attribution-training program would include attention to issues surrounding when it is sensible and correct to attribute failure to limited (but not necessarily low in an absolute sense) ability, and what the implications of such attribution may be. Everyone cannot succeed at everything and students have to be helped to come to terms with that.

Build Intrinsic Motivation/Continuing Motivation

I believe that this approach is both the most important and the least stressed among those considered here. If we really want students to engage in academic activities seriously, it will be important to develop in such students what traditionally has been called "intrinsic motivation" and what Maehr (1976) calls "continuing motivation"—the development of interest in content that generalizes beyond the classroom. This will mean developing students' tendencies to value knowledge and skills for their own sake, as well as to value the exercise of such knowledge and skills. This should lead to enjoyment of the process of learning, pride in craftsmanship when doing assignments, and recognition of the personal benefit that accrues from doing the assignments. It is not reasonable to expect students to be excited or thrilled about their participation in academic activities (except on rare occasions), but we can expect them to find such activities meaningful and valuable, to take them seriously, and to get something out of them. The following methods should help them to do so:

1. Adapt extrinsic reward approaches with an eye toward communicating desirable expectations and attributions, stressing the intrinsic value of task participation and steady gains in knowledge and skills rather than extrinsic rewards or sanctions. Examples of how this can be done with verbal praise are shown in Table 12.1, but the same principles apply to delivery of rewards as well. The key concept is that reinforcement should focus student attention on desired task engagement and problem-solving processes and not on extrinsic factors.

2. Task design. Certain tasks are enjoyed by most people and others are commonly seen as drudgery. We need more attention to the variables of tasks themselves that affect motivation. Some clues have come from analyses of games and recreation. However, as noted previously, school is a work setting.

TABLE 12.2
Classification of 317 Task Presentation Statements Observed in Six
Elementary School Classrooms

Type	Task Introduction Category	N	%
Neutral	None (teacher launches directly into the task with no introduction).	68	21
Neutral	Cues effort (teacher urges students to work hard).	31	10
Neutral	Continuity (teacher notes relationship between this task and previous work students have done, especially recently).	29	9
Neutral	Positive challenge/goal setting (teacher sets goal or challenges the class to try to attain a certain standard of excellence).	18	6
Neutral	Survival value (teacher points out that students will need to learn these skills to get along in life or in our society as it is constructed presently).	13	4
Positive	Recognition (teacher promises that students who do well on the task will be recognized with symbolic rewards, hanging up of good papers in the classroom, etc.).	7	2
Positive	Extrinsic reward (teacher promises reward for good performance).	2	1
Positive	Teacher personalizes (teacher expresses personal beliefs or attitudes directly, or tells the students about personal experiences that illustrate the importance of this task).	3	1
Positive	Teacher enthusiasm (teacher directly expresses his or her own liking for this type of task).	8	3
Positive	Self-actualization value (teacher suggests that students can develop knowledge or skill that will bring pleasure or personal satisfaction).	0	0
Positive	Personal relevance—other (teacher makes some other kind of statement that tries to tie the task to the personal lives or interests of the students).	10	3
Positive	Cues positive expectation (teacher states directly that the students are expected to enjoy the task or to do well on it).	52	16
Negative	Threats/punishment (teacher threatens negative consequences for poor performance).	12	4
Negative	Accountability (teacher reminds students that the work will be carefully checked or that they will be tested on the material soon).	18	6
Negative	Time reminder (teacher reminds students that they only have limited time to get the assignment done so they had better concentrate).	19	6
Negative	Embarrassment (teacher tries to show the importance of the task to the students, but does this in a negative way, indicating that they are likely to be embarrassed at some time in the future if they do not learn the skills involved).	1	<1
Negative	Apology (teacher apologizes to the students for foisting this task on them).	1	<1
Negative	Cues negative expectation (teacher indicates directly that the students are not expected to like the task or to do well on the task).	25	8
		317	100%

Thus, the most valuable clues to design of effective classroom academic tasks probably will come from industrial psychologists' analyses of job characteristics as they relate to job satisfaction, employee turnover, and the like. Employee satisfaction has been found related to such job characteristics as range of variability in the types of tasks included in a job, degree to which the job provides feedback about quality of performance, degree to which the job allows opportunity to complete finished products, and degree to which the job allows opportunity for creativity or decision making. These and other factors that affect worker satisfaction on the job probably have parallels in academic tasks that would affect student satisfaction in school.

3. Teacher presentation variables. Teachers probably affect students' reactions to academic activities by the ways that they present these activities and talk about them (Good & Brophy, 1978, 1980). A given task should be received better by the students of a teacher who presents it by articulating positive expectations and stressing the knowledge or skills that the task should provide than by students of a teacher who presents the task with little enthusiasm or even states that the task is unpleasant but must be done anyway.

Pilot work from my own research on student motivation in the classroom suggests that most teachers could be more positive in presenting tasks to their students. Observations were conducted in six elementary classes (Grades 4–6), during which teachers' comments made about tasks were recorded as they were being presented to the students. In 68 instances, teachers simply launched directly into tasks without describing or characterizing them. They did characterize the tasks in some way most of the time, however, producing 249 presentation statements. These were coded into 17 descriptive categories and tentatively typed as likely to produce neutral, positive, or negative student expectations about tasks. These data are shown in Table 12.2.

Teachers made no introduction to the task at all 21% of the time, made some kind of neutral statement 29% of the time, described the task in positive terms 25% of the time, and said something likely to provoke negative expectations another 25% of the time. Thus, teachers took advantage of their opportunity to engender expectations about tasks only about half the time, and when they did, they were as likely to engender negative expectations as positive ones. Only one of the six teachers attempted to engender positive expectations with any regularity.

Teachers generated quite a variety of task presentations. Ironically, the only category that was not represented even once was that dealing with the intrinsic or self-actualization value of the tasks. More generally, it is clear from the table that these teachers were not doing nearly as much as they could do to foster intrinsic motivation (or continuing motivation) in their students for the knowledge and skills they were learning at school.

CONCLUSION

I believe that traditional sources of advice to teachers about motivating their students need to be supplemented with new research on teachers' communication of expectations and attitudes through their presentations of tasks to students, the nature of tasks themselves, and the affective reactions they engender. In the meantime, we can make teachers more aware of their own roles in shaping student attitudes toward academic activities, we can see that they learn about communicating positive expectations and attitudes through modeling and positive presentation of tasks, and we can insure that they are exposed to recently developed techniques such as cognitive behavior modification and attribution retraining. All this assumes, of course, that teachers have programmed for success by selecting tasks at the right level of difficulty and providing students with sufficient active instruction and follow-up monitoring of independent work activities to allow continuous progress through the curriculum with minimal frustration and failure. Without this, no approach to student motivation can succeed for very long. Thus, although student learning and student motivation to learn have been discussed separately here, they are linked in reality, so that the success of teachers' efforts to foster one will affect the outcomes of their efforts to foster the other.

ACKNOWLEDGMENTS

Parts of this chapter were included in Jere E. Brophy, ''Recent Research on Teaching'' (Occasional Paper No. 40, Institute for Research on Teaching, Michigan State University, November 1980). The author wishes to thank Linda Anderson, Sharon Feiman-Nemser, Tom Good, Susan Melnick, and Mary Rohrkemper for their comments on earlier drafts, and June Smith for her assistance in manuscript preparation. This work is sponsored in part by the Institute for Research on Teaching, College of Education, Michigan State University. The Institute for Research on Teaching is funded primarily by the Program for Teaching and Instruction of the National Institute of Education, United States Department of Education. The opinions expressed in this publication do not necessarily reflect the position, policy, or endorsement of the National Institute of Education. (Contract No. 400–81–0014)

REFERENCES

Acland, H. Stability of teacher effectiveness: A replication. *Journal of Educational Research*, 1976, *69*, 289–292.

Anderson, L., Evertson, C., & Brophy, J. An experimental study of effective teaching in first-grade reading groups. *Elementary School Journal*, 1979, *79*, 193–223.

Berliner, D. Impediments to measuring teacher effectiveness. In G. Borich & K. Fenton (Eds.), *The appraisal of teaching: Concepts and process*. Reading, Mass.: Addison–Wesley, 1977.

Brophy, J. *Child development and socialization.* Chicago: Science Research Associates, 1977.

Brophy, J. Interactions between learner characteristics and optimal instruction. In D. Bar-Tal & L. Saxe (Eds.), *Social psychology of education: Theory and research.* Washington, D.C.: Hemisphere, 1978.

Brophy, J. Advances in teacher effectiveness research. *Journal of Classroom Interaction, 1979, 15,* 1–7. (a)

Brophy, J. Teacher behavior and its effects. *Journal of Educational Psychology, 1979, 71,* 733–750. (b)

Brophy, J. *Recent research on teaching.* Occasional Paper No. 40, Institute for Research on Teaching, Michigan State University, 1980.

Brophy, J. Teacher praise: A functional analysis. *Review of Educational Research, 1981, 51,* 5–32.

Brophy, J., & Evertson, C. *Learning from teaching: A developmental perspective.* Boston: Allyn & Bacon, 1976.

Brophy, J., & Evertson, C. Context variables in teaching. *Educational Psychologist, 1978, 12,* 310–316.

Brophy, J., & Good, T. *Teacher–student relationships: Causes and consequences.* New York: Holt, Rinehart, & Winston, 1974.

Coleman, J., Campbell, E., Hobson, C., McPartland, J., Mood, A., Weinfield, F., & York, R. *Equality of educational opportunity.* Washington, D.C.: U.S. Office of Health, Education, and Welfare, 1966.

Condry, J., & Chambers, J. Intrinsic motivation and the process of learning. In M. Lepper & D. Greene (Eds.), *The hidden costs of reward: New perspectives on the psychology of human motivation.* Hillsdale, N.J.: Lawrence Erlbaum Associates, 1978.

Covington, M. V., & Omelich, C. L. It's best to be able and virtuous too: Student and teacher evaluative responses to successful effort. *Journal of Educational Psychology, 1979, 71,* 688–700.

Crawford, J. Interactions of learner characteristics with the difficulty level of the instruction. *Journal of Educational Psychology, 1978, 70,* 523–531.

Dorsel, T. Preference–success assumption in education. *Journal of Educational Psychology, 1975, 67,* 514–520.

Doyle, W. Paradigms for research on teacher effectiveness. In L. Shulman (Ed.), *Review of research in education* (Vol. 5). Itasca, Ill.: Peacock, 1977.

Dweck, C. S. The role of expectations and attributions in the alleviation of learned helplessness. *Journal of Personality and Social Psychology, 1975, 31,* 674–685.

Emery, R. E., & Marholin, D. An applied behavior analysis of delinquency: The irrelevancy of relevant behavior. *American Psychologist, 1977, 32,* 860–873.

Erlwanger, S. H. Case studies of children's conceptions of mathematics—Part I. *Journal of Children's Mathematical Behavior, 1975, 1*(No. 3), 157–283.

Evertson, C., & Anderson, L. Beginning school. *Educational Horizons, 1979, 57,* 164–168.

Evertson, C., Anderson, C., Anderson, L., & Brophy, J. Relationships between classroom behaviors and student outcomes in junior high mathematics and English classes. *American Educational Research Journal, 1980, 17,* 43–60.

Fisher, C., Berliner, D., Filby, N., Marliave, R., Cahen, L., & Dishaw, M. Teaching behaviors, academic learning time, and student achievement: An overview. In C. Denham & A. Lieberman (Eds.), *Time to learn.* Washington, D.C.: National Institute of Education, 1980.

Frieze, I. H., & Snyder, H. N. Children's beliefs about the causes of successes and failure in school settings. *Journal of Educational Psychology, 1980, 72,* 186–196.

Gage, N. *The scientific basis of the art of teaching.* New York: Teachers College Press, Columbia University, 1978.

Good, T. Teacher effectiveness in the elementary school: What we know about it now. *Journal of Teacher Education, 1979, 30,* 52–64.

Good, T., & Brophy, J. *Looking in classrooms* (2nd ed.). New York: Harper & Row, 1978.

Good, T., & Brophy, J. *Educational psychology: A realistic approach* (2nd ed.). New York: Holt, Rinehart, & Winston, 1980.

Good, T., & Grouws, D. Teaching effects: A process–product study in fourth-grade mathematics classrooms. *Journal of Teacher Education*, 1977, *28*, 49–54.

Good, T., & Grouws, D. The Missouri Mathematics Effectiveness Project: An experimental study in fourth-grade classrooms. *Journal of Educational Psychology*, 1979, *71*, 355–362.

Good, T. L., & Grouws, D. A. *Experimental research in secondary mathematics classrooms: Working with teachers*. Columbia, Mo.: Final Report of Grant NIE–G–79–0103, University of Missouri, 1981.

Harter, S. Effectance motivation reconsidered: Toward a developmental model. *Human Development*, 1978, *21*, 34–64.

Kleinfeld, J. Effective teachers of Eskimo and Indian students. *School Review*, 1975, *83*, 301–344.

Kounin, J. *Discipline and group management in classrooms*. New York: Holt, Rinehart, & Winston, 1970.

Kruglanski, A. Endogenous attribution and intrinsic motivation. In M. Lepper & D. Greene (Eds.), *The hidden costs of reward: New perspectives on the psychology of human motivation*. Hillsdale, N.J.: Lawrence Erlbaum Associates, 1978.

Land, M., & Smith, L. The effect of low inference teacher clarity inhibitors on student achievement. *Journal of Teacher Education*, 1979, *31*, 55–57.

Larkin, J., & Reif, F. Analysis and teaching of a general skill for studying scientific texts. *Journal of Educational Psychology*, 1976, *68*, 431–440.

Lepper, M., & Greene, D. (Eds.). *The hidden costs of reward: New perspectives on the psychology of human motivation*. Hillsdale, N.J.: Lawrence Erlbaum Associates, 1978.

Maehr, M. Continuing motivation: An analysis of a seldom considered educational outcome. *Review of Educational Research*, 1976, *46*, 443–462.

McDonald, F., & Elias, P. *The effects of teaching performance on pupil learning*. Final report (Vol. 1), Beginning Teacher Evaluation Study, Phase II, 1974–1976. Princeton, N.J.: Educational Testing Service, 1976.

McGraw, K. The detrimental effects of reward on performance: A literature review and a prediction model. In M. Lepper & D. Greene (Eds.), *The hidden costs of reward: New perspectives on the psychology of human motivation*. Hillsdale, N.J.: Lawrence Erlbaum Associates, 1978.

Medley, D. The effectiveness of teachers. In P. Peterson & H. Walberg (Eds.), *Research on teaching: Concepts, findings, and implications*. Berkeley, Calif.: McCutchan, 1979.

Meichenbaum, D. H. *Cognitive-behavior modification*. Morristown, N.Y.: Plenum, 1977.

Nicholls, J. Development of perceptions of own attainment and causal attributions for success and failure in reading. *Journal of Educational Psychology*, 1979, *71*, 94–99.

Peterson, P. Interactive effects of student anxiety, achievement orientation, and teacher behavior on student achievement and attitude. *Journal of Educational Psychology*, 1977, *69*, 779–792.

Peterson, P., & Janicki, T. Individual characteristics and children's learning in large-group and small-group approaches. *Journal of Educational Psychology*, 1979, *71*, 677–687.

Peterson, P., & Walberg, H. (Eds.). *Research on teaching: Concepts, findings, and implications*. Berkeley, Calif.: McCutchan, 1979.

Program on Teaching Effectiveness. *An experiment on teacher effectiveness and parent-assisted instruction in the third grade*. Set of five papers presented at the annual meeting of the American Educational Research Association, 1978.

Rosenshine, B. Classroom instruction. In N. Gage (Ed.), *The psychology of teaching methods. Seventy-seventh Yearbook, National Society for the Study of Education*. Chicago: University of Chicago Press, 1976.

Rosenshine, B. Content, time, and direct instruction. In P. Peterson & H. Walberg (Eds.), *Research on teaching: Concepts, findings, and implications*. Berkeley, Calif.: McCutchan, 1979.

Rosenshine, B., & Berliner, D. Academic engaged time. *British Journal of Teacher Education* 1978, *4*, 3–16.

St. John, N. Thirty-six teachers: Their characteristics, and outcomes for black and white pupils. *American Educational Research Journal,* 1971, *8*, 635–648.

Soar, R. S., & Soar, R. M. An empirical analysis of selected Follow-Through programs: An example of a process approach to evaluation. In I. Gordon (Ed.), *Early Childhood Education.* Chicago: National Society for the Study of Education, 1972.

Solomon, D., & Kendall, A. *Children in classrooms: An investigation of person–environment interaction.* New York: Praeger, 1979.

Stallings, J., Cory, R., Fairweather, J., & Needels, M. *A study of basic reading skills taught in secondary schools.* Palo Alto, Calif.: SRI International, 1978.

Stallings, J., & Kaskowitz, D. *Follow-through classroom observation evaluation 1972–1973.* (SRI Project URU-7370) Stanford, Calif.: Stanford Research Institute, 1974.

Stallings, J., Needels, M., & Stayrook, N. *The teaching of basic reading skills in secondary schools, Phase II and Phase III.* Menlo Park, Calif.: SRI International, 1979.

Stephens, J. *The process of schooling.* New York: Holt, Rinehart, & Winston, 1967.

Surber, C. F. The development of reversible operations in judgments of ability, effort, and performance. *Child Development,* 1980, *51,* 1018–1029.

Tennyson, R. Instructional control strategies and content structure as design variables in concept acquisition using computer-based instruction. *Journal of Educational Psychology,* 1980, *72,* 525–532.

Tikunoff, W., Berliner, D., & Rist, R. *An ethnographic study of the forty classrooms of the Beginning Teacher Evaluation Study known sample* (Technical Report No. 75–10–5). San Francisco, Calif.: Far West Laboratory for Educational Research and Development, 1975.

Veldman, D., & Brophy, J. Measuring teacher effects on pupil achievement. *Journal of Educational Psychology,* 1974, *66,* 319–324.

Walker, H. *The acting-out child: Coping with classroom disruption.* Boston: Allyn & Bacon, 1979.

Weiner, B. A theory of motivation for some classroom experiences. *Journal of Educational Psychology,* 1979, *71,* 3–25.

Witkin, H., Moore, C., Goodenough, D., & Cox, P. Field-dependent and field-independent cognitive styles and their educational implications. *Review of Educational Research,* 1977, *47,* 1–64.

Wright, B. The affective and cognitive consequences of an open education elementary school. *American Educational Research Journal,* 1975, *12,* 449–468.

Zimmerman, B., & Jaffe, A. Teaching through demonstration: The effects of structuring, imitation, and age. *Journal of Educational Psychology,* 1977, *69,* 773–778.

13 Social Science and Social Policy: A Role for Universities

Morton W. Weir
University of Illinois at Urbana–Champaign

The term *social policy* is almost always interpreted to mean *public policy*. Such an interpretation is understandable. Social policy decisions that are made, or laws that are written, or regulations that are adopted by public agencies or political entities often affect the lives of large numbers of people and frequently produce their share of controversy. This "public" subset of social policies is therefore often in the news—the busing of pupils to achieve racial balance; Head Start; minimum competency testing; education for the handicapped—to name just a few. So it is not surprising that the terms "social policy" and "public policy" are often used interchangeably; nor is it surprising that when universities develop courses or programs of study in social policy it is the public domain— the domains of the executive, the judicial, and the legislative branches of government—that are stressed and upon which attention is concentrated.

Two arguments are made in this chapter. First, it is argued that universities and social scientists are placing far too much emphasis on the public side of social policy. The successes of social scientists in bringing research to bear in the formation of public policy have been few and far between; and, at least in the short run, much more attention needs to be paid to the private sector if an immediate impact is to be made on decisions that affect the lives of large segments of our society. Second, it will be argued that from a longer term perspective, universities should develop mechanisms to place research findings directly into the hands of those who need them. If the results of social science research are to inform public policy more effectively they must become a part of what Caplan (1979) calls "soft knowledge," or what Lindblom and Cohen (1979) call "ordinary knowledge." These are more general forms of social science knowledge that come through routine channels of communication and come to be accepted by large numbers of people. Much more must be done to add to the body of "soft" or "ordinary" knowledge. In order to accomplish this, a great deal more attention must be paid to the dissemination of the results of research.

Finally, as an offshoot of these two arguments, I express the belief that universities would find better acceptance and endorsement of their activities by people in general if both avenues—attention to the private sector and the dissemination of research-based information—were pursued more vigorously. The public image of colleges and universities suffered in the late 1960s and early 1970s. Since that time there has been an apparent reduction in the value that society attaches to a college education. Now there is an anticipated decline in enrollment at the postsecondary level. Universities must broaden their contributions to the public, in part to overcome the impact of these image-related factors.

These arguments are based on a premise for which some evidence should be presented before moving into the main topics: that social scientists have not been effective in seeing to it that social policies reflect the latest knowledge from their disciplines.

Many authors have written in this vein. Some have conducted studies of the utilization of social science knowledge in the public policy process. Others have observed that process from the "inside" and have described the problem from that perspective. Still others have conducted systematic studies of the public policy process more generally. Nathan Caplan (1979) interviewed 204 upper-level governmental executives regarding their use of social science knowledge in policy-related issues. He concluded: "contact, formal or informal, between social scientists and upper-level decision makers is rare [p. 460]." Dreyfus (1977), after analyzing the legislative process in the United States Congress, wrote: "The observations that have been made strongly suggest the futility of attempting to introduce sophisticated policy research into the congressional decision process [p. 106]." Daniel Patrick Moynihan, in his book *Maximum Feasible Misunderstanding,* concluded that: "The role of social science lies not in the formulation of social policy, but in the measurement of its results [1969, p. 193]." Finally, James Q. Wilson (1978), speaking from the perspective of long governmental experience, joined the array of pessimists when he stated that: "only rarely have I witnessed serious governmental attention being given to social science research [p. 82]."

These views may be extreme in their bleakness, but any reasonable rendering of what is known about the utilization of social science information in the formulation of public policy would, at the very least, lead one to conclude that the record leaves room for much improvement. It is not my contention that scientists in general or social scientists in particular should be responsible for the actual making of policy any more than should any other group of citizens. MacRae (1976) describes the conflict between "expert rule" and "public rule" and concludes that if scientists are favored in the making of public policies, there is a risk of developing a "technocracy." There is, however, a major difference between scientists actually making policy and the policy process being informed by science-based information. The latter is important if policies in such vital areas as education are to reflect the latest relevant knowledge, and the evidence is strong that this process of informing is not occurring effectively.

If we are doing a poor job of bringing social science findings effectively into the public policy process, why is this so? Recently in a graduate seminar the students reviewed much of the literature on the utilization of social science research in the development of public policy. From that review, 14 separate impediments to usage were identified. Some of them seem relevant to the topic of this chapter, and I review them briefly before turning to recommendations for alternative courses of action.

A frequently described problem in using the results of research in the formulation of public policy is that much of social science research is simply not relevant to social problems, let alone to social policies (Davis & Salasin, 1978; Gans, 1971; MacRae, 1976; Weiss, 1978; Williams, 1971). For example, as Williams observes:

> If a Head Start policymaker wants to raise academic achievement levels, the fact that high socioeconomic status is associated with (a high level of) school achievement (even if it causes achievement) is not a particularly meaningful piece of information. Instead, the policymaker needs to know something about factors . . . subject to manipulation [1971, pp. 55–56].

Another example is mentioned by Wilson (1978) in discussing one of the conclusions of the National Commission on the Causes and Prevention of Violence:

> The Commission found that "the preponderance of available research evidence strongly suggests . . . that violence in television programs can and does have adverse effects upon audiences—particularly child audiences." The great bulk of the research relied upon . . . consisted of laboratory studies. . . . It was never shown that . . . the laboratory experiments . . . in any way simulated a reality [p. 84].

The result, of course, was that conclusions based on research of such questionable relevance were treated with skepticism. There are undoubtedly many reasons for the lack of relevance to policymaking of most social science research. The principal reason is that such research is most often done in academic settings, particularly in major research universities, where the reward structure favors "basic" research rather than applied or developmental efforts. As Horowitz and Katz (1975) point out, however, even social science done in settings that encourage application may have little practical value: "Typical is the critique made by the General Accounting Office against the Hudson Institute. . . . Underlining charges made by the Office of Civil Defense, it scored the work of the Hudson Institute in the area of the behavioral sciences for being 'less useful than had been expected' [p. 152].''

When research is relevant, it is often nonprescriptive. That is, it does not contain recommendations but merely criticizes or casts doubt upon some existing policy or program. James Coleman, in commenting on the report *Equality of Educational Opportunity* (often called the ''Coleman Report'') states that because the report contained no recommendations for new policies, the U.S. Office of Education ''simply did not know what to make of it.'' Both the Commissioner of Education and the Secretary of Health, Education, and Welfare, unable to use the report for new policy initiatives treated the report with ''a wariness about how the research might be used by political opponents in ways that could hurt them and a skepticism about how they could use it in any positive way [Coleman, 1978, p. 199].'' Wilson (1978) points to a similar problem in translating Daniel Patrick Moynihan's work on the black family into policy, in that it: ''lacked any clear policy prescription. The study could not say (in retrospect, it is not clear that anyone could have said) what governmental actions would enhance the stability of the black family [p. 86].''

But even if research is relevant and prescriptive, it may never be used because researchers and policymakers are seldom in communication. Policymakers are therefore not informed concerning relevant research (Caplan, 1979; Sundquist, 1978; Weiss, 1978), and researchers are not informed of gaps in knowledge that should be filled to inform policy (Davis & Salasin, 1978; Weiss, 1978). Sundquist (1978) gives three reasons why research results are not likely to appear in a form that is useful to policymakers. First, research reports are likely to be unintelligible to a lay person (''full of gammas and deltas and multiple correlations and regression analyses that are explained in forbidding methodological appendices''). Second, research findings seldom stand alone, but must be carefully pieced together with other results if they are to be meaningful in the policy context. Third, research results are according to Sundquist (1978): ''likely to be inaccessible, published in an obscure journal or simply mimeographed and distributed at conferences [p. 128].'' Weiss (1978) explains why this occurs:

> Dissemination tends to be nobody's job. Neither governmental research managers, project officers, nor researchers win kudos by matching research results with policy needs. Each group gets its rewards in its own bailiwick—from colleagues and fellow professionals or from those who control career chances. Nobody has a stake in ''audience satisfaction'' [p. 57].

In a later section of this chapter, I suggest one method whereby research universities can become more active in such dissemination. All in all, at the present time, the level of communication between social science researchers and policy makers is low and formal mechanisms for improving that condition are rare.

Suppose, however, that a piece of social science research were relevant to policy, prescriptive, and had been communicated to those involved in the decision process. Still another impediment might occur: lack of agreement among researchers. Often researchers, citing findings of others and their own, urge that precisely opposite courses of action should be adopted. Take, for example, the case of PASE versus Hannon involving the use of a standardized intelligence test for placement purposes. In that lawsuit testimony from expert social science witnesses was so contradictory and confusing that the judge decided the case on the basis of his personal, item-by-item analysis of the IQ test and his opinion that only a few of the items were biased. Cohen and Weiss (1977) describe this impediment in the following way:

> Rather than picture the research process as scouts converging on a target, it might make more sense to picture the process as outriders offering different visions of what passes them by. Multiplying the outriders tends to multiply the visions—up to a point of course—and sharpening their sight tends to refine their differences [p. 68].

Horowitz and Katz (1975) extended the same concept somewhat when they concluded that:

> When a genuine, broad-based consensus exists, the social scientists perform major legitimizing and rationalizing services, but when dissensus is present, the social scientists can only serve to reflect that situation in the very polarities of their own professional writings and researches [p. 139].

Such polarities can be seen readily in the arguments and differences of opinion that followed the release of the Coleman Report (*Equality of Educational Opportunity,* 1966). Perhaps the most widely publicized finding of that report was that characteristics of schools (such as curricula and facilities) accounted for relatively little variation in pupil achievement. This unexpected result was quickly attacked by social scientists and educational specialists on a variety of statistical and methodological grounds: deficiencies in the sample, problems with the techniques used to analyze the data, and difficulties with the underlying educational model and the selection of variables to be measured (Williams, 1971). Arguments concerning the analyses of the data were particularly plentiful. Economists preferred one method and sociologists another. Coleman later revised some of the techniques, but the revisions did not overcome still other objections. Cohen and Garet (1975) summarize the sequence of events by saying that the debate: "delighted those hardy souls who digest structural equations with their morning cornflakes, but . . . some . . . have begun to wonder where children and classrooms fit into all this [p. 32]." With all the bickering and confusion among the experts, imagine how mystified the policy makers must have been. It is no wonder that the report, according to Coleman himself, was not used in policy making (Coleman, 1978), at least insofar as school characteristics and pupil achievement were concerned. When complex social issues of great national importance are the subject of research, especially when a popular program or widespread belief is challenged, one wonders if any method of study and analysis would ever be judged to be free of methodological or statistical deficiencies. Probably not, and such deficiencies (alleged or actual) can always serve as grounds for disagreements among experts. Differences of opinion, ideology, and interpretation among social scientists are frequent problems in the acceptance of social science research by policymakers and result in a general undermining of the credibility of social science.

Timing is another frequent impediment. The conduct of research and the development of policy have their own schedules, which seldom coincide. Coleman (1978) describes the difficulties encountered during the Nixon administration in drafting acceptable legislation to aid school districts that were beginning to undertake extensive school desegregation, particularly in the south. The idea stirred so much controversy and opinions were so divided that it was not possible to undertake the short-term research that was needed to inform the legislation concerning ways in which funds could be spent to make integration work. By the time it appeared that political consensus had been reached (though later it turned out that it had not), it was too late to get the research underway. In describing the exceedingly complex nature of congressional decision processes, Dreyfus (1977) alluded to the problem of timing when he wrote:

> Most major congressional issues become full blown without much advance notice and are discovered rather than predicted.
>
> There is seldom any opportunity to do policy analysis in anticipation of future issues, therefore, and little time to do it once congressional action has begun in earnest [p. 104].

Further, when studies of various sorts are timely, they tend to be of a short-range or a narrowly focused nature, lessening their value in making major policy decisions (Williams, 1971). Thus, when the point is reached that certain decisions must be made on legislation, programmatic structure, or regulations, the amount of social science research that is *then* available for use and that fits the needs of the decision maker is very small indeed (Wilson, 1978).

The next two impediments to usage of the results of social science research are somewhat related. One is that the identity of those responsible for policy is not always clear, and the other is that the development of policy is a long process, involving many changes in the policy itself and in the cast of participants along the way. Policies tend to be the product of many individuals, agencies, or committees, in which turnover in membership is high. Sundquist (1978) writes:

In the legislative branch, committee and subcommittee chairmanships change constantly, with major upheavals possible at the beginning of each Congress. . . . In the executive branch, many of the organizations are relatively new and struggling for recognition and influence. Since ambitious people do not seek permanent careers in unstable and insecure surroundings, an almost universal shortcoming . . . is the transient nature of their staffs. They are way stations for persons en route to somewhere else [p. 136].

It is therefore difficult to know who is contributing to the policy process at any particular time. Lynn (1978) calls this the problem of the "elusive" policy maker and cites a specific case:

Power is further fragmented because of specialization by units in the executive and legislative branches of government; thus, for example, 11 committees of the U.S. House of Representatives, 10 of the U.S. Senate, and 9 executive departments or agencies have some jurisdiction over income maintenance programs [p. 16].

Weiss (1978) terms this "diffusion" of policy making and believes that such diffusion makes the use of the results of social science research unlikely, and leads to a lack of clear-cut decisions.

The problem of the "elusive" policy maker is compounded by the fact that policy is a "moving target" (Lynn, 1978). Policies are developed gradually and may change significantly during the process of formulation, implementation, and even evaluation. Thus, even if one could keep track of the cast of characters involved in the policy process, it might not be easy to discover precisely which aspects of the policy were at issue at any particular moment. An example may be found in efforts to adopt policies that are effective in the desegregation of public schools. Early on, the issue seemed simple enough. Dual systems were inherently unequal and would not be tolerated. But that approach quickly was seen as inadequate and the level of complexity increased. The mix of racial and ethnic groups in the schools had to conform to certain standards. Desegregation in many cities was frustrated by shifts in population, and strong objections were raised to solutions in which only minority students were bused in order to achieve balance (Cohen & Weiss, 1977). Intense controversy accompanied plans that required desegregation between school districts, not just within a district. And research results began to call into question the effectiveness of busing as a means of increasing the scholastic performance of minority chidren. As these new issues, complexities, and controversies emerged, the nature of policy questions regarding desegregation changed drastically. Desegregation policy had become a "moving target" and it was virtually impossible to anticipate what research needed doing that would effectively inform the policy process. The situation has not changed today. Weiss points out that policies usually develop through a set of progressively narrowed options and nearly imperceptible choices involving minor steps by many people. She writes: "Without conscious effort, a defined locus of decision, or people charged with responsibility for decisions, a decision accretes [1978, p. 58]." Therefore, it may be exceedingly difficult to know *whom* to contact about *what* at any specific point in the public policy process. Many who have attempted to operate in that environment have felt both confused and frustrated.

But let us suppose for a moment that all the foregoing impediments have been circumvented successfully. You have succeeded in communicating a set of relevant research findings (with suggestions for policy) to the right set of people at precisely the right time and there is no disagreement among experts as to the meaning of those findings. You are then likely to encounter what may be the most intractable impediment of all: Information from the results of social science research is often far less compelling to the decision maker than is information (or pressure) from other sources. In particular, research results are likely to be less persuasive than are practical political considerations. Public policy making is often a complex process of negotiation in which considerations other than those based on research results are very likely to prevail. Consider, for example, the legislative process. The general beliefs of a legislator's constituents in regard to the issues at hand, pressures from a legislator's party or from the executive, and voting trade-offs with other lawmakers are a few of the many considerations that may be more important to developing legislation than the latest research results—no matter how clear and timely they might be.

Even when conditions are favorable and legislative action occurs, political considerations can intervene at the Presidential level to defeat the measure. Steiner (1976) describes in detail the chain of events leading to President Nixon's veto of a comprehensive child care bill in 1971. A combination of circumstances had worked to produce legislation that was approved by both the House and Senate. Uncertainty in the executive branch concerning the nature and extent of the federal role in the child care domain allowed the Congress to take the initiative, led by Representative John Brademas and Senator Walter Mondale. The legislation was strongly and effectively supported by a coalition of child-oriented groups, spearheaded by Marian Wright Edelman. The lobbying effort was based on a broad set of considerations, including the results of research relating to children, youth, and families. Edward Zigler, the newly appointed Director of the Office of Child Development, was supportive even though the bill was not the result of initiatives within his agency or the Department of Health, Education, and Welfare. But when the bill reached the President's desk, it was vetoed with an unusually strong accompanying message: "for the Federal government to plunge headlong financially into supporting child development would commit the vast moral authority of the national government to the side of communal approaches to child rearing over and against the family-controlled approach [as quoted in Steiner, 1976, p. 113]." The President's surprising use of the term "communal" killed all hope for similar legislation in the near future. It is widely believed the strength of President Nixon's veto message and its specific wording were calculated to appease right-wing opponents of his policies toward

China. If this is the case, it is a classic example of the overriding power of political considerations in the policy-making process. Even as late as 1979, legislation related to this earlier child care initiative could not be successfully reported out of committee, apparently because of continuing concerns over its potentially negative impact on the American family.

This can be the most frustrating impediment of all for a researcher. The research case has been presented to the right people at the right time but it has not prevailed. The researcher is likely to complain that the process does not respond in a "rational" way; the legislator is likely to believe that the researcher is naive; and the outcome of the social legislation may be less beneficial than if social science knowledge had played a larger role. This is a grim picture—one that suggests that in our system, research results will seldom have a direct impact on public policy. That leads precisely to the main point of this chapter: *Individual efforts by social scientists and the structure of university programs in social policy are oriented far too much toward the public policy process, and, as a result, a great deal of time is wasted and considerable frustration is produced.*

But what should be done? Surely social scientists cannot abandon the effort to bring social science knowledge to bear on policies that will affect so many people. I have two suggestions. The first is that individual social scientists, especially those involved in programs in social policy, begin to show greater awareness that the private sector is also the source of social policy decisions that have an impact upon millions of Americans. This sector is much more likely to use the results of research in forming policy than is the case in the public sector. Some examples should help to make the point.

Most communities have something akin to United Way. Funds thus collected have a considerable social impact. Often the boards governing such organizations struggle with questions concerning priorities and relative benefits. Kilmer (1980) describes a case in which one such board was uncertain as to how its funds for day care should be allocated. Working with social scientists, and on the basis of a study of local day-care needs, decisions were made concerning the distribution of funds that affected hundreds of families. Furthermore, the United Way board was eager to have this information so that they could base their policy decision on research results and professional advice.

Organizations such as the YMCA, YWCA, and scouting provide services to millions. Program initiatives may occur at the national, regional, or local levels. But how often do social scientists attempt to inform the social policy decisions of such groups? Each organization, for example, is facing the challenges brought by the changing nature of the American family, particularly the one-parent household. The results of research on such families could provide information that would be helpful in determining the programmatic thrusts of such organizations and for making their programs more responsive to these changing needs.

Major businesses and industries face a growing demand that attention be paid to child care arrangements for their employees, a demand fueled in part by the increasing number of households headed by a female or in which both parents must work. Yet it is not likely that information concerning day-care options or the effect of day care on the family finds its way into corporate boardrooms or into executive conferences. In an area such as day care, which is populated by very recent research results, when such information is present, it stands a good chance of being incorrect or incomplete. How often do social scientists consider such an avenue to the formation of social policy?

Of course, research findings will not inevitably win the day in such settings. There will be much competition among ideas and concerns. Community needs, in a broad sense, must be taken into account by social service agencies and their funding sources. Political considerations will intervene, but not as often as in the public sector. Businesses are ever attentive to profit and loss, and tend to look at programs chiefly from that perspective. Typically, however, agencies and corporations do not have access to information from the social sciences. They are not bombarded with lengthy and confusing documents of questionable relevance. Often, social science input is welcomed and can make a difference. Decision makers in these contexts are not continually running for reelection. They are sensitive to community concerns and beliefs, but seldom are dominated by them unless they are pervasive. The issues and programs with which they deal are limited in scope and complexity when compared with those of the federal government. The influence of social science will therefore likewise be limited, but it is far more likely to occur.

In short, my first recommendation is that social science professionals who wish to have an impact on social policy consider the private sector as an appropriate vehicle. Those who are involved in social policy programs must bring the importance of the private sector to students' attention. Material related to the private sector should be covered in our courses and seminars, and internship possibilities should be provided in such organizational settings.

The second suggestion relates to the importance of placing social science information into the hands of large numbers of people. There is evidence that the results of social science research do have an impact on the formation of policy—even public policy. In Caplan's previously mentioned study of upper-level governmental decision makers, he writes: "the strong impression is that more general forms of social science knowledge (soft knowledge) are important far more often in upper-level policy decisions than specialized scientifically premised (hard) knowledge [Caplan, 1979, p. 466]." As sources of this "soft knowledge," decision makers listed newspapers, books, professional journals, magazines, television, and radio. Cohen and Garet (1975) and Weiss (1976) write about the "climate" of opinion and belief that results from the accumulation of research-based information in the public domain. They point out that it would be difficult to identify specific local or national decisions that stemmed from studies such as the Coleman Report or from evaluations of Title I programs, but taken together such reports, evaluations, and related studies have: "gradually eroded the assumptions underlying compensatory (educational) policy," making it "more difficult to maintain or expand" such programs (Cohen & Garet, 1975, p. 23). Cohen and Weiss (1977), also referring to the "changing climates of opinion," point out that both research and policy are influenced by "sea changes" in social thought. "Research and policy affect each other, but both seem to bob along on larger waves [p. 80]."

In a realted vein, Weiss (1976) describes three kinds of usefulness of scientific knowledge: political, intrinsic, and intellectual. Political refers to utility in informing political decisions, whereas intrinsic usefulness relates to the soundness of the research and the importance of the questions addressed. But it is intellectual usefulness—the impact of scientific knowledge on the general understanding of the way in which society functions—that appears most important. In Weiss' (1976) words: "Intellectual usefulness may be the most interesting and, in the long run, most productive way in which social research is useful to government [p. 237]." Similarly, Davis and Salasin (1978) believe that the frequency of use of social research and development is very low in public decision making and that a general awareness of relevant factors on the part of decision makers is more important than their being exposed to specific research findings. Unfortunately, such a viewpoint does not seem to be widely appreciated among social scientists. Finally, Lindblom and Cohen (1979), in arguing that it is "ordinary knowledge," not the results of professional social inquiry that underlies most social policies, state that researchers may not understand: "the necessity, on some policy issues, for an extremely broad diffusion of new knowledge, a requirement to which most researchers seem indifferent, indeed often disdaining those who attempt such a diffusion [p. 70]."

I agree with their assessment, but I also believe that researchers, perhaps especially those in universities, *are* capable of mounting such a diffusion effort and that, in fact, they *must* do so if, in the long run, public policy is to be enlightened by the results of social science research. Perhaps the best way of illustrating what is being proposed is to give a specific example of what a university might attempt.

A group of interested faculty and students could convene as a seminar for the purpose of developing a prototypical dissemination project. It would be advisable, particularly as a first effort, for there to be a fairly broad focus for the seminar—children, youth, and families, for example. It would be desirable, though not necessary, for faculty and students to come from several disciplines.

Such a seminar would doubtless require a full academic year and proceed in a number of stages, following a discussion of the literature relating generally to the role of dissemination of research-based information in the development of social policy. The first stage would include an examination of some areas in which there appear to be pressing informational needs that are of interest to members of the seminar (e.g., minimum competency testing; education of the handicapped) and a consensus would be reached on a topic to be pursued in depth. A target audience would also be identified—that is, a group (or groups) known to be in need of information bearing on the topic and to whom the dissemination would be directed (e.g., parents, teachers, scouting leaders).

Next, the task would be to conduct a thorough review of research that has been done on the topic selected. (There should, of course, have been a preliminary judgment made that the topic has a substantial research base.) For example, suppose the topic were the set of problems experienced by children whose parents are undergoing divorce, especially as revealed in the behavior of such children at school. (In this case, the target audience might be teachers in order to help them understand and deal with such problem behavior.) A review of the research literature relating to children of divorce would be conducted and all relevant information would be catalogued to serve as the basis for the subset of information that would eventually be disseminated.

Concurrently, the group would also be considering the choice of a channel or set of channels for dissemination. If the effort is to be cost effective, it probably would have to rely on an already existing network for distribution. For example, a state or national organization of school principals might serve as the network for the distribution of information concerning ways in which schools might deal more effectively with the problems of children of divorce. If such a channel is to be used effectively, officials from such a state or national organization would have to be involved in the planning at an early point—probably at the time the seminar is choosing a topic and a target audience.

The next stage would involve the selection of a medium for dissemination and a format for the material to be disseminated. Because of costs, it is likely that the print medium would be chosen, and a number of options as to format exist: brochures, brief papers, tabloids, posters, etc. The selection of the medium and the format should be aided by individuals from the target audience and from the organizations forming the network for dissemination. Once the medium and format are decided, the information to be disseminated would be selected from that which has been culled and catalogued from the literature, a draft of the product would be produced, and copies could then be distributed to selected members of the target group for their comments and criticism. Materials would then be revised accordingly, produced in their final format, and distributed via the networks previously selected. Finally, some attempt should be made to evaluate the impact of the materials, and a report on the project and its evaluation could be written.

A project such as that described would have a number of advantages. It would provide a set of experiences in the dissemination of research-based information for a group of faculty and students. It would provide links between the university and individuals from the target audience and the organizations forming the dissemination network. It would add to the base of "ordinary knowledge"—and with many such projects over a long period, have a cumulative impact on social policy. It could serve as a model for the development of similar projects in a variety of fields within the university. (In that respect, I should acknowledge that experience with Cooperative Extension in Agriculture at the University of Illinois has contributed considerably to the development of this idea). Finally, it would provide additional credibility for the university as an important resource at a time when declining enrollments will surely create an additional image problem for higher education.

To summarize, it has been argued that social policy is too often interpreted to mean public policy and that programs in universities related to social policy are likewise oriented too heavily in the public direction. For a variety of reasons already mentioned, social scientists have not been and under current circumstances will not be very effective in bringing research results into the public policy process. Two strategies have been suggested for universities to follow: First, much greater attention is needed to the processes by which social policies flow from the private sector; and second, concentrated effort to place information from the results of research into the hands of those who need it is required. The first strategy should have an immediate impact on social policy, and the latter strategy will influence social policy—both public and private—in the long run.

REFERENCES

Caplan, N. The two-communities theory and knowledge utilization. *American Behavioral Scientist,* 1979, *22,* 459–470.

Cohen, D. K., & Garet, M. S. Reforming educational policy with applied social research. *Harvard Educational Review,* 1975, *45,* No. 1.

Cohen, D. K., & Weiss, J. A. Social science and social policy: Schools and race. In C. H. Weiss (Ed.), *Using social research in public policymaking.* Lexington, Mass.: D. C. Heath, 1977.

Coleman, J. S. The use of social science research in the development of public policy. *The Urban Review,* 1978, *10,* 197–202.

Coleman, J. S. *Equality of educational opportunity.* U.S. Department of Health, Education, and Welfare, 1966.

Davis, H. R., & Salasin, S. E. Strengthening the contribution of social R & D to policymaking. In Lynn, L. E., Jr. (Ed.), *Knowledge and policy: The uncertain connection.* Washington, D.C.: The National Academy of Sciences, 1978.

Dreyfus, D. A. The limitations of policy research in congressional decision making. In C. H. Weiss (Ed.), *Using social research in public policymaking.* Lexington, Mass.: D. C. Heath, 1977.

Gans, H. J. Social science for social policy. In I. L. Horowitz (Ed.), *The use and abuse of social science.* New Brunswick, N.J.: Transaction, 1971.

Horowitz, I. L., & Katz, J. E. *Social science and public policy in the United States.* New York: Praeger, 1975.

Kilmer, S. Early childhood specialists as policymakers. *Education and Urban Society,* 1980, *12,* 241–251.

Lindblom, C. E., & Cohen, D. K. *Usable knowledge: Social science and social problem solving.* New Haven, Conn.: Yale University Press, 1979.

Lynn, L. E., Jr. The question of relevance. In L. E. Lynn, Jr. (Ed.), *Knowledge and policy: The uncertain connection.* Washington, D.C.: The National Academy of Sciences, 1978.

MacRae, D., Jr. *The social function of social science.* New Haven, Conn.: Yale University Press, 1976.

Moynihan, D. P. *Maximum feasible misunderstanding*. New York: The Free Press, 1969.

Steiner, G. Y. *The children's cause*. Washington, D.C.: The Brookings Institution, 1976.

Sundquist, J. L. Research brokerage: The Weak link. In L. E. Lynn, Jr. (Ed.), *Knowledge and policy: The uncertain connection*. Washington, D.C.: The National Academy of Sciences, 1978.

Weiss, J. A. Using social research for social policy. *Policy Studies Journal*, 1976, *4*, 234–238.

Weiss, C. H. Improving the linkage between social research and public policy. In L. E. Lynn, Jr. (Ed.), *Knowledge and policy: The uncertain connection*. Washington, D.C.: The National Academy of Sciences, 1978.

Williams, W. *Social policy research and analysis*. New York: Elsevier, 1971.

Wilson, J. Q. Social science and public policy: A personal note. In L. E. Lynn, Jr. (Ed.), *Knowledge and policy: The uncertain connection*. Washington, D.C.: The National Academy of Sciences, 1978.

Author Index

Subject Index